DRUG POLICY
in the
AMERICAS

edited by

PETER H. SMITH

University of California, San Diego

Westview Press

BOULDER • SAN FRANCISCO • OXFORD

Copyright © 1992 by Westview Press, Inc.

Published in 1992 in the United States of America by Westview Press, Inc., 5500 Central Avenue, Boulder, Colorado 80301-2877, and in the United Kingdom by Westview Press, 36 Lonsdale Road, Summertown, Oxford OX2 7EW

Library of Congress Cataloging-in-Publication Data
Drug policy in the Americas / edited by Peter H. Smith.
     p.   cm.
   Results of a series of workshops held in La Jolla, California,
and Washington, D.C., in 1990–1991 under the auspices of the Project
on Hemispheric Cooperation for the Prevention of Drug Abuse and
Traffic.
   Includes bibliographical references and index.
   ISBN 0-8133-8239-4 (hardcover). — ISBN 0-8133-8240-8
(paperback)
   1. Narcotics, Control of—Latin America.   2. Narcotics, Control of—
International cooperation.   3. Drug traffic—Latin America.
I. Smith, Peter H.
HV5840.L3D77   1992
363.4'5'098—dc20   92-15740
                                                                                      CIP

Printed and bound in the United States of America

The paper used in this publication meets the requirements
of the American National Standard for Permanence of Paper
for Printed Library Materials Z39.48-1984.

10   9   8   7   6   5   4   3   2   1

Contents

Tables and Figures

Figures

Preface

This book results from a series of workshops held in 1990–1991 under the auspices of the Project on Hemispheric Cooperation for the Prevention of Drug Abuse and Traffic, a multiyear program of research and policy analysis sponsored by the Institute of the Americas and the Center for Iberian and Latin American Studies at the University of California, San Diego.

The basic premise of the project has been that illicit drugs present long-term challenges to institutions and governments throughout the Americas—from terrorism and subversion to addiction—and that these problems require a collective international response. No country can deal with these problems alone: Multilateral collaboration is essential.

The project has been overseen by an independent nongovernmental Inter-American Commission on Drug Policy consisting of prominent experts with practical experience in the policy arena: Naya Arbiter, director of services at Amity Inc., a rehabilitation center in Tucson; Bruce Bagley, professor of political science at the University of Miami; Peter Bensinger, former director of the U.S. Drug Enforcement Administration; Paul H. Boeker, former U.S. ambassador to Bolivia and president of the Institute of the Americas; Mathea Falco, former assistant secretary of state for international narcotics matters; Luis Gonzáles Posada, former foreign minister of Peru; José G. Justiniano, former minister of agriculture in Bolivia; Hugo Margáin, twice Mexican ambassador to the United States; and Reginald Smart of the Addiction Research Center in Toronto. It has been my privilege to join this distinguished group as professor of political science at the University of California, San Diego, and as project codirector. Enrique Parejo González, former minister of justice in Colombia, and Peter Reuter, codirector of the Drug Policy Research Center at the RAND Corporation, served as consultants to the commission.

The commission has summarized its views in a policy report entitled *Seizing Opportunities*—in Spanish, *Aprovechando el momento*. Released in June 1991, the document recommends a major revision in antidrug strategies and resources, with greater emphasis on demand reduction than on supply control, and offers a series of practical suggestions for achieving its goals through hemispheric cooperation. The report has been widely distributed to governments and publics throughout the Americas.*

Funding for the Project on Hemispheric Cooperation for the Prevention of Drug Abuse and Traffic has come from the Ford Foundation, the William and Flora Hewlett Foundation, the Bank of America, SERVE San Diego, the University of California Consortium on Mexico and the United States, and the University of California, San Diego.

As volume editor, I want to express my thanks to Paul Boeker, codirector of the Project on Hemispheric Cooperation for the Prevention of Drug Abuse and Traffic; to Mary Uebersax, project coordinator, for her administrative and intellectual contributions to this book; to Guido Belsasso, now a Mexican government official, for his role in helping to initiate the project; to Jeffrey Carmel, Roberto Torres, and Gail Sevrens for assistance on editorial matters; to Barbara Ellington of Westview Press for expert guidance throughout the publication process; to members of the Inter-American Commission on Drug Policy; to authors and conference participants; and to the scores of people throughout the Americas who have given us unstinting encouragement and support.

Peter H. Smith
La Jolla, California

*Copies may be obtained by writing to the Project on Hemispheric Cooperation for the Prevention of Drug Abuse and Traffic, Institute of the Americas, 10111 North Torrey Pines Road, La Jolla, CA 92037.

1

The Political Economy of Drugs: Conceptual Issues and Policy Options

Peter H. Smith

Illicit drugs pose intractable policy problems. Abuse, addiction, and trafficking have inflicted enormous costs on the United States. Annual drug sales in the United States have been estimated at $110 billion in the late 1980s, more than double the combined profits of all *Fortune 500* companies. The economic toll from drug abuse and drug-related accidents approaches $60 billion per year.[1] About 200,000 children are born to drug-dependent mothers every year; nearly half of these infants are "crack babies." Meantime the costs of law enforcement steadily rise while violence mounts in major U.S. cities—most conspicuously in Washington, D.C., but also in Miami, New York, Chicago, Los Angeles.

Within Latin America, especially in producer countries, costs are equally high. The concentration of economic and paramilitary resources in the hands of outlaw trafficking "cartels" has presented a serious challenge to governmental authority. Drug interests have sought to undermine political institutions through bribery, defiance, intimidation, and occasionally through alliances with armed guerrilla movements. Colombia in particular has experienced the pains of "narco-terrorism," an open war by the Medellín cocaine cartel against the political establishment. Declared in August 1989, this bloody confrontation left at least 550 people dead by the end of 1990; after a series of intricate (and highly controversial) negotiations, the deadly rhythm of killings finally subsided during 1991.[2]

Prospects nonetheless seemed bleak. A former president of Colombia, Virgilio Barco, has somewhat ruefully observed that "the only law the narco-terrorists do not break is the law of supply and demand."[3] And ex–Florida governor Bob Martinez, who became head of the U.S. Office of National Drug Control Policy in early 1991, interpreted the drug epidemic as a deadly threat to democratic tendencies within the Western Hemisphere. "Deep down," proclaimed Martinez,

> the American people were aware that this situation was not simply a public policy crisis, but a profound moral crisis. There was a sense that the substance of American society was at stake. The drug crisis raises questions not only about our productivity and efficiency, but about our national character and our fitness to lead the world. Had our ancestors fought valiantly for liberty only to see it squandered in crack houses and

back alleys? Was blood spilled at Gettysburg and in the Argonne and at Normandy to make the world safe for bongs and cocaine parties and marijuana smoke-ins? Were our great cities becoming the world portrayed in *Lord of the Flies?* Were we descending into barbarism and into a world governed only by appetite and instinct?[4]

The governor's hyperbole underscored the frustration of policymakers. Consumption continues, trafficking persists, costs multiply, and political stakes are on the rise. What can governments do?

Customs, Laws, and Substances

The fundamental source of the drug problem, of *narcotráfico* in the Americas, is the presence and power of consumer demand. Demand for drugs is most conspicuous in advanced industrial countries, in Europe, and—especially important for Latin America—in the United States. Demand is what creates the market for drugs. So long as demand continues, there will be people engaged in supply.

Tolerance for the consumption of drugs has developed more from social convention than from scientific deduction. At least two major drugs are permitted under U.S. law: alcohol and tobacco. These two products have had enormous and negative impacts on the physical, psychological, and social health of U.S. citizens. Directly and indirectly, their use has led to hundreds of thousands of deaths every year. But because of history, custom, tradition—and economics—they are legal, and these two drugs are certain to stay that way.

By an equally arbitrary standard, other drugs have been declared illegal. It is essential to distinguish among illicit drugs because their markets, problems, and potential solutions differ.[5] These substances include marijuana, cocaine, heroin, and the so-called dangerous drugs.

- *Marijuana* consists of the dried leaves and flowering tops of the pistillate hemp plant that, when smoked, provide sensations of intoxication and pleasure; variants include cannabis and hashish.
- *Cocaine* is a crystalline alkaloid obtained from coca leaves that tends to induce sensations of stimulation and euphoria; in white powdery form known as cocaine hydrochloride (HC1), it can be ingested through inhalation ("snorting" through the nose or "freebasing" through a pipe or tube) or, dissolved in water, through intravenous injection; combined with baking soda and water and heated—creating a form of cocaine known as "crack"—it can be ingested by either smoking or freebasing.
- *Heroin* is a strongly addictive narcotic derived from the opium poppy, made by acetylation but much more potent than morphine; it is typically administered through intravenous injection but is also suitable for smoking or snorting.
- The term *dangerous drugs* refers to the broad categories of abusable substances, licit and illicit, that include both synthetic and naturally occurring drugs (or

psychoactive substances) such as stimulants other than cocaine, narcotics-analgesics other than opiates, psychomimetics-hallucinogens other than cannabis, depressants-sedatives other than alcohol. Examples include methamphetamine, phencyclidine (PCP), lysergic acid diethylamide (LSD or "acid"), psilocybin, methaqualone (Quaalude).

In effect, the U.S. legal structure declares that two of the world's most harmful and widely used drugs are acceptable whereas other drugs of varying potency and danger are impermissible.

The arbitrary quality of this distinction has had several ramifications. One has been the creation of a credibility gap within younger user populations, who tend to regard such laws as an expression of hypocrisy by a middle-aged (martini-swilling) power establishment. Another has been to obscure the differences among illicit substances by putting them all under the label of "drugs," a catch-all simplification that encourages misplaced efforts to devise uniform policies for a broad array of diverse problems. Yet another has been to establish perverse incentives in favor of participation in drug trafficking, because it is the illegality of the trade that makes it so profitable and therefore attractive. Finally, this logical inconsistency has spawned continuing arguments in favor of legalization, particularly of marijuana, and also some pressure to tighten restrictions on alcohol and tobacco.

Dimensions of Demand

There is considerable uncertainty about the level and location of consumer demand in the United States. Government reports estimate the number of users through a periodic survey conducted by the National Institute on Drug Abuse (NIDA), an official agency whose representatives administer a questionnaire to willing respondents about drug use by household members. As shown in Table 1-1, approximately 37 percent of U.S. citizens (age twelve and older) have used illicit drugs at one time or another. Roughly one-third of the population has tried marijuana, by far the most widely used of the illicit drugs. Between 11 and 12 percent have experimented with cocaine.

Longitudinal comparison shows a substantial decline in the number of current users (defined as those who have taken drugs within the past thirty days) from approximately 23 million in 1985 to 12.9 million in 1990. This implies a drop of 45 percent in overall drug usage, with an even greater reduction in current use of cocaine (from 2.9 percent to 0.8 percent—an estimated 660,000 current users). Not surprisingly, political leaders in the United States have proclaimed that these figures demonstrate the success of current policy. In the words of Governor Martinez, "I can say with confidence that we are moving toward victory, not because of an anecdote here or a story there, but because we have arrayed substantial forces across-the-board."[6] Things seem to be getting better: Press on, and they will get better still.

TABLE 1-1
Prevalence in Use of Selected Drugs in the United States, 1985-1990
(by percent, among population age twelve and older)

Substance	1985		1990	
	Ever Used	Past Month	Ever Used	Past Month
Marijuana	32.5	9.4	33.1	5.1
Cocaine	11.7	2.9	11.3	0.8
Crack	NA	NA	1.4	0.2
Hallucinogens	6.7	<0.5	7.6	0.3
Inhalants	6.8	0.9	5.1	0.6
Psychotherapeutics[a]				
Stimulants	9.2	1.3	6.9	0.5
Sedatives	6.0	0.8	3.7	0.3
Tranquilizers	7.7	1.1	4.3	0.3
Analgesics	6.6	1.1	5.7	0.8
Alcohol	86.1	59.2	83.2	51.2
Cigarettes	75.7	31.5	73.2	26.7
Any illicit drug	36.9	12.0	37.0	6.4

NA = not available.

[a]Indicates nonmedical use.

Sources: Based on data in National Institute on Drug Abuse, *National Household Survey on Drug Abuse: Population Estimates, 1985* (Washington, D.C.: U.S. Government Printing Office, 1987); and NIDA, *National Household Survey on Drug Abuse: Population Estimates, 1990* (Washington, D.C.: U.S. Government Printing Office, 1991).

There are problems with such an assessment. First is a question of measurement. Candor in response might vary over time: The greater the level of social intolerance about drugs, the less likely it is that people will give accurate reports about consumption levels to governmental investigators. Moreover, the NIDA survey deals only with households, which means that it concentrates on people in relatively stable family situations. The NIDA survey misses the homeless, the prison population, students in dormitories, and downtrodden segments of society that are most likely to be engaged in "doing" drugs.

The other standard instrument used to estimate drug use is an annual survey of graduating high-school seniors around the United States. As displayed in Figure 1-1, overall consumption trends appear to have peaked in the late 1970s, at which time nearly 40 percent of graduating seniors acknowledged current use of illicit drugs—most commonly marijuana. Cocaine shows a mildly cyclical pattern—rising in the late 1970s, declining slightly in the early 1980s, rising in the mid-1980s to usage rates of more than 6 percent, then declining sharply after that.

Administered by a top university research team, the high-school surveys none-theless suffer from doubts about their veracity: Everything else being equal, teenagers are reluctant to report how often they violate the law. Moreover, these studies focus only on graduating seniors, whereas the biggest problems exist among those young people who drop out of school and do not reach the point of graduation.

FIGURE 1-1
Trends in Drug Use by U.S. High School Seniors, 1975-1990
(percent who used in past thirty days)

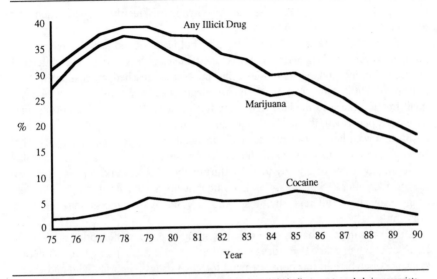

Note: Beginning in 1984, figures for "any illicit drug use" include statistical adjustment to exclude inappropriate reporting of nonprescription stimulants.

Source: Based on data in press release, University of Michigan News and Information Services (January 23, 1991).

By definition, therefore, the two most widely used instruments for measuring drug consumption in the United States fail to assess the most relevant sectors of the U.S. population. What they suggest is that drug consumption appears to be declining within the U.S. middle class, especially the white suburban middle class. But they shed little light on trends or levels within the inner cities, especially black-dominated ghettos.

Here uncertainty abounds. One independent study, based on statistics from hospital emergency admittances and criminal violence, calculates the number of weekly users of cocaine (and presumptive addicts) at 2.2 million—more than three times the NIDA figure.[7] An alternative assessment by another government agency estimates the number of cocaine addicts to be 1.75 million.[8] Yet another calculation indicates that there may be as many cocaine addicts among those excluded from the household survey as there are within the target population.[9]

Despite their imprecision, the NIDA data convey instructive implications. One concerns the much-touted argument that use of so-called soft drugs, particularly marijuana, provides a "gateway" to the consumption of such hard drugs as heroin and crack cocaine. According to this theory, one addiction leads to another; unsatiated appetites lead to intensified cravings and desperate quests for increasing toxic effect.

Confirmation of this hypothesis would seem to require a significant increase in cocaine consumption over time, because substantial numbers of the 18.2 million marijuana users current as of 1985 would move on to cocaine by 1990. And that is not what happened. At best, the gateway hypothesis requires modification and revision.[10]

Further insight emerges from an intriguing but little-noticed fact: There is a large number of *former* drug users in the United States. Measured by the difference between lifetime and current users, this population reached approximately 61.5 million in 1990.[11] How were so many Americans able to stop using drugs? Only a small fraction received medical treatment and therapy. A considerable portion may have been persuaded, through publicity and awareness campaigns, about hazards to health and well-being. Let me advance an additional hypothesis: Drug use and abuse may respond to stages of the life cycle. As George Vaillant has shown, alcohol abuse among U.S. men tends to peak during their thirties and forties, and then decline thereafter.[12] Something similar might happen with illicit drugs. Different drugs may show different rhythms, but the underlying process may be fairly uniform.[13]

Drug consumption has its own dynamic in other parts of the world. Europe and Japan offer major markets for drug-trafficking operations.[14] And in Latin America, as shown elsewhere in this book, demand for illicit drugs is substantial—and almost certainly rising. Beyond the traditional and ceremonial use of peyote, coca leaves, and other natural substances, new processes are at work. One, especially notable in Mexican northern border areas, is the direct influence of the United States. Mexican citizens who have worked in the United States show significantly higher rates of consumption than those who have not.[15] About one-third of heroin users and one-quarter of cocaine users in the Mexican north report that their first experience with these substances came in the United States. A second dynamic, prevalent throughout the Andes as well as Mexico, derives from proximity to production and transit routes. Thus, heroin is often used by young people in poppy-growing areas of northern Mexico, and—in contradiction of the gateway hypothesis—it is sometimes the drug of initiation.[16] Third, and perhaps most disturbing, is the increasing consumption of inhalants by children, especially street children. This does not entail an "illicit" drug in the legal or conventional sense of the term, but it poses a social challenge of considerable magnitude.

Sources of Supply

Over the years, especially since the 1970s, the United States has taken the lead in promoting a policy designed to suppress the production of illicit drugs throughout the hemisphere. According to this logic, a reduction in supply from Latin America will provoke an increase in the street price of illicit drugs throughout the United States—and this in turn will lead to a reduction in demand. Without supply there can be no demand; it is as simple as that. In pursuit of this goal, the United States has advocated two basic approaches: first, elimination of the sources of supply by destroying crops and laboratory facilities; and second, interdiction of shipments bound for the U.S. market by conducting surveillance at the border and on the high seas. The idea has been to reduce the flow of illicit drugs into the United States, drive prices upward, harass the traffickers, and push the users out of the market.[17]

During the 1980s public concern over drug abuse and drug-related violence mounted steadily until, characteristically, the United States chose to declare a "war on drugs." At stake was not only the health of drug users. As William J. Bennett, then head of the Office of National Drug Control Policy, declared in the September 1989 pronouncement of a *National Drug Control Strategy*, it was a matter of national sovereignty: "The source of the most dangerous drugs threatening our nation is principally international. Few foreign threats are more costly to the U.S. economy. None does more damage to our national values and institutions and destroys more American lives. While most international threats are potential, the damage and violence caused by the drug trade are actual and pervasive. Drugs are a major threat to our national security."[18]

To be sure, Bennett and the Bush administration devoted somewhat more attention to the demand for drugs in the United States than had the Reagan administration. In actual practice, however, even under Governor Martinez, U.S. international policy on drugs has retained its longstanding emphasis on supply control.

Almost by definition, this U.S. strategy has focused mainly on Latin America. Countries of the region produce or transship over 80 percent of the cocaine and 90 percent of the marijuana that enters the United States.[19] (It is to be observed that the United States produces at least one-third of the marijuana that is consumed in the United States and is one of the world's leading producers of methamphetamines and so-called "designer" drugs. Many experts therefore believe that a sharp distinction between "producer" and "consumer" nations is misleading and fallacious.[20]) In particular, the concern with cocaine prompted U.S. authorities to devote special attention to coca leaf production in nations of the Andes—Bolivia, Peru, Colombia, and Ecuador to a lesser extent—and to the processing and trafficking "cartels" residing in Colombia. By U.S. government estimates, displayed in Table 1-2, coca leaf production nonetheless continued to increase in most countries in the late 1980s. Despite expanding output within the United States, marijuana cultivation in Latin America increased as well.[21]

Mexico and Guatemala also produce a minor share of the world supply of opium, although they provide perhaps one-third of the market in the United States. From the standpoint of the U.S. government, the major foreign threat comes from the 700 to 890 metric tons of cocaine (HC1) produced in South America. All in all, figures on illicit drug output in Latin America emphasize a basic point: The scale of production is immense, and eradication campaigns face an overwhelming task.

TABLE 1-2
Latin American Production of Coca Leaf and Marijuana, 1987 and 1990
(metric tons)

Country	1987	1990
	Coca Leaf[a]	
Bolivia	79,200	81,000
Colombia	20,500	32,100
Peru	191,000	196,900
Ecuador	400	170
Totals	291,100	310,170
	Marijuana[b]	
Mexico	5,933	19,715
Colombia	5,600	1,500
Jamaica	460	825
Belize	200	60
Others	1,500	3,500
Totals	13,693	25,600

[a]Figures for "mature cultivation estimates."
[b]Figures for 1987 and 1990 not directly comparable because of change in estimation
procedures.

Source: Based on data in U.S. Department of State, Bureau of International Narcotics Matters,
International Narcotics Control Strategy Report, March 1991 (Washington, D.C.: U.S.
Government Printing Office, 1991), 22.

Traffic and Trade

Efforts to reduce supply reveal two key aspects of the international drug market.
First, the production even of natural materials for illicit drugs is extremely mobile.
Under strong pressure from the United States, for instance, Colombia undertook
massive efforts in the late 1970s to eradicate marijuana production—with considerable success. One of the principal effects of this achievement was the expansion of
production in Mexico. Then the United States put pressure on Mexico, which
intensified its own "permanent campaign" against marijuana production. And one
of the most conspicuous responses to Mexico's success in eradication was the rapid
growth of marijuana production in the United States, where domestic production
now fills over one-third of demand. A similar process took place in the heroin
market: After the disruption of the infamous "French connection" in the early
1970s, large-scale production of opium poppies moved from Turkey to Mexico.

Second, product adaptation in the illicit drug market is rapid and tends to generate
new versions with greater toxic effect and lower price, thus finding markets among
new groups—especially the young and the poor. The migration of marijuana

production from Colombia to Mexico and to the United States resulted in the development of more potent strains of the plant. Likewise, the appearance of "crack" cocaine has reflected efforts by producers and distributors to reach a larger market by offering a more powerful product at a lower price.

Product development in Latin America has followed its own course with essentially the same result—broader availability to domestic users of cheaper, more dangerous forms of drugs earlier produced for export. Typical of the hazardous forms of cocaine now marketed in Andean countries are cigarettes laced with cocaine base consumed by poverty-stricken adolescents and homeless street children under various names—*basuco* in Colombia, *pistolas* in Peru, *pitillos* in Bolivia, *pitilios* in Brazil. Almost inevitably, domestic production of drugs leads to domestic demand.

At the same time, conventional wisdom holds that drug-producing nations— especially Colombia, Peru, Bolivia—are addicted to the foreign exchange they obtain through the drug trade. One of the most widely quoted estimates has come from Rensselaer Lee III:

> In the mid-1980s, South American cocaine traffickers probably earned between $5 and $6 billion dollars annually from international sales in the U.S. market. Perhaps $1.5 to $2 billion flowed back to the cocaine-producing countries. Viewed in terms of repatriated dollars, cocaine exports are equivalent to an estimated 10 to 20% of Colombia's 1987 legal exports, 25 to 30% of Peru's, and 50 to 100% of Bolivia's (corresponding dollar figures are, respectively, $500 million–$1 billion, $600–$700 million, and $250–$400 million). Cocaine is almost certainly the most important export in Peru and Bolivia, although in Colombia it probably earns less than coffee and petroleum.[22]

From an economic standpoint coca-cocaine is yet another agricultural commodity for Latin America, except that it is uncommonly profitable. Similarly, marijuana and heroin exports provide substantial foreign exchange for Mexico.[23]

What is the magnitude of earnings from drug exports? Estimates have varied widely. As shown in Table 1-3, for example, experts and media analysts have proposed a broad range of figures. Whereas Rensselaer Lee calculates Colombia's annual intake from coca-cocaine at $500 million–$1 billion, the U.S. media have repeatedly suggested a figure as high as $4 billion. Projections also differ for Peru and Bolivia. In every instance *The Economist*, a respected British journal, falls somewhere in between Lee and the U.S. media. No matter what the estimates, however, the policy problems remain. For poverty-stricken and crisis-ridden economies, such windfalls can only seem to be a blessing. Local governments can hardly be expected to implement eradication with enthusiasm.

Employment appears to be another beneficial consequence of drug production and trafficking. As Lee has argued, cocaine provides jobs: "In Bolivia, where one-fifth of the population is officially unemployed, cocaine employs an estimated

TABLE 1-3
Estimated National Incomes from Coca-Cocaine, Mid-1980s
(U.S. millions $)

Country	Lee	Economist	U.S. Media
Colombia	$ 500-1,000	$ 1,000	$ 4,000
Peru	600-700	750	1,500
Bolivia	250-400	750	1,500

Sources: Based on data in Rensselaer Lee III, "Dimensions of the South American Cocaine Industry," Journal of Interamerican Studies and World Affairs 30, nos. 2-3 (Summer/Fall 1988): 89; Economist (October 8, 1988): 21; and for U.S. media, Mathea Falco, "Beating the Next Drug Crisis," Christian Science Monitor Monthly (February 1990): 52-54.

350,000 to 400,000 people (5 to 6 percent of the population); however, this is just direct employment. There are also incalculable numbers of South Americans in licit occupations—lawyers, accountants, bankers, construction workers, and the like—who benefit from the multiplier effect of the cocaine industry; they prosper by selling goods and services to the industry."[24] For the Andes as a whole, Newsweek has proclaimed that "as many as 1.5 million Colombians, Peruvians, and Bolivians are involved in growing coca, smuggling coca paste, or producing finished cocaine."[25] And employment, like foreign exchange, is especially welcome at a time of economic crisis. Some analysts have even maintained that because of its impact on job creation, cocaine has a more positive impact on income distribution than such traditional export crops as coffee, tobacco, sugar, and bananas.[26]

Distribution systems vary according to the drug. Largely because production has been concentrated within one geographic region, the processing and distribution of cocaine have fallen under the control of centralized organizations—especially the notorious Colombian cartels based in Cali and Medellín. Heroin has been controlled by a number of gangs, from the mafiosi of the 1940s and 1950s to Asian gangs in the 1980s and 1990s. Because of its far-flung and fast-moving production sites, marijuana has been distributed through a large number of channels and organizations. The same holds true for "dangerous drugs," where unscrupulous medical and health professionals have sometimes played a prominent role in production and distribution.

The allocation of profits varies according to distribution channels. In the case of cocaine, earnings tend to be highly concentrated in the hands of the cartels. In 1987, for instance, the price of coca leaves sufficient to produce one kilogram of cocaine oscillated between $500 and $750. As cocaine paste, it was worth $500 to $1,000; as cocaine base, it would fetch $1,000–$2,000. After processing in laboratories, typically within Colombia, the kilo of cocaine would be worth $3,000–$6,000. Once exported to the United States, this same quantity would bring increasingly astronomical prices: $14,000 to $21,000 at the wholesale level, and more than ten times those prices—$160,000 to $240,000—at the retail level (where it would often be diluted with other substances).[27] From farm gate to street sale, the market value of this shipment increased over four hundred times.

Such figures reveal key features of the trafficking phenomenon. First, economic values of drug shipments correlate with perceived levels of risk, which in turn respond to illegality and law enforcement. Second, most of the profits stay in the hands of distributors, or middlemen, rather than the producers. Third, most profits accrue outside of Latin America—in this instance, in the United States—which suggests that a large share of drug money probably remains in the United States.

It is for this reason that money laundering is such a central issue. The retail sale of drugs constitutes a multibillion-dollar business—and almost all transactions are in $5, $10, and $20 bills. As a result, some distributors accumulate 1,000 to 3,000 pounds of bills (quite literally, tons of money) on a monthly basis. The challenge is finding a safe and accessible place for this cash. This leads to a constant and clandestine search for discreet banks and bankers, for ways to transship the money from one country to another, for respectable means of investing the funds. Shipments of cash move by the suitcase, by the trunkful, and by industrial cargo containers.[28]

Finally, trafficking and distribution routes are extremely flexible. In response to new challenges or opportunities, traffickers switch routes from one country to another or from one form of transportation to another. Increased risk of apprehension in the Caribbean led the Colombian cartels to move transit routes from Florida to Mexico. During much of the 1980s, substantial shipments entered the United States on low-flying aircraft using clandestine landing strips. By the late 1980s, distributors were frequently using elaborate hiding devices (such as hollowed-out lumber), cargo containers, and in many cases, individual "swallowers" who carried stashes inside their body—often in condoms filled with cocaine or heroin—while traveling on commercial airlines. In this form a "Nigerian connection" for heroin traffic appeared early in the 1990s. Although ethnic Chinese remained the dominant importers and wholesale distributors of heroin, with networks from the Golden Triangle through Bangkok and Hong Kong to California, highly organized Nigerian groups reportedly controlled as much as 40 percent of the U.S. supply.[29] A new transit route and a new cartel thus emerged almost overnight.

Policies and Wars

Antidrug policies produce complex and contradictory results. In this issue-area, more than in many, political language has come to have a decisive effect on policy options and outcomes. Repeated public declaration of a "war" on drugs has had a remarkable impact on policy debates and discussions. It has led to calls for "total victory" (whatever that might be), prompted appeals for enlistment of the military, and encouraged ostracism of those who disagree with current policy—as though their patriotism were in doubt. And in September 1990, the metaphor prompted then-chief of the Los Angeles police Daryl F. Gates to proclaim that casual users of drugs "ought to be taken out and shot." The police chief's reasoning was that

TABLE 1-4
Anatomy of the Drug Wars

Conflict	Combatants
War no. 1	United States versus suppliers
War no. 2	Latin American governments versus narco-terrorists
War no. 3	Latin American governments versus guerrillas
War no. 4	Latin American governments versus narco-traffickers
War no. 5	Narco-traffickers versus narco-traffickers
War no. 6	Narco-traffickers versus guerrillas
War no. 7	Narco-traffickers versus political Left

the United States has proclaimed a war on drugs; thus, users of drugs are committing the equivalent of treason, and execution is standard wartime treatment for traitors.[30] Rarely has a metaphor had such pronounced effects on public discourse and debate.

Campaigns of repression have erupted in organized violence between armed groups, including the military and the police. These are genuine "wars," and they come in multiple forms. To provide a sense of this complexity, Table 1-4 outlines the anatomy of drug wars being waged in Latin America in the early 1990s. (Note that I am *not* referring to educational or therapeutic campaigns, although politicians frequently describe such activities as part of the antidrug "wars." I am referring to organized violence.)

As the table suggests, there are at least seven simultaneous drug wars in Latin America. In the first, the United States takes on drug suppliers in one way or another, most conspicuously through agents of the Drug Enforcement Administration. In the second, Latin American governments respond to challenges by narco-terrorists—agents of drug cartels who use terror, violence, and intimidation to assert raw political power. (This has been most clearly apparent in Colombia.) In the third drug war, Latin American governments engage in struggles with armed guerrilla movements including such forces as Sendero Luminoso in Peru. In the fourth kind of war, Latin American governments wage armed campaigns against narco-traffickers—those who produce and export illicit drugs but do not engage in systematic political terrorism.

In the fifth kind of war, drug cartels fight among themselves, usually over market share. This explains some of the violence in Colombia, where the Cali and Medellín cartels have skirmished over control of the New York cocaine market. It is this kind of war that has reached into the cities of the United States, where rival dealers and distributors have been waging campaigns of attrition against one another.

In the sixth confrontation, drug traffickers engage in conflict with their sometime-allies, armed guerrilla groups. This often occurs once the *traficantes* begin to purchase significant amounts of real estate, especially in rural areas, thus gaining entry into the landowning class and joining the socioeconomic establishment—against which the guerrillas took arms in the first place. Alliances between traffickers and guerrillas tend to be fragile at best—arrangements of convenience rather than principle—and they can fall apart for many reasons.

In the seventh and last kind of war, unique to Colombia at this point, *narcotraficantes* declare war against ideological opponents—in this case the political Left. To the extent that the Medellín cartel has had any political purpose, it appears to consist of a primitive, reactionary, semi-Fascist project. This tendency has been exacerbated in the case of one well-known ringleader, Fidel Castaño (nicknamed "Rambo"), whose father died while held hostage by guerrillas and who promptly unleashed a violent campaign of retaliation against all left-wing groups. This may help explain the otherwise inexplicable attacks on leaders of the Unión Patriótica and other radical movements in Colombia in 1989–1990.

These wars often overlap with one another, and they can appear in varying combinations. Mexico presents a battleground for the United States to fight against suppliers (war 1) and for its own government to challenge traffickers (war 4). Peru combines a U.S.-led fight against suppliers (war 1) with a government campaign against guerrillas (war 3). Colombia has suffered multiple wars: a fight between the government and narco-terrorists (war 2), between two groups of narco-traffickers (war 5), between narco-traffickers and some guerrilla groups (war 6), and between some narco-traffickers and the political Left (war 7). At various times, too, Colombian authorities have waged campaigns against guerrilla movements (war 3).[31]

The diversity in drug wars underlines the range and variability of interests involved in public policy. The "drug problem" in Colombia is markedly different from the "drug problem" in Peru, Bolivia, or Mexico (not to mention the United States). The goals of governmental policy as well as the choice of instruments therefore are likely to vary, as are the prospects for success.

Also striking is the ubiquity of unintended consequences. It is not always easy to foresee results of public policies. Colombia's crackdown on the Medellín cartel produced a temporary decline in the price of coca leaf in Peru and Bolivia; most observers thought, and many hoped, this would convince coca producers to start cultivating licit crops. On the contrary, however, it encouraged Bolivian peasants to integrate their operations, processing their own products (thus increasing value added) and exporting coca base instead of coca leaves. According to economic logic, this response was entirely rational.

This episode demonstrates that a "success" in the Colombian drug war could exacerbate the problem in Bolivia—or in other neighboring countries. Indeed, it appears that the Colombian crackdown has accelerated the dispersion of drug-trafficking activities throughout the continent, from Chile and Argentina to Costa Rica and Belize, especially as transit routes and as sites for money laundering. "Latin America as a whole is sliding into the drug war," according to Ibán de Rementería of the Comisión Andina de Juristas. "Argentina and Brazil can see their future in Bolivia. Bolivia sees its own [future] in Peru, Peru in Colombia, and Colombia in Lebanon. It's an endless cycle."[32]

TABLE 1-5
Worldwide Cocaine Production:
Quantities Available for Export to the United States, 1986-1990
(metric tons)

Cocaine Production	1986	1987	1988	1989	1990
Worldwide production	606	635	714	776	824
Eradicated	- 2	- 8	- 26	- 21	- 80
Interdicted	- 13	- 45	- 62	- 98	- 152
Consumed overseas	- 50	- 55	- 60	- 65	- 75
Available for export to United States	541	527	566	592	517

Source: Unpublished estimates supplied by U.S. Office of Management and Budget (1990).

Ironically, too, the dismantling of the Medellín cartel may have made trafficking more difficult to stop. By 1991 the Cali group handled 70 percent of the cocaine that came to the United States through Colombia, up from 25–30 percent in 1989. And the Cali group, it turns out, is much more sophisticated than the rough-and-tumble Medellín gang. According to the head of the Drug Enforcement Administration (DEA), in fact, "The Cali cartel is the most powerful criminal organization in the world. No drug organization rivals them today or perhaps any time in history."[33] Meanwhile the Medellín cartel moved much of its operation to Venezuela. In short, the Colombian crackdown led to a transference, a dispersion, and an upgrading of trafficking activities.

Nor have the U.S.-sponsored drug wars achieved the goal of reducing supply and raising prices for illicit drugs in the U.S. market. As plainly suggested by Table 1-5, campaigns for eradication and interdiction of coca-cocaine merely encourage additional production: More and more campesinos become involved in cultivating coca leaves, and the total quantity of cocaine available for export to the U.S. market remains about the same. And because the cost of replacing seized shipments is relatively modest (perhaps 5 percent of the street value), interdiction has little if any observable impact on price.[34] In this respect, drug wars have almost no chance of success.

Yet the wars have altered society and politics in important and far-reaching ways. First, they have subjected the countries and peoples of Latin America to staggering levels of violence and intimidation. The human toll of antidrug campaigns has been extremely high—not only in Colombia but also in Peru and Mexico. Both the power of the drug trade and the violence induced by government efforts to fight that trade have created a widespread sense of fear among the general populace. Ominously, too, antidrug campaigns have produced large-scale violations of human rights.[35]

Second, drugs and drug wars have exposed national institutions to increased temptations of corruption. One of the lessons of antidrug campaigns around the world is that law enforcement agencies risk corruption by drug traffickers and lords;

increased contact with *traficantes*, even in an adversarial manner, increases the possibility of compromise and subversion. This can have a particularly deleterious effect on Latin American police forces, local and national, and on the armed forces as well.

Third, prosecution of the drug wars places increasing autonomy and authority in the hands of the Latin American armed forces. To put it bluntly, drug wars encourage militarization. This can pose a substantial threat to still-fragile democracies, especially in Bolivia and Peru, and alter the political course of the region as a whole.[36]

Finally, the drug wars have created major complications for U.S.–Latin American relations. For reasons of its own, the United States has strongly encouraged Latin American governments to enlist in the antidrug wars. And Latin American leaders respond, also for reasons of their own. Sometimes, as in the case of Bolivia, they are reluctant to precipitate what they regard as all-out wars against the peasantry. Sometimes, as in the case of Colombia, they react to challenges from drug cartels with considerable force—but even then, they are not waging the same war the United States advocates. The U.S. government has been asking Latin American governments to join ranks in a war against the narco-traffickers and thus to forge an alliance with the United States. (In terms of Table 1–4, this would mean a combination of war 1, waged by the United States, with war 4, to be waged by Latin America.) But as successive Colombian presidents have expressed, the concern in Colombia is not so much with narco-traffic as with narco-terror (war 2 in Table 1–4). This entails different purposes, strategies, and policies.[37]

This incongruity in antidrug campaigns leads not only to confusion but also to missed opportunities. As a result of the inevitable tension that accompanies misunderstanding, the United States and Latin America have often found it difficult to collaborate on other pressing issues—such as debt, trade, and development. Drugs have been a particularly conspicuous flashpoint in U.S. relations with Mexico,[38] but the issue has affected other countries as well.

Policy Options

What are the policy alternatives? There is no quick-fix solution, no cost-free outcome. In a sense, policymakers can seek only least-bad solutions. For the sake of simplicity, I present three basic possibilities.[39]

One entails intensification and escalation of the current drug wars. This accepts at face value the claim that the present strategy is starting to work. According to this scenario Colombia should continue its fight, Peru should redouble its efforts, and Bolivia should enter the fray. The U.S. government might increase its overall antidrug investment from $10 billion a year to $20 billion or even $30 billion, but the focus of the effort would remain as it is. The question, of course, is whether the alleged benefits of such a course would outweigh the costs. Some analysts and most policymakers in Washington believe this would be the case.[40]

A second alternative has been called "legalization" of the drug trade. In fact, most such proposals do not envision the straightforward legalization of existing practices; instead, they call for decriminalization of consumption and for governmental regulation of wholesale and retail markets. Most versions would place an age limit on people who purchase drugs, and some advocate state-run monopolies on retail sales. Some would begin only with marijuana; others would embrace virtually all currently illicit substances. One major goal of these schemes would be to curtail the levels of violence and criminality that currently surround drug trafficking and sales. Another would be to reduce health hazards stemming from adulteration or impurities in drugs. As *The Economist* once asserted in a widely quoted editorial, "The worst policy is the present one of making the supply of noxious drugs illegal, so that only dreadful illegals engage in their supply."[41]

In the unlikely event that the United States were to opt for legalization, it should do so only in close consultation with key countries of Latin America. After all this promotion of drug wars, it would be politically and morally untenable to decide on unilateral legalization and thus proclaim that Colombia and other countries had made their sacrifices in vain. It would also be important for the United States to develop a capacity for treatment and therapy sufficient to respond to increased use of currently illicit drugs. (Proponents of legalization generally concede that consumption would rise: The question is how much and for how long.) As things now stand, the United States can provide treatment to only one-third of those who need it.

Responsible proposals for legalization present serious and thoughtful alternatives to the course of current policy. The entire idea is far out of favor with the U.S. public and political establishment, however. It is also inconsistent with the international regime codified in the 1988 United Nations Convention Against Illicit Traffic in Narcotic Drugs and Psychotropic Substances. At least as of the early 1990s, there is virtually no chance of the adoption of legalization within the foreseeable future.

For a third alternative, the United States (and Latin America) could embark on a major rearrangement of priorities. Instead of devoting most resources to supply control and law enforcement, governments could concentrate on the long-term reduction of demand through prevention and treatment programs—education, rehabilitation, and assistance. Instead of allocating 70 percent of its antidrug budget to supply control and law enforcement and 30 percent to demand reduction and prevention, as in recent years, the United States could reverse these percentages— or go even farther—allocating 80–85 percent to treatment, prevention, and the long-term reduction of demand. Ultimately, it is decline in demand that will bring about a decline in supply—and in the power of the Latin American drug cartels. Similarly, the United States could devote assistance not so much to the prosecution of the drug wars as to the creation of viable economic alternatives for campesino growers and to the reduction of demand now incipient in drug-producing countries.

This type of approach has been advocated by the Inter-American Commission on Drug Policy, a blue-ribbon group of experts and policymakers that after two years of study released a policy report in June 1991 entitled *Seizing Opportunities* (in Spanish, *Aprovechando el momento*).[42] Basing its analysis on many of the essays in this book, the commission formed three fundamental premises: (1) Demand, not supply, is the most powerful force underlying the market for illicit drugs; (2) drugs and drug trafficking present a multilateral challenge, and nations of the hemisphere must develop a coordinated, multilateral response; and (3) efforts and resources should be devoted to strategies that are truly effective. As a practical, political matter, legalization (in any form) does not offer a plausible choice.[43]

In the commission's judgment, the early 1990s present policymakers with a special set of opportunities. One comes from the apparent decline in the number of illicit drug users within the United States, at least within the middle class—a trend that demonstrates the workability of demand-reduction programs. Second is the formation of an international consensus against drug trafficking, particularly through the 1988 United Nations (UN) Convention Against Illicit Traffic in Narcotic Drugs and Psychotropic Substances—a document that provides the first coherent set of norms and standards for multilateral collaboration. Third is the development by the U.S. government of an Andean Strategy, a policy that budgets sizable and increasing sums for international programs over the next several years.

The challenge is to assure that public resources are employed in constructive, effective ways. With considerable candor, the Inter-American Commission (composed largely of former policymakers) begins its recommendations with a direct call for the U.S. government to terminate or reduce programs that are ineffective or counterproductive. These programs include interdiction of drug supplies at the U.S. border, which costs a good deal of money and has no observable impact on retail prices for drugs; diplomatic pressure in favor of militarization, which endangers human rights and the consolidation of democracy; advocacy of herbicidal spraying as a primary means for eradication of coca production, which poses excessive environmental (and political) hazards; and congressionally mandated "certification" by the U.S. government of antidrug efforts by other countries, which is demeaning and counterproductive.

Instead, the commission advocates a cooperative and integrated effort throughout the Americas to reduce consumer demand for illicit drugs. Positive steps toward this goal should include the provision of drug treatment in all penal systems (which have large drug-afflicted populations in both the United States and Latin America); publicly funded programs for drug-impaired youth, especially those who have dropped out of school; and the training of specialists (perhaps through the Pan American Health Organization or the Organization of American States) to provide technical assistance to Latin American countries. Especially important in the view of the commission is an emphasis on *prevention*: the promotion of education, counseling, and awareness in all elementary and secondary schools, in community organizations, in the media, and in the workplace. Funding for such efforts could come from two sources. One would be through savings from high-cost but ineffective programs, such as border interdiction; amounts spent on such programs run into billions of dollars per year.[44] Second, the commission proposes the innovative creation of a multilateral fund based on the pooling of economic assets seized from drug traffickers in the United States and in other countries of the hemisphere.

To dissuade campesinos from engaging in illicit production of drugs, especially coca leaves, the commission calls for a realistic economic approach. This entails the withdrawal of incentives for illicit cultivation; practically speaking, this means lowering the market price for such crops. (This can best be achieved by interruption of demand at both the wholesale and retail levels and by the encouragement of market gluts; in actual practice, crop eradication programs have the counterintuitive consequence of supporting prices for coca leaves.) This strategy also calls for the expansion and intensification of rural development programs based on hard-headed evaluation of commercial prospects for specific agricultural products. Only through such efforts will it be possible to offer meaningful economic alternatives to hard-pressed campesinos of Latin America.

Law enforcement would have a key role in the commission's strategy. Instead of concentrating efforts on producers and consumers, however, the Inter-American Commission calls for intensified campaigns against the middlemen: the cartels, the trafficking networks, the wholesale distributors, white-collar criminals engaged in money laundering. By definition, such efforts would require enhanced international cooperation, intelligence-sharing, and coordination. Here the Organization of American States could play an especially constructive role—by guiding the efforts of governments with legal analysis and model legislation and by supporting regional commissions of jurists to consider such crucial issues as the status and security of judges.

These recommendations do not call for increased expenditures of public funds by governments throughout the Western Hemisphere. Instead, they call for a major reallocation of public expenditures, away from interdiction and supply control and toward demand reduction. "In the unending campaign against drugs," the commission concludes, "governments must be flexible enough to draw appropriate lessons from their own experience. They should support the programs that work, not those that do not. It is in this fashion, and only in this fashion, that countries of the region can gain genuine benefit from the increased levels of funding foreseen in the U.S. Andean Strategy. And it is only through effective regional collaboration that nations of the Americas will be able to meet the multiple challenges posed by drug abuse and trafficking."[45]

Notes

1. All estimates about the economic volume of the drug business are rough approximations at best; these figures are from the Office of National Drug Control Policy, *National Drug Control Strategy* 1 (Washington, D.C.: U.S. Government Printing Office, 1989), 2.

2. *Los Angeles Times*, January 16, 1991; and *New York Times*, March 3, 1991.

3. Speech at Institute of the Americas, La Jolla, California, November 1, 1990.

4. Remarks of Governor Bob Martinez on the second anniversary of the president's National Drug Control Strategy, National Press Club, Washington, D.C., September 5, 1991.

5. Technically, only some drugs are "narcotics": those that induce narcosis (sleep, stupor). Many drugs are stimulants.

6. Remarks of Governor Bob Martinez, September 5, 1991.

7. Staff Report, Committee on the Judiciary, United States Senate, *Hard-Core Cocaine Addicts: Measuring—and Fighting—the Epidemic* (Washington, D.C.: U.S. Government Printing Office, 1990).

8. Personal communication from U.S. government official.

9. See Chapter 12.

10. Even then, an increase in cocaine use would not positively confirm the hypothesis; it would not disconfirm it. Nor would prior use of marijuana by a large proportion of cocaine users provide direct confirmation. At most, it might show that consumption of marijuana is a necessary but not sufficient prelude to cocaine consumption.

11. A more conservative estimate, the difference between lifetime users and those who have used drugs within the past year, would put this population at 47.6 million.

12. See the remarkable study by George Vaillant, *The Natural History of Alcoholism: Causes, Patterns, and Paths to Recovery* (Cambridge: Harvard University Press, 1983).

13. The life-cycle hypothesis has yet to receive careful testing. The most conclusive examination would come from a longitudinal panel study; cross-sectional surveys could provide at least a partial test, but published NIDA data—which put all people over age twenty-five into one broad category—cannot shed any light on this question.

14. For perspectives on these markets, see "Latin America, Europe, and the Drug Problem: New Forms of Cooperation?" Dossier 32, Instituto de Relaciones Europeo-Latinoamericanas (Madrid, May 1991); and Peter H. Smith, "Drug Problems and Drug Policies in Japan," unpublished memorandum (Tokyo, August 1990).

15. Víctor Zúñiga, "Uso de drogas e interacción transfronteriza en las ciudades fronterizas de Tamaulipas," *Frontera Norte* 2, no. 3 (January-June 1990): 115–135.

16. María Elena Medina-Mora et al., "El consumo de drogas en la frontera norte de México," paper presented at 1ª Reunión Anual de la Asociación Fronteriza de Salud, Laredo, Texas, April 1991; and María Elena Medina-Mora, "Drug Abuse in the Northern Border Region," unpublished paper, 1991.

17. For a full statement of policy, see James M. Van Wert, "The U.S. State Department's Narcotics Control Policy in the Americas," *Journal of Interamerican Studies and World Affairs* 30, nos. 2–3 (Summer-Fall 1988): 1–18.

18. Office of National Drug Control Policy, *National Drug Control Strategy*, 61.

19. As reported in Abraham F. Lowenthal, "Rediscovering Latin America," *Foreign Affairs* 69, no. 4 (Fall 1990): 27–41, especially 36.

20. It would be equally fallacious to conclude that the United States and Latin American countries therefore have identical national interests with regard to drugs. Considerable variation remains in the relative weight of production and consumption, and, as argued below, the United States and Latin American nations face differing problems and challenges.

21. This is due largely to sharply revised estimates for Mexico, which stirred controversy among experts and created friction in U.S.-Mexican relations.

22. Rensselaer Lee III, "Dimensions of the South American Cocaine Industry," *Journal of Interamerican Studies and World Affairs* 30, nos. 2-3 (Summer-Fall 1988): 87-103, with quote on 89.

23. Bilateral Commission on the Future of United States-Mexican Relations, *The Challenge of Interdependence: Mexico and the United States* (Lanham, Md.: University Press of America, 1988), ch. 4, "The Problem of Drugs," 128; see also Guadalupe González and Marta Tienda, eds., *The Drug Connection in U.S.-Mexican Relations* (La Jolla, Calif.: Center for U.S.-Mexican Studies, University of California, San Diego, 1989).

24. Lee, "Dimensions," 89.

25. "A Mission to Nowhere," *Newsweek* (February 19, 1990): 33.

26. For additional discussion, see Centro para el Estudio de las Relaciones Internacionales y el Desarrollo and Fondo Fiduciario Manuel Pérez-Guerrero para la Cooperación Económica y Técnica entre Países en Desarrollo, *El impacto financiero del narcotráfico en el desarrollo de América Latina: Simposio internacional* (La Paz: Editora Atenea, 1991); Juan G. Tokotlián and Bruce M. Bagley, eds., *Economía y política del narcotráfico* (Bogotá: Universidad de los Andes, 1990), esp. Part II; Bruce M. Bagley, Adrián Bonilla, and Alexei Páez, eds., *La economía política del narcotráfico: El caso ecuatoriano* (Quito: Facultad Latinoamericana de Ciencias Sociales, 1991), esp. essay by Wilson Miño, "El lavado de dólares en el Ecuador," 106-124; Diego García-Sayán, ed., *Coca, cocaína y narcotráfico: Laberinto en los Andes* (Lima: Comisión Andina de Juristas, 1989), esp. essay by Humberto Campodónico, "La política del avestruz," 226-258; and Asociación Peruana de Estudios e Investigación para la Paz, *Cocaína: Problemas y soluciones andinos* (Lima: Asociación Peruana de Estudios e Investigación para la Paz, 1990).

27. U.S. Drug Enforcement Administration, *Intelligence Trends*, vol. 14 (Washington, D.C.: USDEA, 1987): 6.

28. "New Kings of Cover," *Time* (July 1, 1991): 29-33; "How Dirty Money Gets Clean," *San Francisco Chronicle*, July 28, 1991; Statement and Memorandum of James E. Preston before the Committee on Banking, Finance, and Urban Affairs, U.S. House of Representatives, Washington, D.C., November 7, 1989; and for background, President's Report on Organized Crime, *The Cash Connection: Organized Crime, Financial Institutions, and Money Laundering* (Washington, D.C.: U.S. Government Printing Office, 1984).

29. "The Nigerian Connection: The Newest Link in the Growing Heroin Trade," *Newsweek* (October 7, 1991): 43.

30. *Los Angeles Times*, September 6 and 7, 1990.

31. See Peter H. Smith, "Drug Wars in Latin America," *Iberoamericana* [Sophia University, Tokyo] 12, no. 1 (Summer 1990): 1-16, esp. 6-10.

32. Cited in "A Widening Drug War," *Newsweek*/International Edition (July 1, 1991): 9.

33. "New Kings of Coke," *Time* (July 1, 1991): 29.

34. Peter Reuter and associates have shown that interdiction can have only a minor effect on retail price because it is likely to account for no more than 8 percent of the total price of cocaine. See Reuter, "Quantity Illusions and Paradoxes of Drug Interdiction: Federal Intervention into Vice Policy," *RAND Note* N-2929-USDP (April 1989), 11; and Peter Reuter, Gordon Crawford, and Jonathan Cave, *Sealing the Borders: The Effects of Increased Military Participation in Drug Interdiction* (Santa Monica, Calif.: RAND Corporation, 1988).

35. See Americas Watch, *Human Rights in Mexico: A Policy of Impunity* (New York and Washington, D.C.: Americas Watch, 1990); Minnesota Lawyers International Human Rights Committee, *Paper Protection: Human Rights Violations and the Criminal Justice System* (Minneapolis: Minnesota Lawyers International Human Rights Committee, 1990); Americas-Watch Committee, *The "Drug Wars" in Colombia: The Neglected Tragedy of Political Violence* (New York: Americas Watch, 1990); and Peter H. Smith, "Human Rights, Democratization, and U.S. Policy Toward Latin America in the 1990s," paper presented to conference "Setting the North-South Agenda: United States–Latin American Relations in the 1990s" at North-South Center, University of Miami, Miami, June 1991.

36. See Washington Office on Latin America, *Clear and Present Dangers: The U.S. Military and the War on Drugs in the Andes* (Washington, D.C.: Washington Office on Latin America, 1991); and "The Newest War," *Newsweek* (January 6, 1992): 18–23.

37. On Peru, see Gustavo Gorriti, "Misadventures in Cocaland," *New York Times*, September 8, 1991.

38. See González and Tienda, *The Drug Connection in U.S.-Mexican Relations*.

39. For the sake of this discussion I am assuming that antidrug policy will not be distorted by other policy considerations, especially foreign policy considerations, which has not always proven to be the case. See Peter Dale Scott and Jonathan Marshall, *Cocaine Politics: Drugs, Armies, and the CIA in Central America* (Berkeley and Los Angeles: University of California Press, 1991).

40. A statement on current (1990) policy appears in Office of National Drug Control Policy, *National Drug Control Strategy* 2 (Washington, D.C.: U.S. Government Printing Office, 1990).

41. *The Economist* (April 2, 1988): 12. On this subject see the many writings of Ethan A. Nadelmann, especially "The Case for Legalization," *The Public Interest* 92 (Summer 1988): 3–31, and "Drug Prohibition in the United States: Costs, Consequences, and Alternatives," *Science* 245 (September 1, 1989): 939–947; "Thinking the Unthinkable," cover story in *Time* magazine (May 30, 1988): 12–18; a series of op-ed articles in the *Los Angeles Times*, March 12–21, 1990; Richard J. Dennis, "The Economics of Legalizing Drugs," *Atlantic Monthly* (November 1990): 126–132; and Robert J. MacCoun, "Would Drug Legalization 'Open the Floodgates?' Examining the Effects of Legal Sanctions on Psychoactive Drug Consumption," unpublished paper (RAND Drug Policy Research Center, March 1991).

42. *Seizing Opportunities: Report of the Inter-American Commission on Drug Policy* (La Jolla, Calif.: Institute of the Americas and Center for Iberian and Latin American Studies, University of California, San Diego, 1991). Although calling for a major rearrangement of priorities, the commission does not specify a proportional distribution of budgetary allocations.

43. It should be reported that most (but not all) members of the commission objected to the idea of legalization in principle.

44. The commission calls for a reduction in the allocation of funds for border interdiction, not for their complete elimination.

45. *Seizing Opportunities*, 41.

PART
ONE

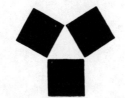

Defining
the
Problem

■◆ Antidrug policies face imposing obstacles—budgetary limitations, imper-
■ fect information, bureaucratic confusion. More fundamental is the broad
array of groups and organizations that have powerful interests in drug trafficking
and its continuation. The criminal cartels that process, transport, and distribute
cocaine and heroin are especially notorious in this regard. But there are others as
well who derive pleasure, sustenance, or profit from illicit drugs. Who are they?
What are their interests? How much power do they have?

First are consumers of illicit drugs, especially in the United States. These
individuals seek enjoyment or solace from the ingestion of narcotic drugs or
psychotropic substances. (Those who suffer from addiction do not exercise the same
degree of choice as casual users, but addicts support their habits until or unless
opportunities for treatment appear.) Drug users have little direct influence on
politics, especially during times of prohibition, but they exert considerable economic
power by determining the size and nature of the retail market.

In the opening chapter of this section, David F. Musto describes cycles of drug
consumption and antidrug policymaking in the United States. The United States
experienced a major drug epidemic around the turn of the century, one that in
some senses foreshadowed the contemporary surge that began in the 1960s and
1970s. Cycles of tolerance and intolerance respond largely to cultural and political
pressures, according to Musto's analysis, although public policy may have played a
significant role in promoting a downturn in marijuana and opium use in the 1920s
and 1930s.

María Elena Medina-Mora and María del Carmen Mariño offer a broad synthesis
of contemporary problems of drug use and abuse in Latin America. The prevalence
of drug use is much lower than in the United States, as shown by a comparative
analysis of national household surveys, though consumption is no doubt on the rise.
Moreover, Medina-Mora and Mariño demonstrate that multiple dynamics are at
work in Latin America: Indigenous communities engage in traditional practices with
peyote and coca leaves; privileged strata tend to indulge in marijuana and (to a
much lesser extent) cocaine; abandoned children living on city streets make extensive
use of diluted coca base or, more frequently, of toxic inhalants.

Producers and traffickers have obvious stakes in the drug trade. Both make more
money than they would from licit pursuits. Somewhat more complicated is the
macroeconomic impact of drug trafficking on "producer" countries, in particular
the cocaine-producing countries of South America—Colombia, Peru, Bolivia.
Remaining chapters in Part One address two sets of fundamental questions. First,
does the drug trade bring economic benefits to producer countries? To whom?
What is the distribution of the benefits? Second, what are the macroeconomic costs
of participation in the drug trade? Do the benefits outweigh the costs or vice versa?

By implication, too, the chapters contemplate a hypothetical postulation: What
would be the social and economic outcomes in Latin American producer countries

of "victory" in the drug wars? Suppose all production and trafficking were brought to a screeching halt—what would happen in these countries? Would they be better off? Chapters 4–7 approach these questions through rigorous analysis of the economic impact of drug production and trafficking on producer countries of the Andes.

Offering an analytical survey of existing estimates about this subject for Colombia, Francisco E. Thoumi argues that (1) the impact of drug trafficking on Colombia is substantial; (2) it is not entirely negative—especially for specific sectors of Colombian society; and (3) much of this activity is beyond the purview of the government. He acknowledges that drug-related violence has discouraged investment and tourism in Colombia but attributes this effect to the illegality of the business rather than to its intrinsic economic character. Thoumi also turns attention to the accumulated overseas assets of the cocaine cartels, multibillion-dollar portfolios that comprise an enormous "overhang" for the Colombian economy. These assets could be anywhere between $39 billion and $66 billion, according to Thoumi's calculations, a sum that could have significant implications not only for Colombia but for international financial markets. Wealth on this scale also helps explain why some cartel ringleaders have pronounced their desires to retire from business with peace, honor, tranquillity—and, of course, prosperity.

Taking up the case of Peru, Elena Alvarez provides an extensive review of methodological efforts to estimate the magnitude of cocaine production and trafficking and focuses on the Upper Huallaga Valley. For the nation as a whole, she establishes an approximate range of $500 million to $1.2 billion for annual coca-cocaine income in the late 1980s. Coca production offers direct employment to roughly 110,000–186,000 peasants and in this sense constitutes a benefit, although it would be almost as profitable—and much less dangerous—for campesinos to raise citrus or other licit cash crops. Moreover, coca leaf production imposes considerable costs, particularly in the degradation of the environment and in the usurpation of governmental authority. Here the political situation is complicated greatly by the existence of a large-scale and intransigent guerrilla movement, Sendero Luminoso, which has declared opposition to crop eradication throughout the Peruvian highlands as part of its claim to represent the cause of campesinos.

For the case of Bolivia, Flavio Machicado stresses both the employment effect and the income effect of coca production in an impoverished economy. In 1987, he asserts, coca leaf production provided direct employment for 150,000 campesinos (and indirect employment for perhaps another 150,000, so the total would be 7 percent of the nation's economically active population). Coca production thus represented one-third of the nation's total agricultural output and over 6 percent of the Bolivian gross national product (GNP); the aggregate value of the entire coca-cocaine production process was equivalent to 31 percent of GNP. In Machicado's view, coca production results from entirely rational economic calculations. The only way to persuade Bolivian campesinos to stop growing coca would be to offer a viable economic alternative; without such an option, it is unrealistic to expect them to forsake such a basic part of their livelihood.

Echoing this basic theme, José Guillermo Justiniano comments on the political resources of coca growers in Peru and especially Bolivia, where farmers articulate their interests through long-established institutional mechanisms in affiliation with the powerful Central Obrera Boliviana. The resulting worker-peasant alliance presents a serious political constraint on governmental policy in Bolivia. This contrasts sharply with Peru, where the growers' occasional alliances with Sendero Luminoso pose a direct paramilitary threat to the existing order rather than a subtle political power within it. It also differs from Colombia: Whereas the narco-terrorism of the Medellín cartel posed a threat to political stability in Colombia, Justiniano suggests, a frontal attack on the coca growers would endanger political stability in Bolivia.

In combination, the chapters in Part One raise several essential points. One relates to methodology. Almost by definition, it is impossible to obtain precise statistical measurements of drug consumption or of illicit economic activity. As a result, researchers—and policymakers—must rely on indirect methods for imprecise estimation of the problems they face. Chapters in Part One survey and review a broad range of methodological approaches—from household surveys to balance-of-payments analysis to aerial photography, from hectare cultivation to migration flows. All these techniques are suggestive; none is conclusive. It therefore seems sensible to use multiple techniques in order to assess the dimensions of drug consumption, production, and trafficking within specific countries.

Second is the problem of comparability. Results from one technique used in Peru are not likely to be comparable to results derived from another technique employed in Bolivia. Because of differences in the availability and collection of data, even use of the same technique in Peru may yield different results in Bolivia. It is questionable, for instance, whether the coca economy of Bolivia is nearly as large as that of Peru, as a comparison of the Alvarez and Machicado chapters seems to suggest.

Third are practical policy implications. Estimations of economic impact are vitally important because they illuminate the magnitude of the drug challenge, the power of the traffickers, and the incentives for governmental policy. Clearly, the goals of the Bolivian government are very different from those of the Colombian government. It is one thing to deal with an extensive and legally organized peasantry; it is quite another to confront a small and illicit criminal cartel. And it is this disparity that complicates the quest for international collaboration.

2

Patterns in U.S. Drug Abuse and Response

David F. Musto

Attitudes toward drug consumption in the United States have undergone a major transformation over the last fifteen or twenty years. Once perceived as a relatively harmless tonic frequently recommended for decriminalization, cocaine has recently come to be seen as a dangerous substance with no redeeming qualities. This turnabout does not represent the first such occurrence in U.S. history. An earlier change in attitude toward cocaine around 1900 closely resembled the popular response to the present cocaine epidemic. Now, as then, the benefits initially ascribed to the drug—euphoria and central nervous system stimulation—were later regarded as seductive dangers and the drug as a menace to society. This pattern of changing attitudes toward cocaine is similar to reactions over time to a number of powerful chemicals and narcotics including opium, morphine, cannabis, and alcohol.

With cocaine as well as other substances, intolerance and condemnation have produced an eventual backlash to this prohibitory mode and a swing toward acceptance and efforts at decriminalization. This relaxation has led to predictably deleterious results for U.S. national health. One might expect that a lesson is learned once and for all, but history chronicles recurring changes in U.S. attitudes. The U.S. public's near-complete ignorance of these earlier episodes may be one reason we have continually repeated this cycle of condemnation and permissiveness.

The history of legislative control in the United States suggests that courses other than decriminalization have been effective. In spite of a substantial addiction rate in the United States around World War I, antinarcotic control measures other than decriminalization accompanied greatly reduced opiate and cocaine consumption. Although the social and legal factors affecting drug use are complex because there is no single influence that determines a particular level of drug use and abuse, study of these early efforts at narcotic limitation may help us approach contemporary

This chapter is adapted from David F. Musto, "The History of Legislative Control over Opium, Cocaine, and Their Derivaties," pp. 37–71 in Ronald Hamowy, ed., *Dealing with Drugs: Consequences of Government Control* (Lexington, Mass.: Lexington Books, 1987) by permission of the Pacific Research Institute.

policy issues with an appreciation of the policy options that reduce or encourage ingestion of these substances.

Legislative control over dangerous drugs began in the early nineteenth century in response to several disturbing trends. Opium was being sold in a crude form containing about 10 percent morphine as well as in concoctions derived from crude opium: paregoric, laudanum, and a solution in acetic acid known as "black drop." Morphine was chemically isolated from opium in 1805, and from the 1830s onward, factories in Germany, Great Britain, and the United States produced it in great quantities. In the early nineteenth century, legislation was passed to prevent acute poisoning from substances that might be purchased in ignorance of their lethal potential or that might be too easily available to those attempting suicide. In 1868 Great Britain enacted pharmacy laws to control dangerous substances, listing "opium and all preparations of opium or of poppies" as commodities that could not be sold without being labeled "poison."[1]

Nineteenth-Century Drug Use

Opium was available in the United States well before the nineteenth century. It was used in various forms derived from crude opium. By the nineteenth century, however, two developments spurred both consumption and concern about opium: (1) the isolation of morphine, which could be injected into the body with hypodermic syringes, and (2) the introduction of smoking opium, which had been brought to the United States mainly by Chinese laborers imported to help build railroads throughout the western United States. Morphine was more addictive than the more dilute forms employed previously, which focused attention on the drug, on medical practitioners, and on modern technology in the form of the hypodermic syringe.

Although the consumption of opium in the United States rose steadily before and after the Civil War, prior to the conflict only a handful of prominent and progressive physicians such as Oliver Wendell Holmes had complained about "opium drunkards." By the latter half of the century many more physicians as well as the general public widely deplored opium and morphine addiction.

Americans received opium and morphine for pain not only from their physicians but they could acquire the substance over the counter or from mail-order catalogues. The U.S. free enterprise system and federalism allowed, quite within the law, a bottle heavily laced with morphine but labeled as containing no morphine whatsoever to be sold across state lines as an "addiction cure."

Despite attempts by a few physicians and pharmacists to strengthen their professions, the U.S. medical and pharmaceutical industries remained largely unorganized throughout the nineteenth century. Moreover, there was no national group of health professionals to which the government could turn for regulation, even if the U.S. constitutional system had permitted such an arrangement.

Whereas in Europe the licensing of pharmacists and physicians was the central government's responsibility, in the United States this power was reserved for individual states. The U.S. Constitution gave states the right to regulate the health professions. In the era of Andrew Jackson—the 1830s—any form of licensing that might lead to a monopoly by the educated classes was criticized as a violation of U.S. democratic ideals. State after state repealed medical licensing laws adopted in earlier days. U.S. medical schools were similarly free from regulation, and many— some no more than "diploma mills"—flourished. States did not reestablish medical licensing until the 1880s, and even then the movement was spotty, with a wide range of standards.[2] Pharmacists—seeking to raise standards and limit their competition—likewise fought at the state level for licensing. In general, the nineteenth- and early twentieth-century interpretation of the Constitution favored a strict division between state and federal powers.

During the nineteenth century, the federal government had no practical control over the health professions; there were no representative national health organizations to aid the government in drafting regulations and no controls on the labeling, composition, or advertising of compounds that might contain opiates or cocaine. In keeping with free market principles, U.S. federal and state governments had virtually no policy concerning narcotics, which were unrestrained at every level of preparation and consumption. State government attempts to control addictive drugs were few and ineffective. The lack of controls facilitated consumption trends.

In the early nineteenth century, the consumption level of opiates in the United States may have been comparable to amounts used in Great Britain, where some areas (notably the fen counties) had a fairly large per-capita consumption.[3] The U.S. annual per-capita consumption rose steadily from about twelve grains in 1840 (an average single dose being one grain) to fifty-two grains per capita annually in the mid-1890s. Statistics show that average individual consumption gradually declined up to 1914, by which time the per-capita rate had fallen back to the level of around 1880.[4] The highest rate of addiction in the United States occurred in the 1890s at the peak rate of 4.59 people per 1,000. Today that rate would be equivalent to 1.1 million addicts, about twice the current official estimate. In short, the nineteenth-century United States faced a serious drug problem.

Drug Control Legislation

Labeling Contents Requirements

In the nation's capital, manufacturers also fought off requirements on content descriptions appearing on nostrum labels. Bills to enact a law requiring labeling under the interstate commerce clause of the Constitution were repeatedly defeated, but in the 1890s a new spirit of reform was evident. The reforms enacted were extensive, ranging from control over the use of forest land to government inspection of meat. The attention given to the danger of narcotics coincided with this era of reform.

The most negative aspects of drug use led to the passage of new legislation. The simplest reform, correct labeling, was part of the Pure Food and Drug Act of 1906. Labels on over-the-counter medicines—usually "patent medicines"—had to list inclusion of any of the following drugs: morphine, cocaine, cannabis, and chloral hydrate (a sleeping medicine). This long-desired reform informed the purchaser if any of these drugs were present in the item. However, it did not prevent purchase or restrict the amount of the drug.

Reports at the time nonetheless indicate a one-half to one-third decline in the use of these substances as a response to public concern.[5] Although the newspapers remained quiet on the subject, widely read magazines such as *Colliers* and *Ladies' Home Journal* railed against patent medicines, especially morphine and cocaine.[6]

State laws were soon amended as laymen and leaders of the health professions became more aware of the growing number of those addicted to opiates, primarily morphine. Meanwhile the professions still lacked organization and continued struggling to achieve mandatory licensing: A threat to take away a license could not be an effective deterrent until a license was required to begin with. Legislators also felt, or at least claimed, a helplessness when neighboring states did not enact strict content and labeling laws—a circumstance more familiar to us with, until recently, variations in the legal drinking age among states. Combined with poorly trained physicians, a lack of professional organizations, and the absence of laws controlling either patent medicine or interstate commerce in drugs, this condition kept local controls more symbolic than effective.

Drug Control and the Progressive Movement

The 1890s saw the rise of what would come to be called the Progressive Movement, a set of reforms typically taking the form of federal laws affecting the entire nation with the ostensible purpose of strengthening the nation's moral fabric or resisting the selfish actions of the rich and powerful. In this climate a movement favoring temperance built up that would eventuate in the Eighteenth Amendment, which outlawed alcohol distribution for nonmedical purposes in the United States.

In many ways the antialcohol movement was part of the Progressive Era; its startling success and later dramatic repeal have contributed to making alcohol a somewhat separate issue, but the interrelationship between the battles against alcohol and narcotics is important. The antialcohol crusade helped establish the beliefs that there could be no compromise with the forces of evil and that "moderation" was a false concept when applied to alcohol: Prohibition was the only logical and moral policy for dealing with this grave national problem.

The significance of prohibition in the control of narcotics was clear. The regulation of alcohol, another dangerous substance, had evolved toward a policy of "no maintenance" and no compromise. Would the same principle be applied to narcotics?

U.S. Drug Policy in the Philippines

The narcotics issue rose to the federal legislative agenda by historical accident. Certainly it would eventually have come to the attention of Congress and the president as a corollary to alcohol prohibition or as an attempt to control addiction, an issue increasingly popular among journalistic reformers and physicians. But it was the acquisition of the Philippines through the Spanish-American War (1898) that prompted decisive action by the federal government because the Philippines, unlike a state, came directly under the control of the federal government. Congress was now forced to wrestle with the issue of the local availability of opium.

Opium had been provided to the Chinese on the Philippine Islands through a Spanish government monopoly. When the islands passed to U.S. control in 1903, Civil Governor William Howard Taft considered whether the monopoly should be reinstituted.[7] It was at this point that the moral question of compromising with "evil" had to be answered. Missionaries in Manila and in the United States strongly urged President Theodore Roosevelt to prevent this moral wrong. Roosevelt ordered Taft to stop the monopoly bill, and that was the end of it. The mood of moral leaders in the United States during the first few years of this century was sufficient to prevent any such "maintenance" program for opium addicts, even if its controlled use was allowed—as originally promised—to the Chinese in the Philippines. This response, coming even before the U.S. Food and Drug Act, gave a hint as to how the federal government would respond to future debates regarding the legal availability of opium for enjoyment or to satisfy addiction rather than for medical purposes.

The Philippine situation forced the federal government to take a stand on opium use for nonmedical purposes, and the decision was made to prohibit this practice. This stance was influenced by Congress's unwillingness to compromise on narcotics policy. According to the Opium Investigating Committee created by Taft to study the issue, the solution to the Philippine problem required the control of international trafficking in opium as well as the curtailment of production in such nations as India, China, Burma, Persia, and Turkey. The Philippines thus placed the United States in the role of leader of the international control of narcotics—a role it holds to this day. Through a series of international conferences in the years before World War I, the United States sought to curtail the drug trade. The State Department took the lead in formulating an antidrug policy for this country.

The Antinarcotics Bills (1910–1914)

The State Department's first attempt to pass an antinarcotics bill failed. The 1910 bill was too stringent for druggists and never even came to a vote in the Sixty-first Congress.[8] The Sixty-second Congress convened in a markedly different political setting. For the first time in almost two decades, Democrats gained control of the House of Representatives, bringing them new power to further the interests especially of Southern Democrats. During this Congress the Foster Bill became the Harrison

Bill, named after Francis Burton Harrison, a New York City Democrat who served on the Foreign Relations Committee. The State Department antidrug specialist, Dr. Hamilton Wright, continued the difficult task of trying to obtain the most stringent bill consistent with winning essential political support from the medical and pharmaceutical interests as well as from the Democratic party. This task prompted the drug industry to establish the National Drug Trade Conference (NDTC), which would represent the major trade associations and try to reach a compromise position on the complex antinarcotics bill. The NDTC, which first met in January 1913 in Washington, D.C., exerted a powerful influence on the writing of what would become known as the Harrison Act.[9]

The attitude of the newly influential Southern Democrats toward any potential invasion of states' rights now had to be taken more seriously. These politicians feared interference with the South's local laws, which enforced racial segregation and disenfranchisement of African-Americans. They bitterly remembered the era of Reconstruction, when the North ruled the South following 1865, and wanted to maintain the authority the white citizenry had won upon the withdrawal of northern troops and "carpetbaggers." Furthermore, the use of the power to tax primarily to achieve a moral end—because the taxes were not intended to bring in a significant revenue but rather to force disclosure and compliance with the rules of narcotics distribution—might set a precedent for other issues brewing in the United States, such as the protection of black voting rights in the South.

Another concern was related to the flourishing prohibition movement. As prohibition was achieved in state after state, the loophole for at least the upper and middle classes was that alcohol could be ordered across state lines and shipped into a dry state, because interstate commerce was regulated by the federal government, which was not yet teetotal. The Webb-Kenyon Act of 1913 was enacted to close this loophole. It survived President Taft's veto and, to the surprise of many, was declared constitutional by the Supreme Court. This removed a stumbling block to the Harrison Bill, because now a national antinarcotics law could not serve as a precedent for curtailing interstate commerce in a dangerous substance.

In the course of all this maneuvering, no one rallied to the defense of any of the drugs under consideration, except that occasionally cannabis was described as not habit-forming or not as serious as opium or cocaine. Perhaps in response to these arguments, cannabis was dropped from the proposed law. Chloral hydrate was also dropped. The attitude toward nonmedical use of opium and cocaine, by contrast, was almost always condemnatory.

The only question was how to control distribution as efficiently as possible. This was problematic because although these drugs were addicting, they had some medicinal value. The government and the trades eventually reached agreement on the proposed law by moderating the record-keeping provision, reducing penalties, and allowing the sale of patent medicines containing small amounts of opiates. Representative Harrison introduced the bill in June 1913, and in December 1914, President Wilson signed it into law—to become effective March 1, 1915. At last the

United States had fulfilled its pledge to the international community that it would enact a stringent law, as it had urged every other nation to do.

The significance of the Harrison Act to State Department strategists, however, was more than just the satisfaction of having redeemed pledges made to incredulous officials of other nations. For them, the Harrison Act was the implementation of the Hague Convention of 1912, which called upon signatories to enact domestic legislation controlling narcotics supplies and distribution. Understood as the fulfillment of treaty obligations, the Harrison Act gave the federal government the authority to usurp the states' police powers because Article Six of the Constitution gives treaties concluded by the United States supremacy over the laws of states. Thus was resolved the problem of states' rights interfering with the ability of a national law to require a uniform compliance with strict narcotics control.[10]

Early Enforcement

Unfortunately, at first the Supreme Court did not concur with the executive branch's interpretation of the Harrison Act. In the first Jin Fuey Moy case (1916), the Court declared by a six-to-two majority that the Harrison Act could not be understood as having been required in every detail by the Hague Convention and that physicians could prescribe substances as they saw fit, even to simple addicts.[11] The decision was a blow to federal enforcement. From the first day of implementation, the act had been directed at pharmacists and physicians who sold prescriptions or treated addicts without any intent to cure them.

World War I, commencing a few months before the enactment of the Harrison Act, profoundly affected U.S. attitudes by creating an intense desire to purify and strengthen the nation as it girded itself to fight for democracy against the barbarism of the Kaiser. The fall of Russia and the spread of Bolshevism intensified fears of contagion and the desire to ensure that the United States remained pure and strong. Not surprisingly, prohibition became a vehicle for such purification and morality-building.

Similarly, a battle was being fought to overturn the Jin Fuey Moy decision, which had weakened the government's intention concerning the Harrison Act. A Treasury Department committee reported that there were over one million addicts in the nation.[12] These exaggerated figures, the fear of returning veterans having become addicted on the battlefield, and the specter of alcohol prohibition—which might drive alcoholics to morphine and cocaine—led to a revived attempt to put teeth into the Harrison Act. This time the government was successful.

In March 1919, two months after the ratification of the Eighteenth Amendment (which would go into effect a year later), the Supreme Court decided five-to-four that a "prescription" for narcotics intended to supply a "mere" addict with maintenance doses was a misnomer because such prescriptions were not intended to cure and thus were not the proper conduct of medical practice. Because it was not a prescription, the issuing physician had conveyed narcotics without the required tax; the doctor therefore had violated the Harrison Act and could be arrested.[13]

At last, the intent of the reformers had been achieved: Simple maintenance was outlawed, and the federal government could take action nationwide to arrest and convict health professionals who practiced it. There was now a no-maintenance policy toward narcotics, which would soon be applied to alcohol. Enforcement of both prohibitions would be the responsibility of a single unit within the Bureau of Internal Revenue Service, reflecting the similarity in the approaches toward these different substances.

The Harrison Act in the 1920s

Perhaps the most important addition to the Harrison Act came in 1924, when the United States banned the importation of opium used for the manufacture of heroin.[14] The observance of federal-state boundaries is evident in this law because it did not ban the manufacture of heroin altogether but only the importation of crude opium for that purpose. More than this seemed to be beyond the power of the federal government.

This law affected several pharmaceutical companies. Heroin had been made available commercially by the Bayer Company of Germany in 1898 as a superior cough suppressant.[15] Heroin had been available in the United States prior to the Harrison Act, and by 1915 in New York City it had replaced morphine as the drug of recreational choice among those admitted to Bellevue Hospital for addiction treatment. The addictive nature of heroin had been recognized rather quickly because the American Medical Association issued a warning in 1902. Heroin was popular because it could be inhaled by sniffing, like cocaine, as well as injected by needle. When injected into the bloodstream, heroin crossed the blood-brain barrier more quickly than morphine, thus delivering a more intense, but briefer, "high." During the years of concern over social control, which began with World War I, heroin became linked with gang violence and the commission of crimes. Some believed that heroin stimulated the user to commit crimes or at least provided the courage to attempt anything from a mugging to a bank robbery. In the early 1920s, most of the crime in New York City was blamed on drug use—principally of opiates, including heroin.[16]

The preference for heroin over morphine by nonmedical users and the belief that other opiates could fulfill heroin's role as a painkiller and a cough suppressant spurred efforts to ban heroin even for medical purposes. The United States put an end to all domestic heroin production in the 1920s but failed to achieve its goals at the Geneva Opium Conferences of 1924 and 1925. Frustrated with the refusal of other nations to agree to curb production of poppies and coca bushes—the ultimate sources of heroin and cocaine—U.S. officials walked out of the conference.[17] Suddenly, the country that had impelled the world antinarcotic movement before World War I now saw the movement taken over by the League of Nations (as the Treaty of Versailles mandated) and controlled by the very nations the United States had sought to shame or force into adopting a more "responsible" narcotics policy.

But this role reversal was not permanent. By the outbreak of World War II, the United States again was marshaling significant participation in international antidrug activities.

The Effects of Drug Control

The use of cocaine, a legitimate ingredient in soft drinks such as Coca-Cola until 1900 and available easily to sniff as a treatment for sinusitis or hay fever, fell after reaching a peak around 1905. By the 1930s cocaine use had declined substantially, and by the 1950s it was practically absent.

Several reasons can be suggested for the decline in cocaine consumption after 1900. Ironically, the drug had initially been introduced as a "wonder" substance. Physicians had praised it as the first medicine that worked as an antidepressant. By 1885 the Parke-Davis Company manufactured coca and cocaine in many forms for drinking, smoking, inhaling, injection, or rubbing into the skin. Although warnings surfaced within a decade, consumption peaked about twenty years after its initial distribution. The peak in consumption occurred around the same time that accounts appeared of cocaine's effect on the lives of users and its popularly believed—although questionable—link with southern blacks. So appalling were the public's perceptions of cocaine's effects that its alleged consequences became the extreme against which other drugs would be compared. Cocaine's association with violence, paranoia, and collapsed careers made laws against it popular by 1900. The first anticocaine law in New York State was enacted in 1907 and was repeatedly strengthened up to the date of the Harrison Act. The combination of strict laws and strong public support of control measures induced a decline in consumption that at the peak of cocaine's legal popularity must have seemed unlikely if not impossible.

The Harrison Act, its court interpretations, and supplementary legislation also appear to have greatly reduced the number of opiate addicts. The medical and pharmacy professions were denied an easy way of providing drugs. Although it is clear that only a fraction of either profession was liberal in the provision of these drugs, this nevertheless had been enough to maintain a large (but declining) number of users. The number of addicts fell from roughly a quarter of a million in 1900 to much less than half that number by World War II. The war effectively reduced supplies of narcotics to the United States, and in 1945 the country probably had the lowest number of opiate addicts since the mid-nineteenth century.

Narcotic Clinics, 1912–1925

Narcotic clinics were intended to deal with addicts who could no longer receive opiate or cocaine supplies from local physicians.[18] The first in the United States was opened in 1912 by Charles Terry, the public health officer of Jacksonville, Florida, where he provided both opiates and cocaine to men and women, blacks and whites. Other clinics followed—especially after the Treasury Department, in enforcement of the Harrison Act, prosecuted or threatened with prosecution health professionals who supplied addicts indefinitely. A series of clinics in New England was established at the suggestion of officials of the Internal Revenue Bureau. In New York State, the crackdown on druggists and physicians emanated from state law, and clinics were established in upper New York State through state planning and authorization. Registration of addicts was permitted so that physicians would restrict maintenance to those already addicted.

In New York City, the Health Department—although it did not wish to provide opiates, morphine, and heroin on an indefinite basis—opened a clinic at the departmental headquarters. This clinic provided heroin but only as an inducement to registration and eventual detoxification and rehabilitation. About 7,500 addicts registered, received their drug of choice in dosages gradually decreased until uncomfortably small (usually three to eight grains of morphine daily), and were offered curative treatment. Unfortunately, most declined to be cured. It was estimated that 95 percent of those who received treatment at North Brother Island were likely to return to narcotics available on the street or from a physician or druggist.

Before their demise, the clinics treated a relatively large number of addicts. The 13,000 addicted registrants in New York State in 1920 are the largest number of legally supplied addicts recorded in any Western country in this century, a number not approached by Great Britain under the so-called British system. Although the "American system" preceded and surpassed in size any scheme attempted at that time or subsequently, it was the large number of addicts in the United States that made maintenance so unwieldy and unpopular.

The relative ease with which addicts could obtain drugs did not last long. Armed with fresh Supreme Court decisions of March 1919, the Treasury Department started to close down the clinics, along with making threats to prosecute the physicians and druggists. One argument was that the availability of easy maintenance inhibited cures. Another was that giving legal permission for maintenance clinics undercut the Treasury Department's position when bringing action against a professional for the reckless provision of drugs. From a legal point of view, the "reckless" provider and the responsible clinic were both obeying the tax laws unless the federal government wanted to get into the question of medical competence, which was a state—not a federal—concern.

Gradually the clinics were closed; the last one was shut down in 1925 in Knoxville, Tennessee. Some had been poorly operated; others functioned quite responsibly with community support. Yet because of the intricacies of the tax powers under federal law, all were closed, even if unfair harassment was necessary to discourage the operation.

The demise of the clinics left drug peddlers and individual members of the health professions as the major targets of the federal government. Generally, physicians neither had any sympathy for nor wished to treat addicts. Those physicians who, for whatever reason, continued to treat addicts with maintenance doses were threatened and at times arrested unless maintenance—determined by individual evaluation by a narcotics agent—had been permitted. Reports prepared by agents investigating narcotic clinics suggest that an acceptable life-style and some medical need or medically caused conditions were requirements for permission.[19]

With maintenance rejected, physicians unfortunately had no effective medical cure available for addiction. Several cures had been promoted in many forms in the nineteenth and early twentieth centuries, but none had been found to have any scientific merit. The issue had turned into a decision of whether to stop opiates abruptly and thereby cause the patient to go directly into full withdrawal—the so-called "cold turkey" approach—or gradually to reduce the opiate over a few days or a few weeks. Two ancient warnings about detoxification—that the patient would die in withdrawal or that a supply cutoff would precipitate a rash of suicides—never materialized.

Marijuana Tax Act of 1937

With the battle against opiate addiction having apparently led to more stable, less alarming levels of use in the 1930s and cocaine use having declined dramatically, a new drug appeared on the U.S. horizon: Marijuana arrived in the United States by way of Mexican agricultural laborers who had crossed the border mostly to harvest fields in the Southwest and Midwest. During the prosperous 1920s, around half a million farm workers came to the United States. But as the Depression's widespread unemployment laid an increasingly heavy burden on the country's citizens, Mexicans became an unwelcome group and were encouraged in all ways to return to Mexico. Among other troubles Mexicans were said to cause local citizens was their custom of growing marijuana for their own use. A strong and negative link thus was made between marijuana and Mexican aliens.[20]

Marijuana use was most prevalent in the western and southwestern United States. The government was importuned to take action, but its recent experience with alcohol prohibition (which had ended in 1933) made the Federal Bureau of Narcotics (FBN) hesitant to get involved in fighting a drug that was grown domestically and prolifically. Because cocaine and heroin were foreign imports, they could—at least theoretically—be regulated more easily and less controversially. Marijuana, on the other hand, appeared to be almost impossible to curb, let alone eradicate. The FBN tried to address this drug by including it in a proposed uniform state narcotics law that would leave to localities the question and allocation of enforcement resources. But a curious law intended to reduce the number of machine guns gave the government the legal means to attack marijuana nationally and at the federal level.

The Firearms Act of 1934 decreed that a change of ownership of machine guns required a transfer tax. This act set the legal precedent for the 1937 passage of a law requiring a transfer tax for marijuana. Enforcement of the marijuana transfer tax law was weak, however, because the FBN did not receive increases in budget or staff and attempted to rely on horrifying descriptions of marijuana to curb the spread in its use. The substance was described to the public as a danger at least equal to cocaine or morphine, and the penalties for its illegal use or possession were severe. Because use of marijuana does not seem to have been great in the 1930s, the law's extraordinary severity did not affect the general public until the 1960s, when thousands of users were arrested as marijuana's popularity burgeoned. Tension between users and drug enforcement officials increased as the inconsistencies between the effects of marijuana observed in the 1960s and the effects long claimed by the FBN became more apparent. These discoveries led to widespread public disbelief in official statements, which still affects popular perceptions today.

Postwar Drug Use and Control

World War II to the 1960s

World War II ended with relatively few opiate addicts and little use of cocaine or marijuana in the United States. The only closely controlled drug increasing in use was alcohol, the consumption of which had increased in per-capita rates since the repeal of Prohibition. During this period, sleeping pills and other barbiturates were prescribed widely but did not appear to be a major problem. The same holds true for amphetamines, which had been made available in the 1930s and continued to be manufactured and prescribed without federal restriction.

Around 1950 a younger age group began to be admitted for heroin addiction, an abuse that reached a very high level by 1970 and remains substantial today. This phenomenon elicited two responses. First, the federal government enacted more stringent laws levying mandatory sentences for conviction of dealing in narcotics. The laws enacted in 1951 and 1956 are the harshest legal penalties against illicit drugs, including marijuana, in the United States to date.[21] The second response reflected the domestic and international tensions of the time. The heroin menace— and it should be reemphasized that cocaine and marijuana were not seen as major problems in the 1950s—was attributed to the infiltration of the drug trade by the Chinese Communists who had taken over mainland China in 1949.

Heroin addicts in the 1950s were mainly young males concentrated in black and Hispanic urban ghettos. Reform-minded lawyers, academics, and physicians found the harsh penalties and the loathing attitude toward addicts to be inhumane. Rather than depriving addicts of heroin, according to this perspective, heroin should be provided to them. Rather than being jailed, addicts should be hospitalized if necessary or simply left alone.[22] This alternative view competed with the more hard-line style of law enforcement.

However, the medical treatment of addicts—popular before World War I but later found to be inadequate for reducing addiction—again became a part of public policy in the 1960s. Methadone, a synthetic opiate developed in Germany during World War II, was used to provide maintenance. This marked a major break in U.S. narcotic control policies: Maintenance again was legal, although not maintenance with heroin or morphine.

1960s to the Present

In the 1960s an enthusiasm for drug consumption of all kinds—"polydrug abuse"—replaced the use of one or two drugs, which had been more common in the past. Marijuana became very popular with young people, although its popularity gradually increased among older age groups as well. Psychedelic drugs, such as LSD, appeared on the scene along with injectable amphetamine, also known as "speed."

Drugs came to symbolize opposition to the government and to traditional mores. Social turmoil and discontent caused by the Vietnam War intensified the sense of alienation many young people felt toward the previous generation, which frowned on drug use other than alcohol and tobacco. In addition to cultural alienation and the rapid increase in multidrug use, the drug problem in the 1960s was augmented by the extraordinarily large number of young people in the age groups most likely to experiment with drugs: The post–World War II "baby boom" generation had reached the teenage years.

By 1970 marijuana was in common use. Research showed that it did not have the horrific effects ascribed to it from the 1930s onward, and various groups and individuals even initiated movements to legalize the substance, perhaps along the lines of tobacco. During the 1970s, however, the drug problem came to be perceived by the public and the federal government to be so serious that it called for a major reevaluation of the nation's entire policy. In 1971 President Richard Nixon established a National Commission on Marijuana and Drug Abuse.

In general, the members of the commission reflected traditional views on the subject of drug control; therefore the commission's recommendation in its first report that marijuana be "decriminalized" had great impact. Decriminalization meant not legalization but one step short of that position: Marijuana possession for individual use would no longer be a crime, but its sale and distribution would. The purpose of control at this stage would be to relieve law enforcement agencies of the nuisance of arresting individual users, thereby allowing more resources to be devoted to the investigation of large-scale crime and more dangerous drugs.[23]

The second and final report, published in 1973, dealt with drugs more broadly.[24] It focused more on the actual, measurable damage done by drugs, reflected in hospital admissions and drug-related deaths, as opposed to the myths that had evolved about many of them. (Heroin, for example, had been misperceived as causing more deaths annually than barbiturates.) This approach was designed to rationalize the discussion over drug policy as well as to lay the groundwork for the inclusion of cigarettes and alcohol in the antidrug crusade. It downplayed, however, the effects of a drug such as cocaine on judgment and efficiency—effects that are less quantifiable but still real aspects of drug use.

The enforcement of laws against individual possession or use of marijuana has fallen to a very low level in the United States. Small-time dealers reportedly are not prosecuted either because the largest dealers and smugglers, who are involved with tons—not ounces or pounds—of marijuana, require all the time of drug enforcement officials. There has been a de facto decriminalization throughout much of the country, even though laws against individual use still exist. Even so, the incidence of marijuana use by high-school seniors has been dropping since 1978. This reduction and a more conservative national mood have slowed further efforts to formally decriminalize marijuana or to soften current drug laws.

Conclusion

The first U.S. cocaine epidemic deserves attention for two basic reasons. First, we can see parallels between the earlier change in attitude and the one we have experienced in the last twenty years or so. Second, the first cocaine epidemic provides a convenient model for analyzing changes in attitude toward seductive drugs.

For the second time in this century, the rise in cocaine's availability and popularity has further complicated the control of drugs in the United States. The fact that an era in which millions used marijuana was followed by a period in which millions more took cocaine raises doubt about the ability of local and national governments to control illicit drugs. The corruption inherent in the drug trade and the restraints on resources that can be allocated to drug control combine to create a sense of frustration with enforcement policy.

Morphine and other opiates have had a more gradual rise in use and a decline perhaps less precipitous than cocaine. Opiate consumption in the United States peaked in the 1890s after rising in an open market throughout the nineteenth century. The lack of state restrictions on opiates until very late in the century and the lack of any significant national controls both were due to the federal form of U.S. government practiced in the last century—that is, a strict reservation of police power, under which antidrug activities generally operate, to the states. Opiate use, furthermore, did not fade as completely as use of cocaine and began a gradual rise in the 1950s—earlier than cocaine, which came back around 1970.

The United States has witnessed recurrent waves of alcohol use, and attitudes about the substance have fluctuated from positive to negative. It is important to stress that the changes in attitude from tolerance to intolerance are not just found in the decades leading up to national Prohibition in 1920 and the backlash to Prohibition that began after 1933. This view inaccurately portrays the antialcohol movement and Prohibition as a mere aberration in our social history, a peculiar event that can safely be forgotten. As I suggested in regard to the first cocaine epidemic, we can easily forget past waves of drug use, but it is to our loss to do so.

The eventual repeal of Prohibition stemmed from a combination of factors. First, unlike for cocaine, there was a cultural acceptance of alcohol among tens of millions of Americans. Although the amount consumed was greatly reduced during Prohibition, the use of alcohol could not be extinguished to the extent that had been accomplished with smoki: g opium, other opiates, or cocaine. The onset of the

Depression made the repeal of the law attractive as a way to stimulate employment and increase badly needed revenue. Repeal, however, came with a backlash: a weariness with talk of alcohol control and alcohol-related problems. Half a century would go by before popular movements such as Mothers Against Drunk Driving and Remove Intoxicated Drivers could again raise questions about alcohol without being apologetic or defensive.

Today, I believe, we are entering a new temperance era, with a growing awareness of the negative side of alcohol. Several crucial elements of earlier temperance movements can be observed. First, an aspect of alcohol's social impact abhorrent to both drinkers and abstainers has been identified and publicized: the drunk-driving problem. Second, the multiple, distinctive forms of alcohol—spirits, wine, and beer—are now perceived as all containing alcohol, with other characteristics deemed irrelevant. Third, alcohol is moving from a substance seen as being helpful, or at least harmless when taken in moderation, toward being a poison. Significant factors in this transformation in attitudes are studies on Fetal Alcohol Syndrome and, more recently, warnings against the male partner's consumption of alcohol near conception.

The battles against alcohol, cocaine, and other chemicals easily become moral contests in which no quarter can be conceded to the hated enemy. The gradual movement toward the prohibition of dangerous substances is both logical and ethical to many Americans. But if we are entering another era of temperance, we will benefit greatly from understanding this country's previous experiences with drug use and control. Expanding the factors we employ in our analysis will make us understand the long-term consequences of outright prohibition.

We are in danger of repeating past mistakes. Perhaps the most unfortunate consequence of Prohibition was the backlash that inhibited direct and frank consideration of the alcohol problem for half a century afterward. The challenge for persons deeply concerned about the impact of alcohol on the health of the born and the unborn is to devise policies that will create lasting changes in behavior that will resist the extreme positions that have characterized past antialcohol campaigns. This task may seem frustrating when the benefits of enforced abstinence seem so obvious, but the most fruitful efforts will be those that produce enduring salubrious changes.

Notes

1. 31 and 32 Vict. ch. 121, 1868: Act to Regulate the Sale of Poison and Alter and Amend the Pharmacy Act 1852 (1868 Pharmacy Act).

2. R. H. Shyrock, *Medical Licensing in America, 1650–1965* (Baltimore: Johns Hopkins Press, 1967), 32ff.

3. Virginia Berridge, "Fenland Opium Eating in the Nineteenth Century," *British Journal of Addiction* 72 (1977): 275–284.

4. David F. Musto, *The American Disease: Origins of Narcotic Control* (New Haven: Yale University Press, 1973), 3.

5. J. P. Street, "The Patent Medicine Situation," *American Journal of Public Health* 7 (1917): 1037–1042.

6. James Harvey Young, *The Toadstool Millionaires: A Social History of Patent Medicines Before Federal Regulation* (Princeton: Princeton University Press, 1961), 213ff.

7. Musto, *American Disease*, 25ff.

8. Musto, *American Disease*, 40–48.

9. Musto, *American Disease*, 54–68.

10. Hamilton Wright to Charles Evans Hughes, June 28, 1916, in Papers of Dr. Hamilton Wright, U.S. National Archives, Record Group 43, entry 36.

11. *U.S. v. Jin Fuey Moy*, 241 U.S. 394 (1916).

12. *Special Committee of Investigation, Appointed March 25, 1918, by the Secretary of the Treasury: Traffic in Narcotic Drugs* (Washington, D.C.: U.S. Government Printing Office, 1919).

13. *Webb et al. v. U.S.*, 249 U.S. 96 (1919); *U.S. v. Doremus*, 249 U.S. 86 (1919).

14. 68th Congress, Public Law no. 274, Section 2. Prohibiting the importation of crude opium for the purposes of manufacturing heroin. Approved June 7, 1924.

15. David F. Musto, "Early History of Heroin in the United States," in P. G. Bourne, ed., *Addiction* (New York: Academic Press, 1974), 175–185.

16. Gerhard Kuhne, "Statement of Gerhard Kuhne, Head of the Identification Bureau, New York City Department of Correction," in *Conference on Narcotic Education: Hearings Before the Committee on Education of the House of Representatives, December 16, 1925* (Washington, D.C.: U.S. Government Printing Office, 1926), 175.

17. Arnold H. Taylor, *American Diplomacy and the Narcotics Traffic, 1900–1939: A Study in International Humanitarian Reform* (Durham, N.C.: Duke University Press, 1969), 200ff.

18. Musto, *American Disease*, 151–181.

19. Musto, *American Disease*, 167ff.

20. David F. Musto, "Marijuana Tax Act of 1937," *Archives of General Psychiatry* 26 (1972): 101–108.

21. 82nd Congress, Public Law no. 255, approved November 2, 1951; 84th Congress, Public Law no. 728, approved July 18, 1956.

22. Alfred R. Lindesmith, *The Addict and the Law* (New York: Vintage Books, 1965); and Rufus King, *The Drug Hang-Up: America's Fifty-Year Folly* (New York: Norton, 1972).

23. *Marijuana: A Signal of Misunderstanding*, First Report of the National Commission on Marijuana and Drug Abuse (Washington, D.C.: U.S. Government Printing Office, 1972), 150ff.

24. *Drug Use in America: Problem in Perspective*, Second Report of the National Commission on Marijuana and Drug Abuse (Washington, D.C.: U.S. Government Printing Office, 1973).

3

Drug Abuse in Latin America

María Elena Medina-Mora
and María del Carmen Mariño

Drug abuse is not a new phenomenon in Latin America, although it has recently acquired new characteristics. The proportion of the population that uses illicit drugs has grown in size. Illegal production and distribution of drugs affect the economies of many nations. Associated crime, violence, and political disruption have no historical precedents. In order to understand the impact of drugs throughout Latin America, we must not only focus on traditional dimensions of supply and demand— we must also consider the social and economic consequences of the production and trafficking of illicit drugs.

Socioeconomic conditions in Latin America are likely to encourage drug consumption. As do other developing areas, Latin America suffers from numerous hazards to health: (1) precarious conditions of personal and environmental hygiene, which often spread infectious disease; (2) susceptibility to degenerative diseases such as heart conditions, cerebrovascular strokes, cancer, diabetes, and mental problems; (3) exposure to chemical products and toxic substances; and (4) pressures within the family and workplace that are associated with violence and alcohol and drug abuse.

Social opportunities are limited. Although the birthrate has declined, it is still one of the highest in the world. As a result, many young people in Latin America will have little chance for education and employment.[1] Urbanization has steadily accelerated, largely as a result of migration, as young people have moved from the countryside to cities in search of jobs and opportunities. Rapid urbanization has led to the consequent formation of "poverty belts" outside major cities; these slumlike areas lack services, pose high risks for health, and create a climate for antisocial behavior and drug abuse among youth.

The rural sector continues to represent a substantial portion of the overall population in Latin America, and it tends to be increasingly poor. It is because of their poverty that country people are often willing to cultivate illegal drugs. In 1988 the rural population of the major drug-producing countries represented 51 percent of the total population in Bolivia, 48 percent in Ecuador, 35 percent in Colombia, 31 percent in Peru, and 30 percent in Mexico—compared with only 26 percent in the United States and 25 percent in Western Europe.[2]

As social problems have intensified, public expenditures on health have declined throughout the region. Spending on health as a proportion of the gross domestic product (GDP) declined between 1980 and 1985 from 1.7 percent to 0.4 percent in Bolivia, from 0.8 percent to 0.7 percent in Colombia, from 1.8 percent to 1.1 percent in Ecuador, and from 1.3 percent to 1.2 percent in Peru.[3] This trend results from the economic crisis of the 1980s. An increase in unemployment and a decrease in health expenditures mean fewer resources are available for treatment and prevention of illness, even though public health needs are more urgent than ever.

Finally, drugs are increasingly available throughout Latin America. Despite the fact that most drugs are destined for export, mostly to the United States, a considerable (and probably increasing) proportion stays within the region. Drugs produced in Latin America include, among others, coca leaf and its derivatives, coca paste and hydrochloride of cocaine; opium and heroin; marijuana; and a variety of natural plants with hallucinogenic effects. The volume of production for cocaine has increased sharply in recent years: Between 1947 and 1980, 35 metric tons were seized throughout the entire world; during the three-year period from 1983 through 1985, 94 metric tons were seized in the Andean region alone. By the mid-1980s, annual U.S. sales of cocaine from Bolivia reached an estimated $6.5 billion, equivalent to more than 70 percent of the entire Bolivian GDP.[4]

Coca leaf is processed into an intermediate product known as base, or paste, which is then transported to such countries as Colombia, where it is transformed into hydrochloride of cocaine. Under the control of highly organized cartels, this product then finds its way to the United States and Europe through a number of Latin American countries. Along these routes the consumption of cocaine is modest but increasing.[5]

Mexico has become an important transit point for cocaine. From 1975 through 1984, over 2,000 kilograms of cocaine were seized in Mexico; in 1985 alone, seizures amounted to more than 2,500 kilograms. More cocaine was seized in Mexico in 1985 than in all of Western Europe combined.[6]

The production and trafficking of cocaine have led to an increase in its visibility, and its availability throughout Latin America. Heroin, by contrast, is scarcely grown in Latin America, with the significant exception of Mexico (and increasingly Central America). Marijuana is cultivated throughout the region. Varieties of hallucinogenic plants are grown in such countries as Peru, Paraguay, Brazil, and Mexico.[7] Methamphetamines and synthetic drugs are manufactured for the most part in Europe and the United States and therefore are not widely available in Latin America.

Prevalence of Drug Use

Drug use in Latin America follows two distinct lines. On the one hand, there exists drug consumption that is essentially similar to that found elsewhere in the Western world. On the other, there is a kind of usage that comes from cultural traditions long established in the region.

As in the United States and Western Europe, alcohol and tobacco are the most common drugs, with usage spread among all ages and social strata. Psychoactive drugs are used in different degrees by young people for recreational purposes; marijuana is consumed widely by youth, especially in cities; tranquilizers and stimulants are used by men and women of all age groups; heroin, morphine, and related drugs do not yet represent a serious problem in Latin America.

Although signs of drug abuse and related health problems are appearing throughout the region, there are no rigorous national estimates for the prevalence of drug consumption. Household surveys (cited fully in the tables in this chapter) have been conducted in only six Latin American countries:

- Peru, 1986 (n, or sample size=7,425) and 1988 (n=6,761)
- Colombia, 1987 (n=2,800)
- Costa Rica, 1989 (n=2,695)
- Mexico, 1988 (n=12,576)
- Ecuador, 1988 (n=6,316)
- Guatemala, 1990 (n=1,807)

Because of variations in survey methodology, population coverage, and age groupings, published results from these studies are not strictly comparable. Moreover, the Latin American surveys have sampled only urban areas, excluding rural sectors. Technically speaking, only the U.S. household surveys are truly national in scope, and even they ignore some of the highest-use populations.

It is nonetheless possible to draw some suggestive comparisons. Fortunately, all the instruments employ conventional distinctions among categories of drug use: "ever use" in the course of a lifetime, use within the past year, and use within the last thirty days. These categories are not mutually exclusive, but they generally reflect increasing levels of use of illicit substances. They do not, however, provide direct information on the amount of substances consumed.

In Table 3-1 prevalence rates for prior use of illicit substances in Mexico are compared with data from the 1990 household survey of the United States (n=9,259). The results are compelling. Prevalence of use in Mexico is less than one-tenth the level in the United States—for virtually every drug, for every age group.

Reported usage rates for Ecuador are slightly higher than those found in Mexico. The prevalence of marijuana use in Ecuador was 7.7 percent for the eighteen to twenty-five age group (versus 4.3 percent for Mexico) and 4.8 percent for the twenty-six to sixty-five bracket (versus 3.02 percent for Mexico). In the older age groups, Ecuador again surpassed Mexico by a margin of about three-to-one. Cocaine use in both countries by the under-eighteen age group was under 0.30 percent, compared with 2.6 percent for the United States.

To broaden the comparison, Table 3-2 shows rates of ever use for marijuana and cocaine in Mexico, Colombia, Ecuador, Costa Rica, and among Hispanics and whites in the United States. For both substances, the lowest reported rates are

TABLE 3-1
Prevalence of Drug Use by Age Cohort: Mexico and the United States
(percent reporting ever use)

Substance	Mexico			United States		
	12-17	18-25	26-65	12-17	18-25	26+
Analgesics	0	0.28	0.12	6.5	8.1	5.1
Tranquilizers	0.51	1.10	0.62	2.7	5.9	4.2
Sedatives	0	0.15	0.11	3.3	4.0	3.7
Stimulants	0.08	0.55	0.93	4.5	9.0	6.9
Inhalants	0.88	1.09	0.54	NA	NA	NA
Marijuana	1.38	4.31	3.02	14.8	52.2	31.8
Hallucinogens	0.09	0.45	0.24	3.3	12.0	7.4
Cocaine	0.29	0.52	0.26	2.6	19.4	10.9
Heroin	0	0	0	0.7	0.6	0.9

NA = not available.

Sources: Based on data in Dirección General de Epidemiología, Instituto Mexicano de Psiquiatría, *Encuesta nacional de adicciones,* 3 vols. (México: Secretaría de Salud Pública, 1989); and National Institute on Drug Abuse, *Overview of the 1990 National Household Survey on Drug Abuse* (Washington, D.C.: December 1990).

observed in Mexico and Costa Rica, whereas the highest are found among whites in the United States. Among Latin American countries, Colombia has the highest reported rates of use (6.5 percent for marijuana and 2.1 percent for cocaine).

Data for current use tend to reduce these differences, as revealed in Table 3-3, but the spreads remain substantial and significant. Colombia has a reported prevalence of 1.1 percent using marijuana within the last thirty days, compared with 7.4 percent for U.S. Hispanics and 9.1 percent for U.S. whites in 1985. The Colombian rate of recent use of cocaine (0.2 percent) was also much lower than the 1985 figures for both U.S. populations (2.4 percent and 3.0 percent, respectively), although there was a significant decline in the reported prevalence of cocaine consumption in the United States by 1990.

TABLE 3-2
Use of Cocaine and Marijuana in Five Countries
(percent reporting ever use)

Substance	Mexico	Colombia	Ecuador	Costa Rica	U.S. Hispanic	U.S. White
Marijuana	3.0	6.5	4.4	3.2	23.5	33.5
Cocaine	0.3	2.1	1.1	0.2	7.3	12.4

Note: Age ranges vary slightly.

Sources: Based on data in Dirección General de Epidemiología, Instituto Nacional de Psiquiatría, *Encuesta nacional de adicciones,* 3 vols. (México: Secretaría de Salud Pública, 1989); Y. Torres de Galvis and L. Murrelle, *Estudio nacional sobre alcoholismo y consumo de sustancias que producen dependencia* (Antioquia: Facultad Nacional de Salud Pública, Universidad de Antioquia, 1987); P. Bonilla and P. Andrade, *El consumo de drogas en el Ecuador: Una aproximación cuantitativa* (Quito: Ministerio de Salud Pública/Fundación Nuestros Jóvenes, 1989); P. Martínez-Lanz and E. Alfaro-Murillo, "Informe preliminar sobre la prevalencia del consumo de drogas en Costa Rica," *Revista Latinoamericana sobre Alcohol y Drogas* 1, no. 1 (1989): 66-72; and National Institute on Drug Abuse, *National Household Survey on Drug Abuse: Population Estimates, 1985* (Washington, D.C.: U.S. Government Printing Office, 1987).

TABLE 3-3
Current Use of Cocaine and Marijuana in Four Countries
(percent reporting use within last thirty days)

Substance	Mexico	Colombia	Ecuador	U.S. Hispanics		U.S. Whites	
				1985	1990	1985	1990
Marijuana	0.5	1.1	0.4	7.4	4.7	9.1	5.0
Cocaine	0.1	0.2	0.1	2.4	1.9	3.0	0.6

Note: Age ranges vary slightly.

Sources: Based on data in Dirección General de Epidemiología, Instituto Nacional de Psiquiatría, *Encuesta nacional de adicciones,* 3 vols. (México: Secretaría de Salud Pública, 1989); and National Institute on Drug Abuse, *Overview of the 1990 National Household Survey on Drug Abuse* (Washington, D.C.: December 1990).

Table 3-4 compares rates of drug use within the previous year by gender among the twelve to sixty-five age group in Mexico and Colombia. Suggestive findings emerge. When both genders are combined, rates of ever use for cocaine and marijuana are higher in Colombia than in Mexico (2.1 percent versus 0.33 percent for cocaine, 6.5 percent versus 2.9 percent for marijuana). Data on recent usage modify these differences. Among males, cocaine use within the previous year was the same for both countries; marijuana use was higher in Mexico. (If the consumption of *basuco* were included in these calculations, however, rates might be higher in Colombia.) The sharpest difference emerges among females, who show substantially more substance use in Colombia than in Mexico: 3.0 percent versus 0.2 percent for marijuana, 0.1 percent versus zero for cocaine.

Turning to young adults, Table 3-5 shows rates of ever use among the twenty to twenty-nine age bracket for four Latin American countries. The results display a broad range of use. Peru has the highest rates of marijuana and cocaine use—8.7 percent and 2.3 percent, respectively. Guatemala has the second-highest rates for

TABLE 3-4
Drug Use by Gender: Mexico and Colombia
(percent reporting use within the past year)

Substance	Mexico			Colombia		
	Male	Female	Total	Male	Female	Total
Alcohol	73.4	36.5	53.5	70.5	41.6	56.0
Tobacco	38.3	14.4	25.8	37.3	22.2	29.7
Tranquilizers	0.5	0.3	0.4	4.6	7.4	6.0
Cocaine	0.4	0	0.2	0.4	0.1	0.3
Marijuana	2.4	0.2	1.2	1.9	3.0	1.1
Basuco	NA	NA	NA	1.0	0.3	0.6

NA = not available.

Sources: Based on data in Dirección General de Epidemiología, Instituto Nacional de Psiquiatría, *Encuesta nacional de adicciones,* 3 vols. (México: Secretaría de Salud Pública, 1989); and Y. Torres de Galvis and L. Murrelle, *Estudio nacional sobre alcoholismo y consumo de sustancias que producen dependencia* (Antioquia: Facultad Nacional de Salud Pública, Universidad de Antioquia, 1987).

TABLE 3-5
Drug Use by Young Adults in Four Countries
(percent reporting ever use)

Substance	Peru	Guatemala		Colombia		Mexico
	20-29	20-24	25-29	20-24	25-29	20-29
Marijuana	8.7	7.6	7.6	2.5	2.0	4.98
Cocaine	2.3	0.4	1.9	0.5	0.5	0.47
Inhalants	2.5	1.9	3.5	NA	NA	1.11
Hallucinogens	1.4	0.8	1.6	NA	NA	0.41
Any illicit use	NA	16.2	15.1	NA	NA	6.89

NA = not available.

Sources: Based on data in R. D. Ferrando, Uso de drogas en las ciudades del Perú (Lima: Centro de Información y Educación para la Prevención del Abuso de Drogas, 1990); U.S. Agency for International Development, Drug Awareness Assessment for Guatemala, Final Report (Guatemala: Development Associates, 1990); Y. Torres de Galvis and L. Murrelle, Estudio nacional sobre alcoholismo y consumo de sustancias que producen dependencia (Antióquia: Facultad Nacional de Salud Pública, Universidad de Antioquia, 1987); and Dirección General de Epidemiología, Instituto Nacional de Psiquiatría, Encuesta nacional de adicciones, 3 vols. (México: Secretaría de Salud Pública, 1989).

both these substances. Colombia and Mexico report lower rates of prevalence, although Mexico shows more exposure to marijuana than does Colombia.

As another indicator of changing consumption patterns, shifts in the utilization of services for substance abuse in Bolivia show a clear increase in reported cases of dependence on cocaine between 1976 and 1987. In 1976 cases of cocaine dependency represented only 10 percent of all medical cases involving drug use; by 1987 the proportion had grown to 33 percent.[8] Increasing rates of experimentation with cocaine have also been reported in Argentina and Mexico.[9] In Peru the total number of users declined from 1986 to 1988, but there was a considerable increase in the proportion of lifetime users who reported using this substance within the last thirty days: In 1986 only 6.2 percent of total users were current users, whereas in 1988 the corresponding proportion was 29 percent.[10] In Mexico, by comparison, 19.7 percent of total users were current users.[11]

At the same time, heroin use is not widespread in Latin America. Modest levels of use have been reported for Mexico,[12] Argentina,[13] and Guatemala.[14] In Mexico the highest rates of drug abuse (other than for tobacco and alcohol) have been found in the northwestern region of the country, where opium poppies are cultivated. Most Mexican users of heroin either lived in this area or obtained the drug for the first time in this region or while in the United States.

Patterns in Drug Use

Among the specific forms of drug use in Latin America that are linked to social and cultural variables we find (1) the ritual use of natural plants with hallucinogenic effects; (2) the chewing of coca leaf, which is widely practiced in the Andean region, especially among lower socioeconomic strata in the rural areas; (3) the smoking of coca paste, which has shown an explosive increase in recent years; and (4) the inhalation of solvents, especially among children from the poorest sectors of society.

Ritual Use of Hallucinogens

The ceremonial use of marijuana has long been observed among indigenous cultures. In Mexico, for example, its use was recorded as long ago as 1772, when it was called the "venerable child."[15] Varieties of hallucinogenic plants are grown and consumed as part of religious ceremonies among indigenous groups in Peru,[16] Paraguay,[17] Brazil,[18] and Mexico. Among the Tarahumaras of Mexico, at least eight different types of cactus with psychotropic properties have been described—the most widely known being peyote, whose active ingredient is mescaline.[19]

Use of these substances is largely restricted to these cultural contexts. Young people who have experimented with hallucinogens generally use natural plants and in a few cases synthetic substances such as LSD.[20]

Coca Chewing

The great majority of coca chewers are Peruvian and Bolivian natives of Quechua and Aymara origin. A declining number of whites and mestizos also share this habit, particularly in northern Peru and in the outskirts of the major cities throughout the Andes. It has been estimated that one-half of the rural population engages in this practice. According to J. C. Negrete, this tradition is being progressively influenced by a general process of acculturation: "The general tendency is for coca chewing to be less prevalent in those sectors of the population who are more involved in the process of modernization and socioeconomic change, and who identify it with what they see as a rather primitive and backward life-style from which they are striving to dissociate themselves."[21]

In urban settings the habit is more actively practiced by people of lower socioeconomic standing. In Lima, for instance, coca chewing has been observed among 5.49 percent of the population in the twelve to forty-five age bracket; most coca chewers are males between thirty-five and thirty-nine years of age with low educational status.[22] But the highest rates of use are found among campesinos, tillers of the soil. Coca leaf chewing is also an integral part of ceremonial festivities; in some villages it is customary to distribute leaves to participants in social gatherings.

There is also widespread consumption of a tea that is made from coca leaves. Coca tea is generally perceived as a soothing medicine, and as such it is socially approved for ingestion by children, women, and the elderly—particularly among mestizos and whites.

Due to its high level of acceptability, coca chewing does not really represent a deviation from community norms. Social standards and cultural perceptions become more restrictive as one moves from rural areas into the cities, which have higher proportions of people of European origin. In this setting coca chewing tends to be accepted for recreational purposes, except in the workplace.

Use of Coca Paste

Increases in the production of coca leaf have led to an increase in the availability of coca paste as an unrefined product that is ingested through smoking, along with either tobacco or marijuana. This practice began in the early 1970s in Bolivia and Peru—first in the capital cities, then in other municipalities, and finally in rural areas. Its use soon extended to Argentina, Brazil, Colombia, and Ecuador.[23] In Colombia it has been estimated that smoking basic paste is as common among students as the use of marijuana.[24] In Peru about 4 percent of the general population reported ever use of coca paste in 1986, compared with 2.6 percent admitting ever use of cocaine; 0.6 percent acknowledged use of basic paste within the previous month.[25] Smoking coca paste leads to a significant number of health complications, and its spread has required increasing levels of medical attention. In Colombia, for example, the number of medical cases resulting from coca paste tripled between 1981 and 1983—by which time about five hundred cases were treated per year.[26] As of 1984, it was estimated that 30 percent of the beds in psychiatric wards in public and private hospitals were occupied by smokers of basic paste.[27]

Inhalant Use by Minors

The inhalation of solvents occurs in most countries of Latin America among all social classes, and gasoline appears to be the substance of choice among the lowest socioeconomic groups. As a general rule, users of inhalants tend to be younger than users of other drugs. Inhalant use is especially conspicuous among children from the poorest sectors of society.

The economic crisis that devastated so much of Latin America during the 1980s led to an increase in the number of children and adolescents who contribute to family incomes by "working" in the streets—washing windows or cars, selling candies or gum, assisting vendors, running errands, begging, and swallowing flames at traffic crossings. In the process of working in this so-called "informal sector," many children drop out of school, leave their family residences, and become involved in the drug subculture.[28]

Surveys of children under age eighteen working in the streets of Mexico City reveal a higher rate of drug use than exists among students of the same age. In one southern section of the city, 27 percent reported ever use of solvents, whereas 22 percent acknowledged daily use; 10 percent reported ever use of marijuana, and 1.5 percent acknowledged daily use. No other drugs were reported.[29] Studies in suburban communities near other cities confirm the high incidence of solvent abuse in Mexico.[30] And although this practice began among children of the poor, it has spread to students and other young people from all socioeconomic backgrounds.

Follow-up studies reveal that the use of solvents is generally abandoned around the age of eighteen. Some users shift to marijuana. The vast majority go on to alcohol.[31] A related phenomenon is the rise of the so-called *bandas juveniles*, contemporary forms of urban gangs. In Mexico City, with a population of 18 million

TABLE 3-6
Solvent Use by Children and Adolescents: Brazil and Mexico
(by percent)

Population	Rates of Use (%)	
	Brazil	Mexico
Homeless children	78.0	36.0
Students of low socioeconomic background	2.5	4.0

Sources: Based on data in B. Carlini-Cotrim and E. A. Carlini, "The Use of Solvents and Other Drugs Among Homeless and Destitute Children Living in the City Streets of São Paulo, Brazil," *Social Pharmacology* 2, no. 1 (1988): 51-52, and "The Use of Solvents and Other Drugs Among Children and Adolescents from a Low Socioeconomic Background: A Study in São Paulo, Brazil," *The International Journal of Addictions* 23, no. 1 (1988): 1145-1156; M. E. Castro and M. A. Maya, "Consumo de sustancias tóxicas y tabaco en la población estudiantil de 14 a 18 años," *Revista Salud Pública de México* 24, no. 5 (1982): 565-574; and M. E. Medina-Mora, A. Ortiz, C. Caudillo, and S. López, "Inhalación deliberada de disolventes en un grupo de menores mexicanos," *Salud Mental* 5, no. 1 (1982): 77-86.

inhabitants, around two thousand youngsters belong to these gangs as a means of acquiring social and political prestige. They have scant opportunity for education or employment. Their lives revolve around various forms of delinquency, from robbery and violence to the habitual use of drugs, especially alcohol and solvents. Among these groups, unfortunately, the inhalation of solvents continues long beyond adolescence, partly because marijuana and alcohol are such expensive items.[32]

Similarly, studies in Brazil show high rates of inhalation among homeless children and among students from low socioeconomic strata. As revealed by Table 3-6, the use of solvents prevails among 78 percent of homeless children in Brazil, more than twice the Mexican figure of 36 percent. Levels of use among students were fairly similar between the two nations and are comparable to results obtained for Costa Rica as well.[33]

The inhalation of a mixture of chloroform and ether, popularly known as *lanca-perfume*, is widespread in Brazil. (Use of this substance has not yet been reported for any other country.) Effects during intoxication include drowsiness and illusions, including hallucinations; use leads to sharp withdrawal symptoms and to strong desires to continue inhaling. Such signs suggest the development of chemical dependence, although this has not yet been confirmed in studies on laboratory animals.[34]

In Mexico, strong predictors of drug abuse have been dropping out of school, lack of family contact, early initiation in informal street work, drug use among brothers and peers, and migration from rural areas. Through a multiple categorical analysis of young people working in streets, these variables strongly differentiated drug users from nonusers ($R^2 = .42$).[35] Among students, involvement in street culture and absence from school in the previous year were positively correlated with drug use.[36] Other empirical predictors were distal perception of family and lack of support.[37]

In contrast to findings for other countries,[38] perceived availability has not correlated strongly with drug use in Mexico. Studies in the northern region of the country also have found little relationship between migration and drug use, although differences become evident when the causes of migration are taken into account: Migration associated with problems in the place of origin, such as delinquent or antisocial behavior among parents, was positively associated with drug use by children.[39]

Similar findings have emerged in Brazil. A disproportionate concentration of drug use has been found among those who were three years behind in their studies. Unemployment was positively associated with solvent use. With regard to family situations, a vast majority of both user and nonuser students tended to live with one or both parents, but a significantly larger number of users reported at least one parent or a sibling "drinking too much."[40]

Even so, research on Brazil and Mexico demonstrates that poverty itself is not causally linked to drug abuse.[41] Children of low-income parents in poverty belts who are raised in a functional family environment and sent to school are much less susceptible to drug abuse than children who are abandoned or removed from school. In Mexico, at least, the disintegration of the family appears to be a determining factor both in the appearance of homeless children and in the use of inhalants.

Notes

1. For example, the birthrate for the Andean region ranges from 2.1 to 2.8, compared with 0.7 for the United States and 0.3 for Western Europe.

2. Population Reference Bureau, Inc., *World Population Data Sheet* (Washington, D.C., 1988).

3. Banco Interamericano de Desarrollo, *Programa económico y social en América Latina, Informe 1987* (Washington, D.C., 1988).

4. Organización Panamericana de la Salud, Organización Mundial de la Salud, *Producción, tráfico y consumo de sustancias psicoactivas en los países de la subregión andina: Indicaciones para el análisis y diseño de las políticas y estrategias de prevención regional de la farmacodependencia* (Washington, D.C., 1988).

5. Department of State, Bureau of International Narcotics Matters, *International Narcotics Control Strategy Report* (Washington, D.C.: U.S. Government Printing Office, 1984–1987).

6. Procuraduría General de la República, *Campaña de México contra el narcotráfico y la farmacodependencia* (México, 1986).

7. H. Leal, L. Mejía, L. Gómez, and O. Salinas, "Estudio naturalístico sobre el fenómeno del consumo de inhalantes en niños de la Ciudad de México," in Charles William Sharp and L. Thomas Carroll, eds., *Inhalación voluntaria de disolventes industriales* (Mexico: Trillas, 1977), 442–459; C. E. Sosa, "El uso de alucinógenos de origen vegetal por las tribus indígenas del Paraguay actual," *Cuadernos Científicos* 4 (CEMEF, 1975): 35–48; J. E. Murad, "El uso indebido de drogas entre los estudiantes del Estado de Minas Gerais, Brasil," *Boletín de Estupefacientes* 31, no. 1 (1979): 49–56; J. L. Díaz, "Ethnopharmacology of Sacred Psychoactive Plants Used by the Indians of Mexico," *Annual Review of Pharmacology and Toxicology* 17 (1977): 647–675.

8. M. M. de la Quintar, "Informe sobre el consumo de sustancias psicoactivas en La Paz, Bolivia," *Salud Pública* (1988).

9. For Argentina: Organización Panamericana de la Salud, Organización Mundial de la Salud, *SIDA: Perfil de una epidémia*, Scientific Publication no. 514 (Washington, D.C.: 1989); for Mexico: M. E. Medina-Mora et al., "Extensión del consumo de drogas en México: Encuesta nacional de adicciones, resultados nacionales," *Salud Mental* 12, no. 2 (June 1989): 7–19; M. E. Castro, E. Rojas, G. García, and J. de la Serna, "Epidemiología del uso de drogas en la población estudiantil. Tendencias en los ultimos 10 años," *Salud Mental* 9, no. 4 (1986): 40–86; J. de la Serna, E. Rojas, M. A. Estrada, and M. E. Medina-Mora, "Uso de drogas en estudiantes de educación media y media superior del Distrito Federal y Zona Conurbana: Medición 1989," *Anales del Instituto Mexicano de Psiquiatría* (1991); A. Ortiz, M. Romano, and A. Soriano, "Desarrollo de un sistema de presentación de informas sobre el uso ilícito de drogas en México," *Boletín de Estupefacientes* 41, nos. 1–2 (1989): 47–60.

10. R. D. Ferrando, *Uso de drogas en las ciudades del Perú* (Lima: Centro de Información y Educación para la Prevención del Abuso de Drogas, 1990).

11. Dirección General de Epidemiología, Instituto Mexicano de Psiquiatría, *Encuesta nacional de adicciones*, 3 vols. (México: Secretaría de Salud, 1989).

12. Dirección General de Epidemiología, *Encuesta nacional de adicciones*.

13. R. F. Jeri, "Coca Paste Smoking in Latin America: A Review of a Severe and Unabated Form of Addiction," paper presented before the meeting of the Advisory Group on the Adverse Effects of Cocaine, Bogotá, Colombia, September 10–14, 1984.

14. R. F. Jeri, "The Cocaine Epidemic in the Americas," paper prepared for the Pride World Conference, April 13–15, 1989.

15. Díaz, "Ethnopharmacology."

16. Jeri, "Cocaine Epidemic in the Americas."

17. Sôsa, "El uso de alucinógenos."

18. Murad, "El uso indebido."

19. Díaz, "Ethnopharmacology."

20. Dirección General de Epidemiología, *Encuesta nacional de adicciones*.

21. J. C. Negrete, "Coca Chewing in the Andes and Coca Paste Smoking in the Cities," in *Drug Dependence in Sociocultural Context* (Geneva: World Health Organization, 1978), 19.

22. C. Carbajal, R. F. Jeri, and C. Sanchez, "Estudio epidemiológico sobre el uso de drogas en Lima," *Revista Sanidad de las Fuerzas Sociales* 41 (1980): 1–38.

23. E. Aguilar, "Investigación nacional sobre consumo indebido de alcohol, drogas y tabaco," unpublished manuscript, Quito, Ecuador, 1988.

24. C. Climent and L. V. Aragón, "Abuso de drogas en cinco colegios de Cali." Archive of the Department of Psychiatry, Division of Health, Universidad del Valle, Cali (March 1982).

25. Joel M. Jutkowitz, *Uso y abuso de drogas en el Perú* (Lima: Centro de Información y Educatión para la Prevención del Abuso de Drogas, 1987).

26. E. Velázquez de Pabón, "Problemas del comportamiento de dependencia en adolescentes y jóvenes en relación con el abuso del alcohol, drogas, cigarrillo y trastornos del peso," *Boletín Informativo, Hospital Mental de Antioquía* 11, no. 1 (January 1984).

27. Jeri, "Coca Paste Smoking in Latin America."

28. M. E. Medina-Mora, M. E. Castro, and Z. G. García, *Drug Use in Latin America: A Review of Literature* (Washington, D.C.: Oficina Panamericana de la Salud, 1985).

29. M. E. Medina-Mora, A. Ortiz, C. Caudillo, and S. Lopez, "Inhalación deliberada de disolventes en un grupo de menores mexicanos," *Salud Mental* 5, no. 1 (1982): 77–86.

30. F. de la Garza, H. I. Mendiola, and S. Rábago, "Psychological Familiar and Social Study of 32 Patients Using Inhalants," in Charles William Sharp and L. Thomas Carroll, eds., *Voluntary Inhalation of Industrial Solvents*, DHEU Publication no. ADM 79–779 (Washington, D.C.: National Institute on Drug Abuse, 1978), 75–89.

31. A. Ortiz, R. Sosa, and C. Caudillo, "Estudio de seguimiento de usuarios y no usuarios de sustancias inhalables en población abierta: Comparación de sus rendimientos cognitivos," *Revista Psiquiatría* 2 (Mayo-Agosto 1988): 165–178.

32. A. Santa María, "Estudio naturalístico del surgimiento de bandas juveniles en una comunidad de alto riesgo," research report (Mexico City: Instituto Mexicano de Psiquiatría, 1988).

33. H. A. Míguez, "Farmacodependencia de la pobreza: Su prevalencia en Costa Rica," *Acta Psiquiátrica y Psicológica de América Latina* 30 (December 1984): 255–263.

34. G. Pryor, "Pharmacological and Neuro-Behavioral Aspects of Solvent Toxicity Based on Animal Studies," paper presented at the Advisory Group Meeting on the Adverse Health Consequences of Volatile Solvents-Inhalants, World Health Organization, 1986.

35. Medina-Mora et al., "Inhalación deliberada de disolventes."

36. Castro et al., "Epidemiología del uso de drogas."

37. M. E. Castro and M. A. Maya, "Consumo de sustancias tóxicas y tabaco en la población estudiantil de 14 a 18 años," *Revista Salud Pública de México* 24, no. 5 (1982): 565–574.

38. R. G. Smart, "Disponibilidad percibida y uso de drogas," *Boletín de Estupefacientes*, Naciones Unidas 29, no. 4 (October-December 1977): 59–64.

39. F. de la Garza, H. I. Mendiola, and S. Rábago, *Adolescencia marginal e inhalantes. Medidas preventivas* (Mexico: Trillas, 1986).

40. B. Carlini-Cotrim and E. A. Carlini, "The Use of Solvents and Other Drugs Among Homeless and Destitute Children Living in the City Streets of São Paulo, Brazil," *Social Pharmacology* 2, no. 1 (1988): 51–62.

41. B. Carlini-Cotrim and E. A. Carlini, "The Use of Solvents and Other Drugs Among Children and Adolescents from a Low Socioeconomic Background: A Study in São Paulo, Brazil," *The International Journal of the Addictions* 23, no. 11 (1988): 1,145–1,156; Carlini-Cotrim et al., "The Use of Solvents and Other Drugs Among Homeless and Destitute Children"; de la Garza et al., *Adolescencia marginal e inhalantes*; Leal et al., "Estudio naturalístico sobre el fenómeno del consumo de inhalantes"; Medina-Mora et al., "Inhalación deliberada de disolventes"; A. Ortiz and C. Caudillo, "Características de familias de sujetos inhaladores en comparación con las de no inhaladores," paper presented at the XXIII Congreso Internacional de Psicología, Acapulco, Mexico, September 2–7, 1984.

4

The Economic Impact
of Narcotics in Colombia

Francisco E. Thoumi

Estimating and analyzing the economic impact of the narcotics industry on producer countries are important but almost impossible tasks. Although there have been some advances in measurement, the difficulty of interpretation and the significance of nonquantifiable factors cast doubt on their validity. This chapter focuses on estimates of the economic impact of the narcotics economy (mainly cocaine and marijuana) on Colombia, the main supplier of cocaine to the U.S. market and a significant supplier of marijuana. I examine available estimates and pertinent methodological issues, indicating why regular cost-benefit techniques are inadequate, why resulting estimates are extremely uncertain, and why it is not possible to determine in a clear-cut way whether the narcotics industry has been "good" or "bad" for Colombia. And I offer some suggestions about the magnitude of various effects of the narco-industry on the Colombian economy.

Methodological Issues

In seeking to determine whether the narcotics industry has been beneficial to a country, we may be tempted to use cost-benefit analysis; yet this does not provide a particularly useful framework for answering many of the most important questions. A cost-benefit analysis of the Colombian narco-industry should measure the opportunity cost of the factors of production used in the industry, the income received by producers and traffickers, and the economic externalities (positive and negative) generated by drug consumption, by money laundering, and by other economic activities that increase as a result of narco-industry growth. Because the negative externalities of drug consumption and money laundering take place mostly outside the country, any cost-benefit calculation for Colombia is likely to come out highly positive.

Such analyses fail on several grounds. First, cost-benefit analysis is applicable to projects that are marginal relative to the size of the economy, so they do not affect income and wealth distribution, but this is not the case with the narco-industry. When a project has substantial income and wealth distribution impacts, there are identifiable gainer and loser groups. In order to decide if benefits exceed costs, it is necessary to compare costs and benefits of different groups—a task that requires value judgments about the desirability of the implied distributive changes. Furthermore, the narco-industry has also affected the power structure of the producer countries, contributed to the overall growth of the underground economy, and weakened the power of the state. Evaluation of all these changes requires further value judgments.

Second, the industry breeds violence, the social costs of which have to be assessed. To do so it is necessary to estimate the value of the lives of different types of people, a process that may yield socially unacceptable results. Measuring the costs of violence also raises a causality issue because it is necessary to decide whether narco-violence results from the intrinsic nature of the industry or from the fact that it is illegal—as most researchers, policymakers, and enforcers believe. If one accepts the latter argument, the costs of the violence should be attributed to the industry's illegality and to governmental attempts at eradication, interdiction, and repression rather than to the activity itself.

A third effect of the large size of the industry is its macroeconomic impact on producer countries. Cost-benefit analysis is not designed to value the costs of the macroeconomic changes caused by an industry or the restrictions the industry imposes on fiscal and monetary policy.

For all these reasons, the impact of the narco-industry on producer countries has frequently been obscured. The first challenge is to understand it. One thus should focus on the most important dimensions of the problem and try to quantify relevant variables. With regard to Colombia, it would be desirable to know:

- How much money do Colombians make a year in the narco-industry?
- How much of that income do the narco-traffickers bring back and spend in Colombia, and how much do they keep abroad?
- What is the net worth of the narco-traffickers, and how much of it is inside and outside of Colombia?
- What has been the impact of narco-capital flows on the Colombian economy and on the government's policies?
- What types of assets have narco-capitalists accumulated?
- Who were the previous owners of those assets?
- What are the long-term implications for Colombian economic policy of the large amount of capital accumulated by narco-capitalists?

Unfortunately, the information available provides only imperfect, incomplete, and indirect responses to these questions. Furthermore, the data may be interpreted in several ways, so the results of any analysis are tentative and uncertain. Thus, it is not surprising that authors who have tried to answer some of these questions warn their readers about the weaknesses and "science fiction" nature of their estimates.

All calculations about the size of the narco-industry begin with estimates by the U.S. National Narcotics Intelligence Consumers Committee (NNICC)—an interagency committee that collects data on drug production and trafficking from such sources as the Central Intelligence Agency, whose satellite pictures are used to estimate the area cultivated with coca, marijuana, and other illicit crops. As shown by Ethan A. Nadelmann, these appraisals are likely to be quite inaccurate because of technical difficulties in determining the nature of an agricultural enterprise and because marijuana and coca plants are frequently grown alongside other crops that hide them from view. And although some authors claim that NNICC figures are the best available, others argue that they are not only inaccurate but that they are biased to protect the particular interests of the agencies represented within the NNICC itself.[1]

After the area under cultivation is assessed, productivity estimates are needed to determine how much marijuana and coca leaf is produced. These estimates vary for different growing systems and for different areas—reflecting the fact that in some areas, marijuana and coca are single crops whereas in others they are mixed with other crops. Also, output per hectare varies among countries and regions. Once the size of the marijuana crop is determined, it is relatively easy to proceed. In the case of coca this is just the beginning, however, because conversion factors are needed to determine how much coca is needed to produce a unit of coca paste, how much is required to produce a unit of cocaine base, and how much base is needed per unit of cocaine. These conversion factors vary with the quality of the leaves and of the preparation. (Bolivian and Peruvian coca leaves yield more cocaine than Colombian and Brazilian varieties.) Moreover, conversion factors may vary through time if there are improvements in cultivation methods or if higher-yield plant varieties are developed. Successive statistical adjustments greatly increase the variance of each estimate.

Determining marijuana prices and the costs at each stage of the cocaine manufacturing process presents another problem. There are no official price series, as one might expect, although the Drug Enforcement Agency publishes annual approximations—which are adjusted from time to time, not only for current years but also retroactively. Narcotics prices are difficult to determine because the markets are highly segmented due to their illegal nature. As Peter Reuter has pointed out, prices vary substantially at any point in time even within the same country because they depend on the availability of distribution and marketing networks.[2] A producer or dealer connected with a good marketing network gets higher prices than one that is unconnected. To arrive at an average price for segmented markets, furthermore, one needs to know not only the prices in each market but also the relative size of each market. Thus, it is not surprising that the Colombian press simultaneously reported 1981 wholesale cocaine prices in Bogotá of $4,000 and $15,000 per kilo and of $40,000 to $55,000 per kilo in New York, whereas wholesale cocaine prices in Europe were reported to be substantially higher.[3] This price uncertainty further increases the variance associated with any estimate of total narcotics revenue.

Costs of chemicals used in the refining process and of transportation at each stage are also required. Some information can be gathered from captured pilots and from the U.S. and European export price of chemicals, but these sources are not always reliable; different pilots may be paid different amounts, and export chemical prices do not necessarily reflect the actual costs to cocaine manufacturers.

Revenue estimates also depend on the amount of coca leaves that are used for domestic consumption in Bolivia and Peru, the amount wasted at each stage of production, the amount of cocaine and by-products consumed in the producing countries, and the amounts seized by authorities. A fairly sound estimate of coca leaf chewing in Bolivia and Peru can be based on traditional consumption, whereas any estimation of *basuco* consumption in Colombia is subject to great uncertainty. Revenue adjustments due to these factors are likely to be relatively small, although they could be important determinants of the amount of narco-profits spent in cocaine-producing countries.

The next step consists of distributing total revenues among the various production and distribution stages. It is generally agreed that prices increase substantially at each marketing stage: The amount received by the farmers who grow the raw materials is fairly small, and high value added at each subsequent stage is basically a payment for the high risks involved rather than a reflection of processing or transportation costs. Because most of the risk occurs in the United States, so do the increases in value added.[4] The distribution of value added yields estimates of factor payments at each stage of production and of the value added in Bolivia, Peru, Colombia, and the United States. These estimates might be useful to determine the contributions of the narcotics industry to gross national product, but they do not show the practical impact the industry has on each country. A large proportion of the profits generated by cocaine processing and exporting from Colombia is likely invested abroad, for example, whereas some of the value added through marketing in the United States is invested in Colombia.

One would thus like to obtain separate appraisals for the amount Colombians make in narcotics and the amount that is invested and spent in Colombia. One would also like to know the size and composition of assets narco-entrepreneurs have accumulated both within and outside Colombia because they relate to the actual and potential influence these entrepreneurs may have on the country.

The amount Colombians make in narcotics is difficult to measure. The value added that is generated in Colombia is only part of the total because Colombians also make money transporting coca paste from Bolivia and Peru and distributing cocaine in the United States. In other words, part of the value added generated outside Colombia belongs to Colombians. Although there is a consensus that Colombians are involved in production and distribution outside the country, however, the *degree* of their involvement is not known. A further complication results from the fact that some Colombians involved in cocaine marketing in the United States are either permanent U.S. residents or naturalized U.S. citizens. Although cocaine and marijuana have received substantial attention from the press and researchers, much less is known about Quaaludes and other drugs Colombia is likely to have produced and exported. Similarly, there is little information about the involvement of Colombians in the European marketing of cocaine, although it is generally believed that their involvement is much less extensive than is the case in the United States.[5]

After estimating narco-business profits, one would like to find how much of these profits is brought back and absorbed by the Colombian economy. Illegal foreign exchange is brought into Colombia and used in several ways: in underinvoicing imports and overinvoicing exports of goods, faking service exports (mainly tourism and labor), financing domestic capital flight, disguising profit remittances by transnational corporations, and promoting contraband and tourism abroad.

Some black market foreign exchange inflows can be detected in the official balance of payments; others cannot. Using balance-of-payments data, it is possible to estimate "normal" levels of tourism flows and labor income and compare those with amounts actually recorded. Although difficult to devise, estimations may be reached for under- and overinvoicing of merchandise trade. But capital flight, contraband, profit remittances by transnational corporations, and tourism expenditures abroad are difficult to estimate, and most of these transactions are not reflected in the official balance of payments. Attempts to link official balance-of-payments data to the drug industry must also take into account alternative factors. Even if one had good estimates of fraudulent trade and contraband, all the foreign exchange used by these activities could not be attributed to the drug industry because they might have come from other sources (such as contraband coffee exports and expatriate worker remittances).

Estimates of illegal flows of capital and goods based on official balance-of-payments data are useful in understanding how these flows affect some important macroeconomic variables, such as the monetary base and international reserves, and to show how the government reacts to changes in those variables. They cannot be used as a measure of the actual narco-income and capital that have been brought back to the country or of their impact on this income and capital.

Assessments of the capital accumulated by Colombian narco-capitalists present further problems. To begin, one would like to have data for the *relevant* group of narco-capitalists, which consists of those whose income and capital either have a direct impact on the country today or could have an impact in the future. This group includes not only the narco-capitalists whose income generates Colombian value added but also Colombians who obtain illegal income outside Colombia and who are likely to bring their capital back to the country. Thus, one would like estimates of the composition and value of the assets this group has in Colombia and abroad and of the return they get from their investments. As mentioned above, a particular problem is presented by Colombians who are either residents or citizens of the United States and who are involved in cocaine marketing in the United States. (Although historically the United States has received a large number of immigrants, the out-migration of foreign-born residents from the United States has also been substantial.[6]) It can be argued that very few immigrants would have stronger emigration incentives than Colombians who have made a few million dollars in cocaine distribution: In the United States they would merely be well-to-do foreigners, only partially assimilated into mainstream society and faced with constant risk of detection; in Colombia they could join the upper tiers of society, especially in small and medium-sized cities.

Reviewing Available Estimates

Existing estimates begin by determining the total output of marijuana and cocaine. Drawing on data supplied by the U.S. Embassy in Bogotá, the pioneering work of Roberto Junguito and Carlos Caballero calculates that in 1978 Colombia exported about 14 tons of cocaine to the United States. Their estimates of marijuana output have a large range because assessments of cultivated area at the time varied from 30,000 to 70,000 hectares. Using alternative wholesale U.S. price assumptions, Junguito and Caballero figured that total cocaine exports did not exceed $154 million, whereas marijuana exports ranged between $435 million and $756 million. They also concluded that real marijuana exports were closer to $500 million than to the upper bound.[7]

Hernando Gómez has used NNICC and State Department data on the cultivated and eradicated marijuana area for the period 1977–1988. In contrast to the Junguito-Caballero study, these figures show a relatively small cultivated area—between 8,000 and 10,000 hectares from 1977 through 1985, increasing to 13,085 in 1987 and falling back to 9,200 in 1988. These data also give very successful eradication rates, beginning with 40 percent in 1984 and rising to 78 percent in 1986 (fading to 56 percent in 1988). For marijuana exports Gómez accordingly calculates about $250 million per year in the late 1970s, declining to around $170 million per year in the early 1980s and dropping sharply in 1985 and 1986 to a minimum of $27.9 million, from which point they rebounded to $88.9 million in 1988.[8]

The Gómez assessments of cocaine exports are based on estimates of coca cultivation in Colombia, on coca paste imports from Bolivia and Peru, and on U.S. wholesale prices. The data suggest that Colombia exported 24–31 tons in 1979, with annual figures ranging between 50 and 99 tons from 1981 through 1988. During these years, wholesale U.S. prices oscillated between $15,000 and $52,000 per kilo. Unfortunately, these two data series are inconsistent in their assumptions about consumer demand for cocaine. If one assumes that the demand function does not change from year to year (or that changes are small), one may argue that the price-quantity data show points on the same demand curve. Using the Gómez data to estimate the arc-elasticity of demand, one finds that the demand curve was perfectly elastic in 1981–1982 and in 1987–1988; that it had negative price elasticities close to zero as expected in 1982–1983 (-0.16), in 1984–1985 (-0.19), and in 1986–1987 (-0.20); that it showed a negative elasticity close to one (-1.03) in 1985–1986; and that it had a large *positive* elasticity (7.80) in 1983–1984, indicating an upward-sloping demand curve. Although these inconsistencies may reflect changes in demand they are difficult to explain—particularly as cocaine exports are shown to increase 90 percent in a year in which the wholesale price remains constant.

Gómez also evaluates the net revenues of Colombian narco-capitalists. He deducts their total input and transportation costs and assumes that they sell the product at the U.S. wholesale price. The difficulty of measurement surfaces through a comparison of his two essays: The first (published in 1988) covers 1981–1985 and the second (1990) stretches from 1981 through 1988. His cumulative estimates for net revenue during 1981–1985 are nearly 40 percent higher in the second paper ($13.7 billion compared to $9.8 billion). His figures for 1986–1988 are, respectively, $1.8 billion, $1.4 billion, and $1.2 billion. These estimates show a net revenue decline as the U.S. wholesale price decreased sharply from 1982 onward.

Using data from the U.S. General Accounting Office, Salomón Kalmanovitz has developed alternative estimates for income from cocaine and marijuana for the period 1976–1989. His figures show much higher cocaine exports from 1984 to 1989 than the Gómez study: 120, 130, 160, 230, 270, and 250 tons, respectively. This series is very confusing because it does not show a decline in 1984 that Kalmanovitz attributes to the destruction of the large Tranquilandia cocaine-refining complex that year. His U.S. wholesale price series shows extremely high prices for the late 1970s ($70,000 per kilo), dropping to $50,000 by 1983 and $18,000 by 1988. He also asserts that in 1987, Colombians were beginning to export to Europe where the wholesale price was higher. Kalmanovitz further assumes that Colombian narco-capitalists control 80 percent of the exports from Colombia, and that losses plus input and production costs represent about 15 percent of revenues. He assumes no participation by Colombians in cocaine distribution in the United States; therefore, Colombian narco-profits should be 65 percent of the total revenue generated by exports from Colombia. (However, his actual calculations show income to be 80 percent of the total, not the 65 percent it should be.) His marijuana estimates come fairly close to those of Gómez. In sum, the Kalmanovitz estimates for total Colombian narco-business annual income are about $2.5 billion in the late 1970s, about $4.3 billion from 1982 through 1985, a bit less in 1986, and over $5 billion every year thereafter.[9]

Other authors have not been as ambitious as Gómez and Kalmanovitz and have tried to develop rough estimates for only one year. Ethan Nadelmann derives general estimates from U.S. government data. Instead of dividing value added by country, Nadelmann offers measurements for different stages of production. His stylized estimations for 1984–1985 assume a U.S. wholesale price of $30,000 per kilo and a total cocaine output of 150 tons—of which 65 tons are exported to the United States. (The balance is assumed to be consumed in the producing countries or exported somewhere else.) The value-added breakdown comes to $400 million for the peasants that grow coca, $133 million for coca paste processors, $360 million for coca paste transportation, $360 million for cocaine base producers, $150 million for cocaine refiners, and $1.37 billion for those who export the Colombian cocaine and sell it wholesale in the United States. These calculations do not include cocaine that is exported elsewhere.[10]

Similarly, W. Rensselaer Lee III provides rough-and-ready approximations. In a well-known article, he asserts that in the early 1980s, "South American cocaine traffickers earned between $5 and $6 billion annually from international sales in the U.S. market. Perhaps $1.5 to $2 billion flowed back to the cocaine-producing countries."[11]

Carlos Caballero makes other broad estimates of net revenues of Colombian narco-capitalists for 1988. However, he uses coca output data from *Fortune International*, which shows total 1988 cocaine exports of 270 tons to the United States and 40 tons to Europe. Using U.S. and European wholesale prices of $19,000 and $50,000 per kilo, together with data on seizures, he estimates that the net income of Colombian cocaine processors and exporters in that year was $4.1 billion.[12]

In separate studies, Hernando Gómez and Miguel Urrutia estimate the amount of illegal foreign exchange that shows up in the income side of the service account of the official Colombian balance of payments. Gómez uses a regression in which the explanatory variables are the black market exchange rate differential, the real exchange rate level, dummy variables to reflect periods of tighter enforcement of foreign exchange laws by the government, and the Venezuelan gross domestic product (GDP)—a proxy variable for contraband sold to Venezuela and for labor income from Colombians working in that country. Only the black market exchange rate differential and the Venezuelan GDP level prove to be statistically significant as independent variables. However, the black market exchange rate differential has a substantial elasticity (1.6) with respect to the amount of black market dollars that show up in the income side of the balance of payments. The resulting estimates are quite low: around $200 million per year in the late 1970s and early 1980s, declining sharply and actually becoming negative in 1983–1984 (when black market exchange rates were above official rates), and becoming slightly positive in 1985 and 1986.[13]

Urrutia follows a simpler approach, looking at the time series for tourism and labor income and concluding that genuine tourism and labor income should contribute about $400 and $150 million a year, respectively. Using these figures, he estimates that in 1987 about $250 million was unexplained on the income side of the balance of payments. In the early 1980s the unexplained amounts were higher— about $500 million, becoming negative in 1983–1984.[14] Both Gómez and Urrutia show that the unexplained amounts fluctuate procyclically, declining sharply when Colombia's international reserves fell abruptly in 1983–1984.

Attempting to throw some light on other uses of narco-dollars, particularly contraband and capital flight financing, Gómez estimates that between 1981 and 1988, drug capitalists made about $14.2 billion. According to the Bank of International Settlements (BIS), the financial assets Colombians accumulated outside the country between 1978 and 1988 came to $4.2 billion. (This figure is based on official balance-of-payments data and, as noted by Gómez, does not include drug monies.) By simple addition, a total of $18.4 billion was therefore available to finance contraband, capital flight, and other black market uses of foreign exchange. Gómez indicates that the National Commerce Federation (FENALCO) figures contraband at about $1.1 billion a year, or $8.8 billion from 1981 through 1988. Subtracting the invested international reserves of the country from the BIS data, he obtains a figure of $2.8 billion as observed capital flight. Then, subtracting both contraband ($8.8 billion) and capital flight ($2.8 billion) from the $18.4 billion, he obtains a balance of $6.8 billion—or $850 million per year. This represents an estimate of the amount available to increase cash foreign-exchange balances in Colombia, nonobserved capital flight, the amount Colombian narco-capitalists and other Colombians have invested abroad, tourism, and other expenditures underestimated in the expenditure side of the balance of payments. This exercise implies that most of the Colombian narco-profits have gone back into the Colombian economy.

Again, Kalmanovitz produces higher estimates than Gómez. Kalmanovitz argues that import underinvoicing has been very large. He assumes that underinvoicing was not important in 1974–1976 and that the value-to-weight ratio of imports tends to be constant. He then notes that this ratio has declined substantially since that time, a fact that he interprets as a statistical mirage attributable to increased underinvoicing discounting the influence of changes in the composition of exports.[15] By this method he estimates increasing import underinvoicing at about $1 billion by 1979 and $2.2 billion by 1983; since then, the estimate has fluctuated between $1.4 and $1.9 billion a year. Kalmanovitz also argues that some of the "nonrefundable" imports are financed with black market funds. Furthermore, in 1977 the Central Bank bought gold worth only $10 million; purchases of gold have increased to an average of around $400 million since 1985.[16] These purchases are supposed to be of domestically produced gold only. Kalmanovitz indicates that during the Belisario Betancur administration (1982–1986), the domestic gold price was substantially above international levels, so gold smuggling financed with narco-dollars was highly profitable.

Kalmanovitz also observes that a different kind of contraband, known as "witches' mail," has grown remarkably in recent years. This is contraband mostly of spare parts and small pieces of equipment. It is reported that many Colombian business professionals and entrepreneurs save on inventory costs through agents in Miami or Panama who can smuggle parts and equipment into Colombia on short notice. Adding to these estimates the regular contraband as well as rough estimates for capital flight and tourism financing, Kalmanovitz concludes that the total amount of black market foreign exchange, mostly narco-currency, that actually comes into the country is over $4.5 billion a year. This figure is dramatically higher than the Gómez estimate of $850 million. The Kalmanovitz calculations also imply that most of the income made by Colombian narco-capitalists finds its way back into the Colombian economy and that the amount they have accumulated abroad is relatively small.

Gómez and F. Giraldo also explore the impact of the narco-industry on the construction sector. Gómez shows that Barranquilla, the reported location of marijuana traders, had a construction boom and low unemployment levels during the late 1970s when the marijuana industry was booming and that Medellín, headquarters for the best-known cocaine cartel, had a construction boom in the early 1980s when cocaine traffic was increasing.[17] Giraldo moreover finds that in recent years, particularly since 1985, the relationship between mortgage loans and new construction permits breaks down. In 1987, for instance, the real value of the construction finance supplied by the official constant-value mortgage system declined by about 20 percent, whereas the licensed construction area increased by 14.6 percent. Giraldo attributes this inconsistency to the fact that narco-capitalists invested heavily in construction with their own financing. Furthermore, he suspects that a fair amount of the construction financed with narco-capital is done without permits, so the total is likely to be even larger. And until 1985, about 75 percent of the construction area licensed was for housing, a figure that dropped to 67 percent in 1988. Giraldo suggests that this increase in nonhousing construction reflects the impact of narco-investments that, according to his estimates, are approximately $1 billion per year.[18]

It is generally agreed that narco-capitalists have invested heavily in rural areas of Colombia—particularly in the middle Magdalena Valley, in the Uraba area of Antioquia and the neighboring department of Córdoba, and in the eastern piedmont and the prairies. These regions have witnessed significant guerrilla activity, have been recently settled, and have frequent and continuing disputes over land property rights.[19] According to Libardo Sarmiento and Carlos Moreno, the cattle and dairy industries increased in areas in which there had been significant guerrilla activity before the narco-investments; narco-business paramilitary groups established effective security, and livestock rustling declined. Their analysis also showed an increase in land concentration, even in areas targeted for official land reform and in which a violent counterreform movement has emerged. Interestingly, narco-investors have had a technologically modernizing effect and a socially regressive one. Their resources have allowed them to increase the capital intensity of the production processes and introduce new technologies, increasing productivity; at the same time, their paramilitary operations have discouraged political participation by the peasantry and have concentrated property. In these same areas, rural wages have increased— perhaps as a result of the higher productivity—and the emigration of rural workers has also increased—probably in response to the violence. In a sense, argue Sarmiento and Moreno, the development of paramilitary groups and accompanying changes pose a dilemma for traditional landlords: If they pay the typical security contributions (the "vaccine" against kidnapping) to the guerrillas as before, then the paramilitary groups will burn their farms and even kill them. If they do not pay, they have to support the paramilitary. Further, the higher wages and the relative lack of investment of these landlords put them at an economically competitive disadvantage. As a result, many traditional landlords sell out to the narco-capitalists, thus increasing the concentration of land tenure in those regions.[20]

Assessing the Estimates

It should be repeated that all of these authors are acutely aware of the limitations and imprecisions of their studies. The Junguito and Caballero, Gómez, and Kalmanovitz estimates focus on the Colombian value added and thus underestimate the amount Colombians make in the drug business (because Colombians are involved in paste transportation out of Peru and Bolivia and in U.S. marketing). These appraisals as well as Nadelmann's produce values of the total drug income of Colombians generated outside the United States that fluctuate between $2 and $4 billion a year. They depend on the accuracy of the estimates of coca and marijuana production. Recent events suggest that these figures have been grossly underestimated, at least during the last few years: Gómez estimates that in 1988, Colombia exported 75.1 tons of cocaine, for example, whereas Caballero provides an upper bound for cocaine production of 310 tons that same year. Reported U.S. seizures of 30 tons of cocaine in one week in the fall of 1989 did not lead to higher cocaine prices at the street level. Furthermore, in March 1990, the U.S. State Department reported that the South American coca crop was sufficient to produce 770 tons of cocaine. Therefore, it seems plausible that during the late 1980s, Colombian narco-capitalists had incomes significantly higher than the $2 to $4 billion range.

The Kalmanovitz study also appears to exclude profits obtained by Colombians by transporting coca paste to Colombia from Peru and Bolivia as well as the profits of Colombians resident in the United States. However, his price figures for the late 1970s are much higher than data in all other sources, and in his assessment of profits he does not appear to have subtracted the 15 percent of export revenue he attributes to production costs and to losses en route. His series for physical output (especially for recent years) is significantly higher than that used by other researchers, as are his estimates of narco-business profits. The Kalmanovitz calculations have biases tending toward both under- and overestimation of total profits, however, so it is impossible to determine how accurate they are.

As mentioned above, the Colombians naturalized or residing in the United States present another methodological challenge. Peter Reuter has estimated 1988 U.S. retail prices of $250,000 per kilo, which had declined from about $600,000 per kilo in the early 1980s.[21] The U.S. retail price for cocaine is thus about ten times the wholesale price. If one assumes that Colombians are involved only in the first marketing stages and that they handle only 50 percent of the cocaine imported, they should be making an amount comparable in magnitude to that made by the Colombian producers and exporters. These are just speculations, but they suggest that the amount of narco-capital that is owned outside the country by Colombians who could consider investing in Colombia is substantially higher than the estimates based only on the value added in Colombia.

There are other sources of underestimation for narco-income. Colombian narco-capitalists are reported to produce and export other narcotics besides cocaine and marijuana, such as Quaaludes and perhaps heroin, and they obtain income from domestic sales. Colombians are involved in the transportation of coca paste from Bolivia and Peru to the laboratories owned by the Colombian cocaine refiners and in the smuggling of chemicals used in the manufacturing process. Therefore, part of the cost of the cocaine inputs also generates Colombian narco-business income. This is not included in any of the standard estimates.

The narco-industry has existed for some time. Narco-capitalists therefore have accumulated income-earning assets in and out of Colombia. Gómez estimates that the total income of narco-capitalists has been around $14.2 billion, but he does not estimate what they might have accumulated. Kalmanovitz argues that the narco-business wealth is much higher than this. Beginning with his estimates of $4 to $5 billion a year for narco-profits throughout the 1980s, Kalmanovitz suggests that if the narco-traffickers have saved and invested $2 billion each year for ten years, capitalized at 10 percent a year, they should command 30 percent of the total wealth Colombians have within and outside the country.[22]

In any case, the amount narco-capitalists have accumulated is likely to be very large in relation to the size of the Colombian economy, and it therefore is likely to exert a significant impact for many years. A simple exercise illustrates this point. Assuming that the narco-capitalists accumulated only $1 billion a year from 1975 to 1979 and $2 billion from 1980 to 1989—and that their investments yielded only 7 percent a year—by 1989 they would have acquired a total of $39 billion. If one assumes a higher asset accumulation of $3 billion per year from 1980 to 1983 and $4 billion from 1984 to 1990, their net worth today would exceed $66 billion.

Figures such as these are just back-of-the-envelope approximations, but they illustrate the point that the narco-capitalists are likely to possess an amount of capital that could yield an income as large as or even larger than direct narco-profits themselves. The scale of narco-wealth is very threatening to the Colombian power structure because it suggests that the narco-capitalists may have a combined drug and capital income that is enormous relative to the size of the country's economy. According to official data, for instance, gross private fixed investment in Colombia ranged from $1.6 to $3.7 billion and averaged $2.8 billion between 1976 and 1986. This means that narco-capitalists had as much capacity to invest in Colombia as did the entire private sector of the country. These figures also suggest that Colombian policymakers are likely to have to take into account a possible very large "narco-capital external overhang," consisting of capital amounts that could be brought into the country sometime in the future.

Balance-of-payments data show that the amount of unexplained foreign exchange received by the Central Bank has not been as large as many would expect because the unexplained tourism and labor income has not exceeded $500 million in any given year. Incoming contraband figures are obviously subject to great uncertainty, but—as noted above—FENALCO indicates that in 1988 this figure was about $1.1 billion. These estimates of illegal inflows do not include the financing of private capital flight and of tourism abroad. It is likely that as political instability, violence, and insecurity increased in recent years, legitimate capital flight has taken place—

at least partially financed by illegal capital inflows; it is consequently probable that "dirty" capital has substituted for "clean" capital. The magnitude of this phenomenon is not known (Kalmanovitz uses $500 million a year but does not explain how he arrived at that figure), and it is not possible to assess its significance.

Similarly, black market foreign exchange is used to finance tourism and other expenditures abroad such as education and health services. These values are not included in the above-mentioned estimates, but they may be important. For example, balance-of-payments data show that the expenditures for trips taken by Colombian residents in 1988 amounted to $601.6 million, and that 541,530 people left the country by air. If one assumes that 75 percent of the departing passengers are Colombian residents, these figures indicate an expenditure of only $1,480 per person—including international airfares—and that is likely too low. Notice that these data do not include the expenditures abroad of tourists who left the country by land. Thus, official tourism imports are likely to be underestimated. (Here Kalmanovitz again uses an estimate of $500 million a year but again does not explain how it was derived.) Therefore, the amount of the narco-capital that has entered the Colombian economy could be substantially larger than the estimates from the income side of the balance of payments plus contraband. However, we should remember that not all illegal capital inflows are drug-originated; some could be generated by export underinvoicing, returning emigrants, and various other means.

Aside from the imprecision of these estimates, narco-business income is so large in relation to some key economic variables in Colombia that narco-capital could easily alter the status quo of the society. For instance, it is acknowledged that narco-capitalists have purchased large tracts of land in the middle Magdalena Valley, in the eastern plains, and in parts of Antioquia and Córdoba—areas in which land prices have been low and guerrilla activity relatively high. According to agricultural experts from the World Bank, prices have ranged from about $500 to $2,000 per hectare. If one accepts the Nadelmann figures for 1985, the profits from one small planeload of 250 kilos of cocaine—after paying $150,000 to the pilot and ditching the $100,000 plane—were enough to purchase between 1,200 and 4,800 hectares of land. The size of the narco-profits is so large relative to the value of many Colombian assets—even if one accepts the lower estimates for narco-income—that the impact of those profits on the Colombian economy can be extraordinary.

Conclusion

Several authors have tackled the difficult task of estimating the impact of the narco-industry on Colombia. Most studies do not attempt traditional cost-benefit analysis because this is not an appropriate methodology. Analysts have concentrated their efforts on the measurement of the volume of narco-exports, the revenues generated, and the level of consequent profits. Although subject to great uncertainty, the findings suggest that Colombian narco-business profits have fluctuated between

$2 and $5 billion per year. However, these estimates are based only on Colombian value added and are likely to underestimate the actual profits of Colombians involved in the drug business in the United States, Bolivia, and Peru. Furthermore, recent cocaine seizures have prompted the U.S. government to greatly increase its estimates of cocaine production, suggesting that narco-profits have been substantially larger than once believed.

There have also been estimates of the narco-money inflow based on official balance-of-payments data. These are useful for analyzing the impact of the narco-industry on some macroeconomic variables and policies, especially as the government reacts to changes in the official balance of payments, but they greatly underestimate the narco-capital inflow into the Colombian economy—which, given the available information, cannot be accurately measured. Estimates have been as high as $4 billion and as low as $500 million a year. Narco-capital inflow could easily have been at least $2 billion per year, however, an extremely large amount relative to the size of private-sector investment in the country.

Narco-capitalists have brought their capital into Colombia through underground channels—increasing the level of contraband, financing legitimate capital flight, and, according to one estimate, greatly increasing underinvoicing of imports. Narco-capital has been invested in several sectors but has had a particularly noticeable impact on urban construction and rural land purchases, especially in areas of recent settlement where property rights are still questioned and the state's presence is weak. These investments altered patterns in urban construction and have concentrated rural property significantly in some regions.

Even according to the lower estimates, the amount of narco-capital accumulated inside and outside Colombia is extremely large in relation to the size of the Colombian economy. The full impact of this wealth has yet to be felt. It could be truly dramatic, and narco-capitalists could eventually become the dominant economic group within Colombia.

Notes

1. See Ethan A. Nadelmann, "Latinoamérica: Economía política del comercio de cocaína," *Texto y Contexto* 9 (September-December 1986): 27–49; Hernando J. Gómez, "Colombian Illegal Economy: Size, Evolution, and Economic Impact," mimeo (Washington, D.C.: Brookings Institution, 1985); and Peter Reuter, "The (Continued) Vitality of Mythical Numbers," *The Public Interest* 75 (Spring 1984): 135–147.

2. Peter Reuter, "Eternal Hope: America's Quest for Narcotics Control," *The Public Interest* 79 (Spring 1985): 79–95, esp. 88.

3. See Roberto Junguito and Carlos Caballero, "Illegal Trade Transactions and the Underground Economy of Colombia," in V. Tanzi, ed., *The Underground Economy in the United States and Abroad* (Lexington: Lexington Books, 1982), 291.

4. Reuter, "Eternal Hope."

5. Peter Reuter has argued that Colombians are involved in distributing cocaine in the United States because the large number of Colombians living there facilitates the development

of trusted marketing relationships. By this logic one would not expect Colombians to be involved in Europe, where few Colombians reside. Thus, Reuter observes that most South American cocaine that reaches the European market passes through Brazil. See Reuter, "Eternal Hope," 89.

6. R. Warren and J. M. Peck, "Foreign-Born Emigration from the United States: 1960 to 1970," *Demography* 17, no. 1 (February 1980): 71–84.

7. Junguito and Caballero, "Illegal Trade Transactions."

8. Hernando J. Gómez, "El tamaño del narcotráfico," *Economía Colombiana* 226–227 (February-March 1990): 8–17; and "La economía ilegal en Colombia: Tamaño, evolución e impacto económico," *Coyuntura Económica* 18, no. 3 (September 1988): 93–113.

9. Salomón Kalmanovitz, "La economía del narcotráfico en Colombia," *Economía Colombiana* 226–227 (February-March 1990): 18–28.

10. Nadelmann, "Latinoamérica: Economía política del comercio de cocaína."

11. W. Rensselaer Lee III, "Dimensions of the South American Cocaine Industry," *Journal of Interamerican Studies and World Affairs* 30, nos. 2–3 (Summer-Fall 1988): 89.

12. C. A. Caballero, "La economía de la cocaína," *Coyuntura Económica* 18, no. 3 (September 1988): 179–184.

13. Gómez, "Colombian Illegal Economy."

14. Miguel Urrutia, "Análisis costo-beneficio del tráfico de drogas para la economía colombiana," *Coyuntura Económica* 20, no. 3 (October 1990): 115–126.

15. Average Colombian exports are likely to have become of lower value per unit of weight because of the development of coal exports.

16. Kalmanovitz, "La economía del narcotráfico."

17. Gómez, "La economía ilegal," and "Colombian Illegal Economy."

18. F. Giraldo, "Narcotráfico y construcción," *Economía Colombiana* 226–227 (February-March 1990): 38–49.

19. Alejandro Reyes, "Geografía de los conflictos sociales y de la violencia en Colombia," paper presented at conference on the Contemporary Crisis in Colombia, Center for Iberian and Latin American Studies, University of California, San Diego, December 1989.

20. Libardo Sarmiento and Carlos Moreno, "Narcotráfico y sector agropecuario en Colombia," *Economía Colombiana* 226–227 (February-March 1990): 29–37.

21. Peter Reuter, "Can the Borders Be Sealed?" *The Public Interest* 92 (Summer 1988): 51–66.

22. Kalmanovitz, "La economía del narcotráfico."

5

Coca Production in Peru

Elena Alvarez

Peru has often been cited as a classic (if not always successful) example of an export-led economy. The celebrated "guano age" in the mid-nineteenth century made Peru a monoproduct export economy that failed to achieve self-sustaining growth. The rubber boom of the 1890s and 1900s had its impact in the jungle region, with little effect on the remainder of the country.[1] Prosperity in the jungle was entirely dependent on monoproduct rubber exports. There was no attempt to diversify or develop the local economy; once deprived of its import capacity, the region sank immediately into stagnation.[2]

In the late 1970s and throughout the 1980s, coca leaf—cultivated in the Andes for thousands of years—suddenly became the country's most profitable export crop. Coca profitability is linked to the production of cocaine, an illegal commodity. Most of the domestic coca economy is an underground operation, and consequently information about it is scant. Does the export economy generated by coca follow the pattern of previous experiences in Peru? As Francisco E. Thoumi has shown for the case of Colombia in Chapter 4, the fragmentary information currently available does not always allow answers to this question—and when it does, the answer may not be very accurate. I will nonetheless try to assess the data in a cautious, conservative fashion.

Preconditions for Coca Expansion

It is essential to understand the reasons for illegal coca expansion because many of these factors still persist and could lead to the resurgence of this activity. Aside from strong external demand and Peru's comparative advantage for coca production,[3] there are internal reasons for the expansion of coca. One concerns a pattern of agricultural development that has yielded very low levels of income in the Andean region, where the majority of the farms are *minifundios* of less than 5 hectares. As a result, Peru has levels of poverty comparable to those in the least developed areas of Asia and even Africa. Studies estimate per-capita income for Andean peasants at around $50 in the early 1970s and somewhere between $157 and $620 in the early 1980s.[4]

In addition, food consumption patterns in Peru have undergone drastic change. The traditional emphasis on Andean goods (sweet potato, barley, soft maize, soft wheat) has gradually been replaced by a more Westernized diet in the urban areas (rice, white potato, chicken, dairy products, bread, noodles, and other processed foods). Thus, in the last decades Andean farmers have faced a declining market for the type of foodstuffs they can produce within the ecological zones they inhabit.

Output has been affected by the agrarian reform of 1969, which excluded the Andean *minifundios*, or the majority of the poor agricultural producers in the country. It did affect the best lands, however—about 10 million of the total 30 million hectares in farm properties. These lands and other assets were transferred to former workers in the previous hacienda and modern plantation systems.[5] In the meantime, most nonland reform policies applied to the agricultural sector before and after 1969 were planned and implemented for the purpose of supplying cheap foodstuffs for the urban areas. As a result, profitability for most of the agricultural sector sharply declined.[6]

As a result of poverty and its exacerbation, there was continual rural-to-urban migration from the Andes to the coast until the late 1960s; probably as a result of agrarian reform as well, this migration later turned toward the jungle in the Amazon regions. An area of colonization since at least the 1960s, the jungle could produce some of the food items sought by urban areas (rice, yellow corn, palm oil). And during the 1970s, coca exports soared. By the 1980s, the jungle thus became the second-most important agricultural region in Peru.

The Coca Economy: How Big?

Given the illegal nature of the coca crop, it is difficult to determine accurate production figures. Output has been estimated on the basis of aerial photographs of known producing areas, which give an approximate number of hectares devoted to the crop and to which an imputed yield is applied. Yields seem to fluctuate between less than one and over two metric tons per hectare per year—depending on the variety and age of the plant, altitude, atmospheric conditions of production, and other factors.

Available estimates for cultivation range from 26,000 hectares for the Upper Huallaga Valley (UHV), the presumed largest producing area, to 380,000 hectares for the entire country (a figure quoted to the press by a former minister).[7] Responsible analysts have placed the "most likely" figure for the entire country in the vicinity of 200,000 hectares.[8]

Many studies have concentrated on the Upper Huallaga Valley, where most of the illegal coca expansion in the 1970s and 1980s is believed to have occurred. Although the empirical evidence is not clear, recent estimates seem to indicate that illegal expansion in other areas of the country has been as large as or even more significant than that in the Upper Huallaga.

A study by Inés Astete and David Tejada for the United Nations Development Programme (UNDP) (hereinafter UNDP study) is the only one in existence that develops a framework of analysis based on alternative methods to determine the proper range of the coca hectareage in the Upper Huallaga Valley. Once the authors determine the range for the UHV, they infer the size for the rest of the country.[9] J. Laity used the UNDP methodology to reassess the possible hectareage cultivated with coca in the Upper Huallaga during 1988; because he compares his estimates with alternative sources, his calculations seem to be more realistic than those of the UNDP study itself.[10]

The UNDP study uses four alternative methods to estimate maximum possible coca hectareage in the UHV, focusing on land use potential, labor availability, aerial photography, and kerosene requirements. They merit recapitulation here.

Land Use Potential

In the Upper Huallaga Valley, this approach divides agricultural land into different zones: agricultural land (suitable for annuals or perennials), including some fallow areas, pasture land, forest land, and land not suited to agro-forestry exploitation (mountains and woods). Coca production is then estimated according to the feasibility of cultivation in each category of land. Results appear in Table 5-1.

Prevailing estimates about potential coca production may be too low. First, as witnessed by anthropologists and other observers, farmers often disguise coca production with their legal crops. By overlooking this deception, the land use technique underestimates the quantity of illegal coca production. Second, many experts agree that much illegal coca is cultivated on land not suitable for conventional agricultural purposes; if so, this qualification would increase the feasible scale of production. Third, it is possible that there is no fallow land, thus adding another 54,340 hectares for coca cultivation. And instead of assuming that only 10 percent of the "land potentially usable for agriculture within a short time" is currently planted in coca, one could as well assume 25 percent. These changed assumptions would result in a total of 139,286 hectares devoted to coca production in the Upper Huallaga Valley—rather than 66,155—thus doubling the original estimate.

Labor Availability

This method estimates labor requirements for legitimate crops in the valley, subtracts this from the total amount of labor available, and finally—using an estimate of labor required per hectare of coca—calculates the maximum amount of coca that could be cultivated by the remaining workers. Applied to the Upper Huallaga Valley, the method takes demographic projections from the 1981 population census, hypothetical labor requirements provided by the Banco Agrícola del Perú (BAP) branch in Tingo María, and actual labor requirements determined by interviews with cultivators. As shown in Table 5-2, data on the extent of migration from

TABLE 5-1
Availability of Land for Coca Production in Upper Huallaga Valley (UHV)

Type of Land	Hectares	
Total area of UHV		1,859,000
Total agricultural surface area		192,598
Land in use for legitimate crops	69,381	
Official estimate of land in use for coca	**30,183**	
Pasture land	10,238	
Fallow land	82,796	
Fallow land required to stabilize production of legitimate crops (.78 x 69,381)	54,340	
Land available for additional coca production	**28,456**	
Additional forest land potentially usable for agriculture within a short time		100,163
Natural pasture in use	25,000	
Mountains and woods	61,731	
Other land	13,432	
Maximum amount for future coca cultivation [(61,731 + 13,432) x 10%]	**7,516**	
Total land potentially available for coca production (30,183 + 28,456 + 7,516)		**66,155**

Sources: Based on data in Inés Astete and David Tejada, "Elementos para una economía política de la coca en el Alto Huallaga," Project AD/PER/86/459 OSP-PNUD (Lima, 1988), 35-45; and J. Laity, "The Coca Economy in the Upper Huallaga," mimeo (Lima, 1989).

neighboring provinces and labor requirements for cultivation provide supporting information for this technique.

The UNDP study concludes that approximately 30,000 workers were cultivating just over 42,000 hectares of coca leaf in the Upper Huallaga Valley in 1987. Let us review the assumptions behind these calculations. BAP lends money to agricultural producers according to loan types for ideal predetermined classes of technology for various products. The UNDP study takes its labor requirements from BAP estimates for "techniques designed to produce a high yield per hectare." These requirements are considerably higher than the ones established through direct interviews with cultivators. According to BAP, the total number of workers required to produce the legitimate crops grown in 1987 was 22,107; interviews suggest that the actual figure was only 12,789. The UNDP researchers use the higher labor requirement per hectare of coca production (or 208 worker days per hectare per year divided by 300 work days per worker per year = 0.7 workers per hectare) *and* an average of interview and BAP requirements for legitimate crops (= 17,448 workers). They also assume a figure of 10 percent (= 7,738) rather than 20 percent for migrant labor of the neighboring economically active population (EAP) provinces.

TABLE 5-2
Demographic Projections for Upper Huallaga Valley[a]

Population		Figures
Total population (1987)		169,758
Rural	103,510	
Urban	66,248	
Economically active population (EAP)		63,954
Rural	39,894	
Urban	24,060	
EAP in agriculture		36,817
Migrant labor from neighboring provinces[b]		15,477
Total potential agricultural workers in UHV (36,817 + 15,477)		52,294

[a]As derived from 1981 population census and potential work force estimates (1987).

[b]Estimated as 20 percent of EAP of neighboring provinces: Huánuco, Huamaliés, Marañón, Pataz, and Coronel Portillo.

Sources: Based on data in J. Laity, "Coca Economy in the Upper Huallaga," mimeo (Lima, 1989), 6; as derived from Inés Astete and David Tejada, "Elementos para una economía política de la coca en el Alto Huallaga," Project AD/PER/86/459 OSP-PNUD (Lima, 1988), 46-74.

The same methodology with different assumptions can yield remarkably different results. Working with the lower labor requirements, for example, J. Laity obtains a maximum cultivable area of 94,060 hectares.[11] This estimate is consistent with findings from other studies based on alternative methodologies.

Aerial Photography

This approach is based on aerial photography performed from 1985 through 1988 by the General Directorate of Aerial Photography under contract to the Special Project for Control and Coca Crop Reduction in the Upper Huallaga Valley. As summarized in Table 5-3, the UNDP study applies this technique to obtain a maximum estimated coca-producing area of 44,715 hectares for the Upper Huallaga.

Astete and Tejada state that the coca fields could not be quantified accurately through this methodology because (1) the photographs corresponded to different years (1986, 1987, and 1988), and (2) coca production has grown very quickly— particularly on forest reserves (*bosques de protección*). Using the same photographs, moreover, the U.S. Narcotics Assistance Unit reached estimates of 60,000 to 70,000 hectares devoted to coca production in the Upper Huallaga.[12] The discrepancy between these conclusions indicates how difficult it is to generate data from this type of source.

Kerosene Requirements

The last method in the UNDP study concentrates on a key input in the production of basic paste. In theory, and in the normal practice of producing national

TABLE 5-3
Coca Hectareage Estimated by Aerial Photography, 1985-1988

Area	%	Hectares
Total area to be photographed[a]		963,000
Area completed at time of study		455,850
Area identified as either "coca fields" or "potential coca fields"		29,501
Percent coca fields in area photographed	6.5	
Area not yet photographed		507,150
Estimated percent coca fields in area not yet photographed[b]	2.0-3.0	
Estimated coca hectareage in areas not yet photographed (507,150 x 3%)		15,214
Maximum coca hectareage (29,501 + 15,214)		**44,715**

[a]Excludes area unsuited for forestry and agriculture.

[b]Shares assumed without explanation.

Source: Based on data in Inés Astete and David Tejada, "Elementos para una economía política de la coca en el Alto Huallaga," Project AD/PER/86/459 OSP-PNUD (Lima, 1988).

accounts, one could determine the size of the overall illegal coca activity by determining the "production function" of coca paste and the availability of inputs in the producing areas. If all the information on the various inputs were available and the usage of the same inputs in other industries were determined, one could easily determine the size of the illegal activity.

According to the UNDP report, the availability of kerosene in the upper jungle increased by 55 percent between 1984 and 1987, if it is assumed that 25 percent of the 1984 production levels plus *all* of the additional increment of kerosene were used in the production of coca paste in 1987—that is, about 50 percent of kerosene production in neighboring refineries. This would make a total of 305,500 barrels (or 47,963,500 liters) available for coca paste production. According to Edmundo Morales, 110 kilos of dry coca leaf for the production of 1 kilo of coca paste requires 25.2 liters of kerosene; processing 1,000 kilos of coca leaf would therefore require 229 liters of kerosene.[13] Half of the available kerosene in 1987 would permit the processing (or production) of 209,448 metric tons of coca leaf—or, in other words, the cultivation of 209,448 hectares (if yields are assumed to be 1 ton per hectare). Because the same kerosene can be recycled at least twice, however, the actual production of coca leaf and coca paste could have been at least twice as high.[14]

Beginning with a much higher estimate of kerosene availability, the UNDP study reaches a significantly smaller production figure of 32,353 metric tons of coca leaf. This calculation is based on a "recipe" for coca paste that appears to be clearly inaccurate, because it calls for several times the kerosene cited by Morales on the

TABLE 5-4
Potential Coca Hectareage in Upper Huallaga Valley

Technique	UNDP	Laity	Other
Land use potential	66,155	≤100,000	NA
Labor availability	42,000	94,060	NA
Aerial photography	44,715	NA	60,000-70,000
Kerosene requirements	32,353	65,000	≤200,000

NA = not available.

Sources: Based on data in Inés Astete and David Tejada, "Elementos para una economía política de la coca en el Alto Huallaga," Project AD/PER/86/459 OSP-PNUD (Lima, 1988); J. Laity, "The Coca Economy in the Upper Huallaga," mimeo (Lima, 1989); data supplied by U.S. Narcotics Assistance Unit; and author's estimates.

basis of first-hand observation. (The authors did not visit the Upper Huallaga, so I will rely on the Morales recipe.)

Clearly, the key input method is not very reliable. Better estimates might be obtained assessing the utilization of more than one input—for instance, sulfuric acid as well as kerosene. In any case, the procedure can provide an alternative means for determining a plausible range of figures for production.

Table 5-4 presents a summary of hectareage availability estimated by the four methods. Because of several restrictive assumptions, the UNDP study arrives at rather low hectareage figures, ranging between 32,353 and 66,155 hectares. The recalculations by Laity and my own assessments seem somewhat more realistic; they give a hectareage range for the Upper Huallaga of between 60,000 and 100,000 hectares. The upper limit of 100,000 hectares in the Laity estimate is based on labor requirements, which seem to be a crucial limitation for coca production; this seems to represent a valid upper bound.

Although projections for 1990 by the National Plan for the Elimination of Narco-trafficking and the National Planning Institute indicate that the Upper Huallaga Valley cultivates only 27 percent of the total coca cultivated in the country, most of the best studies assume that the Upper Huallaga accounts for 50–80 percent of the country's total production. With this background, I now turn to production estimates for the nation as a whole.

Values for National Coca Production:
Direct and Indirect Effects

Here I seek to assess the *possible* magnitude of the overall coca export economy in Peru, including the direct and indirect effects. I also try to assess the importance of the coca economy at the regional level. In so doing, I hope to convey some of the "flavor" of what it is like to analyze an underground economy.

Parenthetically, the national balance of payments sheds little light on this question. A brief analysis of the Peruvian balance of payments during the 1980s, particularly the "errors and omissions" account, does not provide any hint that $1 billion or more may have been missing from official records. Furthermore, the level of aggregation in the balance of payments did not permit analysis of other accounts that might have been used to disguise illegal incomes; nor was it possible to assess negative income effects that illegal drug activity might have had on other accounts, such as tourist revenues.

Working with production data instead, I begin by assuming that the Upper Huallaga Valley contained one-half the area available in Peru for coca exports in 1988—that is, 100,000 hectares; another 100,000 hectares are distributed throughout the rest of the country, so the total available hectareage comes to 200,000 hectares. I exclude from the coca export hectareage those areas for domestic consumption and those that have been eradicated. Although it may be a conservative guess, I assume that coca yields one metric ton per hectare. (This partly offsets the upper-bound assumption of available hectareage in the Upper Huallaga.) I further assume that 10 percent of the coca paste is consumed domestically, that 40 percent of coca paste is converted into coca base, and that 50 percent of the paste is exported. The prices used for every stage of production are very conservative, which explains the relatively small value added at the coca paste and coca base stages. The resulting estimates of coca base and paste exported from Peru range between $382 and $942 million. This is equivalent to 14.3 to 35.4 percent of the total legal exports of the country for 1988.

The income multiplier assumed for the coca leaf stage is 2.0, an assumption that appears to be somewhat low (propensity to consume, or PC = 50 percent). Although still a very preliminary analysis, at least one account of expenditures in the local producing areas seems to indicate an even lower multiplier effect.[15] A significant share of the income also seems to be leaving the country. The assumed multiplier for the coca base stage is even smaller, 1.5, partly because the income per capita at this point is presumably higher and much of the income may leave the country (thus PC = 33 percent). The total coca export income effect raises the overall income to a range of $498 million to $1,219 million, which would make its share of overall GDP between 1.5 and 3.7 percent.

The employment effect is difficult to determine because there are no studies of labor requirements at each stage of the production process. Lacking better data, I assumed the same employment multiplier used by Clark Joel in the Bolivian case, or 1.5.[16] The total employment effect may therefore range between 165,000 and 279,000 workers. This would amount to 2.7–4.5 percent of total employment in Peru and 6.8–11.5 percent of the nation's agricultural employment. Without superior data, some other studies estimate that several times more workers are involved in coca production.[17]

Despite inconsistencies among existing studies, it is clear that the legal agricultural activity in the Upper Huallaga Valley is small in comparison to that of coca. According to ECONSULT, the agricultural GDP share of the area was 7.2 percent in 1985, whereas the UNDP study indicated 13.5 percent for 1986. Rice, coffee, bananas, and tea experienced substantial decreases in production in the early 1980s, but legal agricultural growth performance between 1985 and 1987 was significant.

One effect of the eradication program in the Upper Huallaga seems to have been to discourage coca growers in the valley—many of whom kept their families in their legal plots, which might explain the growth in legal agriculture. A related effect of the eradication program is to foster extensive cultivation of the type that entails deforestation, a point I take up below.

I believe the employment effect is ambiguous. On the one hand, according to literature on labor availability in the Upper Huallaga, legal agriculture appears to employ the dominant share of the work force in the valley. On the other hand, in view of the wide wage differentials between coca cultivation and other crops, coca appears to employ the larger share. Furthermore, because many legal cultivators grow coca in their legal plots, the net effect may be that coca employs more workers than surveys and educated guesses usually suggest. More research is needed on this issue.

In terms of the income generated by coca, it is not clear how and where it is distributed and spent. It seems, however, that much of the locally generated value added does not remain in the valley.[18] From the figures calculated by Laity on value added for coca leaf ($312 million), paste ($63 million), and base ($165 million) in the Upper Huallaga, together with his assessment of the commerce sector in the valley, a large share of the income appears to be spent on contraband merchandise— either in larger cities (such as Lima) or elsewhere.[19] In this case the multiplier for coca leaf in the Upper Huallaga would fall between 1.25 and 1.50.

Obviously, the workers directly affiliated with the coca export activity are much better off, at least in monetary terms, than the rest of the rural workers. According to Laity's figures, coca leaf value added per capita comes to an average of $7,800 per person ($312 million per 40,000 cultivators). This would place these workers well within the upper quartile of Peru's overall income distribution.

In sum, despite my very conservative assumptions, the figures indicate that the underground coca economy is substantial in size and importance. Table 5-5 displays a summary of estimates.

For the cultivators directly involved, in particular, coca export activity appears to be very significant for both rural employment and income. It is not clear, however, how this income is distributed in the country or how it is spent. This last point is especially problematic in reference to the Upper Huallaga Valley. As will be shown below, there are related costs that tend to offset many of the benefits.

Costs Affiliated with Illegal Coca Exports

Many costs related to the illegal coca activity cannot be quantified. Difficulties in measurement arise from problems in acquiring information and defining clearly the opportunity costs. I group these costs into four categories: (1) economic costs— activities that do not take place because the illegal activities discourage them,

TABLE 5-5
Coca Economy in Peru: Summary Estimates for 1988

Cultivation and production[a]	
Total hectares under cultivation	200,000
Less hectares for domestic consumption	17,914
Less eradicated hectares	15,587
Total hectares in production	166,499
Value of production and exports[b]	
Values of coca leaf	
Minimum	158.2
Maximum	474.5
Values of coca paste	
Minimum	215.7
Maximum	575.2
Values of coca base	
Minimum	274.5
Maximum	653.6
Value of total exports	
Minimum	382.3
Maximum	941.2
Economic value added[b]	
Direct value added	
Minimum	279.0
Maximum	654.0
Indirect value added	
Minimum	219.0
Maximum	565.0
Total value added	
Minimum	498.0
Maximum	1,219.0
Employment[c]	
Direct employment	
Minimum	110,000
Maximum	186,000
Indirect employment	
Minimum	55,000
Maximum	93,000
Total employment	
Minimum	165,000
Maximum	279,000

[a]In hectares.
[b]In U.S. millions $.
[c]By number of workers.

implicit appreciation of Peruvian currency vis-à-vis other currencies caused by significant inflows of illegal foreign exchange, and the cost for the government to replace drug production; (2) ecological costs—destruction of natural resources and pollution of the environment; (3) political costs—alliances of different illegal activities tending toward political instability and eventual destruction of the state; and (4) social costs—institutional deterioration, criminal violence, and growing consumer addiction.

Economic Costs

We are unable to measure directly losses of income associated with the coca activity. Tourist receipts and foreign investment behavior have probably been more affected by the guerrilla actions of Sendero Luminoso (Shining Path), starting in the 1980s, than by drug activity. We are still studying the impact on the economy of the large inflow of illegal foreign exchange. As of early 1990, the exchange rate for the new Peruvian sol (1 sol per U.S. dollar) appeared to be higher than would otherwise have been the case. It was not clear whether this resulted from explicit government policy or from the coca underground economy.

The cost of crop substitution between 1981 and 1988 was $34.5 million,[20] a very small amount compared with the incomes produced by coca in Peru. The program has not been very successful, however, if measured by the fact that fewer than 16,000 hectares were actually eradicated through 1988 (see Table 5-5).

Ecological Costs

Several recent studies have documented the deforestation process in the Amazon region and attempted preliminary assessments of the hectareage lost by deforestation and of the environmental pollution. E. Bedoya explains that the illegality of the coca crops has encouraged extensive agriculture by both titled legal cultivators and illegal coca producers. Extensive slash-and-burn agriculture promotes deforestation. Legal cultivators do not have enough wage laborers available to help in permanent agriculture because coca crops pay higher wages; eradication programs also force producers to migrate greater distances and in the process to deforest the jungle. Another factor in the deforestation process is Sendero Luminoso, which forces cultivators to plant coca along with self-subsistence crops. The guerrillas charge a "tax" (*cupo*) for protection that is financed by coca production.[21]

According to M. Dourojeanni, coca is cultivated mainly on lands that are appropriate for forestry or for reserves, which has serious effects on the environment. The deforested areas include actual coca plantations; plantations of subsistence crops (cassava, bananas, and corn) by the coca growers; areas used by peasants who have fled those regions dominated by narcotics traffickers and terrorists; land used by coca growers fleeing police repression; and areas deforested for landing strips, camps, and laboratories. Dourojeanni calculates that about 700,000 hectares may have been deforested directly and indirectly due to coca.[22] This represents about 10 percent of the total deforestation in the Peruvian Amazon region during the twentieth century. Dourojeanni describes the environmental results: "the loss of soil through sudden or cumulative erosion; the extinction of genetic resources; the alteration of the hydrological system; flooding; the reduction of the hydroelectrical potential; increased difficulty in river navigation; the lack of wood and firewood; the lack of game animals for hunting, etc. Moreover, under these circumstances burning off the woods and ground cover produced by clearing the land is almost obligatory, bringing other consequences like air pollution, the loss of soil nutrients, and damage to topsoil."[23] Even though there is evidence from pre-Hispanic times that coca can be planted in such a way as to preserve natural resources, Dourojeanni explains, cultivation methods in use today promote erosion. Modern coca-growing practices have won the plant the epithet Attila of Tropical Agriculture.

B. Marcelo has studied the impact of the chemical waste dumped by the coca paste producers into the rivers. In 1986 the volume of toxic waste dumped into rivers was estimated at 57 million liters of kerosene, 32 million liters of sulfuric acid, 16 thousand metric tons of lime, 3,200 metric tons of carbide, 16 thousand metric tons of toilet paper, 6.4 million liters of acetone, and 6.4 million liters of toluene. The result poses a grave threat to the survival of the region's aquatic resources. Many species of fish, amphibians, aquatic reptiles, and crustaceans have already completely disappeared from the rivers and streams in areas in which maceration pits are located.[24] The contamination of these rivers in the Upper Huallaga Valley already exceeds pollution standards for fresh and inland water established by the World Health Organization (WHO). The WHO designates as polluted or contaminated those bodies of water that have been altered in such a manner that they can no longer be put to the normal uses that would correspond to their natural state.

It can be argued that legal production has caused as much damage to the Amazon environment as has illegal coca production. It can also be argued that the people in Peru are not preoccupied by this "environmental issue," which tends to be a concern of the advanced industrial world. Yet this cannot justify the destruction of the Amazon environment. First, legal production can always be taxed, and the consequent revenues could be used to alleviate the situation. Second, the environment is not an "issue" in Peru and other Third World countries only because real incomes for the majority of the population are so low that survival is more important than anything else.

It is difficult to put a price on losses in nature. Some of the deforested land may be recovered, but vanished animal species areas may not. What price do we use to assess the value of 700,000 deforested hectares? One report quotes a value of $600 per hectare in lands producing legal crops in the UHV.[25] This is estimated to be the annual earnings on an average hectare through the cultivation of such legal crops as coffee or cacao—compared with $4,500 per hectare per year earned cultivating coca in 1985. A more recent UNDP study quotes prices per hectare per year of possible coca substitutes—such as cocoa ($1,615), coffee ($1,114), palm oil ($833), and rice ($885)—using the best available technologies.[26] In the absence of firm data, I will use $600 and the 1990 data for the coca substitutes mentioned above as lower and upper limits, respectively, to value the hectareage losses or the income that cannot be produced. This yields boundaries of $420 million (i.e., US$600 x 700,000 hectares = $420 million lost income) and $778 million (or [US$1,615 x 175,000 hectares] + [US$1,114 x 175,000 hectares] + [US$885 x 175,000 hectares] + [US$833 x 175,000 hectares] = $778.225 million).

In other words, although coca produced between $498 million and $1,219 million, it may have created losses on the order of $420 to $778 million. A figure in between these two is probably realistic because the higher estimate assumes that Peru encounters no obstacles in selling its extra production.

Political Costs

The eradication program initiated in Peru in 1981 has been identified as one of the causes that indirectly triggered the alliance between Sendero Luminoso and the coca growers.[27] The guerrillas found an excellent source of revenues by serving as a protective army for coca producers. There is no way of knowing how this income may have sustained or strengthened Sendero, but it definitely contributed to the escalation of violence throughout the 1980s. Government budget appropriations for army expenditures and policy enforcement add yet another cost. All in all, illegal drug trafficking has accelerated the deterioration of the political situation in Peru.

Social Costs

Current Peruvian surveys do not show an addiction of epidemic proportions caused by the smoking of coca paste. Domestic usage is nonetheless growing, as María Elena Medina-Mora and María del Carmen Mariño have shown in Chapter 3, and it is cause for potential concern.[28]

Illegal coca activity contributes directly to institutionalized corruption. One sign of this is the fact that current statistics do not indicate any increases in arrests and sentences for coca production or trafficking. On the contrary, there seems to be a regression in drug-related crimes in Peru.[29] This simply shows that the illegal drug activity contributes to a further deterioration of the state, which is already a weak institution in Peru. This weakness in turn explains why the illegal activity became so large and so prosperous in Peru in the first place.

Conclusion

I have presented a preliminary assessment of the benefits derived from the illegal exports of coca by-products on the Peruvian economy. Economic historians have shown that Peru has had several "export booms" that did not move the nation into a path of self-sustained development. The coca boom may be another such experience, except that here the illegal trade may create more poverty and political chaos in the long run.

Because of the illegality of the activity, it is difficult to assess actual benefits and costs, which is why I tried to establish at least one piece of fairly solid information: production data for the main coca-producing area, the Upper Huallaga Valley. From this I constructed reasonable ranges of production for the country as a whole.

The production data, based on estimates of hectareage, thus constitute the major building block for developing other parameters to assess direct and indirect income and employment effects in the country and in the major producing area. My analysis has shown that the illegal coca activity in Peru is important. Its aggregate value added may fall between $498 and $1,219 million—between 2 and 4 percent of Peru's GDP—while generating 3 to 4 percent of the country's total employment.

Costs created by the illegal coca trade are multiple, complex, and extremely difficult to measure. These costs may offset the benefits derived from coca and create more poverty for the country in the long run. Principal among them are the ecological destruction of the Peruvian jungle and the alliance of convenience between the guerrillas and those in the illegal coca trade against the state.

Notes

I thank the Friedrich Ebert Foundation for its support of field research in Peru; Martín Alvarez for help with data gathering; and Bruce Bagley, Paul Boeker, Fernando Eguren, Alvaro Salazar, Donor Lion, Peter Smith, Francisco Thoumi, Jeryl Mumpower, and Jolyne M. Sanjak for their helpful comments on previous drafts.

1. G. Pennano, *La economía del caucho* (Iquitos, Peru: Centro de Estudios Teológicos de la Amazonia, 1988), 180.

2. Rosemary Thorpe and Geoffrey Bertram, *Peru 1890–1977: Growth and Policy in an Open Economy* (New York: Columbia University Press, 1978), 3, 67–70.

3. The Bolivian Chapare and the Peruvian Upper Huallaga Valley areas, where coca production for export has expanded so greatly in the past decade, seem to be perfect habitats for the highly valued Huánuco variety of coca leaf. This is a shrub one to three meters tall that grows principally at between 500 and 1,500 meters of elevation, although it may be found at up to 2,000 meters altitude. Geographically, the production of this variety extends from Ecuador to Bolivia; it is unknown in Colombia and in the Amazonian lowlands. Another aspect of Peru's "comparative advantage" is the remoteness of the cultivation areas, which makes policing very difficult. See T. Plowman, "Coca Chewing and Botanical Origins of Coca (Erythroxylon) in South America," in D. Pacini and C. Franquemont, eds., *Coca and Cocaine: Effects on People and Policy in Latin America* (Boston: Cultural Survival, 1986), 5–33; and T. Plowman, "Aspectos botánicos de la coca," in R. F. Jerí, ed., *Cocaína 1980* (Lima: Pacific Press, 1980), 90–105.

4. See J. M. Caballero, *Economía agraria de la sierra peruana* (Lima: Instituto de Estudios Peruanos, 1981), esp. 208; and D. Cotlear, "La economía campesina en las regiones modernas y tradicionales de la sierra," unpublished manuscript (Lima, July 1987).

5. J. M. Caballero and E. Alvarez, *Aspectos cuantitativos de la reforma agraria (1969–1979)* (Lima: Instituto de Estudios Peruanos, 1981).

6. E. Alvarez, *Política económica y agricultura en el Perú, 1969–1979* (Lima: Instituto de Estudios Peruanos, 1983).

7. The statement was made by former Interior Minister Abel Salinas to *El Comercio* (February 17, 1987). A journalistic assessment places the cultivated area at between 570,000 and 760,000 hectares, producing an income for Peru of $3 to $6 billion. See "Coca, ese becerro de oro," *Actualidad Económica* 88 (March 1987).

8. M. Dourojeanni, "Impactos ambientales del cultivo de coca y la producción de cocaína en la amazonia peruana," in F. León and R. Castro de la Mata, eds., *Pasta básica de cocaína* (Lima: Centro de Información y Educación para la Prevención del Abuso de Drogas, 1989), 281–299.

9. Inés Astete and David Tejada, "Elementos para una economía política de la coca en el Alto Huallaga," Project AD/PER/86/459 OSP-PNUD (Lima, 1988).

10. J. Laity, "The Coca Economy in the Upper Huallaga," mimeo (Lima, 1989).

11. Laity, "Coca Economy," 6.

12. As reported in Laity, "Coca Economy," 9.

13. See Edmundo Morales, *Cocaine: White Gold Rush in Peru* (Tucson: University of Arizona Press, 1989), 74 (esp. Table 3).

14. Morales has explained to me that kerosene is recycled two or three times until its flavor turns "sweet." After that the kerosene can be used for domestic purposes.

15. Laity, "Coca Economy."

16. Clark Joel, "Importance of the Coca/Narcotrafficking Industry to Bolivia's Economy," mimeo (August 1988).

17. For example, see J. Briceño and J. Martínez, "El ciclo operativo del tráfico ilícito de la coca y sus derivados: Implicancias en la liquidez del sistema financiero," in León and Castro de la Mata, *Pasta básica*, 261–279

18. See Morales, *Cocaine*; and Briceño and Martínez, "El ciclo operativo."

19. Laity, "Coca Economy."

20. ECONSULT, *Informe final de la evaluación del Proyecto AID No. 527–0244: Desarrollo del area del Alto Huallaga* (Lima: ECONSULT, 1986), paragraph 10.

21. E. Bedoya, *Las causas de la deforestación en la amazonia peruana: Un problema estructural* (Binghamton, N.Y.: Clark University and Institute for Development Anthropology, 1990).

22. Dourojeanni, "Impactos ambientales."

23. Dourojeanni, "Impactos ambientales," 5–6.

24. B. Marceló, "Víctimas del narcotráfico," *Medio Ambiente* 23 (1987), esp. 2, 4.

25. ECONSULT, *Informe final*.

26. A. Salazar, "Análisis económico de cultivos alternativos a la coca en la región del Alto Huallaga," Project AD/PER/86/459 OSP-PNUD (Lima, 1990).

27. M. Reid, "Una región amenazada por el narcotráfico," and J. Gonzáles, "Perú: Sendero Luminoso en el Valle de la Coca," in D. García-Sayán, ed., *Coca, cocaína y narcotráfico* (Lima: Comisión Andina de Juristas, 1989), 135–169 and 207–222; and Gustavo Gorriti, "Democracia, narcotráfico y la insurrección de Sendero Luminoso," in L. Pasara and J. Parodi, eds., *Democracia, sociedad y gobierno en el Perú* (Lima: Centro de Estudios de Democracia y Sociedad, 1988), 193–212.

28. See J. Jutkowitz et al., *Uso y abuso de drogas en el Perú* (Lima: CEDRO, 1987); and F. León, "Epidemiología del uso y abuso de la pasta básica de cocaína en el Perú: 1976–1989," in León and Castro de la Mata, eds., *Pasta básica*, 29–111.

29. L. Bustamante, "Corrupción y descomposición del Estado," in León and Castro de la Mata, eds., *Pasta básica*, esp. 313–315.

6

Coca Production in Bolivia

Flavio Machicado

Coca production has a long and complex history in Bolivia. Originally grown for traditional consumption by highland campesinos, coca leaf—for better or worse—has become a mainstay of the national economy. Its impact on Bolivian society has varied greatly—according to region, sector, and location in the production cycle. To a considerable extent, coca-cocaine in Bolivia displays the characteristics of an economic enclave, analogous to mining in generations past.

Patterns of Production

Bolivia is located in the center of South America and basically has two major coca-producing zones, the Yungas and the Chapare. (A third zone, Yapacani, is of modest significance.) Because these areas have different characteristics, the repercussions of coca production (or eradication) will be quite different for the regional economy, the national economy, and drug-trafficking activity.

In the Yungas, a high-mountain area with uneven terrain, coca represents only 35 percent of agricultural production, as shown in Table 6-1. Although coca leaf production for domestic consumption originated there, the region nonetheless has a rather diversified economy. In the case of the Chapare, the situation is reversed: 92.5 percent of production is concentrated in the dry leaf coca crop. Chapare's extensive area and its location in the Amazon belt are very advantageous for air and river transportation, making the region suitable, therefore, to the establishment of laboratories for coca sulfate and chloride production. Unlike the Yungas, the Chapare offers excellent conditions for drug processing, trafficking, and smuggling. It is estimated that there are over 1,500 clandestine landing strips in the Chapare—in addition to other tropical areas of the country such as the Beni, Pando, and Santa Cruz—areas where much of the coca chloride, or cocaine, is manufactured. It is also estimated that there are 4,500 laboratories producing paste and chloride in small quantities, and their geographical dispersion makes suppression difficult.

Although major increases in the production of coca leaf have taken place since 1975, this process acquired its current dimension in the decade of the 1980s. As can be seen in Table 6-2, from 3,000 hectares cultivated in 1963 with a dry leaf volume equivalent to 4,822 metric tons, production jumped to 11,285 hectares in

TABLE 6-1
Agricultural Production in Leading Coca Regions
(by percent)

Yungas		Chapare	
Crop	%	Crop	%
Coffee	55.0	Bananas	3.2
Citrus	5.0	Citrus	2.5
Other	5.0	Other	1.8
Coca	**35.0**	**Coca**	**92.5**
Totals	100.0		100.0

Source: Based on data in Jairo Morales, *Plan Integral de Desarrollo y Substitución (PIDYS)* (La Paz: Programa de Naciones Unidas para el Desarrollo, 1989).

1975 with a volume equivalent to 26,961 metric tons. This means that within a twelve-year period, the area of cultivation almost quadrupled. And from 1975 to 1987, a period of similar length, production increased fivefold—increasing to 60,956 hectares, equivalent to a production of 151,992 metric tons. Most of this increase in hectares cultivated occurred within the Chapare zone. Whereas the cultivated area in the Yungas increased by 7,213 hectares between 1963 and 1987, reaching a total of 8,913, the cultivated area in the Chapare increased from 1,300 to 52,043 hectares.

Impact on Agriculture

Coca production represented nearly one-third of the total agricultural national output in 1987. As shown in Table 6-3, the situation is more pronounced in Cochabamba, traditionally known as the "national breadbasket," where coca repre-

TABLE 6-2
Growth of Coca Production, 1963-1987

	La Paz		Cochabamba[a]		Bolivia	
	Area[b]	Tons	Area[b]	Tons	Area[b]	Tons
1963	1,700	1,377	1,300	3,445	3,000	4,822
1970	1,800	1,458	2,650	7,022	4,450	8,840
1975	1,600	1,296	9,685	25,665	11,285	26,961
1980	6,418	5,198	16,370	43,380	22,788	48,578
1985	6,675	5,406	37,611	101,285	44,286	106,691
1987	8,913	8,343	52,043	143,649	60,956	151,992

[a]Cochabamba figures include Yapacani, with a maximum area of 845 hectares in 1987.
[b]In hectares.

Source: Based on data in Jairo Morales, *Plan Integral de Desarrollo y Substitución (PIDYS)* (La Paz: Programa de Naciones Unidas para el Desarrollo, 1989).

TABLE 6-3
Cultivation of Coca and Other Products, 1987
(percentages of value)

Product	La Paz	Cochabamba	Bolivia
Cereals	5.6	6.9	15.0
Vegetables and garden products	4.6	7.0	8.4
Tubers (potatoes)	22.5	14.4	19.8
Other	34.1	8.9	28.3
Coca	**33.2**	**62.8**	**28.5**
Totals	100.0	100.0	100.0

Source: Data supplied by Unidad de Análisis de Políticas Económicas (UDAPE), Instituto de Estadística, 1989.

sents 62.8 percent of total production—a startling increase over previous years (in 1980 it was only 24.7 percent). In the department of La Paz, which includes the Yungas region, the incidence of coca cultivation in total production reached 33.2 percent, compared with 18.2 percent in 1980.

The influence of coca leaf production in the agricultural sector is readily apparent. It becomes even more pronounced when output is measured in relation to the country's gross national product. Farming and animal husbandry have traditionally amounted to one-fifth of total production, but their growth has stagnated in recent years—to the point that food donations now represent 25 percent of the daily diet. It is within this context that the economics of coca production have become a dynamic factor within the agricultural sector—no doubt subtracting from important resources that would otherwise go toward the cultivation of essential foodstuffs and economic growth. Table 6-4 reveals that coca production was estimated to account for 6.38 percent of Bolivia's GNP in 1988. In other words, coca production was equivalent to 50 percent of the combined production of the mining and hydrocarbon sectors and almost 60 percent of the total manufacturing sector.

TABLE 6-4
Coca and Bolivian GNP, 1988
(by percent)

Sector	% of GNP
Agriculture (without coca)	16.01
Coca	**6.38**
Manufacturing	10.79
Mining and hydrocarbons	12.84
Services	37.01
Other	16.97
Total	100.00

Source: Data supplied by Unidad de Análisis de Políticas Económicas (UDAPE), Instituto de Estadística, 1989.

TABLE 6-5
Families and Workers in Coca-Cocaine Cycle

Employment	Chapare	Yungas	Yapacani	Bolivia
Families producing coca	35,492	23,299[a]	2,400	61,641
People employed in coca production	105,003	14,091	1,733	120,827
People employed in sulfate production	9,780	410	110	10,300
People employed in processing paste[b]	NA	NA	NA	20,000
Total employment in cycle[c]	201,275	150,000	13,440	364,715

NA = not available.

[a]With very diversified production.

[b]Author's estimate (see text).

[c]Direct plus indirect employment.

Source: Data supplied by Unidad de Análisis de Políticas Económicas (UDAPE), Instituto de Estadística, 1989.

There is no question that coca cultivation has a major economic impact. It also generates substantial indirect effects. Here we are concerned not only with linkages between coca and specific economic sectors; we are also dealing with the implications of coca for foreign trade, for employment (especially informal employment), and for monetary economics in general.

According to the social accounting matrix elaborated by the Unidad de Análisis de Políticas Económicas (UDAPE), each $U.S. worth of coca production creates an intermediate demand for inputs equivalent to merely $0.04. For intermediate consumption of each dollar produced in other sectors, such as modern agriculture, this figure increases to US$0.27; in traditional agriculture to $0.07; in hydrocarbons to $0.10; and in mining to $0.13. The same profile occurs in relation to labor costs. In the case of mining, the amount reaches $0.38 for each production unit; in the case of coca, it comes to only $0.06 per production unit. This figure refers only to the direct economic impact of coca-cocaine production, however; the indirect impact is much greater than occurs in other economic sectors.

Levels of employment are difficult to estimate. According to unofficial information, the number of people engaged in coca cultivation appears to exceed 120,000; to this we would have to add at least 10,000 engaged in sulfate production. There has been no quantitative study of employment in the production of base sulfate (paste) or of chloride. Given the existence of 4,500 clandestine laboratories, we can presume that the processing industry employs perhaps 20,000 people.

Overall, this means that employment in the coca-cocaine cycle directly involves approximately 150,000 people, or 7 percent of the economically active population. Assuming a one-to-one relationship for indirect employment as well, we could add as many as another 150,000 people—without considering the informal labor involved in the domestic laundering of narco-dollars. Although fairly imprecise, the estimated number of persons who depend on coca for their livelihood represents a significant portion of the economically active population (see Table 6-5 for estimates). The elimination of that source of income would therefore entail serious social and political consequences.

It has been estimated that total eradication of coca would cost the country $490 million directly and $449 million indirectly, or a total of nearly $1 billion—equivalent to one-fifth of Bolivia's GNP. This would happen gradually, of course, if current programs of crop substitution were to continue at the rate of 6,000 hectares per year. The total effect on the economy thus would be distributed over a period of eight years. Note that this is a *hypothetical* rate of coca crop substitution that would be difficult to accomplish in practice. Besides, production might shift to another illicit substance (such as marijuana or opium poppies). Even more likely is the possibility that coca cultivation would simply be transferred to another country.

In the 1987–1988 eradication campaign, for example, only 2,516 hectares were substituted; between 1985 and 1989, 31.6 metric tons of cocaine were confiscated. During the same period, however, 6,817 new hectares were planted, so the net effect was an *increase* of 4,300 hectares of coca—this in the midst of an eradication program. Meanwhile, the Bolivian government requested $1.6 billion for its three-year eradication plan of 1987–1989; only $300 million was obtained, of which $15 million was disbursed. Substitution of coca crops thus is not easily accomplished, especially in view of coca's relatively high economic yield.

One has only to compare the income level generated by one hectare cultivated with coca to that of alternate crops. In the Yungas region, the agricultural yield for coca is relatively low and the agricultural production structure is fairly diversified. Under such conditions, a crop substitution program might be reasonably successful. In the Chapare, by contrast, the price per kilo in mid-1990 was $1.57; this would produce a profit of $4,340 per hectare. (At this time, I should note, coca leaf prices were in a state of depression.) This is far higher than the yield from coffee, where income is approximately $800 per hectare; citrus fruits, where income increases to $2,000; or cacao, where income would be approximately $2,700 per hectare.

Export costs also vary. For every dollar's worth of nontraditional export products, $0.60 in transportation and related costs, $0.51 for mining, and $0.15 for oil and gas are required. By contrast, only $0.10 is needed to export $1 worth of coca derivatives. This alone helps explain coca's high profitability—and its weak connections with the domestic economy.

To evaluate the impact of coca-cocaine production on the national economy, Table 6-6 presents data on the entire production cycle. As the figures indicate, only 16 percent of total leaf production is destined for traditional internal consumption (chewing) and for legal pharmaceutical uses. At the same time, only 40 percent of the sulfate base production (paste) is used in the manufacturing of cocaine chloride in the country. This means that Bolivia exports the remaining 60 percent, a total of 410.2 metric tons, in the form of base sulfate (paste). Hydrochloride, or cocaine, production in the country reached 218.8 metric tons, almost all of which is exported. Judging from paste exports and cocaine production, we conclude that Bolivia has a production capacity of hydrochloride (HC1) of nearly 550 metric tons.

Table 6-7 translates these values into monetary terms. These calculations suggest that the total aggregate value of the coca-cocaine production process in Bolivia is

TABLE 6-6
Coca and Cocaine Production

	Quantities (metric tons)			
Product	Chapare	Yungas	Yapacani	Bolivia
Dry leaf production	141,511.0	8,343.0	2,138.0	151,992.0
Destined for internal				
consumption	19,812.0	4,755.0	214.0	24,781.0
Raw material for sulfate	121,700.0	3,587.0	1,924.0	127,211.0
Sulfate production	1,268.0	66.0	20.0	1,354.0
Sulfate base	633.9	39.9	10.0	683.8
Exports of sulfate base	380.3	23.9	6.0	410.2
Raw material for hydrochloride	253.6	16.0	4.0	273.6
Hydrochloride production	202.8	12.8	3.2	218.8
Total potential hydrochloride				
production	507.0	31.9	8.0	546.9

Source: Data supplied by Unidad de Análisis de Políticas Económicas (UDAPE), Instituto de Estadística, 1989.

TABLE 6-7
Coca-Cocaine Production Process
(U.S. millions $)

	Chapare	Yungas	Yapacani	Bolivia
Coca production				
Gross value	221.7	13.1	3.4	238.2
Input cost	- 2.7	- 0.5	- 0.0	- 3.2
Aggregate value	219.0	12.6	3.4	235.0
Sulfate production				
Gross value[a]	332.2	17.4	5.3	354.9
Dry coca leaf	- 190.7	- 5.6	- 3.0	- 199.3
Transportation	- 0.0	- 0.3	- 0.0	- 0.3
Inputs, national industries	- 3.1	- 0.1	- 0.1	- 3.3
Imported materials	- 8.0	- 0.2	- 0.1	- 8.3
Hydrocarbons	- 14.0	- 0.4	- 0.3	- 14.7
Aggregate value	116.4	10.8	1.8	129.0
Sulfate base production				
Gross value	950.8	56.8	15.0	1,022.6
Sulfate	- 332.2	- 17.4	- 5.3	- 354.9
Transportation	- 5.1	- 0.3	- 0.1	- 5.5
Imported materials	- 11.4	- 0.6	- 0.2	- 12.2
Aggregate value	602.1	38.5	9.4	650.0
Hydrochloride production				
Gross value	794.5	50.5	12.6	857.6
Sulfate base (paste)	- 380.3	- 23.9	- 6.0	- 410.2
Domestic materials	- 2.0	- 0.1	- 0.0	- 2.1
Imported materials	- 37.0	- 2.3	- 0.6	- 39.9
Aggregate value	375.2	24.2	6.0	405.4
Total aggregate value	1,312.7	86.1	20.6	1,419.4

[a]Estimated 60 percent exportation of paste.

Source: Data supplied by Unidad de Análisis de Políticas Económicas (UDAPE), Instituto de Estadística, 1989.

TABLE 6-8
Distribution of Aggregate Value
(U.S. millions $)

	Region			
Source/Distribution	Chapare	Yungas	Yapacani	Bolivia
From coca production				
Salaries	113.4	7.4	1.9	122.7
Rent	105.6	6.2	1.5	113.3
From sulfate production				
Salaries	20.8	0.6	0.3	21.7
Rent	95.6	10.2	1.5	107.3
From sulfate base production				
Salaries[a]	63.4	4.0	1.0	68.4
Rent	538.7	34.5	8.4	581.6
From hydrochloride production				
Salaries[a]	20.3	1.3	0.3	21.9
Rent	354.9	22.9	5.7	383.5
Total value	1,312.7	87.1	20.6	1,420.4
Salaries[a]	217.9	13.3	3.5	234.7

[a]In specie and in kind.

Source: Data supplied by Unidad de Análisis de Políticas Económicas (UDAPE), Instituto de Estadística, 1989.

$1.4 billion. This is equivalent to 31 percent of the national GNP. The figures also show that imported inputs are modest in scale, representing only $60 million within the entire process. Further, except for the coca leaf production, domestic inputs amount to merely $30 million. This underscores a point already made above: This activity has little relation to the domestic economy, with low intermediate consumption and high profitability. In reality, the coca-cocaine production cycle displays the characteristics of an economic enclave, a situation in which coca-producing campesinos benefit the least. It is even worse for those who transform leaves into paste and do their work at great risk to their health.

Table 6-8 explores the distribution of this aggregate value. The figures reveal that salaries, in money and in chemicals, total $234.7 million. The income accruing to those who work in the production of sulfate and cocaine hydrochloride, however, is nearly $1.2 billion—about five times the earnings of the large coca-producing masses of the countryside. This explains why subsistence levels for campesinos are so low, even when they are engaged in such a lucrative field. Indeed, it is estimated that the bulk of the cocaine business in Bolivia is in the hands of only twenty-five entrepreneurial groups.

The relationship between unit costs and prices for coca plus its derivatives sheds additional light on this situation. As shown in Table 6-9, by mid-1990 the price per kilogram for coca reached $1.57, with a profit margin of $0.74; for sulfate the price was $262, with a profit of $79.30; for sulfate base it was $1,500 per kilo, with a profit margin of $856. For hydrochloride, the kilogram value reached $3,917, with a profit margin of $1,749. Marginal yields accelerate at every stage of the production process.

TABLE 6-9
Cost-Price Relationship per Kilo
(U.S. $)

Product	Cost	Price	Margin
Coca	0.83	1.57	0.74
Sulfate paste	182.70	262.00	79.30
Sulfate base	644.00	1,500.00	856.00

Source: Data supplied by Unidad de Análisis de Políticas Económicas (UDAPE), Instituto de Estadística, 1989.

A comparison between figures and the international cocaine market yields astonishing results. For 1990 the price of cocaine per kilogram in the New York wholesale market fluctuated between $20,000 and $25,000; the retail price (on the street) ranged between $500,000 and $600,000. Total sales at the wholesale level therefore fluctuated between $2.1 and $2.7 billion and between $53.0 and $64.2 billion at the retail level.

Impact on Foreign Trade

There is little information on the role of drug traffic on exports, and more research needs to be done specifically for Bolivia. One approach is to estimate outgoing contraband, including drugs and other illegal products, which generate income for goods and services that in turn comes back into the country illegally. Another approach has yielded two types of estimates—one dealing with private consumption at the aggregate level and another for consumption by urban and rural populations.

It has been estimated that Bolivian private consumption per capita was $500 in 1978 and $583 in 1987. Given population size, this means total private consumption would have been $2.65 billion in 1978 and $3.91 billion in 1987. Subtracting the officially registered money supply as well as legal imports from both consumption levels, as in Table 6-10, we find over $470 million resulting from contraband for 1987. (With a different technique, data from a household survey yield a comparable estimate for contraband in the mid-1980s at $490 million a year.)

Once the level of contraband has been established, it becomes easier to estimate the incidence of narco-dollars in foreign trade and also to evaluate corresponding capital flight. Official figures indicate that Bolivia's total exports came to $652.7 million in 1987. This suggests that exports of coca derivatives were equivalent to 41 percent of total exports, a proportion that seems much too high. Indeed, such figures suggest that Bolivia's entire foreign trade is based on coca derivatives. The real importance of this external linkage is much more modest.

Capital flight accounts for the discrepancy. According to Table 6-11, based on official figures, capital flight in 1987 came to almost $1.1 billion. This sum represents

TABLE 6-10
Private Consumption and Contraband
(U.S. millions $)

Data and Estimates	1978	1987
Population (millions)	5.3	6.7[a]
Per capita consumption	500.0	583.0
Total consumption (TC)	2,649.8	3,907.6
Goods, national origin (GN)	2,111.7	3,124.7
Goods, imported (GI)	538.1[b]	309.0[c]
Estimate for contraband (= TC - GN - GI)	NA	473.9

NA = not available.

[a]Projection.
[b]Registered including contraband.
[c]Not including contraband.

Source: Data supplied by Unidad de Análisis de Políticas Económicas (UDAPE), Instituto de Estadística, 1989.

almost 70 percent of the value of sulfate base and coca hydrochloride exports and leaves $490 million available for domestic uses. Because there are other contraband export goods—unpolished gold and woods as well as animal species—the total income from these other exports balances the sources and usage of funds, which according to the balance sheet show a deficit of $114.4 million.

The incidence of the narco-dollars is manifest not only in the foreign exchange balance but also in the internal monetary equilibrium. Due to the government's contractional policy, the low domestic monetary supply barely allows a relationship between the money supply and the GNP of between 5 and 7 percent—under circumstances in which this relationship would usually increase from 12 to 14 percent. The total was fluctuating between $540 and $639 million at a juncture when internal money supply was between $225 and $315 million. Drug money was compensating for the difference. This economic effect is highly significant because, as is well known, a restriction in the domestic monetary supply depends mostly on the country's monetary stability.

Impact on Public Finance

The impact of drug production and trafficking on public finances appears to be nil or very indirect, if it exists at all. This is because coca production, although officially recognized, makes no contribution to agricultural taxes. And because of the modest income level for coca-producing campesinos, they would be exempt from any taxation.

With regard to derivative products, which are illegal, it is inconceivable that they could ever be taxable. Nor would money laundering become taxable. Narco-dollars

TABLE 6-11
Balance of Foreign Exchange, 1987
(U.S. millions $)

Sources of official foreign exchange	
Goods and services exports	652.7
Unilateral transference	135.5
Direct investment and credits	309.5
Official inflow	1,097.7
Use of official foreign exchange	
Private and public imports	919.6
Rent	152.9
Debt service	197.3
Less variation in reserves	- 57.7
Official outflow	1,212.1
Official balance (official inflow - official outflow)	- 114.4
Nonofficial sources of foreign exchange	
Contraband exports (excluding coca)	113.0
Coca derivatives exports	1,584.6
Nonofficial inflow	1,697.6
Nonofficial uses of foreign exchange	
Contraband imports	490.0
Capital drain	1,094.2
Nonofficial outflow	1,584.2
Final balance (nonofficial inflow - nonofficial outflow)	113.4

Sources: Based on data in Banco Central de Bolivia, *Cuentas nacionales* (La Paz: Banco Central, 1989); and on data supplied by Unidad de Análisis de Políticas Económicas (UDAPE), Instituto de Estadística, 1989.

circulate within the underground economy, and they make no contribution to public revenues.

Coca Substitution

Despite the popularity of the thesis that alternative crops can substitute for coca, such a development seems unlikely, at least in the short term. It seems somehow utopian to imagine that Bolivia will receive a capital inflow of $3.5 billion with a profitability equal to that of coca. I say "utopian" because even were the investment capital available, it would require an average real profit rate of 27 percent—and such rates are inconceivable in the present Bolivian context. These levels of productivity and profitability would require major subsidies from foreign markets, which are also unlikely to appear.

Although the UN Agro-Yungas project has developed feasibility models for crop substitution, this could occur only in that region because of its agricultural variety and versatility. The idea of substitution implies not only greater diversification in crops but also an increase in productivity—in coffee, citrus, and other goods. In sum, it is necessary to analyze the problem not only with regard to capital yield but also from the standpoint of labor. Above all, it is necessary to evaluate developmental prospects in the light of cold, hard economic facts.

7

The Power of Coca Producers

José Guillermo Justiniano

Why do peasants grow coca? As previous chapters have shown, coca production responds to an overwhelming logic: There is a lucrative market, and farmers have the productive capacity to meet that market. Peasant organizations throughout the Andes have a long history of common struggle for economic and sociocultural rights. Coca production is but one more link in the long chain of their fight for survival.

Establishing a Conceptual Framework

Any serious analysis of drug trafficking must address the economic reasons campesinos produce coca. There is a strong world demand, driven by cocaine consumption, which in turn makes coca production a profitable enterprise for the campesino. Like any other *homo economicus*, the coca producer is making a rational decision in response to signals from the market. This is an economic choice, not a moral or a political one. Accustomed to chewing coca, campesinos tend to be unaware of and unconcerned about hazards to the health of far-distant consumers. Andean peasants thus make "portfolio" decisions about the use of labor and land. There is a need for a cash crop to complement foodstuffs, and coca meets that need.

Further, the price elasticity of supply is very high because the availability of land, labor, and technology enables campesinos to react to market prices. In highland areas of Bolivia, campesinos have considerable extensions of land (an average of 50 hectares in recently colonized areas), which permit them to grow foodstuffs alongside cash crops. Coca can also be grown on land on which other crops might not be successful; at the same time, coca shrubs develop and grow very quickly so that, in the short term, production can be increased to meet market demands. Labor is also not an issue: Individual campesino families can take care of both types of crops, and in indigenous communities households work together by pooling resources. Finally, the requisite technology for production is well-known by campesinos.

Despite short-term oscillations in prices for coca leaves, profits from coca remain far superior to those from any alternative crop. After the frontal attack by the Colombian government against the drug mafias in late 1989, the coca price fell to the lowest levels ever experienced ($10 per hundredweight, equivalent to 46 kilograms), which provided a brief opportunity for the establishment of alternative development programs. The equilibrium, or break-even, price is estimated to be around $30 per hundredweight. In recent years, the price has generally oscillated between $30 and $150 per hundredweight. Even so, this profit margin has not materially altered the fundamental poverty of peasants, who tend to be exploited by intermediaries in the process of coca commercialization.

Coca-producing areas are generally located in tropical or subtropical zones, which have very difficult access, resulting in high transportation costs. These areas are consequently inadequate for perishable crops with low bulk sale value. Further, the internal market for foodstuffs is small, because campesinos tend to grow their own food and urban workers have very low purchasing power. Coca, by contrast, is easy to transport; it does not deteriorate easily due to climatic conditions; and it has wide demand in foreign markets. It is therefore difficult for other crops to be competitive.

Coca Production and the Rural Problem

The production of coca is intimately linked to the larger problem of rural poverty in the Andes. In Peru and Bolivia, indigenous campesinos of Aymara and Quechua origin make up half of the national population; together with mestizos they account for roughly 80 percent of the total population. Bolivia, unlike Peru, underwent a profound revolution in 1952 that totally modified the economic, social, and political structures of the country. Campesinos actively participated in the revolutionary movement and recovered nearly all available lands in highland areas, which had been in the hands of a few powerful landowners. In Peru the government of General Juan Velasco Alvarado (1968–1975) attempted revolutionary changes, including agrarian reform through the creation of campesino cooperatives.

Despite these attempts at reform, the rural question has never been squarely addressed. The standard of living for Andean campesinos is comparable to the lowest levels in Africa. Childhood mortality indicators, life expectancy, general health, malnutrition, and educational deficits reach alarming proportions. Critical poverty in both countries is an essentially rural phenomenon. In general, the majority of the campesino population has not been integrated into national society. The permanent weakness of the states plus the lack of vision on the part of longtime ruling classes have failed to provide adequate solutions to the historic problem of rural poverty.

Under these conditions young people in the countryside are likely to migrate— either to lowland areas, where they can grow tropical or subtropical agricultural products, or to marginal neighborhoods in or near the urban centers. Agriculture developed in the lowland areas by campesino migrants from the highlands tends to be unsustainable due to the fragility of the soil and is destructive to forests and fauna as well. Facing an unfamiliar environment and lacking technical or economic help from the state, campesinos exploit the land as best they can.

Within this context, many campesinos turn to coca production. Approximately 200,000 hectares of coca in Peru and 60,000 hectares in Bolivia are providing, however temporarily, a remedy to mitigate the hardships of rural life. As Elena Alvarez and Flavio Machicado have demonstrated in Chapters 5 and 6, hundreds of thousands of campesinos depend on coca-derived income for their livelihood. In economic terms, the gross value of coca represents around 25 percent of the total agricultural output of Bolivia.

For these reasons, it is difficult to imagine that coercive measures against campesinos could ever have positive results. Peasants producing coca have nothing to lose. As long as coca provides a family livelihood, they will protect their coca crop at all costs.

Campesino Organizations and Political Power

The history of the campesino organizations and their struggle to defend their interests in Peru and Bolivia is very old and is very important for understanding contemporary phenomena. We need only remember Tupak Katari and Tupac Amaru and their fights for *reivindicación* of campesino rights.

Bolivia probably has the most developed and powerful campesino organizations in Latin America. Peasants played a fundamental role in the 1952 revolution when they joined forces with miners and overthrew the mining feudal oligarchy. The Confederación Nacional de Campesinos Bolivianos (CNCB) and the campesino-armed Militias for the Defense of the Revolution were established at that time. Campesino unions were organized throughout the country, and they became the basic cells for political organizations formed on behalf of campesino interests. During that period the influence of the Movimiento Nacional Revolucionario (MNR), the political party that led the 1952 revolution, was crucial in defining the ideological orientation of the campesino movement. In time the link between the MNR and the campesino movement grew weaker—until the 1980s when the Confederación Sindical Única de Trabajadores y Campesinos de Bolivia was established as an organization independent from political parties but with a strong Katarista orientation toward economic and racial vindication.

What was new was that for the first time, the campesino movement joined the powerful Central Obrera Boliviana (COB). This resulted in a labor-campesino alliance. In Bolivia the campesino organizations, through their affiliation with the COB (regardless of what appears to be a relative loss of power at present), constitute a genuine force within the country's power structures.

Campesino theses on coca have been fully and formally adopted by the COB. These theses are, first, that coca chewing is an ancestral custom and must be defended. Second, coca crops must be protected. Also, there is a juridical and legal difference between coca and cocaine. Next, the use of herbicides must be forbidden in the destruction of coca plantations. Finally, crop substitution must be voluntary and integrated within economic programs for alternative crop development.

A clear indication of campesino organizational power came through the difficult and long negotiations among the government, the CNCB, and the COB on proposed legislation against coca and controlled substances during the late 1980s. Before the law was passed, there were protest marches, roadblocks, and assaults on the headquarters of special drug-traffic fighting forces, which resulted in several deaths and injuries. Mobilization on the part of the campesino unions proved to be highly effective.

Over a period of two years, almost half of the cabinet members became involved in discussions about the proposed legislation; congress also provided a forum on several occasions when campesino leaders and their advisers were present. Thus, the law and other institutional mechanisms that were passed toward the adoption of the Plan Integral de Desarrollo y Sustitución had key input from campesino leadership. The campesino presence has been institutionalized in legal form in all decisions regarding coca.

In the implementation phase of crop substitution programs, there has been considerable resistance from many campesino leaders who are permanently opposed to any such programs, even on a voluntary basis. Pressure and tactics have varied. In some instances, rumors are spread that a price increase for coca leaf is imminent; in others, campesinos receiving credits for abandoning coca are forced to pay a fine (or a kind of tax) to the union; finally, leaders proclaim that those who participate in crop substitution may suffer confiscation of their land. All these mechanisms have been highly effective, given the cellular organization of campesino unions throughout the rural sector.

In addition, all political parties assign great importance to the electoral power of the campesino bloc. In preelection periods, it is worth noting, most campaign promises concern issues facing coca growers. All this makes it hard for the legislature to analyze the problem, and it further hinders the decision-making process.

Campesino links to narco-traffickers may be undergoing change. There is fragmentary evidence that some campesino leaders receive economic help from narco-traffickers to finance activities to pressure the government. It also appears that campesinos have begun to produce cocaine base (*pasta básica*), partly in response to the 1989–1990 decline in price for coca leaves. This suggests a change in strategy on the part of narco-traffickers, who are passing on to thousands of campesinos the risk of producing cocaine base. This is a truly dangerous development; it would mean a large number of campesinos may eventually prefer to manufacture cocaine base rather than harvest coca leaves. Up until now the core leaders, especially those of Central Obrera Boliviana, have clearly defined their opposition to the manufacture of cocaine; they now tolerate it, however, and justify this process on socioeconomic grounds. Their next step might be to defend campesinos engaged in the production of coca base for humanitarian or social reasons. Should this occur, the battle against drug traffic would become increasingly difficult.

The situation in Peru is even more complex. Despite the fact that campesino organizations do not have the tradition of their Bolivian counterparts and are not formally attached to national power groups, they have a working relationship with Sendero Luminoso—the terrorist movement committed to the total destruction of the social, economic, and political systems of the country. Given this situation, drug traffickers and guerrillas become tactical and strategic allies in a united front against the established order. Indirectly, the campesinos who grow coca are participating in that agreement, because they accept armed protection from the drug traffickers. As a result, the coca-producing areas in Peru are even harder to access and control than those of Bolivia.

Development Projects and International Aid

Until now, bilateral and multilateral aid for rural development programs geared toward changing coca crops for legitimate production has not been very successful, for various reasons. First, it is difficult to persuade campesinos to reduce or destroy coca crops when profits are high. To some extent there is a close correlation between interdiction of traffic and coca prices. The microeconomic explanation is that when drug traffickers suspend coca purchases (totally or partially), the supply curve becomes lower, as does the equilibrium point. The most dramatic expression of this came with the declaration of war against the cartels by the Colombian government in 1989–1990, which resulted in the price decrease for coca from $80 to approximately $10 per hundredweight. But this was a short-term phenomenon. As such, it underscores the fragility of alternative crop development programs.

Second, most development projects have been pilot programs on a reduced scale due to scarce resources. For that reason it has not been possible to distribute resources to all the relevant producers. In some cases, friction has arisen because of perceived discrimination in favor of coca producers who participate in reduction programs.

Third, technical and economic solutions in coca-production areas take a relatively long time—five to ten years—to achieve concrete and positive results. In subtropical areas, due to the quality of the soil and the climatic conditions, the majority of the programs—if they are to be feasible—must be based on long-cycle perennial crops and on commercialization processes that require a slow maturation process. This time frame is too remote, and it creates uncertainty and reluctance on the part of campesinos.

Conclusion

The power of coca producers is expressed in different ways in different countries. In Bolivia it comes through the campesino organizations allied with the Central Obrera Boliviana and through the formal mechanisms of a democratic system, which allow great influence on decision making but not direct control over national policy. Peru presents a different situation. Campesinos rely heavily on informal mechanisms, such as their relationship with Sendero Luminoso and with *narcotraficantes*.

In both Bolivia and Peru, political parties and the armed forces firmly intend to prevent a campesino war at all costs. Such a war would have serious effects on the fragile economies and political systems of the two countries. Furthermore, the campesino vote is very important for the politicians, and it poses an additional impediment to the use of force against coca-producing campesinos. In the long run, the electoral power of the campesinos may constitute their most effective political resource.

PART TWO

Assessing
Policy
Alternatives

Has there been any clear progress in campaigns against drug abuse and trafficking? What has failed? What has worked? What have been the outcomes, intended and unintended, of governmental intervention in this area? Chapters in Part Two offer penetrating assessments of three types of public policy: (1) efforts to reduce or eliminate the production and supply of illicit drugs; (2) efforts to reduce or eliminate consumer demand for illicit drugs; and, in a more hypothetical vein, (3) potential strategies for the decriminalization, regulation, or "legalization" of the drug market. Only through such analysis will it be possible to design effective public policy. Especially in this area, it is vitally important to discard ideological preference, to learn from past failures, to contemplate a broad range of policy options, and to monitor outcomes in a long-term, rigorous fashion.

Opening the inquiry into supply-control policies, Guy Gugliotta traces the evolution of campaigns against cocaine cartels in Colombia. From historical and theoretical standpoints, Gugliotta explores a broad variety of alternative strategies— accommodation, frontal war, decapitation, divide-and-conquer tactics. He convincingly demonstrates that these strategies have differential consequences. Decapitation of the cartels might reduce the level of narco-terrorism, for instance, but it is unlikely to have any appreciable impact on the workings of the cocaine market. Through his discussion of the range of instruments available to policymakers, one conclusion emerges with utmost clarity: Selection of the strategy must be consistent with policy goals.

Focusing primarily on U.S. policy, Bruce M. Bagley then describes efforts to militarize the war on drugs—with participation of both U.S. and Latin American armed forces. In Bagley's estimation this strategy is shortsighted, dangerous, and counterproductive. It distorted the mission of the U.S. military (restored by Operation Desert Storm in early 1991). It exposed the Latin American military to continuing corruption and subversion. And in so doing, it posed a profound threat to democracies throughout the region, especially the fragile regimes in the Andean countries.

From a similar perspective Miguel Ruiz-Cabañas explores the Permanent Campaign in Mexico, a case in which the military has been deeply involved in antidrug strategies for more than a decade. This involvement has not led to outright military intervention in the political arena. But as Ruiz-Cabañas points out, the *campaña* has been unable to stem the flow of drugs from and through Mexico to the United States largely because of continuing demand in the U.S. market. And although the Permanent Campaign does not seem to threaten the stability of the political system itself, it has had a corrosive effect on law enforcement agencies: "One of the most negative consequences brought on by the drug-trafficking problem," according to Ruiz-Cabañas, "has been to delay and hinder the much-needed professionalization of the Mexican police corps." Conceived largely as a response to pressure from the United States, the so-called Permanent Campaign cannot continue forever.

107

From a demand-side perspective, Peter Reuter then takes up a counterfactual question: What if the drug wars succeed? What would be the impact on the U.S. market? Would U.S. consumers turn to other drugs or drop their habits altogether? The answer, according to Reuter, lies somewhere in between these possibilities. Examining three episodes of supply reduction, he finds that stoppage of supply would lead to partial reduction in overall consumption. Like other consumers, some drug users have strong "brand loyalties" and are reluctant to turn to substitute products; this may be more true for casual users than for abusers and addicts, however, and it is difficult to pinpoint the *degree* of substitution for each kind of drug. Whether the ensuing decline in consumption would be worth the cost of eliminating the supply of any given drug is an entirely different question.

Moving on to demand-reduction strategies, Rod Mullen and Naya Arbiter describe the challenges of providing treatment for the U.S. underclass, a population that is "increasingly separate from middle-class experience and deviant from middle-class values. It will not and cannot respond to programs designed for the mainstream middle class." Deprived in almost every way, this population requires opportunities not for rehabilitation but for *habilitation*. Mullen and Arbiter present a persuasive argument that therapeutic communities can provide effective means for salvaging drug addicts in the United States. Length of time in treatment is "almost universally correlated with posttreatment success," they point out, especially when therapeutic approaches consider drug abuse as only one part of a large-scale societal problem. For this reason U.S. prisons present both a problem (with the high number of incarcerated addicts) and an opportunity (for the institutionalization of systematic treatment). "Ironically," say Mullen and Arbiter, "the costs of such [therapeutic community] intervention are minimal when compared with the escalating costs that result from ignoring these problems." They conclude with an eloquent plea for Latin American policymakers to avoid the errors and mistakes that have so long characterized U.S. approaches to illicit drug abuse.

To this Michael C. Hoffmann adds a brief but instructive statement about the utility of community mobilization programs. Such efforts can be especially effective, he says, if outside professionals encourage community members to take charge of local campaigns. The transfer of knowledge and training of leaders—"human technological development," as it is sometimes called—can provide further essential resources.

Turning to Latin America, Roberto Lerner offers a comprehensive overview of drug prevention programs in practice throughout the region. He demonstrates the existence of a variety of approaches, including public awareness campaigns and community development strategies, and acknowledges the special difficulties of improving the social conditions of Latin America's street children. Lerner is pointedly critical of "the conspicuous absence of rigorous methodology" in research purporting to evaluate prevention programs. And he notes that there is a movement toward community participation models, in keeping with the Mullen-Arbiter and Hoffmann assessments, but that this has yet to reach maturity: "In practice," Lerner writes, "these programs often resemble political platforms, and one has to wonder whether such broad promises of social salvation have not interfered with the realization of more concrete but less ambitious actions." And ill-informed hysteria about cocaine, largely imposed by the United States, may actually lead to increased patterns of consumption: "In short, we will have created a self-fulfilling prophecy."

Concluding the discussion of demand-reduction policies, Mathea Falco provides a review and a synthesis of demand-reduction strategies. Because the United States has placed such long-standing emphasis on supply-side policies, in Falco's judgment, research on prevention and treatment has been "very limited." In fact, U.S. policy may have exacerbated consumption problems in Latin America because eradication and interdiction may have encouraged traffickers to turn their operations away from marijuana toward less bulky (and more profitable) cocaine—including the development of local markets for such items as *basuco*. In the future, Falco speculates, the United States may lose interest in Latin America's drug problems as U.S. demand either continues to decline or shifts toward drugs produced elsewhere. Past experience offers scant hope that the U.S. government will exhibit much concern about demand reduction within Latin America. As a result, she concludes, "Perhaps the so-called 'supplier' countries in Latin America will be the ones to lead the way to a more effective regional and hemispheric policy based on the importance of demand reduction."

Finally, Mark A.R. Kleiman and Aaron Saiger turn to the question of legalization. Describing the current debate on the subject as "surprisingly muddled," they explore the idea (used in favor of legalization) that prohibition and its enforcement impose excessive costs in relation to benefits. According to its advocates, legalization thus "would make the streets safer, put the black market dealers out of business, and focus attention on the medical problem of addiction rather than the legal problem of drug dealing." Opponents tend to stress the likelihood of expanding consumption and growing threats to public health. As Kleiman and Saiger indicate, reasonable assessment of any legalization scenario depends on specifics: which drugs would be legalized, for consumption by whom, under what circumstances. Prohibition of purchase by minors would pose special challenges for enforcement. Not all legalization schemes have proven positive: The U.S. regime for alcohol offers "a superb example of legalization gone awry," in their judgment—hardly an encouraging model for cocaine or heroin. Even marijuana poses difficult questions because it is essential to distinguish between legalization and decriminalization: "Rational marijuana traffickers ought to fear legalization above all things but should regard decriminalization as an entirely good idea." One possible form of legalization, for alcohol as well as perhaps for marijuana, might entail positive licensing, as in the case of automobile driving. At most, say Kleiman and Saiger, the United States might adopt a posture of "grudging toleration."

Cocaine constitutes a separate matter, however, especially since the advent of crack. Legalization might lead to a reduction in violence and lawlessness but to an increase in consumption. Thus, there might be less predatory crime but more pharmacologically generated violent crime. Benefits from legalization of cocaine do not appear obvious.

In sum, chapters in Part Two clearly demonstrate that supply-control strategies cannot by themselves eliminate the drug problem—on the contrary, they may merely exacerbate the problem. Legalization presents suggestive possibilities, at least in some forms, but it is unlikely to come to pass within the foreseeable future. The most promising feasible path therefore leads in the direction of demand reduction, but this in itself is not a simple panacea: Effective programs require considerable analysis, investment, and commitment.

8

The Colombian Cartels
and How to Stop Them

Guy Gugliotta

The sparse evidence available suggests that a true cartel—collusion among producers to control the supply of a commodity and thereby its price—existed only briefly in the cocaine business. Beginning in 1981, U.S. Drug Enforcement Administration (DEA) intelligence reports—known as "sixes"—spoke of traffickers brokering cocaine at "conventions" held in Medellín at spots frequented by the traffickers, such as the Intercontinental Hotel and Kevin's Nightclub. Large crime families—the Ochoa Clan of Jorge Ochoa, Los Pablos of Pablo Escobar, Los Chemas of Cali's Rodríguez Orejuela brothers, and a few others—assembled large shipments of cocaine destined for the U.S. market. Small processors and traffickers, of which there were dozens, were invited to ship with the big gangs—that is, to "piggy-back" small loads on the same airplane with the big producers' large loads (between 800 kilograms and 1 metric ton in 1981). Ochoa, Escobar, and the others, DEA agents said, encouraged and facilitated this process—charging little for transportation and offering a package of guarantees to the small producer. Most notable among these was "insurance," whereby the large traffickers promised to replace a small producer's load if police seized it or to reimburse a small producer at market prices if the load were stolen or otherwise lost. At the time, DEA agents speculated that the large traffickers were using the brokering process to control the volume of cocaine entering the United States, keeping the price high ($45,000–$55,000 per kilo wholesale in Miami at the end of 1981) and thus maximizing their unit profit. In other words, they sought to form a cartel.

And it worked, at least through 1983 and apparently even as late as May 1984, when the large traffickers still claimed to control 70 to 80 percent of Colombia's cocaine trade. This contention was made in a trafficker "peace proposal" submitted to the Colombian attorney general at a Panama City meeting, and there was no reason to doubt it. What seemed remarkable at the time was the bosses' ability to exert continued domination over a business that had grown helter-skelter from a cottage industry in the mid-1970s to a spectacular, fully integrated, multinational enterprise less than ten years later.

The mythology suggests that the large traffickers bent the smaller ones to their will by murdering or otherwise intimidating dissenters. Although there is undoubtedly some truth to this (Medellín's scale of violence eclipses that of any other "peaceful" city in the world), the large traffickers' success as a cartel was probably due to a more mundane factor—the members controlled cocaine's infrastructure. The cartel leaders had begun trafficking in the mid-1970s and by the early 1980s had established vertically integrated processing networks that could move cocaine by the hundred-weight. The large traffickers had the laboratories, the precursor chemicals, the aircraft (Pilotos Ejecutivos was the Ochoas's charter airline), the shipping routes, the transshipment points, and the stateside wholesale warehousing and distribution facilities. Carlos Lehder, the cartel's fixer extraordinaire, made a fortune during this period largely by providing ancillary services to the drug bosses. Indeed, law enforcement throughout the history of big-time drug trafficking consistently under-estimated the importance of logistics in the cocaine pipeline. The infrastructure is elaborate and expensive, and when the industry took off in the early 1980s, only the cartel members had developed it.

In later years, however, the picture changed. The supply of available cocaine skyrocketed in 1984–1985, and the per-kilo price plunged. Cheap cocaine sought and found new markets. The crack epidemic began in the United States, and *basuco* abuse became widespread in the South American producer countries. The cartel—as a mechanism to control supply and price—ceased to exist. We do not know why this happened, but two possible reasons suggest themselves.

First, the cocaine industry in the mid-1980s may simply have become too lucrative, too large, and too diffuse for the large traffickers to control it or to even want to control it. By 1985 yesterday's piggy-backers had become entrepreneurs in their own right and had built their own factories, bought their own airplanes, and bribed their own officials. There were too many rich players in the game, and the onetime cartel members were simply the biggest in a growing school of big fish.

Second, in the mid-1980s the cartel may have made a conscious decision to allow the supply of cocaine to grow in response to burgeoning consumer country demand, hoping the market would expand as the price went down—in other words, they decided to dismantle the cartel and let market forces dictate the nature of the business. My research suggests that this probably happened sometime in 1983, perhaps at a Medellín convention, but I have not been able to confirm the information. In any case, once the large traffickers saw the wisdom of this decision, they simply let the market explode—reaping profits along with the rest of Colombia's expanding pool of large traffickers. By the end of the 1980s, the old cartel members probably controlled a significantly smaller slice of the total market but were making a lot more money because the pie had grown greatly.

Cartels as Gangs

With the departure of cocaine's true cartel, the view that a cartel-focused analysis of the industry no longer made sense gained popularity. The removal or survival of the cartels, this reasoning went, would have no effect on the cocaine market, because so many big-time traffickers were in the business. Why waste time studying the cartels? In fact, however, the events of 1989–1990 suggest that the cartels continued to exert tremendous power and, equally important, that the fortunes of the Colombian cocaine trade remained as closely tied to those of the large traffickers as they ever were.

Thus, another reevaluation was necessary because after the August 18, 1989, murder of Luis Carlos Galán, the cartels reemerged dramatically and became far more visible in the drug wars than at any time since 1984. If there had been an atomization of economic power among the traffickers, the axis of drug-trafficker political and military power nevertheless remained with the cartel bosses.

Within days of the Galán shooting the Extraditables, the *nom de guerre* the Medellín cartel first used in communiqués in 1982, declared "total and absolute war" against the Colombian government—inviting it to participate in a contest for state power. A series of terrorist bombings followed; targets included the offices of *El Espectador* (a newspaper), an Avianca commuter flight, and the Bogotá headquarters of the Department of Administrative Security, which is Colombia's FBI. As the terrorism evolved, the government's efforts to bring the Extraditables to account focused on Escobar and Gonzalo Rodríguez Gacha, the one-time Escobar lieutenant who became a major cartel boss during the late 1980s. Rodríguez Gacha seemed uniquely qualified to fight a terrorist grudge war. His falling-out with guerrillas of the Revolutionary Armed Forces of Colombia had prompted a four-year vendetta against the Patriotic Union, the guerrillas' political stepchild. Indiscriminate violence was his trademark.

This analysis proved true. After police and soldiers finally cornered and killed Rodríguez Gacha in mid-December 1989, at a ranch near Cartagena, the bombings immediately stopped. Clearly Rodríguez Gacha, acting as the post-Galán strategist for the Medellín cartel Extraditables, had inspired a nationwide terrorism campaign to embarrass the government and demonstrate cartel strength. Rodríguez Gacha had ordered a war, and his soldiers had dueled the government to a standstill for nearly four months—this from an organization whose power and influence had supposedly dissipated during the previous few years.

With Rodríguez Gacha dead, the cartel bosses launched a new carrot-and-stick strategy, kidnapping prominent Colombians (among them the son of President Virgilio Barco's closest adviser) and using the hostages to blackmail the government into negotiating a peaceful settlement to the war. This strategy—employing terrorism to enhance the traffickers' bargaining position—smacked of Pablo Escobar. In the past he had often posed as a wronged innocent forced to take desperate action to protect himself.

Carrot and stick dominated the war into 1990, but in the absence of a public response from the government, the Extraditables changed tactics again. They began to release hostages, turned over some laboratory complexes, and formally "surrendered"—issuing yet another communiqué. Here finally was the hand of Jorge Ochoa, who—according to DEA intelligence reports—had been trying to get out of the cocaine business ever since his sojourn in jail at the end of 1987. In the surrender phase, beginning in January 1990 and lasting into mid-March of that same year, the Extraditables offered Barco a chance to proclaim victory and end the war, suggesting (not demanding) only that the government grant "considerations" to the traffickers—that is, let them retire and live in peace.

The Medellín cartel clearly remained active and powerful enough to stamp the antigovernment campaign with its personal signature. It was also able to focus the attention and the wrath of the Colombian government to the exclusion of all other actors (in the latest campaign, virtually no attention was paid to the Rodríguez Orejuela cartel in Cali). Finally, as is seen below, its military and political decisions dictated the tempo of the entire cocaine industry for at least the first seven months following Galán's death. In short, the cartels seemed as strong as ever. Although they no longer functioned as true economic cartels, they remained in the spotlight as extremely powerful criminal organizations able to affect the political balance of power in Colombia almost at will. One suspects that the only reason they did not exert the same control over the cocaine market in 1990 that they had in the early 1980s was that they simply chose not to do so.

The cartels in mid-1990, then, could be seen primarily as criminal gangs with a significant political-military component. Their members and affiliates remained prime targets of law enforcement in both the United States and Colombia. One year earlier, perhaps, this emphasis would have seemed misplaced, but in early 1990— given the events of the post-Galán crackdown—a cartel-focused strategy again seemed to offer significant possibilities. Before investigating these, it seems useful to analyze the structure of the cartels in the post-Galán period and to catalog their vulnerabilities and potential weaknesses.

Rodríguez Gacha's death left the Medellín cartel with only two original members, Escobar and Ochoa. Both men began their criminal careers in the 1970s, working for traditional Medellín smugglers who trafficked in liquor, cigarettes, and electronic equipment—most of it bought at the duty-free emporia of the Panama Canal Zone. Escobar started as an enforcer and a hired gun, earned some investment capital from a kidnapping, and went into the smuggling business for himself—probably in 1975. A year later he was known in the Medellín underworld as an important cocaine trafficker, and within three years he had become one of the city's biggest and richest criminals. Like all the Medellín bosses, he preferred to employ *antioqueños* and had no foreigners in any positions of trust. His chief lieutenant was his first cousin Gustavo Gaviria. Pablo Correa Arroyave, the third member of the original Los Pablos, was murdered in 1986.

Ochoa came from a middle-class Medellín family. He began as a courier for his uncle, Fabio Restrepo Ochoa—an old-time Medellín smuggler—and gradually took over the business. How he accomplished this is not known, but Restrepo died in 1978 and by 1979, Ochoa was in control of the Restrepo organization. Ochoa grew reclusive after his 1987 arrest and was largely ignored in the post-Galán crackdown. His principal lieutenant was his brother Fabio.

The Medellín cartel (which also included Rodríguez Gacha and Carlos Lehder before his 1987 arrest and extradition to the United States) gained notoriety for its use of violence and terrorism and its repeated confrontations with the government. Violence was the trademark of Escobar and Rodríguez Gacha, a tool both men used effectively throughout their careers. The confrontations, however, defied easy explanation. They probably resulted from the bosses' desire to recover the public stature they enjoyed prior to the murder of Justice Minister Rodrigo Lara Bonilla in April 1984. Before that time, Escobar served as an alternate member of the Colombian congress and had budding ambitions as a philanthropist; Lehder had founded a political party; the Ochoas were prominent horse breeders; Rodríguez Gacha owned a soccer team. The Lara Bonilla assassination, however, turned the Medellín bosses into outlaws for all time, demonstrating that they could not be both drug traffickers and respected members of society. The cartel's periodic wars after the murder appeared to be attempts to recover lost legitimacy through violence. By 1990 Ochoa seemed ready to settle for amnesty and quiet retirement; Escobar, however, still seemed to want some sort of vindication, although it was not clear why. Regardless of motive, the Medellín cartel's propensity to challenge the government brought the bosses their greatest successes and their greatest failures: success because confrontation contributed to the cartel mystique and further weakened Colombia's democratic institutions; failure because repeated government crackdowns caused the cartel to lose two of its members, hurt its operations significantly, and made it extremely difficult for the cartel to enjoy the fruits of its labor.

The Rodríguez Orejuela group in Cali presented a marked contrast to the Medellín cartel. Gilberto Rodríguez and his younger brother Miguel began their working lives as pharmacists (in 1990 the brothers owned a chain of drugstores). Miguel remained a more-or-less legitimate businessman, but Gilberto began showing up on police blotters in 1969—first as a kidnapper and later as a drug smuggler and even a suspected guerrilla terrorist. His closest associate both in the early days and throughout his career was José Santacruz Londoño. In 1990 both Rodríguez and Santacruz were under indictment in the United States for drug trafficking, but neither man was wanted in Colombia. Miguel, as far as is known, had never been arrested, and in 1990 he managed the Rodríguez Orejuelas's substantial business empire. The family's most visible asset was the América de Cali soccer club, the best team drug money could buy.

Unlike the Medellín traffickers, the Cali cartel always sought a low profile, managing its operations quietly and seeking to maximize its legitimate business holdings. In this sense it was similar to the U.S. mafia. It avoided confrontation with the government and until late 1987, appeared to get along comfortably with its colleagues from Medellín. In that year, however, apparent disagreements over market share and accusations of double-dealing by both sides led to a prolonged, bloody "war of the cartels." Meanwhile, the Cali cartel benefited dramatically from the post-Galán crackdown, because as the government focused on the Medellín traffickers, the Cali bosses remained virtually untouched. By February 1990 U.S. drug agents estimated that the Cali traffickers controlled half of the cocaine coming into the United States, achieving parity with the Medellín cartel for the first time in history.

Points of Vulnerability

Despite the cartels' seeming omnipotence, the traffickers did have weaknesses and had shown vulnerability at several stations along the cocaine trail. I describe these weak points, then examine some of the strategies that might be used to exploit them.

Colombianness

Throughout their history, the cartels insisted on living in Colombia—maintaining their corporate headquarters there and building most of their laboratory facilities in the Colombian backlands. Colombianness had several advantages. Colombians were easy for other Colombians to control and intimidate, and their families could be held hostage—which is why no high-level Colombian arrested in the United States up until 1990 had ever "flipped" to become an informant for U.S. authorities.

Also, it was easy to maintain the illusion of invulnerability closer to home. The cartel members became legends in their own time, and their names struck fear into the hearts of local law enforcement officials. It would take years to build this mystique in a new environment.

Finally and most important, security was easier to achieve in Colombia. Ill-fated adventures in Panama and Spain in 1984 prompted the cartels to develop a tried-and-true crisis management policy under which the bosses ran for prearranged safe houses and hideouts in Colombia until crackdowns subsided. Indeed, all available evidence suggests that the more closely the traffickers were pursued, the less inclined they were to leave the country.

The weaknesses of the cartels' Colombianness became apparent in the post-Galán crackdown. First, it was always easy to know where the traffickers were, and it was shown that concerted effort could produce results. Before his death in 1986, police colonel Jaime Ramírez had demonstrated the value of stubbornness, three times stalking and nearly capturing Carlos Lehder in *llanos* hideouts. Lehder's life became so unpleasant that he began to take foolhardy risks and was eventually captured in a safe house outside Medellín in 1987. On two occasions similar police pressure after Galán's death nearly resulted in Escobar's capture.

Second, law enforcement agents outside Colombia could understand that any white-collar Colombian they arrested was likely important in the cartel organization. With the exception of some assassins and bodyguards, almost any Colombian seized in the United States or any other consumer country was likely to be a major cartel wholesale cocaine distributor or money launderer. These jobs were never entrusted to foreigners.

Finally, the cartels showed reluctance to move their operations to other countries. Nothing good ever happened to them outside Colombia, and they tried everything they could to ensure that they would never have to go into exile. The Lehder case showed that continued pressure in Colombia amplified the traffickers' feeling of being trapped. When—and if—they decided to leave, they would be particularly vulnerable.

The Hourglass

Imagine the cocaine industry as an hourglass lying on its side. In one large end are several hundred thousand campesino growers producing coca in Bolivia and Peru. In the other end are hundreds of thousands of consumers who sniff cocaine and smoke crack in the United States and other consumer countries. In between is the narrow neck in which the cartels operate. Here the processing, shipment, and wholesale distribution take place.

Traditionally, interdiction efforts focused on the neck of the hourglass, where the fewest people at the highest level handled the largest amount of cocaine. In attacking the cocaine trade there, in theory law enforcement got the biggest bang for its buck. The neck of the hourglass theoretically offered the best opportunities to capture the cartel members, seize their cocaine, ground their planes, or take away their money. The trouble with the concept was that the cartels made the same calculation. They were prepared to lose a certain amount of cocaine or money in the neck of the hourglass and had factored these seizures into their economic equation. This was the price of doing business.

At the same time, they screened themselves and their trusted associates from serious damage. Most of the cocaine pilots or ship captains—the most dangerous jobs in the pipeline—were Americans, third-country nationals, or low-level Colombians with no status in the cartel hierarchy. They were expendable. Also, the enormous volume of cocaine coming out of Colombia meant that law enforcement was spread thin, and in many cases authorities seized cocaine that did not belong to the cartels. Whatever the reason, the arithmetic clearly still made sense to the big traffickers. The losses were acceptable; cocaine was still profitable.

Nonetheless, there were gains to be made by working in the hourglass neck. It was no accident, for instance, that the two most effective anticartel informants ever developed by the DEA were an airplane pilot and an aircraft dispatcher—both U.S. citizens. The transporters are the only foreigners who have a chance to interact directly with the cartel members over any length of time, and foreigners can be flipped and used.

Also, pressure can force important cartel figures into the open. Rodríguez Gacha was trapped and killed primarily because he was forced to handle a large shipment of cocaine by himself. His principal transportation expert had already been caught in the post-Galán crackdown and extradited.

Nature

Up until 1990, the cartels' efforts to broaden the cultivation of high-yield coca beyond parochial areas of Bolivia and Peru had proved unsuccessful. Some coca was grown in Ecuador in the late 1980s, and Rodríguez Gacha tried to produce high-alkaloid coca in the Guaviare *llanos* of eastern Colombia, but neither venture proved to be economically useful. Despite these and other efforts to expand production, in 1990 coca grew principally on the eastern slopes of the Peruvian Andes, especially in the Upper Huallaga Valley; in the Chapare region of central Bolivia; and in the Yungas, on the edges of the Bolivian *altiplano*. It grew nowhere else.

The Yungas is a traditional growing area (filling the coca needs of the Andean mountain people), whereas the Chapare and the Upper Huallaga Valley were created exclusively to produce coca for the international cocaine market. The identity of the person or persons who brought coca to these two regions remains a fascinating mystery in the history of cocaine.

What is important is that in 1990, everyone—cartels, law enforcement agents, and governments—knew where coca was grown. All traffickers—small, medium, and large—bought coca and coca paste in the same places from the same people. And all traffickers took the paste to Colombia to process it into cocaine. Coca was geographically vulnerable. Apart from economic, political, and ecological considerations, there was no doubt that an effective herbicide or parasite would have an immense impact on the amount of coca available for the market.

More important for our purposes, however, coca's geographical imperative offered further opportunities to pursue cartel operatives outside Colombia. Like the pilots who flew cocaine from Colombia to the United States, the pilots who flew paste from Peru to the cartel's jungle laboratories were particularly vulnerable. Follow the pilot, find the lab; arrest the pilot, find the lab, and find out who owns the lab.

Monopsony

In 1990 the traffic in coca and coca paste was a buyers' market. The campesino growers had to sell to Colombian traffickers because no other nation could absorb the enormous tonnage of coca leaves available. The coca fields of the Upper Huallaga were satellites of the Colombian industry.

In good times, a campesino could sell coca for as much as $200 per 100 pounds of leaf. Campesinos did not become millionaires growing coca, but they made more money than they could doing anything else. At $200 per hundredweight, no crop substitution program could be as effective.

But when this equation was somehow disturbed, interesting things happened. Law enforcement agents first got an inkling of how this could work in 1986 during Operation Blast Furnace, a four-month deployment of U.S. Army Blackhawk helicopters to the Beni region of Bolivia. The Blackhawks' mission was to transport and support Bolivian police and soldiers in efforts to seize major back-country cocaine laboratories and capture traffickers. Results were disappointing. The helicopters found only two labs and arrested around two hundred low-level drug offenders.

During the time the Blackhawks were in Bolivia, however, no coca was bought, no paste was processed, and no cocaine was shipped. Coca prices plunged, and campesinos became desperate. The industry stopped because the traffickers were content to wait for the helicopters to depart, which they did when funding for the program ran out. Soon the cocaine business was back to normal.

A similar phenomenon occurred in both Bolivia and Peru in 1990. The post-Galán crackdown forced the Colombian traffickers to curtail their business activities. Coca-growing campesinos—not just in the Chapare but everywhere—felt the effects of the traffickers' decision. No one was doing business, and the price of coca began to drop precipitously at the beginning of 1990. By the first week of February, coca leaves in the Upper Huallaga Valley were selling for $10 per hundredweight and in the Chapare for $7 per hundredweight. To break even, campesinos needed to sell the leaves for at least $30 per hundredweight. In these circumstances, crop substitution looked much more attractive. If the acreage devoted to coca began to shrink, the cartel could experience supply bottlenecks.

Money

In 1981 in a background interview a U.S. Internal Revenue Service investigator described the cocaine industry as "a billion-dollar-a-year business conducted in $20 bills," and the characterization was as true in the 1990s as in the early 1980s. Cocaine is a cash business, and in 1990 cartels devoted incredible amounts of time and resources to the care and handling of money: hiding it, counting it, laundering it, and making payoffs. Cash is bulky and freely convertible, and it has no history.

Law enforcement agencies made a lot of money fighting the cocaine war. For years the DEA boasted that it was the only U.S. government agency outside the IRS that operated at a profit. In 1989 the DEA seized $1.1 billion in cash on a budget of $500 million. Antidrug enforcement, like the cocaine traffic itself, paid well.

Traditionally, however, authorities gave only limited attention to money. Law authorities were interested in seizing cocaine and traffickers; cash was regarded as only peripherally important. Only in 1987 did law enforcement agencies begin to reevaluate and refine their cash seizure techniques when they realized that money investigations could be the wave of the future. Traffickers were insulated against cocaine seizures and against the arrests of even mid- to high-level helpers and associates, but serious cash shortages could cripple every aspect of the industry. The Peruvian coca market plunged into depression in 1990 in part because traffickers had no money to pay campesinos for coca leaf. The post-Galán crackdown had curtailed cash flow, and everyone in the cocaine business—the campesino in Peru, the hired assassin in Medellín, the pilot in Miami, the distributor in Queens, and the street corner crack peddler in Washington, D.C.—worked in cash.

Further, money was the reason traffickers were in the cocaine business. If law enforcement agents seized their bank accounts, froze their assets, or otherwise prevented them from tapping their wealth, they could not buy the properties and pleasures that caused them to become cocaine traffickers. Denial could be an effective deterrent. What good was the money if it could not be enjoyed?

Strategies for Fighting the Cartels

By the 1990s law enforcement agencies in both producing and consuming countries could choose from many options in combating the cocaine cartels. These had never been used with any consistency, however; indeed, some had been used only sporadically and others not at all. For this reason, when the U.S. government spoke (as it had for decades) of a "war on drugs," it was doing little more than blowing hot air. The United States never had a plan to combat drugs, and the so-called "war" did not exist.

This perhaps changed with the advent of the so-called Cartagena agreement in February 1990. This document—signed by the presidents of the United States, Colombia, Peru, and Bolivia—envisioned a comprehensive strategy combining demand reduction in consumer countries with a producer country program based on increased law enforcement and interdiction, economic development, and crop substitution to wean poor people away from coca cultivation and cocaine processing.

The principles of the Andean Strategy, which evolved from the Cartagena agreement, were sound. Successful implementation would probably depend on the rapidity with which portions of the plan were implemented and the degree to which tactics in different countries could complement each other. For U.S. drug czar William Bennett, the potential for success was high because, as one staffer put it in an off-the-record statement, "we have a foot on every base." In other words, the Andean Strategy attempted to do something about every section of the cocaine pipeline.

Unfortunately, different tactics do not necessarily go together and indeed could work at cross purposes. For instance, a policy of coca eradication would be almost impossible to implement given the Cartagena document's emphasis on crop substitution. Worse, talk in the United States of developing a parasite that would eat coca leaves had the effect of undermining the Cartagena accord. The Andean countries liked the idea of crop substitution because it proposed to destroy coca cultivation and replace it with something else. They disliked eradication (through herbicides or parasites) because it destroyed coca cultivation and replaced it with nothing, creating great potential for social and political unrest. The Andean presidents sold the idea of crop substitution to the United States at Cartagena, but talk in Washington of new eradication projects called into question the sincerity of the U.S. commitment to the accord.

Generally speaking, any program that hurts cocaine trafficking hurts the Colombian cartels to some degree. What is not always clear is how particular policies, if aimed specifically at the cartels, can do serious damage to the entire cocaine industry. Nevertheless, in 1990 there were three reasons targeting the cartels made sense. First, the cartels were still the world's biggest drug traffickers. Damage to them by definition was damage to the industry. Second, the cartels had tremendous prestige. Damage to them destroyed the myth of trafficker invincibility, restored confidence in Colombia's democratic institutions, and helped convince people that the war against drugs was winnable. For example, celebrations were held throughout Colombia the evening after Rodríguez Gacha's death was announced. Third, evidence from the post-Galán crackdown suggests that cartel policies still drove the cocaine industry. A serious disruption of the cartel's activities could cause a serious disruption in the entire business.

What follow are some possible strategies to use against the cartels and discussion of the effects they have had and might have on cartel activities. When possible, a strategy will be considered as it relates specifically to the cartels and also as it relates to the entire industry.

Interdiction

Interdiction means the seizures of drugs and money and the arrests of traffickers anywhere in the neck of the cocaine hourglass—from the Colombian labs to the wholesale distributors and buyers in major consuming country entry points. It is clear from past history that no one has been particularly satisfied with the results of interdiction-based strategies. It is equally clear from the Cartagena agreement, however, that interdiction would form a major component of any future strategy.

It is my opinion that interdiction must be maintained, if for no other reason than to keep the traffickers "honest." Traffickers expect to lose cocaine and to risk arrest. Interdiction keeps the costs of doing business high and thus may discourage some people from getting involved in the cocaine industry.

I also believe, however, that interdiction is unlikely to do any serious damage to the cartels. The biggest traffickers are too well screened to risk capture, and there is too much cocaine being shipped by too many people for law enforcement to inflict a mortal blow against the cartels simply by seizing dope. Capture of the Medellín cartel's Tranquilandia factory complex in 1984 did cause a rise in the wholesale price of cocaine, but only for about five weeks.

Conventional interdiction can put small traffickers out of business—wiping out their capital in a single seizure. Extreme measures, such as stationing an aircraft carrier off the Colombian coast, can put even more small traffickers out of business—especially if Tomcats shoot down every Cessna that leaves a Colombian airstrip. But none of these strategies will hurt the cartels. Throughout history the big traffickers have accepted the losses inherent in conventional interdiction. Further, an aircraft carrier could do nothing to halt the massive quantities of cocaine being sent by the big traffickers by way of container ship. And finally, although the carrier would indeed work against air transport, it would only do so as long as it took the traffickers to find an alternate Pacific coast route—perhaps five weeks.

Yet, interdiction can inflict financial damage to the cartels. In matters of money, they are particularly vulnerable because the same volume business that insulates them from damage due to large cocaine seizures requires that they take substantial risks with cash. The cartels need a lot more money than small traffickers and have a lot more trouble hiding it. The cartels launder money in consumer countries, transfer it across international borders, and reclaim it—either as cash in Colombia or as bank deposits in Europe or the Caribbean. Seizing cartel money hurts the traffickers much more than seizing their cocaine.

Finally, law enforcement agencies could pay greater attention to the cartels' clients in the United States and other consuming countries. Through the early 1990s, cocaine arriving in U.S. ports of entry was still owned by Colombians in most cases. At some point, however, the cartels' distributors transferred ownership to and took payment from the U.S.-based criminal organizations that controlled the traffic in most U.S. cities. Even after years of cocaine interdiction, as of 1990 almost nothing was known about this crucial moment—the last transaction in the neck of the hourglass. Several stateside Colombian distributors (high-level messengers of the cartels) were arrested and imprisoned, but the U.S. wholesalers (high-level messengers of the U.S. gangs) were largely ignored. Seizing the Americans was not likely to hurt the Colombian cartels, but it could be extremely useful in unraveling U.S. cocaine distribution networks. U.S. distributors would also be much more likely to accept plea bargaining arrangements than their Colombian colleagues.

Frontal War

After the Lara Bonilla assassination, the Colombian government ordered five crackdowns against the cartels through mid-1990. But only one of these—the 1989–1990 post-Galán offensive—could be described as anything resembling a "frontal war" against the cartels. The characteristics of the post-Galán offensive were much different from the earlier crackdowns, and so were the results. It will be useful to examine all the crackdowns in some detail.

The first (after Lara Bonilla in May 1984) was ordered by then-president Belisario Betancur, and the other four came during the 1986–1990 administration of President Virgilio Barco. The first three Barco crackdowns, like the Lara Bonilla offensive, were provoked by particular events: the release of Jorge Ochoa from jail on bail (August 1986), the murder of *El Espectador* newspaper editor Guillermo Cano (December 1986), and the kidnap-murder of Attorney General Carlos Mauro Hoyos (January 1988). Although the post-Galán crackdown (August 1989) also appeared to have been ordered because of an assassination, most of the measures called into force after Galán's killing had been contemplated for some time as a response to a number of earlier high-profile murders. All five crackdowns specifically targeted the Medellín cartel, the government believing (probably correctly) that cartel killers were responsible for each of the key crimes.

The post–Lara Bonilla crackdown took the cartels by surprise. The Betancur government—which had been passive and unconcerned about drug trafficking during its first two years in office—turned suddenly aggressive after Lara Bonilla's death, and the traffickers were not prepared for the change in attitude. They immediately slid across the border into Panama and went to safe houses allegedly protected by General Manuel Antonio Noriega. Former Colombian president Alfonso López Michelsen met with Escobar and Ochoa in Panama less than a week after Lara Bonilla's death.

It is not known exactly how long the traffickers stayed outside Colombia, but their sojourn clearly lasted several months. During that time, everything went wrong for the cartels. The meetings with López and later with the Colombian attorney general were widely publicized. Cartel problems with the Panamanian operations eventually escalated into at least one acrimonious disagreement with Noriega. After the cartel had struck a deal with Noriega, the Panamanian Defense Forces seized and destroyed a supposedly "protected" cocaine lab in the Darien jungle. The cartel's new initiative in Nicaragua blew up in its face when its leading pilot turned out to be a DEA informant who was able to link Pablo Escobar and the Sandinista government in a large cocaine deal. And worst of all, Ochoa and Gilberto Rodríguez Orejuela went into exile in Spain only to be captured and jailed for nearly two years.

It appears that on the basis of these experiences, the cartel decided that exile was not the safest response to government repression. Instead, the bosses built safe houses in Colombia, hired more bodyguards, and put enough police and other public officials on the payroll so they would always be forewarned about new crackdowns. Escobar and Rodríguez Gacha were back in Colombia by November 1984, and, as far as is known, neither man ever again left the country for any length of time.

The next three crackdowns caused no visible damage to the cartels. In each case Barco invoked special state-of-siege measures to facilitate search, seizure, and arrest; and on each occasion some low- and mid-level traffickers were picked up and subsequently released. A few laboratories were destroyed and some cocaine was seized, but drug-trafficking operations were not impaired. The traffickers had done their work well: Their security arrangements were in place, and they were able to terrorize Colombian officialdom at will. Police did capture Lehder during the Cano crackdown, but Lehder had been a fugitive since late 1983 and had not played a major role in cartel operations for at least three years prior to his arrest.

At no time during the first four crackdowns did the Colombian government have any comprehensive strategy for dealing with the cartels. Escobar's zoo at Puerto Triunfo was seized then handed back on three occasions; Jorge Ochoa's father Fabio was arrested and released twice, as was Escobar underboss Evaristo Porras. No systematic attempt was made to reform Colombian law enforcement, reinforce the courts, or enact new laws more congenial to the arrest and prosecution of drug cases. The entire justice system was crippled or hopelessly compromised. In short, the crackdowns were a waste of time. Law enforcement without institutional underpinning was worse than useless: Not only did it not produce results, but it allowed the traffickers to flout the justice system and call into question the government's ability to govern.

On the surface, the post-Galán crackdown closely resembled the earlier fiascos; but there were differences. Most important, Barco decided to extradite drug suspects by executive fiat and began doing so within three weeks of the Galán killing. This decision—to let U.S. courts serve as a surrogate justice system—gave Colombia a credible legal threat against the cartel for the first time in more than two years. When the Supreme Court subsequently ruled that the extradition decrees did not violate the Colombian constitution, Barco had won the first great Colombian victory of the drug wars.

The crackdown's second success, not fully understood even months later, was due to the fact that constant pressure against the cartel took the bosses out of circulation. Escobar was almost captured twice; the second time he ran out the back door of a jungle safe house wearing nothing but underwear and an Uzi submachine gun. Gonzalo Rodríguez Gacha lost at least twenty-two pieces of property—including apartment houses, ranches, and mansions. Police seized several tons of his cocaine and froze millions of his dollars in overseas bank accounts. When security forces finally caught him, he had been on the run for four months.

In effect, the post-Galán crackdown began to approach frontal war. There was a strategy: Seize the cartel's property, capture the bosses, and extradite them. There was tenacity: The pressure did not dissipate after six weeks but lasted through 1989 and well into 1990. And there was commitment: Barco—regarded for much of his term as little more than an opaque, colorless bureaucrat—had become the scourge of the Medellín cartel.

The sustained pressure had some astonishing effects. As mentioned earlier, the traffickers' inability to operate normally caused a profound depression in the Peruvian and Bolivian coca market. The entire industry slowed to a near halt. In addition, the Extraditables were twice forced to change their strategy, moving from "total and absolute war" to kidnapping and finally to "surrender." For the first time in history the Colombian government was dictating the rhythm of the drug war.

Several lessons can be learned from the post-Galán offensive, at least during its first months. First, frontal war against the cartels not only damages the cartels but damages the entire cocaine industry. Second, constant harassment neutralizes cartel members and makes them more apt to be captured or killed, a lesson that should have been learned during the years spent pursuing Lehder. Third, suppressing the Colombian cocaine industry can result in opportunities elsewhere, such as making crop substitution much more attractive to Peruvian and Bolivian campesinos whose coca profits have tumbled because no Colombian traffickers are buying coca leaf.

At the same time, frontal war has its own dangers. Most of all, it creates unreasonable expectations if it is not accompanied by supplementary strategies. Without important outside financial assistance, the Colombian government could not be expected to maintain the post-Galán pressure indefinitely; unless the cartels can be dealt a death blow, they will simply wait until the crackdown runs out of steam.

Also, the Colombians should have used the crackdown as an opportunity to reform and revamp their laws and legal system and to develop effective control mechanisms that went beyond the naked use of force. The crackdown gave Colombia's damaged institutions a breather, but if the government failed to take advantage of it, the crackdown would have few lasting results.

Finally, complementary strategies were necessary outside Colombia. Without working crop substitution programs (there was only one small program in existence, in Bolivia, during the first six months of the post-Galán crackdown), campesinos had nowhere to turn if they decided to abandon coca and take up legitimate farming. Governments were missing the opportunity presented by the coca depression.

Decapitation

Between 1984 and 1991, law enforcement agents killed or captured all of the major cartel leaders. Gonzalo Rodríguez Gacha was killed by police, and Carlos Lehder was extradited. Jorge Ochoa spent a little over two years in jail on two separate occasions, and Gilberto Rodríguez Orejuela was imprisoned for two-and-a-half years in Spain and Colombia. After extensive negotiations with the government, Pablo Escobar finally turned himself in to Colombian authorities in 1991.

There is no evidence, however, that "decapitation" has any effect on the world cocaine traffic. There were price fluctuations and major disruptions in the flow of cocaine as a result of interdiction (Tranquilandia) and frontal war (the post-Galán crackdown), but capturing or killing drug bosses by itself did not influence the market. It did dramatically improve the security climate in Colombia. Before Rodríguez Gacha's death, bombs were exploding all over the country; after his death, there were no more bombings. In removing Rodríguez Gacha, the Colombian government had eliminated its greatest enemy.

The importance of this cannot be overstated. The Barco government's enthusiasm for the drug war, in my view, resulted principally from its perception that the Medellín cartel threatened Colombia's national security. Eliminate the threat and Colombia's reason for fighting the drug war would disappear. The death of Rodríguez Gacha demonstrated to Colombia that there was indeed a causal relationship between the activities of the cartel members and the nation's institutional well-being.

A decapitation strategy thus offered tremendous potential benefits to Colombia. By replacing the Rodríguez Gachas of the cocaine trade with "kinder, gentler" drug traffickers uninterested in competing with the government for state power, Colombia would eliminate the institutional threat. The victory would be won.

On the other hand, decapitation offered no help to the United States and other consuming countries. First, the flow of cocaine would remain unaffected; thus, consuming countries would gain no relief from the tide of drug abuse and its attendant social problems. Second, Colombia's enthusiasm for the drug war could dim. Its problem—national security—would be solved. Drug abuse is a problem of the consuming countries.

Divide and Conquer

As with decapitation, a policy of divide and conquer is unlikely to have any lasting effect on the world supply of cocaine. Were the Medellín cartel to be eliminated, new traffickers would undoubtedly arise to take the places of the old bosses, which would also occur if Rodríguez Orejuela and his colleagues were removed from the Cali cartel.

What did happen, as described above, was that the Medellín cartel's losses during the post-Galán crackdown were the Cali cartel's gains. The Cali bosses never challenged the government to a "war," nor did they ever directly threaten Colombian institutions. And with the post-Galán crackdown, their soft line was finally vindicated. The crackdown's emphasis on the Medellín cartel left the Cali traffickers in an excellent position to pick up the pieces when and if the pressure finally subsided.

Curiously, law enforcement agencies have never seriously attempted to play one cartel against the other—a tactic that, if handled properly, could perhaps cause both cartels great damage. The so-called "war of the cartels" showed how this might work. Ostensibly, the war began in late 1987 when Rodríguez Gacha tried to muscle in on the Cali cartel's wholesale distribution networks in New York. Other events that could be attributed to the war—based on sketchy information and a plethora of unsubstantiated rumor—included the arrest of Jorge Ochoa outside a highway toll booth near Cali in November 1987, the machine gun death of Ochoa lieutenant Rafael Cardona Salazar a month later, and the bombing of Pablo Escobar's residential high rise in the El Poblado section of Medellín in January 1988.

Although it was not clear how many of these and other events were tied directly to the war of the cartels, there nonetheless was plenty of evidence that beginning in late 1987 the cartels caused each other plenty of aggravation. This was particularly significant because until the "war," the two cartels appeared to get along quite amiably—as evidenced by the Ochoa–Rodríguez Orejuela joint venture in Spain in 1984. How the cartels' peaceful coexistence foundered remains an important and potentially useful question for law enforcement agencies to answer. Law enforcement agents could find out why the cartels quarreled and encourage them to continue doing so.

Negotiations

The Extraditables' January 1990 "surrender document" represented the third publicized, full-scale attempt by the Medellín cartel to negotiate a peace treaty with the Colombian government. Besides the formal proposals, the government and the traffickers were also known to have had several other informal or private contacts and were rumored to be constantly in communication.

The first question regarding negotiated settlements is whether a proposal is serious. The answers here are probably no in 1984, possibly yes in 1989, and probably yes by 1990. The 1984 document appeared to be drafted by Escobar and designed to establish a "state-to-state" relationship between the traffickers and the government. The traffickers promised to get out of the cocaine trade in return for amnesty, freedom from extradition, and the government's specific guarantees that the bosses would be able to live unmolested lives outside the drug business. This was the Medellín cartel leaders' earliest bid to recover their lost prestige. By the time of the second document in 1989, the traffickers had dropped the specific language regarding amnesty and had made their other wishes less explicit. By the third document in January 1990, the traffickers had eliminated all explicit demands and had "surrendered."

The third document was important because it suggested that the post-Galán crackdown had been successful enough to cause the traffickers to regret that they had ever challenged the government to total and absolute war. It also suggested that Escobar may not have been setting the strategy; his response to adversity had always been more violence rather than less. Negotiations may finally have been put in Ochoa's hands or, as was also rumored, in the hands of a public relations firm.

The third document was also perceptive on two grounds. First, it spoke to national security—the Barco government's major concern. The surrender effectively guaranteed that the Medellín cartel would no longer fight to overthrow the government. It thus offered Barco a classic opportunity to proclaim victory, end the crackdown, and end his administration on a high note.

Second, the document should be read not as a surrender, but as a bid by the Medellín cartel to retire. This interpretation gained force in February 1990, when the traffickers turned over several large laboratory complexes as a demonstration of their bona fide desire to get out of the drug business. Retirement was also the underlying theme of the 1984 document, but the sentiment seemed more sincere by 1990–1991. The later proposal lacked the earlier desire for vindication and respectability. Instead, all the traffickers wanted in the early 1990s was to get out of the cocaine business, retire, and quietly enjoy their millions.

Seen in this light, the proposal could probably have been taken seriously, but it was difficult to see what advantage the Colombian government could obtain by engaging the traffickers in negotiations. First, there was no assurance that the traffickers could stop Colombia's cocaine traffic. Significantly, the 1990 proposal did not make fresh mention of the Extraditables' 1984 contention that they controlled 70 to 80 percent of Colombia's cocaine. It also specifically excluded the Cali cartel from the agreement. In other words, the Extraditables did not speak for Cali and indeed may not have spoken for anyone beyond the Escobar and Ochoa crime families. Chances that a negotiated settlement would result in any serious diminution of the cocaine traffic or a decline in drug-related crime thus appeared to be nil.

On the positive side, the agreement appeared to offer the government guarantees that the traffickers would no longer directly menace Colombian institutions. A settlement could serve the government well in a divide-and-conquer strategy: Take Medellín out of the picture, then turn to Cali. Signs were, however, that Barco felt he could neutralize the Medellín cartel without a treaty. Thus, why negotiate? Also, why risk international ridicule? It was hard to imagine the president of a sovereign nation negotiating a public peace treaty with organized crime.

International Cooperation

Clearly, international cooperation is the key to any long-term producer country strategy. We have seen how much more effective Colombia's frontal war could have been if crop substitution programs had been in place in Peru and Bolivia and been ready to woo campesinos from coca growing when the depression hit. Similarly, without the promise of extradition, the frontal war strategy would have been little more than tilting at windmills.

With better exchange of information, earlier lessons could be passed on to neighboring countries and used to greater effect. Peruvian and Colombian officials could have better anticipated the coca depression if they had kept in mind the lessons of Operation Blast Furnace. Also, the 1984 Panama example shows that harassment in one country can lead to mistakes in another. In 1984 no one was on Colombia's geographical perimeter seeking to take advantage of cartel blunders. Closer attention then might have resulted in the captures of all members of the Medellín and Cali cartels.

The Cartagena document suggested very specific areas in which producer and consumer countries might cooperate—among them the licensing of precursor chemicals, the shipment of firearms, and the sale of aircraft. It was a testament to the growing sophistication of law enforcement agencies that these ideas—which did not exist a decade ago—had become realistic possibilities.

Two other areas that demand international accords are extradition and money laundering. The existence of a working international extradition document would probably eliminate half of the bickering and recriminations that now plague the domestic politics and diplomatic relations of the drug war. If extradition were automatic in drug cases, national legal systems would not have to be perpetually under siege. The traffickers, however—finely attuned to the dangers of extradition— have proved to be particularly expert at inflaming nationalist sentiments against it. For this reason, a multilateral extradition accord seems unrealistic at present.

Money laundering has greater promise for elimination. Both consuming and producing nations have evinced considerable enthusiasm for accords that facilitate the movement of banking information across international borders. Also, countries understand that unlike cocaine, money is extremely useful. The DEA fights its drug war with its enemies' profits. There is no reason other nations cannot do the same.

9

Myths of Militarization: Enlisting Armed Forces in the War on Drugs

Bruce M. Bagley

Mounting frustration with the failure of the Reagan administration's "war on drugs" to curb the burgeoning U.S. drug plague in the early and mid-1980s generated rising political pressure in Washington to expand the role of the U.S. military and its counterparts in source and trafficking countries in Latin America in antidrug efforts during the late 1980s. This chapter examines the rationale, scope, and effectiveness of the U.S. and Latin American militaries in drug interdiction and enforcement in the 1980s and explores the problems and prospects of the trend toward "militarization" as of mid-1990.

The Politics of U.S. Military Involvement

In the 1980s advocates of greater U.S. military involvement in the war on drugs ranged across the U.S. political spectrum from liberal Democrats, such as former New York City Mayor Edward Koch and Representative Charles Rangel (D-NY), to conservative Republicans, such as Senator Alfonse D'Amato (R-NY) and Representative Duncan Hunter (R-CA). Despite their many differences, proponents of expanded military involvement generally advocated increasing resources for military interdiction at U.S. borders and on the high seas—empowering members of the U.S. armed services to interdict drug shipments and apprehend drug smugglers and deploying U.S. military forces in foreign countries to stop drug production and processing at the "source." Their justification for increased military participation was grounded in their common claim that drug trafficking constituted a major threat to U.S. national security: an especially insidious form of foreign invasion that warranted nothing less than the full-scale mobilization of the U.S. armed forces.[1]

An eclectic coalition of fiscal conservatives, civil libertarians, and Department of Defense (DOD) officials opposed expanded involvement of the U.S. military in the war on drugs. In effect, their basic argument was that the assumption that the military could halt the flow of drugs into the United States from abroad was largely wishful thinking—a myth—with potentially harmful side effects for the U.S. forces as an institution for civil rights and democratic freedoms in the United States. Their principal contentions:

Interdiction Will Not Work. During Reagan's presidency, secretaries of defense Caspar Weinberger and Frank Carlucci maintained that the only effective way to reduce the flow of drugs into the United States was to reduce demand. They contended that expansion of interdiction efforts might raise the traffickers' risks and costs but would never halt drug smuggling into the United States completely or permanently.[2]

Readiness Would Be Impaired. Both Weinberger and Carlucci, along with many top Pentagon military officers, also feared that deployment of U.S. military personnel and equipment to fight the drug war might impair DOD's ability to perform its primary missions: defending the United States from foreign nuclear or conventional attack and projecting U.S. military power abroad in defense of U.S. national interests. They worried that DOD could not afford to take on this new mission unless substantial additional funding was allocated.[3]

The Military Should Not Be Involved in Civilian Law Enforcement. Many DOD officials objected because they felt military personnel lacked the training and expertise needed to carry out law enforcement activities. Secretary Weinberger underscored the possibility that deviations from the military's principal missions could seriously damage morale.[4] Lieutenant General Stephen Olmstead, deputy assistant secretary of defense for drug policy and enforcement, expressed concern that expanded military involvement in civilian affairs might undermine civil liberties and erode popular support at home for the U.S. armed forces.[5] The American Civil Liberties Union voiced similar fears about the potential for undermining civil rights and legal guarantees in the United States if the military became actively involved in law enforcement.[6]

The U.S. Military Would Be Exposed to Corruption. Many Latin American militaries have been plagued by drug-related bribery and corruption. Some opponents of a broader U.S. military role in drug control warned that U.S. military forces might be similarly corrupted, thereby seriously disrupting military discipline and the chain of command.

The U.S. Military and Drug Interdiction

Historically, U.S. military involvement in civilian law enforcement was legally proscribed by the 1878 Posse Comitatus Act. Although it specifically prohibited only the use of the army to "execute the laws," through the early 1980s U.S. authorities consistently interpreted the act's restrictions as binding on the navy, marines, and air force as well.[7]

Responding to the explosive growth of the U.S.-Andean cocaine trade, in 1981 Senator Sam Nunn (D-GA) led a bipartisan effort to amend the Posse Comitatus Act (attached to the 1982 Defense Authorization Act) to authorize the U.S. armed forces to share drug-related intelligence from military sources with civilian officials, lend military equipment to U.S. law enforcement agencies, assist in the operation of this equipment, and make military facilities available to federal agents. The Nunn

amendment, however, did maintain existing prohibitions regarding the direct involvement of U.S. military forces in searches or arrests of civilians. In addition, any
assistance that would "adversely" affect military preparedness was explicitly prohibited. To activate military assistance, the new legislation required that the secretary
of state, the secretary of defense, and the attorney general declare that a "serious
threat" existed to the interests of the United States. Although the act did not
specifically state that military assistance could be provided to foreign law enforcement
officials, it was broadly interpreted by the Reagan administration during the 1980s
to permit such aid.[8]

Reflecting continuing DOD reluctance, resource limitations, and the restrictions
specified in the 1982 act, the U.S. military's role in federal drug control remained
relatively limited during Ronald Reagan's first term in office. In fiscal year (FY)
1982—the first in which the relaxation of Posse Comitatus took effect—DOD
spent only $4.9 million on drug interdiction. By FY 1985 the military's drug budget
had risen to over $100 million—mostly for underwriting DOD equipment loans to
civilian drug enforcement agencies—but was still not considered a major priority by
DOD.[9]

Congressional pressures on the Reagan administration to increase military
involvement intensified steadily in advance of the November 1986 midterm elections.
Responding to these rising political pressures, in April 1986 President Reagan issued
a National Security Decision Directive (NSDD) declaring drug trafficking a
"lethal" threat to U.S. national security, thus setting the stage for rapid expansion
of U.S. military participation in drug interdiction at U.S. borders and abroad in the
second half of 1986 and beyond.[10] Existing restraints on the direct involvement of
U.S. military forces in domestic law enforcement nonetheless were preserved, and
similar limits were extended to cover U.S. military activities overseas. The guidelines
regulating U.S. military participation in drug enforcement operations abroad specifically stipulated that (1) U.S. forces had to be invited by the host government; (2)
the forces were to be directed and coordinated by U.S. civilian agencies; and (3)
their role was to be limited to support functions.[11]

Indicating strong bipartisan support for Reagan's new national security directive,
Congress almost doubled DOD's annual drug budget for FY 1987 to $379 million.
As in the earlier 1982 Defense Authorization Act, the 1986 legislation emphasized
increased DOD support for civilian law enforcement through the provision of
equipment and facilities, training, and intelligence-gathering. As of late 1988, the
accumulated value of military lending from all service branches since FY 1982
totaled $300 million—an average of approximately US$41.5 million a year. Coast
Guard, Customs, and DEA requests for specialized military equipment had been
regularly filled by DOD from FY 1982 onward, although resource limitations and
readiness considerations had sometimes compelled DOD officials to turn down
some specific requests, restrict levels of assistance, or delay delivery prior to FY
1987.[12]

President Reagan's 1986 NSDD and Congress's FY 1987 funding increases enabled DOD to expand its assistance to U.S. law enforcement agencies substantially in 1987–1988. One example of DOD's stepped-up support was the creation of the joint Coast Guard–navy Tactical Law Enforcement Teams (TACLETS)—also known as the Law Enforcement Detachment (LEDET) program—which assigned Coast Guard officers to navy vessels for drug interdiction operations. Navy ships were assigned to interdict vessels suspected of transporting illegal drugs; on-board Coast Guard personnel then carried out searches, seizures, and arrests. In 1987–1988, the navy provided approximately 2,500 ship days in support of the program, which resulted in 20 vessel seizures, 110 arrests, and confiscation of 225,000 pounds of marijuana and 550 pounds of cocaine—at a total cost of $540 million. Beyond normal operating costs, the Coast Guard spent an additional $13 million and the navy $27 million. A second example of increased support was the establishment of the air force drug surveillance program. In FY 1987 the air force flew 591 hours in support of drug interdiction, producing ten arrests and six seizures at an incremental cost of $2.6 million. In FY 1988 further funding increases for military antidrug operations permitted the navy and marines to provide 2,037 ship days in support of LEDET at an increased cost of $24 million.[13]

Beyond equipment loans, provision of drug-trafficking intelligence to U.S. law enforcement agencies was widely regarded as the most significant contribution the U.S. military made to civilian drug enforcement efforts in the 1980s. In 1986, for example, the navy provided 1,638 hours of aerial surveillance over the Caribbean, the Mexican border, and the Gulf of Mexico and gradually increased the total every year thereafter. Using its E-2s, P-3s, and S-3s, the navy relayed information on suspected smuggler movements to Customs, the Coast Guard, and the DEA. The marines also provided both aerial surveillance (from OV-10s) and ground surveillance (through mobile ground radar equipment). The air force contributed information from its Aerostat radars to command, control, and communication facilities operated by Customs and monitoring support from its AWACS planes—often with Customs officials on board. The national and air guards transmitted intelligence from both aerial and ground surveillance equipment as well. In combination, military surveillance substantially improved U.S. intelligence on traditional sea and airborne drug smuggling routes across the Caribbean into south Florida and the southeastern United States.[14]

In 1987–1988, DOD also conducted joint operations with U.S. law enforcement agencies: Operations Hawkeye, Groundhog, Alliance, and Autumn Harvest. In Operations Hawkeye and Groundhog, army personnel learned to fly OV-O1D Mohawks in "selected target areas" and to transmit the information gathered to the U.S. Customs Service. In Operation Alliance, army trainees learned to use ground surveillance equipment along the Mexican border. Operation Autumn Harvest involved Customs officials and the Arizona National Guard in joint interdiction efforts along the Arizona-Mexico border. The guard units' mission was to relay ground-based radar to identify possible airborne smugglers and communicate their information to Customs. Customs used P-3 and E-2C aircraft to track suspected aircraft to their U.S. destinations and then called in "bust planes" (such as the B200, King Air E90, Cessna 404, and Blackhawk helicopters) to search, seize, and apprehend drug traffickers and their cargos.[15]

The Effectiveness of U.S. Military Border Interdiction

Because military assistance was provided mainly on a nonreimbursable basis, in mid-1988 anticipated constraints on the FY 1989 defense budget threatened the Pentagon's ability to sustain its expanded assistance to federal drug enforcement agencies. Indeed, in FY 1988 budgetary shortfalls caused the navy to cut back joint operations with the Coast Guard. According to DOD, any future expansion of military antidrug assistance in FY 1989 and beyond would require either modifications of the armed forces' mission priorities or additional resources from Congress.[16]

Hard-line rhetoric and bureaucratic politics aside, the military's insistence on its need for more funding to underwrite its drug interdiction activities raised the issue of whether such expenditures were cost-effective. In practice, however, accurate measurement of the impact of military involvement in U.S. drug interdiction efforts was not feasible. The U.S. government simply did not have reliable estimates of the total amounts of illicit drugs smuggled into the United States each year, so it was impossible to calculate the percentage of the total that U.S. agencies in general—or the U.S. military in particular—had managed to interdict. Moreover, even if U.S. past military support programs had increased the overall effectiveness of U.S. interdiction operations, it was still uncertain "whether more DOD support . . . [would] achieve significant results or if the law enforcement agencies could effectively absorb more support."[17]

Nonetheless, using official reports, the General Accounting Office (GAO) in 1988 found "no direct correlation between resources spent to interdict and the long-term availability of imported drugs in the domestic market."[18] The major reason for the apparent ineffectiveness of U.S. interdiction efforts may be that transportation costs constituted only a relatively minor part (less than 10 percent) of final street prices; hence interdiction efforts, even if well conceived and implemented, ultimately affected retail prices only marginally.[19]

However marginal their overall impact, some military drug assistance programs were clearly more ineffective than others. One factor was the reduced absorptive capacities of specific law enforcement agencies. Enhanced flows of military intelligence on suspected drug shipments could not be put to optimum use unless enforcement agencies (for example, the Coast Guard, DEA, or the Federal Bureau of Investigation [FBI]) could mobilize sufficient personnel and equipment to follow up in a timely fashion. They often could not.

A second limitation on military effectiveness resulted from the alternative priorities, or "missions," combined with bureaucratic "turf" rivalries over authority and resources typical of U.S. enforcement agencies. The Central Intelligence Agency

(CIA), for example, withheld sensitive data on drug smuggling activities in Mexico from the DEA, FBI, and Customs investigators assigned to investigate the 1985 murder of DEA agent Enrique Camarena; the CIA feared release of these data might compromise CIA sources connected with traffickers who provided intelligence on Communist insurgencies and arms trafficking in Central America or funds and logistical support for U.S. covert aid to the Nicaraguan Contras during 1985–1986. CIA reluctance came in large part from U.S. law enforcement agencies' propensity to expose intelligence sources in court during prosecutions of suspected traffickers. It was National Security Counsel adviser Oliver North's 1986 decision to "leak" to the U.S. press DEA photographs, purportedly revealing Sandinista complicity in cocaine trafficking through Nicaraguan territory, that exposed the DEA's surveillance operations in Nicaragua.[20]

A third constraint on military effectiveness involved resource bottlenecks that forced the DOD to withhold key assets from civilian agencies. The TACLET-LEDET program, for example, did not function optimally in 1987–1988 because the Coast Guard was forced to station most of its three hundred TACLET personnel on the navy's so-called "ships of opportunity," which deviated from their preestablished course only if a vessel suspected of drug smuggling were spotted. Although as of mid-1988 the navy's ships of opportunity had been involved in only one seizure, Coast Guard officials defended the program on the grounds that the mere presence of Coast Guard personnel aboard naval vessels had deterred drug smugglers from air and sea routes across the Caribbean.[21]

The U.S. Military and International Narcotics Control

Paralleling its expanded support of civilian drug interdiction programs at U.S. borders during the 1980s, DOD also broadened its role in U.S. narcotics control programs in the Caribbean and Latin America. From 1982 through 1985, the U.S. military was used mainly in Caribbean operations—such as HAT Trick I, HAT Trick II, and Operation Bahamas and Turks (OPBAT)—to support U.S. and local Caribbean law enforcement officials. The numbers of U.S. military personnel that took part in these operations were small, usually between ten and twenty. Both OPBAT and HAT Trick II, for example, relied on air force and army helicopters for "quick insertion" of Bahamian law enforcement teams carrying out seizure and arrest missions. Some DOD personnel also participated in operational planning, development of interagency radio networks, and collection of intelligence for Operation HAT Trick II.[22]

U.S. government officials claimed that the military's participation in these Caribbean operations was particularly effective in deterring drug smugglers from using Caribbean routes. David Westrate, assistant DEA administrator for operations, for example, claimed that OPBAT was highly successful and was the primary reason that up to a third or more of the cocaine coming into the United States now flowed through Mexico and across the U.S.-Mexican border rather than through the traditional routes across the Caribbean.[23]

Official Washington's enthusiasm notwithstanding, claims of success for these early military interdiction operations in the Caribbean must be tempered by the fact that they did not permanently disrupt, much less halt, drug smuggling into the United States; they merely shifted trafficking methods and routes. In practice, new routes through Central America and Mexico were soon established, and neither availability nor prices were seriously affected.

Even if merely shifting the traffic away from the Caribbean into Central America and Mexico can be viewed as a success, some operations were patently less effective than others. Operation Autumn Harvest, for example, did not produce any seizures or arrests. Only six of thirty-three targets were successfully intercepted, and none was smuggling drugs. Reagan administration officials attributed this lack of results to premature newspaper publicity, limited coordination between the national guard and Customs, and inadequate radar capability. Nonetheless, they stressed that the operation resembled a realistic war-time scenario and provided valuable training to national guard personnel (at an estimated cost of $900,000).[24]

Despite serious questions about the long-term effectiveness of U.S. interdiction efforts—civilian and military—in the Caribbean, in mid-1986 President Reagan ordered the U.S. military to participate in Operation Blast Furnace in Bolivia in response to President Victor Paz Estensorro's appeal for U.S. assistance in halting the production, processing, and trafficking of cocaine. Paz's request was motivated largely by Washington's threat to cut off U.S. aid because of Bolivia's failure to carry out credible coca eradication and crop substitution programs. It also reflected his fears that the country's powerful drug smugglers posed a growing threat to state authority and control.[25]

On July 14, 1986, six U.S. Army Blackhawk helicopters with their associated flight crews and logistical support personnel (150 U.S. troops) arrived in Bolivia. Their four-month mission involved provision of air transportation and communications support to Bolivian police forces and DEA agents assigned to locate and destroy cocaine laboratories. U.S. Army pilots transported Bolivian Rural Mobile Patrol Units (UMOPAR) and U.S. DEA personnel to preselected sites and remained with the helicopters while the UMOPAR-DEA teams secured the area, arrested the traffickers, and destroyed the facilities.

The Bolivian government plan targeted laboratories rather than coca growers and their fields in hopes that such a strategy would disrupt the drug trade and thus meet U.S. demands for compliance without alienating the hundreds of thousands of peasants dependent on coca farming for their livelihood. The idea was that a disruption of cocaine processing would decrease the illicit demand for coca leaf, push prices down below the costs of production, and thus make Bolivia's coca growers more amenable to state-sponsored crop substitution programs.[26]

In practice, Operation Blast Furnace proved only partially and temporarily successful. Coca leaf prices did fall below the farmers' break-even point and remained at record lows for the duration of the exercise, thereby heightening peasant interest in crop substitution programs largely financed by the U.S. Agency for International Development (USAID). Despite the decline in leaf prices and the parallel decline in cocaine refining in Bolivia during Operation Blast Furnace, however, there was no discernible impact on the availability of cocaine in the United States, and coca leaf prices rapidly rebounded to pre–Blast Furnace levels after U.S. forces withdrew in November 1986.

Moreover, even the short-term "success" of the operation was offset by the heavy political costs it imposed on the Paz government. Mass protests against U.S. troop presence in Bolivia occurred in rural zones such as the Chapare and the Beni and in urban centers throughout the country. President Paz Estensorro was vilified by his domestic critics for authorizing U.S. intervention and barely escaped impeachment proceedings in the Bolivian congress. Although he ultimately weathered these political storms, his administration was virtually paralyzed by intense political opposition during the first month of the operation and continued to confront harsh nationalist criticism long after U.S. forces had left. In light of the severe political fallout, the U.S. military's direct involvement in Bolivia's Operation Blast Furnace was unquestionably a diplomatic failure, independent of its short-term disruptive effect on the country's coca industry.

In the wake of Operation Blast Furnace, the U.S. military continued to assist Bolivia's UMOPAR, albeit with a much lower profile. The State Department's Bureau of International Narcotics Matters (INM) followed up by leasing six UH-1H "Huey" helicopters from DOD and providing them to the Bolivian government to allow UMOPAR to continue its interdiction activities. INM also paid for the maintenance of these aircraft while the U.S. military trained Bolivian Air Force pilots to fly them. The UMOPAR police received additional training from U.S. Army Special Forces (Mobile Training Teams) in a series of five-week courses on small-unit tactics, map reading, jungle survival, and communications. Furthermore, U.S. Special Forces medics and communications personnel continued to accompany UMOPAR on interdiction operations.[27]

By lowering its profile, in late 1986 and beyond the U.S. military was able to defuse the public outcry against U.S. antidrug assistance programs in Bolivia while continuing to support Bolivian drug enforcement efforts. Perhaps the key lesson to be gleaned from this experience is that high-profile U.S. military involvement in drug interdiction in Latin America is controversial, unsustainable, and politically counterproductive. Indirect forms of assistance that provoke less anti-U.S. hostility and facilitate long-term cooperation are more effective and appropriate.[28]

From Reagan to Bush: Militarizing the War on Drugs

In late October 1988, frustrated by and on the political defensive because of the lack of tangible progress in curbing drug production, trafficking, consumption, and related violence in the United States—and once again faced with intense U.S. public pressure to "do something" about the nation's drug problem in advance of the November 1988 presidential and congressional elections—the U.S. Congress enacted the Omnibus Anti-Drug Abuse Act of 1988. Although retaining the long-standing emphasis on supply-side strategies and interdiction typical of previous U.S. drug policies, this law also incorporated a new focus on demand and called for increasing allocations of federal antidrug budgets for domestic demand-control programs over the next several years.[29]

This shift was not merely cosmetic nor simply a function of election-year politics: It revealed growing disillusionment in Congress with the ineffectiveness of the supply-control–interdiction tactics pursued during the Reagan administration. In effect, the shift was driven by failure. The heightened priority assigned to demand-side measures in the 1988 law suggested that a conceptual transition away from supply-side policies was under way in Washington as President Bush began his term in office. The transition, however, was at best partial and incomplete. The new legislation did not abandon supply-side programs but rather increased federal funding for them while simultaneously opening a "second front" directed at demand reduction in the United States.[30]

George Bush consistently reaffirmed his commitment to further escalation of the war on drugs—from his inaugural promise that "this scourge will end" through his September 1989 presentation of a new National Drug Strategy (prepared by "drug czar" William Bennett) to his authorization of a U.S. invasion of Panama in December 1989. In keeping with this commitment, during 1989–1990 his administration sponsored a steady expansion of the U.S. military's role (along U.S. borders and overseas) and intensified U.S. pressures on other governments in the hemisphere to assign a greater role to their own armed forces in combating drug trafficking.[31]

Putting an end to rear-guard Pentagon resistance to expanded U.S. military involvement, in mid-September 1989 Secretary of Defense Richard Cheney declared that "detecting and countering the production and trafficking of illegal drugs is a high-priority, national security mission" for the Pentagon.[32] Presaging Bush's heightened emphasis on greater military involvement in drug control efforts, in October 1988 Congress passed the 1989 National Defense Authorization Act—which ordered DOD to serve as the "single" lead agency of the U.S. government in the detection and monitoring of aerial and maritime transit of illegal drugs into the United States and to assume responsibility for integrating federal command, control, communications, and technical intelligence assets involved in drug interdiction into an effective communications network. The same act also approved and funded various state plans for expanded use of National Guard personnel in support of federal drug interdiction and enforcement activities at U.S. borders.[33]

In FY 1989, funding for DOD's antidrug activities reached $450 million. The bulk of these resources (70 percent) was earmarked for support of civilian law enforcement in the United States, especially in the areas of equipment lending and intelligence-gathering. At the same time, however, the military's budget for international narcotics control assistance also grew substantially. The Bush administration's inclination to expand the role of the U.S. military in the war on drugs in Latin America became clear during Bush's first year in office. Most dramatic was his December 1989 decision to authorize U.S. military intervention in Panama to oust accused drug trafficker and money launderer General Manuel Noriega. Less draconian but equally revealing were Washington's deployment of U.S. ships off the Colombian coast without Bogotá's prior permission, its construction of Vietnam-style fire bases for DEA operations in Peru's Upper Huallaga Valley, Bennett's often-repeated statements that U.S. Special Forces might be sent to the Andean countries, the use of intelligence satellites over Mexican territory without informing the Mexican government, and U.S. support for the creation of a multinational drug "strike force" despite almost unanimous rejection by Latin American leaders.[34]

U.S. emphasis on greater Latin American military involvement in drug control efforts was also unmistakably in evidence in the Bush government's highly publicized Andean Strategy, announced in September 1989. The first phase of this initiative—the $65 million emergency U.S. aid package sent to Colombia in late September to support President Virgilio Barco's "total" war against the Medellín cartel—primarily contained conventional military arms, even though the Barco administration had requested police equipment, electronic intelligence-gathering devices, and technical assistance for Colombia's hard-hit judicial system. The second phase—the Bush administration's FY 1990 request for $261 million in antidrug assistance programs for Peru, Colombia, and Bolivia—which funded military and police activities almost exclusively despite the Andean governments' appeals for economic development aid and trade incentives, reaffirmed Washington's emphasis on enhanced military involvement in the war on drugs in the region.[35]

Militarization and U.S.–Latin American Drug Diplomacy

To defuse the widespread (albeit short-lived) condemnations of the U.S. direct intervention in Panama throughout the region and the Andean leaders' vehement complaints regarding the lack of trade and aid components in Washington's Andean Strategy, in early 1990 U.S. spokespersons underscored U.S. interest in promoting hemispheric cooperation on drug issues. To dramatize this commitment to multi-nationalism, President Bush reaffirmed his determination to attend an Andean Summit at Cartagena, Colombia, in February 1990 despite the potential security risks and despite Peruvian President Alan García's strident declarations that he would boycott the meeting to protest the U.S. "occupation" of Panama.[36]

To persuade García to reconsider his decision, Bush announced in mid-January that U.S. troops would begin a phased withdrawal from Panama prior to the summit. To soften region-wide criticism of the Andean Strategy's overemphasis on repressive military tactics to halt cocaine trafficking, Bush highlighted his administration's intention to request $2.2 billion in development funds for the Andean countries for the 1991–1995 period to assist their transition away from coca cultivation. Finally, to ensure a joint summit statement acceptable to all the Andean presidents, U.S.

negotiators met repeatedly with their Andean counterparts in advance of the meeting to hammer out a compromise document; the final version significantly watered down the original U.S. emphasis on the importance of increasing the role of the Andean militaries in the war on drugs and accepted Andean demands for additional provisions, emphasizing the need to reduce consumption in the United States.

At the summit President Bush did not publicly press the Andean leaders on the sensitive issues of greater foreign and domestic military involvement in their nation's antidrug campaigns. Moreover, he explicitly recognized that continuing U.S. demand was a key factor in the hemispheric drug trade. In short, President Bush went to considerable lengths before and during the Andean Summit to reassure the Andean leaders that Washington sought cooperation, not conflict; that it recognized the socioeconomic and political costs and consequences of their antidrug efforts; and that his administration was prepared to provide not only police and military assistance but also development aid to help ameliorate the disruptive effects of suppressing the drug trade.[37]

Within weeks after this widely publicized presidential summit, however, the cordiality and cooperative spirit in evidence at this symbolically important meeting began to fade. Colombian authorities were deeply offended by the U.S. Navy's March 1990 seizure of two Colombian freighters within the country's two-hundred-mile maritime limit without prior approval from Bogotá. They also resented President Bush's failure to make good on his promise to help restore the International Coffee Agreement and his administration's decision to apply additional countervailing duties on Colombian cut flower exports to the United States during the final months of Barco's presidency (February-August 1990). In an unofficial visit to Washington in July 1990, just a few weeks prior to his August 7 inauguration, President-elect César Gaviria Trujillo emphatically reiterated that Colombia sought expanded trade with the United States rather than increased antidrug aid. He also specifically rejected U.S. emphasis on a broader role for the Colombian military in his country's antidrug campaign. Instead, he highlighted the importance of additional international assistance to reform and strengthen Colombia's weakened judicial system. After taking office, Gaviria reaffirmed Bogotá's resolve to continue fighting drug trafficking but underscored that his government's highest priority was to end domestic narco-terrorism rather than to combat international drug smuggling.[38]

Reflecting his administration's strategic priorities, in mid-August Gaviria announced that his government would not extradite Colombian drug traffickers if they abandoned their terrorist tactics and submitted to criminal trials in Colombia. He also called on the United States to do more to lower domestic drug consumption, to stop U.S.-based money laundering activities, and to curtail arms and chemical precursor chemicals used by Colombia's drug cartel that originated in the United States. Gaviria's underlying—but unmistakable—message was that although his administration would not abandon its commitments in the hemispheric war against drug trafficking, he did not intend to sacrifice Colombia's social and political stability in a quixotic attempt to prosecute the war unilaterally. Other nations would have to do their fair share to achieve any progress against the international traders.

Responding to demands from Bogotá and other Latin American governments for expanded trade opportunities, President Bush unveiled his administration's Enterprise for the Americas initiative in June 1990. This initiative proposed the establishment of free trade agreements with Latin American countries or associated groups of countries interested in trade liberalization. It also included provisions under which the U.S. Treasury would forgive up to $7 billion of official Latin American foreign debt owed to the U.S. government. In September 1990, Bush formally requested legislative authority from the U.S. Congress for a free trade pact with the Andean nations. President Gaviria in particular lauded the Bush "initiative" effusively but also noted that U.S. congressional delay or dilution of the White House's Andean trade initiative (in response to domestic protectionist lobbies) could seriously undercut future U.S.-Colombian cooperation in the war on drugs specifically and U.S.–Latin American relations generally.[39]

Because their economies were much weaker than Colombia's and were more dependent on foreign exchange derived from the cocaine trade, the Bolivian and Peruvian governments placed far more emphasis on increased U.S. aid to combat coca cultivation and trafficking than did Bogotá. By September 1990, both President Jaime Paz Zamora of Bolivia and President Alberto Fujimori of Peru had nonetheless declared that their governments remained reluctant to accept the FY 1990 assistance offered by Washington in the Andean Strategy because of the plan's excessive emphasis on military strategies and tactics and the absence of funds for socioeconomic development.[40]

Bolivia's President Paz explicitly denounced Washington's insistence on tying U.S. aid to La Paz's acceptance of an expanded role for Bolivia's armed forces in the nation's antidrug campaign. Nationalist resentments of U.S. "interference" in Bolivian affairs certainly influenced his decision. More fundamental, however, were his fears that acquiescence might undermine civilian control over the military, increase levels of state repression and social violence in the Bolivian countryside, and thus pave the way for a future military coup against his democratically elected government. As an alternative, he called on the U.S. government to help underwrite Bolivia's crop substitution–rural development initiatives, thereby providing Bolivian coca farmers with viable economic alternatives, and to support his efforts to reform and strengthen civilian law enforcement in Bolivia. In the end, however, he agreed to accept U.S. conditionality.[41]

Fujimori's rejection of U.S. antidrug aid to Peru was driven by a similar calculus. In contrast to his Bolivian counterpart, from the outset Peru's newly inaugurated president confronted a serious challenge to state authority and control from a formidable rebel force—the Maoist-oriented Sendero Luminoso guerrillas—which had extensive ties to Peru's coca-growing peasantry in the Upper Huallaga and other rural areas. From his perspective, Washington's emphasis on broadening the role of the Peruvian armed forces in the nation's antidrug campaign, given the absence of resources to offer real alternatives to coca-dependent farmers, would inevitably drive Peru's rural poor into the ranks of Sendero and further inflame rural violence and rebellion. This would also undermine the legitimacy of his government and the stability of Peru's fragile democratic regime.[42]

The Politics of Militarization

By late 1990 the Bush administration's Andean Strategy, the cornerstone of its regional narcotics control policies, was clearly in disarray. Why was Washington so emphatic about the militarization of the war on drugs in the face of Andean resistance? Pentagon officials hotly denied that DOD was intent on militarizing the war on drugs in the Andean region or elsewhere in Latin America and the Caribbean. The public record lends credence to their denials. First, DOD leaders— both civilian and military—repeatedly testified in 1989–1990 that enhanced military interdiction and enforcement operations could not be expected to stop U.S.–Latin American drug trafficking completely. At best, they claimed, expanded interdiction efforts could only "buy time" for U.S. authorities to undertake more effective demand-reduction programs. Second, they underscored that the bulk of U.S. military antidrug funds was spent on improving intelligence-gathering activities and assisting U.S. law enforcement at U.S. borders, not abroad. Finally, they noted that the U.S. military's principal role in U.S. international narcotics control efforts in Latin America and the Caribbean involved provision of equipment and training to local law enforcement personnel rather than to military forces: U.S. troops did not generally participate in field operations, except in support roles (for example, pilots, communications, surveillance).[43]

Reinforcing the Pentagon's claims that the U.S. armed forces were not militarizing the war on drugs in Latin America, in-depth, off-the-record personal interviews with senior U.S. military officers in 1990 revealed widespread doubts and skepticism regarding the real effectiveness of U.S. (and Latin American) military involvement in drug interdiction and enforcement. A major cause of concern was the lack of clarity surrounding the mission assigned to the U.S. armed forces: What would constitute "victory" in this sort of war? A closely related concern involved how the effectiveness of U.S. military participation was to be measured—especially when the institution's impact ultimately depended on the performance of civilian law enforcement agencies, both domestic and foreign.[44]

In view of the ill-defined parameters of the mission and the lack of precise standards of evaluation, many officers worried that the U.S. military could become a scapegoat for civilian politicians seeking to blame the armed forces for failing to end the U.S. drug "scourge" and in the process to exonerate themselves before an angry and frustrated U.S. public. Some speculated that such political scapegoating might contribute to an overall decline in public support and congressional funding for the U.S. military. Even if the DOD budget were not cut, many expressed profound concern over the possibility that overall military readiness might be affected adversely—especially in the context of declining East-West tensions, serious U.S. fiscal deficits, and the massive U.S. deployment to the Gulf.

DOD's budgetary and institutional-political reluctance to militarize the war on drugs also reflected senior officers' awareness of the limitations and weaknesses of Latin American militaries. They were referring primarily to institutional vulnerability to drug-related corruption and to the dangers of military usurpation of civilian authority and democratic processes.

U.S. military leaders frequently attributed the "distorted" image of their current role in the war on drugs in Latin America to inaccurate and sensationalist media coverage—often magnified by leftist propaganda, exaggerated nationalist sensitivities, and unfounded speculation sparked by leaks of unofficial military contingency plans. The July 1990 revelations by *Newsweek* of General Maxwell Thurman's (Southern Command) proposal for U.S.-supported simultaneous military raids on drug-trafficker targets throughout the Andean region were commonly cited as an example of such distortions. Although only unofficial recommendations, Thurman's plans were reported in both the U.S. and Latin American press as if they were official statements of DOD strategy in the region. In fact, Thurman's notorious proposals had been drawn up by civilian consultants after he had purged all military regional experts from the Southern Command staff in Panama and were never endorsed as official DOD policy.[45]

Although Pentagon denials that it was not militarizing U.S. drug programs in Latin America are convincing overall, General Thurman's advocacy of U.S.-backed military raids in the Andes indicated that there were high-ranking officers within the U.S. armed forces who favored such tactics. Because careers of the growing number of middle-level officers assigned to drug interdiction activities inevitably depend on their efficiency in carrying out drug-related tasks, it is not unreasonable to anticipate that additional pressures for wider use of U.S. military forces in Latin America and the Caribbean could emerge from the Pentagon bureaucracy in the early 1990s.[46]

Even if such considerations are discounted, however, DOD protests that the U.S. military is not engaged in militarizing the U.S. war on drugs in the hemisphere basically overlook the central point. In the Andean region, the Bush administration's antidrug assistance in 1989–1990 was conditioned on expanded local military involvement in drug control efforts. Given this reality, it mattered little to the Andean governments that U.S. drug enforcement agents active in the region were civilians—DEA, State Department, CIA, or contractees—supported by the U.S. military rather than uniformed U.S. forces. The point is that U.S. strategy and tactics emphasize repressive action over economic development, civilian institution-building, and multilateral cooperation.

In fact, during the first two years of the Bush administration, the impetus toward increased militarization came mostly from civilian politicians in Congress and executive branch appointees, not from DOD or the Joint Chiefs of Staff. Frustrated with the ineffectiveness of existing programs at home and overseas and sensitive to electoral pressures to do more, both the Bush administration and the U.S. Congress proved increasingly disposed to endorse the strategies and tactics of militarization, even if the U.S. military did not fully back such an approach.[47]

Alternatives to Militarization

The key to an effective international drug control program in the Andes and throughout the hemisphere is to find ways to support and strengthen governmental-institutional capabilities to maintain public order, administer justice, and meet the basic needs of their citizenries. The virtually complete collapse of Colombia's judicial system in the 1980s is the most dramatic but by no means the only manifestation of regional institutional deficiencies. Colombia, like its Andean neighbors and most other Latin American and Caribbean countries, needs sustained foreign assistance to rebuild and extend state authority and control throughout its national territory. This will be a delicate, difficult, and long-term enterprise. The U.S. government, the U.S. people, and other international donors should entertain no illusions that it can be achieved quickly, easily, or cheaply.

Equipping and training Latin American and Caribbean militaries is an important dimension of any comprehensive institution-building effort, but it should not be the first or only priority. As in the United States, drug enforcement is primarily a civilian rather than a military function. The police and the courts, not the military, must assume the lead roles in law enforcement programs generally and in drug enforcement in particular; otherwise, civilian and democratic regimes may not survive in some countries in the hemisphere.[48]

Efforts to bolster the capacity of the states in the region to penetrate remote, conflict-ridden rural areas beset by drug traffic, to rein in paramilitary and guerrilla violence, and to deliver essential government services must be strengthened along with law enforcement if antidrug efforts are to be effective over the long run. Most governments in the region are convinced of the need for such initiatives. The U.S. government could and should provide support for comprehensive development programs as part of its overall antidrug strategy. The United States clearly will not be able to foot the entire bill for the Andean countries, much less for the entire hemisphere, but it could and should contribute significantly to such efforts and encourage other developed nations to do so as well.

Although Washington's leadership and resources are indispensable to effective hemispheric drug control efforts, primarily bilateral initiatives and programs are inherently inadequate for several reasons:

1. They run the risk of fueling nationalist resentment and raise fears of U.S. political domination.
2. They are circumscribed by the limited availability of U.S. aid funds.

3. They preempt the participation of extra hemispheric powers (such as Western Europe) that are also affected by drug trafficking and that have resources and expertise to contribute.
4. U.S. projects and personnel constitute prime targets for narco-terrorists and leftist revolutionaries.[49]

Without downplaying the coordination problems that confront multilateral coop-eration, in the long run U.S. resources will be more effective if channeled through inter-American and international organizations. The United Nations Development Programme, for example, is already actively involved in the design and implemen-tation of regional development plans in the areas of crop eradication, crop substitu-tion, and rural development. Interpol is a potentially useful channel for regional police training. The Italian and British governments, among others, have consider-able expertise in combating terrorist violence against the judiciary. The Organization of American States could serve as a clearinghouse and training center for drug education, prevention, treatment, and rehabilitation programs; for judicial reform; and for information-sharing. The Inter-American Development Bank and the World Bank could be used as key channels for rural development programs in source countries.

Channeling U.S. aid primarily through U.S. agencies—such as USAID, the DEA, or the U.S. military—implies costly bureaucratic expansion, duplication, coordination problems, and high-risk exposure of U.S. personnel to terrorist reprisals. Ever since the Alliance for Progress was launched in the early 1960s, U.S. government programs in Latin America have not proved particularly cost-effective in promoting permanent national or regional institutional capabilities. U.S. leadership in launching and coordinating international aid for the Andean countries is critical, but purely bilateral or subregional initiatives and programs should give way to multilateral efforts that could maximize resource use, distribute international assis-tance responsibilities more equitably, and promote better coordination and fuller hemispheric and extrahemispheric cooperation in the war on international drug trafficking.

The Bush administration's September 1989 proposal to step up U.S. police and military assistance to the Andean source and trafficking countries represented a halting first step toward improving regional narcotics control assistance programs. The absence of economic development aid at the outset, however, was shortsighted. Police and military programs for the Andean republics must be complemented with substantial U.S. assistance and trade incentives.[50]

Disbursement of U.S. assistance should be contingent on periodic evaluations of foreign country–government cooperation and performance. Although U.S. monitor-ing is essential, regional and international evaluations should be encouraged as well. In place of negative sanctions, such as the U.S. Congress's flawed and controversial decertification ritual, a system of positive inducements should be developed in which continued disbursements and future increments would be contingent on fulfillment of multilaterally established evaluative criteria. The U.S. government, in tandem with other hemispheric and extrahemispheric governments involved in the multilateral campaign, should be involved in specifying project objectives and monitoring progress. It thus could maintain control over U.S. aid and ensure accountability while defusing the issue of U.S. unilateralism.[51]

Substantial increases in U.S. economic assistance for international drug control programs, especially in the Andean and the Caribbean Basin countries, are arguably the sine qua non of any serious drug control effort in the hemisphere. In economic areas such funds should target transportation, basic infrastructure, rural development, job training, and export promotion programs (not just eradication and crop substitution). To be sure, poverty and lack of viable economic alternatives are not the only reasons millions of Andean peasants grow coca (many coca growers are not poor peasants); but unless governments in the region can offer realistic options, there will be continued incentives to cultivate illicit crops.

Governments must also stress the modernization of law enforcement and judicial systems, regulation of chemical exports and money laundering operations, enhanced intelligence-gathering, and multilateral law enforcement coordination. Less often contemplated but no less important, U.S. trade policies toward the Andean countries should be modified to encourage or at least not actively discourage their exports to U.S. markets and thus their ability to finance antidrug programs and offer real economic alternatives to coca growers. The Bush administration's proposed legislation to authorize a new U.S.–Andean Free Trade Pact proposed under the Enterprise for the Americas initiative, if passed by Congress, will eliminate many current U.S. protectionist barriers—especially against Andean agricultural exports such as cut flowers, sugar, vegetables, and fruits.[52]

Conclusion

The Bush administration must move beyond symbolism to serious and sustained cooperation with the Andean and other source and trafficking countries in Latin America. Excessive emphasis on military and police repression will not work and poses multiple risks to civilian leadership, human rights, and democracy in the Andes and elsewhere in the hemisphere. Institution-building, multilateral coordination, and economic development must all be incorporated into a comprehensive response to the regional drug trade.

Equally if not more important, unless the United States addresses the demand side of the equation—thereby reducing the profitability of drug trafficking—supply-side efforts in Latin America and the Caribbean may ultimately prove fruitless. Although an in-depth discussion of demand-reduction policies is beyond the scope of this chapter, the major strategies now being discussed in Washington fall into two basic categories: (1) prevention, education, treatment, and rehabilitation programs; and (2) intensified law enforcement efforts directed against both dealers and users.[53]

In the FY 1990 budget, Bush proposed just under $8 billion for drug programs: 70 percent for enforcement and 30 percent for education and treatment. The Democrat-controlled Senate added over $1 billion to Bush's proposal and assigned more resources to education, treatment, and local law enforcement. Demand reduction in the United States will be a long and expensive effort that could take years and cost billions of dollars. Without such efforts, however, the scourge of drug abuse and trafficking in the hemisphere and in other Western countries will surely continue to spread. As the Bush administration and the U.S. Congress maneuver to respond to short-term hysteria about drugs and demands for tougher measures in the United States, there is a serious danger that U.S. policy could get sidetracked into a one-dimensional military and police-oriented response—both at home and abroad—that would not only be ineffective but that could become counterproductive and destabilizing for democratic governments in the region, including the United States.[54]

The real challenge for U.S. policymakers in the area of international narcotics control is to fashion a balanced long-term strategy that addresses both the demand and supply sides of the equation. No other response offers anything but temporary relief. To "win" the war against drugs will require permanent changes in both U.S. and Latin American societies that cannot be achieved quickly or cheaply and certainly not by law enforcement and military tactics alone. The United States and other Western nations could best help Latin American and Caribbean countries plagued with drug trafficking by providing the resources needed to fund demand-reduction programs at home and by backing international economic assistance programs, multilateral cooperation, and institution-building efforts throughout the region.

Notes

1. Donald J. Mabry, "Narcotics and National Security," in Donald J. Mabry, ed., *The Latin American Narcotics Trade and U.S. National Security* (New York: Greenwood Press, 1989), 3–10; and in the same volume, Bruce Michael Bagley, "The New Hundred Years War? U.S. National Security and the War on Drugs in Latin America," 43–58.

2. The empirical basis for this position was provided by a report contracted by DOD from the RAND Corporation. See Peter Reuter, Gordon Crawford, and Jonathan Cave, *Sealing the Borders: The Effects of Increased Military Participation in Drug Interdiction* (Santa Monica, Calif.: RAND Corporation, 1988).

3. See Caspar W. Weinberger, "Our Troops Shouldn't Be Drug Cops," *Washington Post*, May 22, 1987, C2. See also George C. Wilson and M. Moore, "Pentagon Warns of No-Win Mission," *Washington Post*, May 13, 1988, A4; and Michael H. Abbott, "The Army and the Drug War: Politics or National Security," *Parameters* (December 1988): 95–112.

4. Weinberger, "Our Troops," C2; Donald Mabry, "The U.S. Military and the War on Drugs in Latin America," *Journal of Interamerican Studies and World Affairs* 30, nos. 2–3 (Summer-Fall 1988): 53–76.

5. Lt. General Stephen Olmstead, USMC, Deputy Assistant Secretary of Defense for Drug Policy and Enforcement, "Statement," in Congressional Research Service, *Narcotics Interdiction and the Use of the Military: Issues for Congress* (Washington, D.C.: U.S. Government Printing Office, 1988), 15.

6. For the ACLU perspective, see Loren Siegel, "The War on Drugs," *Civil Liberties* (Spring-Summer 1988): 4–5. Civil liberties and democracy are also core concerns of M. J. Blackman and K. E. Sharpe, "Stopping U.S. Military Intervention—in the U.S.," *Boston Globe*, September 18, 1990; Ethan A. Nadelmann, "U.S. Drug Policy: A Bad Export," *Foreign Policy* 70 (Spring 1988), 108; and Juan G. Tokatlián, "National Security and Drugs: Their Impact on Colombian-U.S. Relations," *Journal of Interamerican Studies and World Affairs* 30, no. 1 (1988): 133–160.

7. Paul J. Rice, "New Laws and Insights Encircle the Posse Comitatus Act," *Military Law Review* 104 (Spring 1984): 109–138; Major Aleksandra M. Rohde, "Pushing the Limits of Posse Comitatus," *National Guard* (August 1989): 30–34.

8. Rohde, "Pushing the Limits," 31–34.

9. U.S. Congress, Senate Committee on Appropriations, *Department of Defense Support for Drug Interdiction*, Hearing, 99th Congress, 2nd Session (Washington, D.C.: U.S. Government Printing Office, 1985).

10. Keith B. Richburg, "Reagan Order Defines Drug Trade as Security Threat, Widens Military Role," *Washington Post*, June 8, 1986, A28; Julie Rovner, "Reagan, Senate Republicans Join Drug War," *Congressional Quarterly Weekly Report* 44 (September 20, 1986): 2,191–2,197.

11. Rovner, "Reagan," 2,192–2,195.

12. General Accounting Office, *Drug Control: Issues Surrounding Increased Use of the Military in Drug Interdiction*, GAO/NSIAD-88-156 (Washington, D.C.: U.S. Government Printing Office, April 1988), 29–30.

13. GAO, *Drug Control*, 23–25.

14. GAO, *Drug Control*, 28–29.

15. David Morrison, "The Pentagon's War on Drugs," *National Journal* (September 6, 1986): 2,109; GAO, *Drug Law Enforcement: Military Assistance for Anti-Drug Agencies* (Washington, D.C.: U.S. Government Printing Office, 1987).

16. GAO, *Drug Control*, 25, 29; Admiral Paul A. Yost, "Coast Guard Has a Key Role in Major Elements of National Security," *ROA National Security Report* 6, no. 8 (August 1988): 3; U.S. Congress, House Committee on Merchant Marine and Fisheries, Subcommittee on Coast Guard and Navigation, *Coast Guard Drug Activities*, Hearing, 100th Congress, 2nd Session (Washington, D.C.: U.S. Government Printing Office, 1988).

17. GAO, *Drug Control*, 26–27.

18. GAO, *Drug Control*, 17.

19. GAO, *Drug Control*, 17–18; and Reuter et al., *Sealing the Borders*.

20. E. Sciolino and S. Endelberg, "Narcotics Efforts Failed by U.S. Security Goals," *New York Times*, April 10, 1988, A1, A14; Richard L. Barke, "Foreign Policy Said to Hinder Drug War," *New York Times*, April 14, 1989, A5.

21. GAO, *Drug Control*, 28.

22. U.S. Congress, House of Representatives, Committee on Government Operations, *Initiatives in Drug Interdiction (Parts 1 and 2)*, Hearings, 99th Congress, 1st and 2nd Sessions (Washington, D.C.: U.S. Government Printing Office, 1986).

23. David Westrate, U.S. Congress House Committee on Foreign Affairs, "Review of the International Narcotics Control Strategy Report," Hearing, 100th Congress, 1st Session (Washington, D.C.: U.S. Government Printing Office, October 7, 1987), 41.

24. GAO, *Drug Control*, 50–52.

25. GAO, *Drug Control: U.S. Supported Efforts in Colombia and Bolivia*, GAO/ NSIAD-89-24 (Washington, D.C.: U.S. Government Printing Office, November 1988), 48–51; also Eduardo Gamarra, "Drugs, Politics, and Foreign Policy in Bolivia," paper prepared for the International Conference on Money Laundering, University of Miami, Coral Gables, Florida, October 27–29, 1989.

26. GAO, *Drug Control: U.S. Supported Efforts*, 52; and Raphael N. Perl, *Policy Alert: Narcotics Control and the Use of U.S. Military Personnel: Operations in Bolivia and Issues for Congress* (Washington, D.C.: Congressional Research Service, 1986).

27. GAO, *Drug Control: U.S. Supported Effort*, 53–57.

28. Dennis J. Dugan, "Operation Blast Furnace: Attacking the Source," seminar paper, University of Miami, Coral Gables, Florida, December 5, 1989, 34.

29. See Charles Doyle et al., *Anti-Drug Abuse Act of 1988 (HR5210, 100th Congress): Highlights of Enacted Bill* (Washington, D.C.: Congressional Research Service, Library of Congress, November 16, 1988).

30. Despite authorizing additional resources for demand-side programs, in FY 1989 Congress did not fully fund these new initiatives.

31. For the text of President George Bush's speech, see "Address to the Nation on the National Drug Control Strategy," September 5, 1989, in *Public Papers of the Presidents: George Bush*, vol. 2 (Washington, D.C.: U.S. Government Printing Office, 1989), 1,136–1,140. On the Bush administration's emphasis on an increased role for the military in antinarcotics efforts both at home and in Latin America, see Bernard Trainor, "Military's Widening Role in the Anti-Drug Effort," *New York Times*, August 27, 1989, A24; Peter Grier, "Pentagon's Support Role Increases," *Christian Science Monitor*, September 1, 1989, 8; and Coletta Youngers, "The War in the Andes: The Military Role in U.S. International Drug Policy," paper prepared for conference, Violence and Democracy in Colombia and Peru, Columbia University, New York, November–December 1990.

32. Dick Cheney, "DOD and Its Role in the War Against Drugs," *Defense* (November–December 1989): 2–7; Andrés Oppenheimer, "Military to Boost Drug-Fighting Role, New Chief Says," *Miami Herald*, October 1, 1989.

33. Raphael F. Perl, *Congress and International Narcotics Control* (Washington, D.C.: Congressional Research Service, September 13, 1989), 13–14; Jerry Thomas, "DEA Enlists Guard Units in Drug War," *Boston Globe*, July 28, 1989, 13; Captain Jean Marie Brawders, "Guard Expands Role in Drug War," *National Guard* (August 1989): 30.

34. Ethan Bronner, "U.S. Aide Talks of Troop Help for Colombia," *Baltimore Sun*, August 21, 1989, 1; Jay Mallin, "Bennett: Drug War Will Test Congress," *Washington Times*, August 14, 1989, 3; Ron Howell, "Anti-Drug Military Force Urged," *Long Island Newsday*, August 19, 1989, 7; Richard L. Berke, "Bennett Calls Use of Army Possible," *New York Times*, September 9, 1989, A5.

35. U.S. Congress, House Committee on Armed Services, *The Andean Drug Strategy and the Role of the U.S. Military*, 101st Congress, 1st Session (Washington, D.C.: U.S. Government Printing Office, January 1990); Washington Office on Latin America, *Andean Initiative: Legislative Update* (Washington, D.C.: WOLA, December 1990).

36. Associated Press, "Latin Allies Prefer U.S. Money to Military in Drug-Fight Role," *Miami Herald*, January 17, 1990, 10A; and Juan G. Tokatlián, "¿Será un fiasco la cumbre?" *Semana* (February 6–13, 1990).

37. Andrés Oppenheimer, "U.S., Andean Nations Form 'Anti-Drug Cartel'—U.S. Offers Resources to Battle Trafficking," *Miami Herald*, February 16, 1990, 14.

38. Andrés Oppenheimer, "The Colombian Takes Office, Demands U.S. Help," *Miami Herald*, August 8, 1990, 9A; also Bruce Michael Bagley and Juan Gabriel Tokatlián, "Colombia's Drug Dilemma," *Hemisfile* 1, no. 3 (April 1990): 4.

39. Andrés Oppenheimer, "Trading Blocs," *Miami Herald*, October 7, 1990, 36; Dory Owens, "Latin Observers Temper Their Hopes," *Miami Herald*, June 28, 1990, 18A.

40. Christopher Marquis, "Coca-Growing Nations Shun U.S. Military Aid," *Miami Herald*, August 11, 1990, 12A.

41. Pedro Sevcec and Iván Román, "Reacciones a condiciones impuestas a Bolivia," *El Nuevo Heraldo*, July 11, 1990, 4A; Melvin Burke, "Bolivia: The Politics of Cocaine," *Current History* 90, no. 553 (February 1991): 65–68, 90.

42. Michael Isikoff, "Talks Between U.S., Peru on Military Aid Collapse," *Washington Post*, September 26, 1990, 29A; David P. Werlich, "Fujimori and the Disaster in Peru," *Current History* 90, no. 553 (February 1991): 61–64, 81–83.

43. Stephen M. Duncan, "Prepared Statement of the Assistant Secretary of Defense for Reserve Affairs, DOD Coordinator for Drug Enforcement Policy and Support," U.S. Government Anti-Narcotics Activities in the Andean Region of South America, Hearing Before the Permanent Subcommittee on Investigations, Senate Committee on Governmental Affairs (September 29, 1989): 17. See also Rowan Scarborough, "Pentagon Memo Opposes Military's Role in Drug War," *Washington Times*, August 24, 1989, 3; Committee on Armed Services, U.S. House of Representatives, *The Andean Strategy and the Role of the U.S. Military*, 100th Congress, 1st Session (Washington, D.C.: U.S. Government Printing Office, 1990).

44. Interviews conducted by the author of an off-the-record basis during 1990 at the Pentagon, the Naval Post Graduate School (Monterey, California), the Center for Naval Analysis (Arlington, Virginia), and the National Defense University (Washington, D.C.).

45. Douglas Waller with Mark Miller and John Barry in Washington, Spencer Reiss in Miami, and Bureau Reports, "Risky Business," *Newsweek* (July 16, 1990): 16–19; personal interviews, 1990.

46. Personal interviews, 1990; Douglas Jehl, "GIs Escalate Attack and Drugs in South America," *Los Angeles Times*, July 2, 1990, Jeff Leen, "Drug War Unhurt by Gulf Build-up," *Miami Herald*, September 11, 1990.

47. Rowan Scarborough, "Congress Plots Wider Role for Military in Drug War," *Washington Times*, August 23, 1989, 3; R. W. Apple, "The Capital: With Talk of Troops to Colombia, a Trial Balloon Serves Its Purpose—and the Administration's," *New York Times*, August 23, 1989, 18; Elaine Shannon, "Attacking the Source: Bennett's Plan to Send Military Advisers to Aid Anti-Narcotics Campaigns in Peru and Bolivia Arouses Serious Worries in Washington," *Time* (August 28, 1989): 10; Rick Maze, "Lawmakers Like Military Profile in War on Drugs," *Air Force Times* (September 4, 1989): 6.

48. Peter H. Smith, "Drugs Great Burden on Foreign Policy: High Political Price Extracted for Any Potential Benefits," *Los Angeles Times*, March 16, 1990, B-7; Inter-American Dialogue, *The Americas in a New World: The 1990 Report of the Inter-American Dialogue* (Washington, D.C.: Aspen Institute, 1990), 43–56.

49. General Accounting Office, *Drug Control: How Drug-Consuming Nations Are Organized for the War on Drugs*, GAO/NSIAD-90-133 (Washington, D.C.: U.S. Government Printing Office, 1990).

50. See Rensselaer Lee III, *The White Labyrinth: Cocaine and Political Power in the Andes* (New Brunswick, N.J.: Transaction Press, 1989).

51. U.S. Congress, House Select Committee on Narcotics Abuse and Control, *Drugs and Latin America: Economic and Political Impact and U.S. Policy Options*, 101st Congress, 1st Session (Washington, D.C.: U.S. Government Printing Office, 1989), 56–74.

52. On the pros and cons of economic aid, see House Select Committee on Narcotics Abuse and Control, *Drugs and Latin America*, 1–52. Also Gustavo A. Gorriti, "How to Fight a Drug War," *Atlantic* 263, no. 1 (July 1989): 70–76.

53. See the White House, *National Drug Control Strategy* (Washington, D.C.: U.S. Government Printing Office, January 1990), 13–64.

54. Mark A.R. Kleiman, "The Cocaine Blizzard: Snowed In," *New Republic* (April 23, 1990): 14–16.

10

Mexico's Permanent Campaign:
Costs, Benefits, Implications

Miguel Ruiz-Cabañas I.

From its beginnings the antidrug policy of the Mexican government has been linked to U.S.-Mexican relations and to U.S. antidrug policy. Its earliest antecedent dates back to 1912 when, at the request of its northern neighbor, Mexico adhered to the Hague Convention for the control of opium sales.[1] After World War I, Mexico joined international conventions adopted within the League of Nations. At the end of World War II, the United Nations inherited the task of enforcing these agreements. Later, the United Nations decided to summarize the principal resolutions in a single treaty, the Single Convention of 1961, to which Mexico adhered in 1967.[2]

On the home front, since the 1920s Mexico has passed legislation intended to suppress the cultivation, production, selling, and trafficking of narcotics. Gradually the nation's legal framework has been modified in minor ways to comply with terms of international conventions. As a result, since the 1940s Mexico has pursued a clear antidrug policy in keeping with the standards of the international community.[3]

A historical antecedent of Mexico's so-called *Campaña Permanente* (Permanent Campaign) against drug production originated in 1948 with the Great Campaign, a manual crop eradication program implemented by the army.[4] From that time until the end of the 1960s, according to some historians, Mexico carried on a half-hearted crop eradication campaign. In response to exponential growth in U.S. demand and, it has been argued, increasing exports of cannabis and heroin, the campaign was curtailed. This led to constant friction between the governments of Mexico and the United States during these years—including the so-called Operation Intercept of 1969—until the administration of Luis Echeverría launched a Permanent Campaign against the cultivation, processing, and trafficking of narcotics in 1975.[5]

Since then and in increasing cooperation with U.S. authorities, subsequent Mexican administrations have supported the Permanent Campaign primarily for two reasons: international concerns, especially about Mexico's fulfillment of international contractual obligations and the need to ensure adequate relations with the United States; and domestic concerns, in particular about public health and the threat posed to national security by powerful criminal groups in certain areas of the country. This chapter analyzes the costs, benefits, and implications of continuation of the Permanent Campaign.

The International Drug Control Regime

Mexico's narcotics policy and specifically the Permanent Campaign must be understood within the context of the international drug control regime. At the insistence of the U.S. government, the International Opium Convention of 1912 articulated for the first time the fundamental principle that remains the basis of the international drug control regime: to reserve and limit the production and use of narcotics exclusively to medical and scientific purposes—thus establishing a prohibitionist regime against the unauthorized production, distribution, and sale of opium. This principle was later extended to other drugs, specifically to cannabis and cocaine.[6] With the support of the United States, the League of Nations also adopted a series of international conventions whose principal aims were to eliminate production, trafficking, distribution, and sale of narcotics not destined for medical and scientific use.[7]

Although these resolutions were frequently violated, by the late 1930s the free trade of narcotics—widespread at the turn of the century—was no longer regarded as legal. Most countries gradually began to adopt legislation in keeping with this new position.[8] The Convention to Limit the Manufacture and Regulate the Distribution of Narcotics, adopted in Geneva in 1931, asserted that the best way to control the illegal production and distribution of narcotics was to do it at "the source"—that is, in the country of origin.[9] Inspired mainly by the United States, this approach implied a conceptual separation of supply from demand. Cultivation and illegal trafficking were seen as the causes of drug abuse. Consumption, or demand, was not regarded as the cause of the supply. The international prohibitionist drug control regime of the early twentieth century thus provided for the *control* and *regulation* of legal cultivation, production, and distribution (for medical and scientific purposes) and for the *elimination* of illegal cultivation, production, and distribution while leaving aside the issues of drug consumption and abuse.

On its foundation, the United Nations inherited the function of enforcing the international conventions drafted by the League of Nations. After adopting additional agreements to reduce the world's legal production of opium, in 1961 the General Assembly approved a Single Convention that summarized the main international regulations adopted to that date. The 1961 convention was designed to eliminate the supply of narcotics while ignoring the role of consumption.

> Subject to the requirement of their Constitution, each of the Parts agrees to adopt the necessary measures so that the cultivation and production, manufacture, extraction, preparation, possession, supplies in general, offers of sale, distribution, purchase and sale, forwarding of any kind, brokerage, shipment, in-transit shipment, transportation, import and export of drugs not in agreement with the regulations of this Convention

or of any other acts which in the opinion of the Part may be carried out in infringement of the regulations of the present Convention, be considered as crimes if committed intentionally, and that the serious crimes be punished adequately, especially with prison terms or other freedom-depriving penalties.[10]

The convention did not establish any kind of criminal sanction for the consumption of narcotics; on the contrary, it adopted a remarkably tolerant regime for narcotics users: "Notwithstanding the dispositions of the previous section, when those people making undue use of narcotics have committed these crimes, the Parts, instead of declaring them guilty or imposing criminal sanctions, or in addition to declaring them guilty or sanctioning them, shall be able to submit them to treatment, education, after-treatment, rehabilitation and social readjustment according to the dispositions set forth in paragraph 1 of article 38."[11] By repressing supply and tolerating demand, as Samuel del Villar has pointed out, the Single Convention "set the basis for the spectacular growth of the illegal narcotics market during the sixties and seventies in the United States, for the uncontrollable and corrupting flow of drug money toward Mexico, and for the advent of great criminal organizations which have controlled these flows."[12]

The 1961 convention and its subsequent 1972 protocol consolidated an international regime with two central characteristics: first, a conceptual separation of supply from demand, which are seen as separate phenomena and not as functional elements within a single market; second, repression of supply and tolerance of demand, which tend to produce an artificial rise in prices (especially when demand is inelastic). As a result, the obligations imposed on drug-producing countries by the convention are out of proportion to the obligations for consuming countries. In other words, the main costs—economic, political, social, and human—of the international drug control regime lie on the shoulders of producer nations, not consumer countries.

The international regime helps to explain the nature and magnitude of the problems faced by Mexico's antidrug policy. In more than one sense, Mexico has been forced to apply a Permanent Campaign against drug traffic. Yet, the international regime cannot explain the special characteristics of the campaign that have developed over time. To do so it is necessary to analyze this campaign in the light of U.S.-Mexican relations and of Mexico's internal motivations: national security and protection of public health.

U.S. Policy and Mexico's Permanent Campaign

Ever since its inception, the international antidrug movement led by the United States has had a single touchstone: the elimination of all kinds of drugs—either at their place of origin or while in transit to consumption centers (with the exception of drugs for medical and scientific use).[13] This U.S.-dominated strategy tends to underline the supply side of the phenomenon while giving little or no attention to demand. As the President's Commission on Organized Crime established by

President Ronald Reagan pointed out in 1986: "The history of federal drug policy . . . shows that the preferred and dominant approaches in federal response during the past 75 years have aimed at reducing supply. Only recently has the dynamic nature of supply-demand of illegal drugs been fully understood, leading to a new appreciation of programs to reduce demand, and to a renewed insistence on these programs."[14]

Due to Mexico's geographical position and its propitious conditions for the cultivation of narcotics, the United States has always wanted Mexican drug policy to adhere to the U.S. stance as closely as possible. From the time it convinced President Francisco Madero to subscribe to the 1912 Hague Convention, the United States has consistently sought to circumscribe Mexican antidrug policy to its own criteria—either through bilateral agreements or through multilateral conventions.[15]

For nearly a century U.S. antidrug authorities and perhaps a great majority of citizens have tended to associate drug consumption with racial minorities (Chinese, blacks, Mexicans), lower classes, and such undesirable groups as prostitutes and thugs.[16] Partly because of these popular perceptions, until the 1960s U.S. policymakers promoted a punitive approach against drug distributors and consumers alike. Only when drug consumption spread to the offspring of middle- and upper-class Americans did the official approach show significant change. Drug abuse then came to be considered more a problem of public health than a problem of criminal behavior. This change implied a reinterpretation of U.S. laws against illegal drug trafficking.[17]

In essence, the new approach meant that drug consumption would not be strictly penalized whereas cultivation, production, trafficking, and distribution would be prosecuted with intensified vigor. Followed in general terms by Western Europe and Latin America, including Mexico, this posture was linked in multiple and profound ways to the exponential development of global illegal drug markets. It tended to restrict even further the sale of illegal drugs to those individuals and organizations willing to accept high levels of risk. Inadvertently, the new policy thus set the foundations for the development of the largest and most powerful international mafias the world has ever seen.[18]

As long as U.S. authorities associated the consumption of marijuana with minorities, perhaps, the drug trade between the United States and Mexico did not create serious problems for bilateral relations. Until the 1960s almost all U.S. consumption of marijuana was drawn from Mexican sources. Historically, Mexico also supplied about 10 or 15 percent of the total U.S. market for opium and heroin, except for a brief period during World War II when Asian and European sources were closed and the U.S. government officially requested that Mexico allow the cultivation of poppies for the production of morphine.[19]

Exponential growth in U.S. consumption of marijuana and heroin during the 1960s radically changed public opinion about the abuse of drugs in general and of Mexican marijuana in particular. Drugs suddenly came to play an important role in the 1968 presidential campaign that brought Richard Nixon to power. Soon after taking office, Nixon launched the so-called Operation Intercept to elicit greater efforts from the Mexican government to stop the flow of drugs to the United States.[20] Operation Intercept entailed high political and diplomatic costs and was widely criticized in both countries. Even so, it gave the issue of drug traffic higher priority on the bilateral agenda and led to a new period of sustained collaboration.

From 1970 to 1975, this cooperation centered on crop eradication in Mexico and on confiscation programs at the border. Then in July 1972, the government of Turkey—under enormous pressure from the United States—prohibited the cultivation of opium within its own territory. A few months later, modest quantities of Mexican heroin began to appear in the U.S. market. From 1972 to 1975, according to U.S. government estimates, the supply of Mexican heroin increased from 10–15 percent to 80 percent of·the total available in the United States.[21] It is important to emphasize this "supplier substitution" phenomenon because it demonstrates a recurrent pattern in the international drug market: Each time an illicit drug source is eliminated or substantially reduced, the vacuum tends to be filled by a new source within a brief period of time.[22]

Faced with substantial increases in poppy and marijuana cultivation and heroin production, the Mexican government decided to step up its antidrug activities and declared its Permanent Campaign.[23] At first, the campaign entailed the use of more modern technology and equipment for the detection and destruction of drugs, such as the multispectral detection system for opium poppies. Likewise, a system was introduced for large-scale crop eradication through aerial spray of chemical substances. Thus began Operation Condor. The country was divided into 13 zones and 344 sectors by the attorney general. Communications networks were established, and outposts were built in areas of intensive opium cultivation. For this operation the Mexican government invested US$35 million, 2,500 soldiers, 250 agents from the federal legal police, and additional forces from the army, from the navy, and from state and municipal police.[24]

During the late 1970s the Permanent Campaign, through Operation Condor, was highly successful. According to U.S. government data, the supply of Mexican marijuana for the U.S. market declined from 75 percent in 1976 to around 4 percent in 1981 (from 6,500 to 400 tons). The supply of opium and heroin from Mexico was reduced from 67 percent of the U.S. total in 1976 to 25 percent in 1980 (from 40 to 17 tons). The success of the Mexican eradication program drew considerable praise from U.S. officials. In its 1980 report, for example, the National Narcotics Intelligence Consumers Committee stated that "as far as eradication is concerned, Mexico remains a bright spot in a disheartening scenario."[25]

These reductions in Mexican supply did not lead to a similar reduction in U.S. consumption. Mexican supply was quickly replaced by production in other countries, including the United States. Indeed, the 1970s saw great increases in acknowledged drug consumption in the United States.[26]

It can nonetheless be said that Mexico had to declare its Permanent Campaign in the mid-1970s because in addition to the continued growth of marijuana cultivation for the U.S. market, international drug lords began to use Mexican territory to replace Turkish opium and heroin. The presence and power of these drug lords posed a direct threat to social and political stability in major production areas—specifically in the states of Sinaloa, Durango, and Chihuahua.

The decision to launch the Permanent Campaign also stemmed from the needs to maintain adequate relations with the United States and to abide by international conventions. Drug trafficking was not a source of friction between the United States and Mexico until November 1984, when several tons of marijuana were found in the state of Chihuahua. U.S. authorities immediately interpreted this confiscation as a sign that the Mexican crop eradication campaign was weakened. For the first time in many years, moreover, spokespersons from the Reagan administration publicly pointed to the corruption of Mexican officials as the main reason for the deterioration of the campaign.[27]

What was the source of this problem? Analysts have cited several possibilities, including (1) extraordinary weather conditions in 1984 that led to abundant crops, reduced adherence of herbicides to plants, and posed obstacles to aerial fumigation; (2) bureaucratic inertia or corruption at the end of the 1976–1982 presidential administration; (3) an economic crisis that led many peasants to grow more lucrative crops—that is, illicit drugs; (4) U.S. carelessness in trusting that the Mexican campaign would always be successful; and (5) changes in the routes used by drug lords as links emerged between Mexican and Colombian traffickers.[28]

These factors cannot be dismissed lightly, but they do not provide a convincing explanation. Historical experience has shown that when a source of narcotics is significantly reduced without parallel reductions in demand, other sources will fill the gap—and sooner or later the original source will emerge once again. Thus, the main cause of the campaign's deterioration was that U.S. demand for illegal drugs not only failed to decline but actually grew considerably.

This observation prompts reflection on the nature of the Permanent Campaign. At its inception, the adjective "permanent" meant that crop destruction activities led by the army would be carried out throughout the entire year and not only during times of planting and harvest, as had been the case until then. In addition, the campaign originally comprised a series of extraordinary measures by the Mexican government against drug traffickers in Sinaloa, Durango, and Chihuahua in an effort to eliminate their economic, social, and political influences. The campaign thus was construed as permanent in the sense that it would last until the problem was solved, not in the sense that it would continue in perpetuity. As with any other "campaign"—political, electoral, financial, or educational—the Permanent Campaign could not be sustained forever without losing its effectiveness.

Results of the Permanent Campaign

Drug traffic has perhaps caused the greatest tension in U.S.-Mexican relations during the past decade or so. The problem had drastically undermined bilateral relations, contaminating the diplomatic climate necessary for negotiating other issues between the two countries. This became abundantly clear in March 1985 when a DEA agent was kidnapped and murdered by Mexican drug traffickers. Regarding the incident as a failure of the Permanent Campaign,[29] the United States responded with a second Operation Intercept. To the Mexican government, such criticism seemed unjustified. Despite a growing economic crisis, after all, Mexico was still allocating a significant share of governmental resources to address the drug problem.[30]

I will not undertake here an in-depth appraisal of President Miguel de la Madrid's policy and its results. In order to analyze the political implications of the Permanent Campaign, however, we must begin with basic facts.

- By constitutional decree, in Mexico the responsibility to investigate and prosecute "crimes against health" through drugs and psychotropic substances lies solely with the Office of the Attorney General because these are considered federal crimes.
- The Army and the Navy are responsible for guaranteeing national security, which includes cooperation with the Office of the Attorney General in the eradication of illegal drug trafficking. To fulfill these tasks and to assist the national government and the Federal Judicial Police, the army "locates and destroys illegal plantings. It dismantles clandestine laboratories and breaks up drug networks which traffic, distribute, sell, and consume narcotics and psychotropic substances." It is important to point out that the armed forces arrest drug traffickers "only when caught in the act," on the basis of a constitutional decree that allows any person to arrest a criminal and his or her accomplices and bring them immediately into custody of the federal authorities.
- Government agents in the states and the Judicial Police agents also collaborate with the attorney general.[31]

Thus, by constitutional decree the Mexican state's administrative structure for fighting drug traffic is centralized in the attorney general's office. At different levels, both the armed forces and the state offices of the attorney general participate in the Permanent Campaign as auxiliaries in support of activities and policies determined by the central Office of the Attorney General.

According to official data, during President de la Madrid's administration 1,200 federal agents and more than 22,000 members of the armed forces participated continually in the Permanent Campaign. Funding increased from 32.5 percent of the budget of the Office of the Attorney General in 1985 to more than 60 percent in 1988. During de la Madrid's *sexenio*, or six-year presidential term, the Office of the Attorney General and the National Defense Department allocated to the campaign $631.7 billion pesos—at the prevalent rate of exchange, about US$230 million.[32]

This investment led to the eradication of 307,536 plants over an area of 34,871 hectares; the seizure of 726.9 kilograms of heroin and opium gum, 33,176.6

kilograms of cocaine, and 9,660 tons of marijuana; the destruction of 47 laboratories; and the confiscation of 6,414 ground vehicles, 125 aircraft, and 75 marine vessels—plus 9,978 weapons. Furthermore, 70,460 people (almost 0.1 percent of the population) were detained and handed over to judicial authorities for crimes related to drug trafficking; 43,895 judicial proceedings were initiated; and 47 federal agents lost their lives in direct actions against drug trafficking (which brings the total number of deaths since the beginning of the campaign to over 400).[33] By any standard, this constituted an extraordinary effort.

According to U.S. government reports, however, drug trafficking had far from diminished. By the late 1980s, Mexico continued to be the main exporter of marijuana and heroin to the United States and remained an important transit point for cocaine from South America. After a decade and a half, in other words, the solution to the problem of drug traffic remained as elusive as it had been in 1975 when the Permanent Campaign began.

Official and unofficial sources clearly suggest that the campaign's economic, political, and social costs—both direct and indirect—have steadily mounted. Judicial efforts have focused on drug-related crimes in spite of the fact that, at least until recently, drug consumption within Mexico has been limited.[34] Similarly, the armed forces have been forced to allocate increasing economic and human resources to an enterprise that, in principle, does not fall within their normal scope of action.[35]

On the other hand, to the degree that drug traffic tends to generate corruption and violence wherever it operates—as a result of the almost unlimited flow of "drug dollars" produced by U.S. consumers—the Mexican police corps has been constantly exposed to situations that encourage corruption. Some of these cases involve middle- to high-ranking officials. In my estimation, one of the most negative consequences brought on by the drug-trafficking problem has been to delay and hinder the much-needed professionalization of the Mexican police corps.[36]

In this sense, the indefinite continuation of the campaign does not promote the professionalization of Mexican police officers: There can be no breathing space for new approaches and techniques in the midst of continuing crisis. This situation is particularly lamentable in view of the well-known need for better public security services throughout the nation's cities.

Prosecution under the Permanent Campaign in rural areas for an extended period tends to wear out the state's image among the peasantry, which assumes the risk of cultivating illegal drugs. Depending on the specific circumstances, the government agents in charge of eradicating crops—the army and the Federal Judicial Police—tend to be viewed with mistrust and suspicion by campesinos.

It is for this reason that the de la Madrid government emphasized the idea that drug trafficking "has become a part of our times, affecting both culture and the economy, and with the potential, as we have seen in other countries, of affecting the political structures and organizations of nations. . . . Thus, the fight against drug traffic, the prevention of drug addiction, and its adequate treatment are in the interests of the state and of Mexican society."[37] Likewise, the government of President

Carlos Salinas de Gortari has declared drug traffic to be a threat to national security.[38]

It is difficult to determine how the Mexican Army as an institution has been affected by its participation in the antidrug campaign. Numerous difficulties stand in the way of such analysis. First, the Mexican Army and the military as a whole remain relatively unstudied institutions. No corpus of academic studies exists showing the recent evolution of the Mexican Army and its influence on the political system that is comparable to those studies on such countries as Brazil, Argentina, or Chile. Second, the few extant studies on the Mexican Army do not refer to its role in the fight against drug traffic.[39]

According to the National Defense Department's reports, the fight against drug traffic has not required an increase in its budget: "Drug traffic is fought solely with its own resources, without demanding any additional support." According to military sources, Mexico has been involved in drug trafficking for three reasons: (1) its geopolitical location bordering the largest consumer market; (2) the existence of "complex international criminal networks, involved in drug traffic coming from Central and South America"; and (3) the precarious social and economic conditions of some sectors of the population. Within this context, the army has pursued four interrelated goals: to prevent rural inhabitants from being persuaded or pressured to cultivate poppies or marijuana; to prevent the processing of raw material; to halt drug trafficking; and to identify and dismantle criminal organizations involved in these illegal activities. The army clearly regards its attempts to prevent rural peasants from becoming involved in the illegal drug market as a topmost priority. It is also apparent that the army sees these efforts, especially its "depistolization" campaign, as contributing to the maintenance of peace and stability in the Mexican countryside.[40]

Yet, these activities do not indicate whether the army as an institution has been strengthened (or weakened) within the political system. If, as some believe, the Mexican Army has gained political strength over the past two decades, this is not necessarily due to its participation in the Permanent Campaign. It is more likely a result of its institutional modernization and economic and internal policy changes that require greater army participation.

On the other hand, it is impossible for any government anywhere to sustain a permanent campaign against a specific target without losing strength and suffering a loss of image. To the degree that the drug problem remains unsolved, citizens come to question and eventually to challenge the continuation of a costly enterprise that seems to have no possibility of victory. Opposition becomes even more intense as the government is accused, justly or unjustly, of errors in judgment and tactics.

This may already have happened with Mexico's Permanent Campaign against drug traffic. Indeed, I suspect that some sectors of the population question the prudence of continuing a campaign that, after fifteen years, has not achieved any clear-cut victories. It is very important to keep this possibility in mind in order to analyze antidrug-trafficking policy implemented by the current government.

What have been the achievements of the campaign for the state and for Mexican society? In my view, there have been two benefits: First, further progression of drug trafficking has been halted; and second, diplomatic relations with the United States— in spite of numerous incidents—have remained adequate for dialog and negotiations on this and other key issues. A traditional cost-benefit analysis of the campaign is not applicable because Mexico has no realistic alternatives due to its contractual agreements with the international community and to the influence of U.S. antidrug policy.

The Salinas Policy on Drugs

The Salinas administration has insisted that Mexico fight drug traffic for three main reasons, in order of priority: "for the health of Mexicans, for national security, and for international cooperation." With these aims in mind, President Salinas reinforced governmental structures by creating an Assistant Office of the Attorney General for the coordination of antidrug activities and by increasing the allocation of material and human resources. He also amended the Criminal Legal Code to increase the penalties for crimes linked to drug traffic, especially for public officials.[41]

Initial results, from December 1988 through January 1990, were impressive: the eradication of 86,401 plants over a surface of 7,845 hectares and the confiscation of 36 tons of cocaine, 586 tons of marijuana, and 687 kilograms of heroin. Likewise, 11,661 people have been handed over to judicial authorities, 280 criminal groups have been dismantled, and 45 public servants have been killed in confrontations with drug traffickers.[42]

There is little doubt that the Salinas government has decided to intensify the Permanent Campaign. In general terms, the strategy remains the same, with one important exception: High priority is now given to disbanding criminal organizations. The army continues its activities, and the Office of the Attorney General has expanded operations.

The Salinas administration seems willing to give crop eradication and antitrafficking policies a new chance while waiting for the U.S. government to do its part: achieve substantial reductions in the U.S. domestic level of consumption. Without demand reduction, the result will be clear: a simple substitution of suppliers. Furthermore, the economic, political, and social costs of the campaign will escalate sharply in proportion to increasing efforts.

All these efforts and sacrifices have nonetheless failed to impress the U.S. government because the levels of production, trafficking, and consumption of drugs continue to be very high. Frankly, Mexican public opinion resents this attitude. Criticism from the United States tends to destroy the public support the Mexican government needs to carry forth this campaign. We must remember that the consumption of illegal drugs in Mexico, in spite of recent increases, remains miniscule in comparison with that of the United States. The key problem for Mexico is not the addiction of its population but the criminal activity that is caused by the flow of drug money into the country.

Notes

1. See William O. Walker III, *Drug Control in the Americas* (Albuquerque: University of New Mexico Press, 1981).

2. See text of the convention in United Nations, *Convención única de 1961 sobre estupefacientes* (New York: United Nations, 1967).

3. "El problema de las drogas," *El desafío de la interdependencia: México y Estados Unidos*, Informe de la Comisión Bilateral sobre el Futuro de las Relaciones Mexico-Estados Unidos (México: Fondo de Cultura Económica, 1988), 123.

4. Richard Craig, "La Campaña Permanente, Mexico's Anti-Drug Campaign," *Journal of Interamerican Studies and World Affairs* 20, no. 2 (May 1978): 108.

5. Craig, "La Campaña Permanente."

6. See United Nations, *The United Nations and Drug Abuse Control*, Publication no. E.87.I.8 (New York: United Nations, 1987), 63.

7. On U.S. roles in international drug policy, see Arnold H. Taylor, *American Diplomacy and the Narcotics Traffic, 1900–1939: A Study in International Humanitarian Reform* (Durham: Duke University Press, 1969).

8. Taylor, *American Diplomacy.*

9. The convention's text can be found in United Nations, *The United Nations and Drug Abuse Control.*

10. See United Nations, *Convención única sobre estupefacientes*, especially article 36, paragraph 1a.

11. United Nations, *Convención única sobre estupefacientes*, article 36, paragraph 1b.

12. Samuel del Villar, "Perspectivas del control del mercado de narcóticos: México y Estados Unidos," in Guadalupe González and Marta Tienda, eds., *México y Estados Unidos en la cadena internacional del narcotráfico* (México: Fondo de Cultura Económica, 1989), 139; for English version, see Guadalupe González and Marta Tienda, eds., *The Drug Connection in U.S.-Mexican Relations* (La Jolla: Center for U.S.-Mexican Studies, University of California, San Diego, 1989).

13. See Taylor, *American Diplomacy.*

14. See President's Commission on Organized Crime, Report to the President and Attorney General, *America's Habit: Drug Abuse, Drug Trafficking, and Organized Crime* (Washington, D.C.: U.S. Government Printing Office, 1986), 187.

15. See Taylor, *American Diplomacy.*

16. See Ann J. Blanken, "Las pautas cambiantes del consumo de estupefacientes en Estados Unidos," in González and Tienda, *Cadena internacional*, 38–40.

17. Blanken, "Las pautas cambiantes."

18. For this argument, see *The Economist* (April 6, 1988): 7–8, and del Villar, "Perspectivas."

19. See President's Commission on Organized Crime, *America's Habit.*

20. See Richard Craig, "La política antidrogas de Estados Unidos hacia México: Consecuencia en la sociedad estadounidense y en las relaciones bilaterales," in González and Tienda, *Cadena internacional*, 97–122.

21. See Morgan Murphy and Robert H. Steele, *The World Narcotics Problem: The Latin American Perspective*, Report of Special Study Mission to Latin America and the Federal Republic of Germany, 93rd Congress, Committee on Foreign Affairs (Washington, D.C.: U.S. Government Printing Office, 1973), 14; and Comisión Bilateral, "El problema," 125–126.

22. See Miguel Ruíz-Cabañas, "La oferta de drogas ilícitas hacia Estados Unidos: El papel fluctuante de México," in González and Tienda, *Cadena internacional*, 72–77.

23. See Craig, "La Campaña Permanente," 115–120.

24. See Richard Craig, "Operation Condor: Mexico's Anti-Drug Campaign Enters a New Era," *Journal of Interamerican Studies and World Affairs* 22, no. 3 (August 1980): 345–363.

25. See *The Supply of Illicit Drugs to the United States from Foreign and Domestic Sources (with Near Term Projections)*, 1980 Annual Report of the National Narcotics Intelligence Consumers Committee (Washington, D.C.: U.S. Government Printing Office, 1980), 91.

26. See Ruíz-Cabañas, "La oferta," 82.

27. See Richard Meislin, "Mexican Linked to U.S. Abducted," *New York Times*, February 13, 1985.

28. See Craig, "La política antidrogas de Estados Unidos hacia México," 97–105.

29. See the report of the Comisión Bilateral, *El desafío*, 123.

30. See Guadalupe González, "El problema del narcotráfico en el contexto de la relación entre México y Estados Unidos," Centro de Investigación y Docencia Económicas, *Carta de Política Exterior Mexicana* 5, nos. 2–3 (April-September 1985): 20–28.

31. See Mexico, Attorney General of the Republic, Office of the Assistant Attorney General for Investigation and Combat of Drug Trafficking, *Mexico's Efforts in the Fight Against Drug Trafficking* (Mexico City: Office of the Attorney General, June 1989), 7.

32. Mexico, Attorney General, *Mexico's Efforts*, 8–9.

33. Mexico, Attorney General of the Republic, Office of the Assistant Attorney General for Investigation and Combat of Drug Trafficking, *Mexico's Efforts in the Fight Against Drug Trafficking* (Mexico City: Office of the Attorney General, 1990).

34. See *Programa contra la farmacodependencia*, Secretaría de Salud, Consejo Nacional contra la Farmacodependencia, Instituto Mexicano de Psiquiatría (México: Secretaría de Salud, 1985), especially 14–31; and Chapter 3 in this volume.

35. See Juan Arévalo Gardoqui, *El ejército mexicano en la campaña contra el narcotráfico* (México: Procuraduría General de la República, 1987).

36. See Sergio García Ramírez, *El narcotráfico: Un punto de vista mexicano* (México: Editorial Porrúa, 1989).

37. Address by President Miguel de la Madrid Hurtado at the conclusion of the governors' meeting, Tijuana, Baja California, January 28, 1987 (México: Procuraduría General de la República, 1987).

38. See Mexico, Attorney General, *Mexico's Efforts*, 1990.

39. See, for example, David Ronfeldt, ed., *The Modern Mexican Military: A Reassessment* (La Jolla: Center for U.S.-Mexican Studies, University of California, San Diego, 1984).

40. Secretaría de la Defensa Nacional, *Memorias de la campaña contra el narcotráfico, diciembre 1982–noviembre 1987* (México: Secretaría de la Defensa Nacional, 1988), 7–57.

41. Mexico, Attorney General, *Mexico's Efforts*, 1990.

42. Mexico, Attorney General, *Mexico's Efforts*, 1990.

11

After the Borders Are Sealed:
Can Domestic Sources Substitute
for Imported Drugs?

Peter Reuter

The principal illicit drugs consumed in the United States are produced outside its borders. An increasing share of marijuana consumption is provided domestically, but even most of that drug seems still to be grown in Mexico, Colombia, and Jamaica. All of the cocaine and heroin for U.S. consumption is supplied by other nations, some of them far from the United States.

Two factors may explain the dominance of foreign producers. First, the risks faced by producers in the United States in terms of exposure to incarceration and seizure of assets seem to be much higher than those in the producer countries. In many countries the judiciary is intimidated and the police corrupted by traffickers.[1] Second, the factors of production of the raw materials—namely land and unskilled labor—are much cheaper abroad, and transportation costs (per dollar of retail sales) are very low.[2] As discussed below, interdiction can increase those costs substantially under some circumstances.

The dominance of foreign production has affected U.S. drug policy. Considerable effort is given either to preventing the production overseas, through eradication and crop substitution schemes, or to interdicting smugglers of these drugs.[3] At times, corrupt foreign governments have been made scapegoats for the U.S. drug problems; this was particularly the case with respect to heroin control around 1970.[4]

This in turn leads to two charges against current U.S. policy. The first, an element in almost all critiques of the federal effort, is that foreign production and smuggling cannot be controlled.[5] The industry is too profitable for poor peasants to be prevented or discouraged from entering it, and, it is commonly said, the control of international commerce and traffic into the United States is too difficult.

The second charge is made less frequently, but it is a claim implicit in the more pessimistic essays about drug policy—particularly those by advocates of drug legalization. They suggest that even if the borders were sealed, the result would

Preparation of this paper was supported by RAND's Drug Policy Research Center, which is funded by the Ford and Weinart foundations.

merely be a change in the nature of the drugs consumed.[6] Instead of foreign-source natural-based drugs (marijuana, cocaine, and heroin), U.S. consumers would turn to domestically produced synthetics. A wide variety of such synthetics have become widely used, at least in some places in some periods. Moreover, many synthetics appear (pharmacologically) to be substitutes for the natural-based drugs.

This chapter examines this second claim about the effect of "sealing the borders." What would be the consequences for the extent of drug abuse and the mix (and resulting harms) of drugs used? To what extent would domestic sources replace imports, either with the same drug or with a substitute?

Given that the borders have been very porous, at least in recent times, this chapter is inevitably highly speculative. However, some relevant historical experiences are worth examining, periods during which specific imported drugs became substantially less available. My central conclusion is that the evidence favors the proposition that total drug consumption would decline if the natural products were no longer available but that the harms associated with drug use (that is, the damages incurred by the average drug user) might increase because of the greater dangers caused by synthetics. The primary basis for the conclusion is that pharmacological notions of substitutability turn out not to be descriptive of actual behavior; there is instead (weak) evidence of enduring preferences for the imported drugs.

I next introduce the relevant data and analytic concepts. The subsequent portion, the heart of the argument, examines successively three episodes in which imports have been seriously disrupted: the heroin drought of the mid-1970s; the elimination of methaqualone (Quaalude) imports in the early 1980s; and the substantial reduction in Colombian-source marijuana during the same period. In each case I describe the evidence pointing to sharply reduced availability and then examine data concerning consumption of substitute (illicit) drugs[7] and changes in rates of initiation into use of the drug now in restricted supply. The final section summarizes the evidence and draws the lessons.

Data Sources and Other Preliminaries

Substitution Among Drugs

Substitution has many meanings. For a physician, drugs may be substitutes if they accomplish similar therapeutic goals; ether may be a substitute for morphine if both drugs can rapidly induce a sleep-like state for a specified period of time. Mode of administration may be a minor consideration, the choice perhaps depending on the risks of side effects associated with each.

For those who use a drug for pleasure rather than therapy, substitution may be quite a different concept. The desirability of a drug is a function not simply of its pharmacological properties but also of the "set" and "setting" associated with it.[8] Two euphoriants that have the same therapeutic value may not appear to be substitutes to users, either because they do not believe the two drugs produce the same sensations or because they have had different experiences with the two. And those experiences and beliefs may be heavily influenced by the setting in which the drug is used (with whom and with what expectations) and by the mode of administration.

Ronald Siegel offers a different and interesting interpretation of the meaning of substitution based on the notion that animals, including humans, have a natural craving for mood-altering substances similar to the drives for food and sex. According to Siegel, different natural and synthetic substances can satisfy this drive so that changing the menu of available substances will not change the propensity for drug abuse. The evidence for this comes largely from clinical and observational studies, and it gives little weight to analyses of aggregate data that reflect changes in actual availability.[9]

A related but more specific notion of drug substitutes is based on the neurobiological explanation for so-called "psychological" addiction. Certain drugs stimulate the chemical pleasure centers of the brain, and each succeeding use of these drugs reinforces the positive stimulus and conditions the users to seek their use. Even after a period of abstinence, memory of past positive reinforcement can trigger this drug "craving." Roy Wise succinctly describes the implications for drug substitution: "If a variety of addictive substances have positive reinforcing effects through a common biological mechanism, then one drug should have some of the same subjective consequences of, and partially satisfy the urge for, another."[10] In this view, psychological dependence is dependence not on a particular substance but on the "high" that numerous substances can provide.

Substitution also has an economic meaning. Two goods are substitutes when a rise in the price of one increases demand for the other; they are complements when the rise in the price of one decreases the demand for the other. This may have little to do with the sensations the drugs produce. Marijuana and chocolate, for example, may be complements or substitutes for different individuals. Many marijuana users seek certain taste sensations while under the influence, so they might consume candy bars after smoking a joint. For them, a rise in marijuana price may reduce chocolate consumption because they consume less marijuana and hence have reduced cravings for chocolate. For others, marijuana and chocolate may be alternative ways of gratifying their need for (mildly) disapproved sensations; a higher marijuana price may shift them to greater consumption of chocolate.

All of these interpretations of substitution have their uses. The latter two both play a role in our analysis. In illegal markets, knowledge about the effects of drugs not in common supply may be very limited. Decisions about the acceptability of one drug when another becomes hard to get may depend largely on reputation rather than actual knowledge. Moreover, decisions about substitutability may change with experience of those drugs, as is true of other consumer goods. The experiences of a group may affect the preferences of an individual. But price will also play a role, particularly in a setting in which heavy drug use is increasingly associated with polydrug use[11] and many users are familiar with a range of drugs.

Data

Evaluation relies on available data systems. Three are of particular significance: the DAWN (Drug Abuse Warning Network) system, the High School Senior Survey (HSSS), and the *Narcotics Intelligence Estimate*. DAWN collects data from a selected sample of emergency rooms (ER) and medical examiners (ME) in about twenty-five metropolitan areas. Each participating facility provides data on all episodes in which illicit drugs played a contributing role in the event that led to the emergency room visit. The HSSS, briefly mentioned in Chapter 1, is an annual survey of approximately fifteen thousand students in the twelfth grade; it includes questions on the respondents' drug use. The *Narcotics Intelligence Estimate* is a publication of an interagency committee (the National Narcotics Intelligence Consumers Committee) headed by the Drug Enforcement Administration; the report presents estimates of the total quantities of drugs produced in various source countries along with comments on drug consumption and trafficking patterns in the United States.

The unit of analysis presented here for DAWN is the "mention" of a drug; an individual who enters an emergency room may list more than one drug as being related to the episode (the alternative unit of analysis). Especially useful is a special publication entitled A *Decade of DAWN*, which presents a consistent and comparable series of data on emergency room observations for the ten-year period 1976 through 1985 (many other DAWN facilities had reported only episodically). The analysis here is admittedly crude. It constitutes (at best) an effort at "pattern recognition," attempting to see if a break in the trend of one series is reflected in other potentially related series. It cannot be considered dispositive—although I attempt to ameliorate the problem by use of multiple indicators—because many factors other than the number of drug users affect the DAWN figures.

For example, I examine evidence on the number of DAWN episodes involving drugs in the same therapeutic class. Drugs show up in the DAWN system through a number of channels, not just reflecting use of drugs for recreation purposes. Some DAWN episodes are the consequence of suicide attempts; in 1988, 11.4 percent of all ER mentions of narcotic analgesics (the class including heroin) were classified as suicide attempts, and 62.8 percent of tranquilizer mentions were so classified. (Because an episode can involve more than one drug, each drug mentioned was not necessarily taken as part of the suicide attempt.) If suicide attempts increase, perhaps as a result of worsening economic conditions, that fact may show up in the form of increased DAWN mentions of a particular drug. Other admissions to ERs are people trying to detoxify from the effects of chronic use, and the quantity of these incidents may be driven by different factors.

Similarly, the likelihood of an episode of drug use resulting in an emergency room mention is partially a function of the age and career length of the user population. As users age and expose their bodies to a rising total amount of damage from drug use, each episode is increasingly likely to lead to either death or a need for medical treatment. The analyses that follow cannot control for this effect, although in the relatively short time periods used it is not likely to be a major factor.

Finally, drugs vary in their degree of dangerousness. In a given population, a heroin-use episode may have, say, a 1 in 10,000 chance of engendering an emergency room visit, while a codeine-use episode may have only a 1 in 50,000 chance of producing such a visit. Because these probabilities are not precisely known, it is not possible to create a scale of total drug use based on the numbers of episodes involving different drugs.

Local Variation in Drug Consumption Patterns

One striking feature of the illicit U.S. drug market is its fragmentation. There is enormous local variation in the popularity of specific drugs. For example, through most of the 1980s, PCP (phencyclidine, an illicitly manufactured hallucinogen) was widely used in the Washington, D.C., metropolitan area but was almost unknown in Baltimore—a mere thirty-five miles away—or in most other metropolitan areas.[12] In 1988, 29 percent of Washington, D.C., arrestees tested positive for PCP, compared with 13 percent in the next-highest city (Chicago); most cities had prevalence rates of less than 5 percent.[13] In the same year, of all treatment admissions that listed PCP as the primary drug of abuse, 45 percent were from the District of Columbia or Maryland.[14] In recent years, the prevalence of PCP in Washington has given way to crack in a sober reminder of how rapidly drug preferences can change.

Methamphetamines have been widely used in the San Diego metropolitan area for many years but have little use in most other cities. Three-quarters of all amphetamine mentions in the DAWN medical examiners data occur in three cities: Dallas, Philadelphia, and San Diego.

Even with respect to heroin there is substantial variation across cities. In Miami heroin is seldom found in the criminally active population (as indicated by the Drug Use Forecasting System), whereas in Washington, D.C., between 10 and 20 percent of arrestees have tested positive for heroin in recent years. Similarly, as is noted in the next section, there is considerable variation across cities in the nature of the drugs used as substitutes for heroin.

Although the following analysis focuses on national responses to reduced availability of illicit drugs, it also gives some attention to variation across cities. In some cities, the elimination of cocaine imports might result primarily in the expansion of the already-substantial market for synthetic or diverted stimulants. In others, without an established network of suppliers of these drugs, those who are currently dependent on cocaine may have difficulty finding any satisfactory alternatives—at least in the medium run.

Note that many of the locally popular drugs are primarily illicitly manufactured rather than diverted from legal distribution or imported. The United States has a large and innovative illicit drug-production industry, with a long history of efficient and experimental clandestine manufacture. Among the drugs that have been produced clandestinely are PCP, amphetamines, fentanyl, and MDMA (Ecstasy). Diversion has been a persistent problem, but it is one that seems more amenable to control than does domestic illicit manufacture.

Import-Reduction Experiences

The Heroin Drought of the Mid-1970s

A combination of events led to a sharp reduction in the availability of heroin to U.S. consumers in the mid-1970s. Although there has been a remarkable dearth of scholarship on this signal experience, the basic story entails a range of near-simultaneous events: Turkish opium-control efforts, Mexican opium eradication programs, droughts in Southeast Asia and Mexico, and the departure of U.S. troops from Indochina. As a result, it appears that the price of heroin rose dramatically and street purity declined sharply. The drug became much less attractive.

This is best reflected in the DAWN data. Mentions of heroin in emergency room admissions, after rising rapidly between 1974 and 1976, fell over the next four years. According to one major study, heroin ER mentions fell from a peak of 11,156 in 1976 to a floor of 4,889 in 1979; the decline was almost 60 percent. Medical examiner reports showed a similar trend, declining from a peak of 1,437 in 1976 to only 424 in 1979.[15]

Other indicators also pointed to declining heroin use. There was evidence of declines in the number of persons initiating heroin use in the late 1970s. Heroin purity, after rising from 5.1 percent in 1973 to 6.3 percent in 1976, fell to 3.6 percent in 1979 and 3.8 percent in 1980.[16] Admissions to treatment facilities rose from 14,746 in 1977 to 22,348 in 1980. Despite these indicators of declining use, prices rose at the retail level—from $1,400 per pure gram in 1976 to $2,290 in 1979—suggesting that reduced availability rather than changing tastes was producing these results.

DAWN includes heroin as one member of the category of opiates. Pharmacologically, there are numerous substitutes for heroin, which is a highly refined form of opium. Morphine, codeine, oxycodone, and hydromorphone (marketed under the name Dilaudid) are just some of those substitutes—all available through diversion from licit distribution.[17] And indeed there were increases for use of some of these drugs. As shown in Table 11-1, mentions of Dilaudid and pentazocine (most often combined with triplennamine and referred to as "Ts and Blues") rose substantially between 1976 and 1980. Codeine (often combined with the sedative gluthemide and called "fours and doors") mentions did not consistently rise, whereas oxycodone increased each year from 1976 to 1985.

Parenthetically, the decline in methadone mentions in the same period is perhaps harder to explain. Methadone is provided as an alternative narcotic to heroin addicts who seek treatment; taken orally (under supervision), it is longer lasting and produces

TABLE 11-1
Emergency Room Episodes Involving Heroin and Substitutes, 1976-1985

Substance	1976	1978	1980	1982	1984	1985
Heroin/Morphine	11,156	5,669	5,536	7,873	8,934	10,561
Hydromorphone	214	321	479	596	650	557
Pentazocine	800	1,159	1,503	1,961	643	542
Codeine	833	925	848	805	746	646
Oxycodone	775	1,042	1,086	1,143	1,149	1,341
Methadone	2,669	1,942	1,592	1,507	1,368	1,341

Source: Based on data in National Institute on Drug Abuse, A Decade of DAWN (Rockville, Md.: NIDA, 1986).

a milder high. It appears in the DAWN system largely because the drug is sometimes diverted from treatment facilities to street markets, where it is injected. This gives a sharper and shorter high than does oral ingestion; it also creates higher risks of an adverse reaction. As heroin becomes less available, *ceteris paribus*, methadone is more attractive as an alternative narcotic. However, it appears that the late 1970s saw a tightening of control of methadone, reducing the ease with which it could leak from treatment programs into the illicit market.

These figures mask interesting variations across cities. Some cities in which a drug had been almost unknown saw dramatic increases; in Philadelphia pentazocine mentions rose from 31 in 1976 to 258 in 1982 and in New Orleans they rose from 2 to 595 between 1976 and 1981. In Chicago, however, where the drug was already well established, the rise was much more modest—from 185 to 339 between 1976 and 1981—and in New York there was scarcely any movement. (Some of this variation may be explained by the location of production and distribution; diversion is easier in cities close to large-scale production and distribution facilities.)

Just as relevant is the pattern of drug mentions after the heroin drought ended in the early 1980s, when Southwest Asian heroin (predominantly from Afghanistan and Pakistan) became more available.[18] Heroin mentions rose, almost reaching their 1976 peak by 1985 and rising thereafter. Pentazocine mentions—peaking in 1981, a year after the heroin mentions—then fell sharply over the following five years.[19] Codeine and hydromorphone mentions showed quite a different pattern; codeine fell by 25 percent from its peak and hydromorphone mentions actually peaked in 1984, falling only in 1985. Methadone mentions continued to fall throughout the period.

Additional information also pointing to partial substitution can be found in the annual reports of the National Narcotics Intelligence Consumers Committee (NNICC). In 1980 NNICC stated that the percentage of heroin users reporting secondary drug use had grown steadily from 44 percent in 1976 to 55 percent in the first half of 1980. NNICC also asserted that a 52 percent rise in the price of Dilaudid between 1979 and 1980 was partially the consequence of declining heroin availability and hence of increased demand for a substitute. There was considerable regional variation in the particular substitutes that became widely used in illicit markets. Dilaudid was most frequently reported in Miami, New York, and Washington; in the Midwest, Talwin and pyribenzamine were more common.

In 1981 NNICC observed that the narcotics-using population had apparently changed its preferences among drugs. Many now either preferred the pharmaceutical analogues to heroin or preferred to use them in combination with heroin rather than using heroin alone. Note that these observations were made as the drought was coming to its end and may have reflected the slow spread of information (and development of supply channels) for these substitute narcotics during the drought. Observations recorded in the deliberations of the Community Epidemiological Workshop Group (consisting of experts from twenty-one cities, meeting twice a year) also point to a complicated pattern of substitution that varied across cities.

These patterns of substitution refer largely to those who were already heroin-dependent before the drought began. There is little doubt that the heroin epidemic ended before the drought. The number of new users showing up in treatment programs fell sharply well before 1976, and the average age of those entering treatment started to rise. Richard Clayton and Harwin Voss report that the annual prevalence of drug use among young men in Manhattan, after climbing from 3 percent in 1963 to 20 percent in 1970, had declined to 13 percent by 1974.[20] This may have been a consequence of the tougher enforcement in the early 1970s or of increasing awareness of the dangers of heroin use. The drought period was marked by continued decline in the initiation of new heroin users in the period 1976–1980; nor is there any evidence of the growth of a new addict population dependent on the heroin substitutes.

In summary, although there was some shift to other narcotics and narcotic-type drugs, the reduced availability of heroin in the second half of the 1970s seems to have reduced the use of illicit drugs among heroin addicts. This effect was reversible; when heroin became more available, many of those who had entered treatment, reduced their heroin consumption, or shifted to other drugs returned to heroin use.

Elimination of Methaqualone Imports

Methaqualone was widely distributed as an illicit drug in the late 1970s. The drug is a nonbarbiturate sedative, manufactured primarily in Germany and Hungary. It entered the illicit U.S. market through Colombia, which imported startlingly large quantities in powder form. It was always highly implausible that the domestic Colombian market could account for this quantity, and apparently the bulk of it was transshipped to the United States after being processed into pill form.

The U.S. government put pressure on the European manufacturers to control their shipments to Colombia. As a consequence, Colombian imports declined from approximately 120 tons in 1980 to virtually zero in 1985. Correspondingly, U.S. government seizures dropped from 58 metric tons in 1981 to 2.2 metric tons in 1985. Given that the drug is difficult to manufacture illicitly because it requires relatively elaborate production facilities, this meant that methaqualone was no longer

TABLE 11-2
Emergency Room Episodes Involving Methaqualone and Substitutes, 1976-1985

Substance	1976	1978	1980	1982	1984	1985
Methaqualone	1,858	1,839	4,045	2,479	806	379
Diazepam	17,448	15,192	11,188	8,751	6,908	6,295
Flurazepam	3,447	3,551	3,238	2,722	1,706	1,404
Diphenhydramine	832	986	913	1,068	1,124	1,235
Phenobarbitol	2,477	2,171	1,953	1,892	1,550	1,346

Source: Based on data in National Institute on Drug Abuse, *A Decade of DAWN* (Rockville, Md.: NIDA, 1986).

available for U.S. consumers, although counterfeit Quaaludes continued to be marketed.

The cycle is clearly registered in DAWN figures. In the *Decade of DAWN* series, ER admissions with mention of Quaaludes first rose, from 1,858 mentions in 1976 to a peak of 4,045 in 1980 (more than double the 1976 figure), and then declined precipitously to 379 in 1985—a fall of more than 90 percent. The number of mentions in the ME data showed a similar pattern, rising from 73 in 1976 to a peak of 123 in 1981 and then falling to only 10 in 1985; the initial rise was less sharp, but the later decline was equally precipitate.

There is no evidence of substitution in the DAWN data. Two other important drugs in the same therapeutic class (diazepam, or Valium, and flurazepam) also showed declines throughout the entire 1976–1985 period, whereas a third (diphenhydramine) increased throughout that period; Table 11-2 presents the ER figures. Phenobarbitol, a key ingredient in some counterfeit Quaaludes, declined—although rather slowly—throughout the period.

Interpretation of these data is complicated by the clear evidence, reflected in other sources as well, that tranquilizer use was on the decline by the late 1970s. Consider the thirty-day prevalence rates in the High School Senior Survey. Methaqualone shows a fairly steady upward trend from 1976 (1.6 percent) to 1981 (3.3 percent) and then a sharp decline to 1985 (1.0 percent). For the other sedatives, however—namely barbiturates—the pattern is one of steady decline from 3.9 percent in 1976 to 2.0 percent in 1985. The DAWN data simply show no change in the trend as a result of changes in methaqualone availability. Even the one member of the therapeutic class that showed a different pattern, diphenhydramine, rose constantly during the entire cycle of methaqualone abuse.

NNICC reported in 1981 that as a result of reduced availability of methaqualone powder, "there has been a trend to substitute other depressant substances, such as phenobarbitol and diazepam (Valium) in the illicit manufacturing process."[21] For some years there was considerable "counterfeiting" of Quaaludes with other depressants or sedative hypnotics, but because of low quality and inconsistency, the counterfeits gained little popularity. DAWN data confirm that this use of counterfeits was not of a scale to compensate substantially for the decline in genuine methaqualone consumption.

Eliminating Colombian Marijuana

This case is not as clear an illustration of the impact of sealing the borders, but it does provide some interesting insights into the consequences of effective interdiction—the most heavily funded of the programs aimed at isolating the United States from foreign drug production. In the late 1970s, when U.S. marijuana consumption was at its peak—at least as measured by prevalence—the bulk of that marijuana was imported from Colombia, apparently by sea. Seizures of fifty tons or more were not uncommon, with large seagoing vessels carrying the drug to within about fifty miles of the Florida coast—at which point they off-loaded to smaller and faster "cigarette boats." The latter brought the drug into the numerous bays that dot the coastline and make interdiction so difficult.

The coast guard and Customs Service employed increasing resources, including airborne radar and a large number of fast ships, against this mode of smuggling. Quantities seized had already begun to decline by 1981, as had the average size of seizures; in 1981 coast guard marijuana seizures averaged 9 tons compared to 4.6 tons in 1985.[22] The farm gate price of marijuana in Colombia also began to decline, presumably reflecting reduced export demand. It appears that Colombian maritime smugglers may have shifted to cocaine from marijuana, because the more compact cocaine was much less readily detected in sea traffic; it could be carried on smaller and less conspicuous boats, and high-value shipments could be concealed in hidden compartments that apparently were difficult for interdiction agents to detect. Certainly, coast guard seizures of maritime-borne cocaine rose rapidly.

This interdiction success had four consequences:

1. New sources of marijuana replaced Colombia. Mexico, whose marijuana industry had been badly affected by an eradication campaign in the mid-1970s and by an associated paraquat herbicide scare, reappeared in a more dispersed and covert form.[23] By 1986 Mexico was supplying an estimated 30 percent of the U.S. market, or 40 percent of total imports.
2. Domestic commercial producers became significant for the first time. In 1985 the NNICC estimated that 19 percent of U.S. consumption was supplied from domestic sources; by 1989 that figure had risen to 25 percent. Given the higher potency and price of domestic marijuana, it accounted for a larger share of total revenues.
3. The potency of marijuana increased markedly. The federal laboratory at the University of Mississippi, which does chemical analyses of a sample of federal and local seizures, reported an increase in average THC (tetrahydrocannabinol, the active ingredient in marijuana) content every year after 1973. By 1988 the average content was 3.6 percent, compared with 0.2 percent in 1972.
4. The price of marijuana, even when adjusted for inflation and potency, seems to have increased. After having fluctuated around a constant level during the

period 1975–1978, a period of increasing demand, prices began to increase sharply thereafter when demand seems to have turned down.[24]

We can reasonably attribute these changes to the increased interdiction effort, because Colombia continued to be the low-cost producer of marijuana, with much lower domestic wholesale prices than those found in Mexico and the United States. Moreover, Colombian domestic prices actually declined from the late 1970s, whereas those in Mexico and the United States increased substantially. Roger Warner presents an interesting description of how interdiction affected patterns of production and trafficking.[25]

The rise in potency, the shift to domestic sources, and price increases are all of interest for this analysis. Domestic growers incur much higher costs than those in the poorer traditional source countries. However, they avoid the costs of risky (expensive) smuggling across international borders into the United States and thus are able to compete with these producers when offered the protection of aggressive interdiction. Marijuana, which is relatively bulky and has a distinctive odor, is more vulnerable to interdiction than either cocaine or heroin.

For domestic producers, the primary cost of production is the risk associated with detection of the plants. To minimize that risk they have moved to the development and cultivation of progressively higher-potency strains, permitting higher yields per square meter. In recent years some sophisticated production facilities have been found, including one with acres of underground cultivation.

Nonetheless, despite the expansion of domestic production, marijuana use has continued to decline. This seems to be primarily a function of changing attitudes toward health and perceptions of the dangers of drugs rather than of the rise in prices.[26] This makes the price evidence even stronger. Effective interdiction of marijuana from the low-cost producer, although its effects were ameliorated by the existence of domestic and other less vulnerable producers, was indeed able to increase the price of marijuana even in the face of declining demand.

I present no data on the extent of substitution because there is no literature as to what in fact are the substitutes for marijuana. The shift to more potent forms may be seen as one form of substitution because they are not necessarily the desired forms; very high-potency marijuana is harder to titrate. Nor, even at recent high prices, is there a comparably cheap source of intoxication per unit hour. Mark Moore estimates the price of a joint in the mid-1980s at ninety-five cents.[27] One joint, particularly of high-potency marijuana, can yield two hours of intoxication.

Conclusion

Although the evidence is scarcely overwhelming, it fairly consistently supports the proposition that declines in imports caused by major disturbances overseas or by the risks faced by smugglers are by no means fully compensated for by domestic production or diversion. In each of the three cases examined in this chapter, reducing the availability of foreign-source drugs apparently had positive consequences on the reduction of U.S. drug consumption. Although heroin addicts did search for substitutes, there was clearly a decline in the number of addicts, and the extent of effective substitution was modest. When heroin again became readily available, many of those who had reduced their consumption of heroin returned to that drug. Methaqualone abuse does not seem to have been replaced by abuse of a substitute drug following its virtual elimination from the U.S. market. Effective interdiction of Colombian marijuana, although it led to the growth of domestic production, did make marijuana substantially more expensive.

None of this constitutes an endorsement of the cost-effectiveness of interdiction or other programs outside U.S. borders. But when such programs are successful, they can have an effect on U.S. drug consumption.

In conclusion, I take up three points: explanations for incomplete substitution; additional consequences of declining imports; and finally, the likelihood of accomplishing a major decline in cocaine imports through external supply control programs.

Why is there not more complete substitution? The heroin episode is perhaps the most interesting because the users of that drug were the most committed or dependent and were heavily involved in criminal activity; if criminal energy could establish channels for substitutes, it would do so for this drug. As suggested above, many apparently good substitutes for heroin already exist in the pharmacopoeia of prescription drugs. In addition, it is always rumored that some basement chemist has developed a new, more powerful analogue to heroin—for example, fentanyl, up to one thousand times more powerful than morphine; and MPPP, a mepiridine (Demarol)-like drug. Yet none of these analogues seems to have gained widespread acceptance when heroin became markedly less available.

Explanations can be found on both sides of the market. Users may have experimented with other drugs and simply not found the sensations comparable enough to accept the substitutes. Frequently, counterfeit or substitute drugs are of inconsistent and poor quality. The available literature does not allow an examination of that possibility.

On the supply side, we need to consider separately diversion and illicit production. It may be that diversion cannot readily be expanded in face of increased demand without a large increase in risks and hence in the prices of the diverted drugs. And the substitutes available from illicit chemists have frequently had dangerous side effects; in particular, the synthetic opiates that are so much more powerful than heroin present problems in terms of control of dosage. Moreover, slight errors in production can result in toxic by-products: MPTP—a by-product of careless MPPP production—caused numerous deaths and serious injuries, damaging the reputation of clandestine laboratory suppliers.

Declines in imports will do more than just affect the composition of illicit drugs consumed; they will also affect trafficking patterns within the United States. Typically, domestic production has occurred through more decentralized modes than those that brought in imports. There is no counterpart in the domestic marijuana or PCP markets to the large-scale importing groups involved in the cocaine industry. This may explain the observation, based solely on anecdote, that there is less violence associated with the high-level trafficking of domestically produced drugs.

Note that it may be easier to control diversion from licit commerce than from the import of natural-based drugs or the manufacture of illicits. The reformulation of Talwin, the evidence that triplicate forms for prescription drugs have reduced ER admissions related to such drugs, and the effectiveness of the methaqualone controls all point to the potential effectiveness of such efforts. Control of domestic manufacture, typically through registration and monitoring of precursor chemicals, apparently has not managed to greatly reduce illicit manufacture of drugs such as PCP and methamphetamine.

The analysis here is highly speculative. Is it likely to be subject to a test in the near future? Is there any basis to expect that interdiction or foreign-control programs will have much impact on the availability of cocaine? In the first half of 1990, many cities reported a sharp increase in prices at the wholesale level, despite other evidence that demand was declining. This price increase was apparently triggered by the Colombian government's crackdown against the Medellín trafficking group. As expected, the crackdown also led to a sharp decline in coca leaf prices in both Bolivia and Peru, driven by an abrupt reduction in refining activity.

By the third quarter of 1990, leaf prices were reported to have risen again, suggesting that the effect of the crackdown was temporary; refining activity had returned to previous levels. Indeed, the best explanation for the earlier import price rise may be that the Cali traffickers, who were not targeted in the crackdown, took advantage of the elimination of the competition to raise their product prices. There is some evidence that the Medellín group has established new refining and export facilities in Bolivia. All this presages a likely decline in import prices—perhaps back to the 1988 levels.

But if it were possible to achieve a lasting reduction in the availability of foreign-source cocaine to the United States—not only from the Andes but from all other potential growing areas around the world—then the result might be a substantial reduction in both the consumption of cocaine and the recruitment of new users into stimulant abuse. The existence of substitutes such as methamphetamines is not enough to justify nihilistic skepticism about the worth of international control programs. The fundamental question is whether in fact these programs have any prospect of achieving their proclaimed goals.

Notes

1. For example, see Bruce M. Bagley, "Colombia and the War on Drugs," *Foreign Affairs* 67, no. 1 (Fall 1988): 70–92.

2. These statements are true with current technology. It is possible that given effective international control programs, higher-technology modes of production might be developed that would allow U.S. growers to compete internationally.

3. Source country control programs receive more rhetorical than fiscal support; these programs accounted for only about 5 percent of the federal government's drug budgets throughout the 1980s. As a share of the nation's total drug control expenditures (including those of state and local governments), they might have accounted for no more than 2 percent in the late 1980s. Interdiction does account for substantial expenditures; it typically accounted for 25 percent of federal expenditures in the same period.

4. See Edward Jay Epstein, *Agency of Fear* (New York: G. P. Putnam, 1978).

5. See Ethan Nadelmann, "Drug Prohibition in the United States: Costs, Consequences, and Alternatives," *Science* 245 (1989): 939–947.

6. See James Ostrowski, "Thinking About Drug Legalization," *Cato Institute Policy Analysis* 121 (May 25, 1989).

7. Alcohol may be an important substitute for many illicit drugs. However, with the existing data systems, it is impossible to detect changes in alcohol consumption by current and potential users of a particular illicit drug. Douglas Anglin, who has followed a cohort of heroin addicts over a twenty-year period, suggests that alcohol is the drug to which they turn when it becomes difficult (that is, time-consuming and risky) to obtain heroin or close substitutes. Note that I am including as illicit drugs those that can be medically prescribed; it is the nonmedically prescribed use of the drug that is illicit.

8. Norman Zinberg, *Drug, Set, and Setting* (Cambridge: Harvard University Press, 1980).

9. Ronald Siegel, *Intoxication: The Search for Altered Consciousness* (New York: Simon and Schuster, 1989).

10. Roy Wise, "The Neurobiology of Craving: Implications for the Understanding and Treatment of Addiction," *Journal of Abnormal Psychology* 92, no. 2 (1988): 125.

11. M. Douglas Anglin and Yih-ing Hser, "Treatment of Drug Abuse," in Michael Tonry and James Q. Wilson, eds., *Drugs and Crime* (Chicago: University of Chicago Press, 1990).

12. Peter Reuter, John Haaga, Patrick Murphy, and Amy Praskac, *Drug Use and Drug Programs in the Washington Metropolitan Area* (Santa Monica, Calif.: RAND Corporation, 1988).

13. National Institute of Justice, *Drug Use Forecasting: Annual Report* (Washington, D.C.: U.S. Government Printing Office, 1990).

14. See William Butyniski and Diane Canova, *State Resources and Services for Alcohol and Drug Abuse Programs* (Rockville, Md.: Alcohol, Drug Abuse, and Mental Health Administration, 1988). Since 1987 the prevalence of PCP in Washington has declined sharply, apparently pushed out as the result of the availability of crack. Whereas in July 1987 approximately half of all arrestees tested positive for PCP, that figure had fallen below 10 percent by July 1990.

15. In the absence of consistent panel data, the rise for 1974–1976 is derived from the fraction of all ER episodes that were heroin related: 0.65 per 1,000 in 1974 and 0.95 per 1,000 in 1976. See Nicholas Kozel, Raquel Crider, Mark Bordsky, and Edgar Adams, *Epidemiology of Heroin: 1964–1984* (Rockville, Md.: National Institute on Drug Abuse, 1985).

16. Kozel et al., *Epidemiology of Heroin*, especially Figures 9B and 9H and Appendix 2.

17. Heroin is a Schedule I drug; it has high abuse potential and there is no therapeutic use for which it is the preferred drug. Morphine, codeine, and the like are generally Schedule II drugs; they have high abuse potential but also have therapeutic uses.

18. Annual reports of the National Narcotics Intelligence Consumers Committee, *Narcotics Intelligence Estimate* (Washington, D.C.), especially 1983 and 1985.

19. This decline almost certainly reflected the decision to reformulate the commercially marketed form Talwin with a narcotic antagonist, naxolone. The antagonist caused serious adverse reactions in narcotics addicts, the people for whom pentazocine had previously served as a substitute. In the period just before the reformulated Talwin was introduced, Ts and Blues suppliers apparently hoarded any available pentazocine. This raised pentazocine prices above heroin prices, which were just beginning to decline in the fall of 1983. This illustrates well short-term price effects of substitution and the facility with which the problem could be controlled "at the source" when the drug was licitly manufactured in the United States.

20. Richard Clayton and Harwin Voss, *Young Men and Drugs in Manhattan: A Causal Analysis* (Rockville, Md.: National Institute on Drug Abuse, 1981).

21. National Narcotics Intelligence Consumers Committee, *The Supply of Illicit Drugs to the United States from Foreign and Domestic Sources in 1979 and 1980* (Washington, D.C.: NNICC, 1981).

22. Peter Reuter, Gordon Crawford, and Jonathan Cave, *Sealing the Borders: The Effect of Increased Military Involvement in Drug Interdiction* (Santa Monica, Calif.: RAND Corporation, 1988).

23. Peter Reuter and David Ronfeldt, *Quest for Integrity: The Mexico-U.S. Drug Problem* (Santa Monica, Calif.: RAND Corporation, 1991).

24. The nominal price per gram was $0.64 in 1976 and $5.00 in 1988. When adjusted for inflation and potency changes since 1976, the 1988 figure was $0.75—a 17 percent increase. Mark Moore, "Supply Reduction and Drug Law Enforcement," in Tonry and Wilson, *Drugs and Crime*, 109–158.

25. Roger Warner, *Invisible Hand: The Marijuana Business* (New York: Beech Tree Books, 1986), 28–44.

26. Jerald G. Bachman, Lloyd D. Johnston, and Patrick M. O'Malley, "Explaining the Recent Decline in Marihuana Use: Differentiating the Effects of Perceived Risks, Disapproval, and General Lifestyle Factors," *Journal of Health and Social Behavior* 29 (March 1988): 92–112.

27. Moore, "Supply Reduction."

12

Against the Odds: Therapeutic Community Approaches to Underclass Drug Abuse

Rod Mullen and Naya Arbiter

As the tide of casual drug use that crested in 1985 recedes, the United States must face what it has long ignored: the intractable and entangled wreckage of inner-city social ills. Addiction-driven criminality among the urban "underclass" is the force behind the dramatic growth of prisons, jails, probation, and parole. Always marginal, this population is increasingly separate from the middle-class experience and deviant from middle-class values. It will not and cannot respond to programs designed for mainstream society.

Effective interventions for urban underclass drug users must focus on methodology that is "habilitative" rather than rehabilitative, providing the very basics of healthy living. Emphasis must shift from individual recovery to community and institutional recovery. These community models must be long-term, comprehensive programs; they must include health care, basic education, job training, parenting skills, moral development, and community-building skills. Ironically, the cost of such intervention is minimal when compared with the escalating costs that result from ignoring these problems.

During the turn-of-the-century flirtation with cocaine in the United States, described by David Musto in Chapter 2, drug use was almost equally divided among the advantaged and disadvantaged. Despite cocaine's status as the glamour drug of the 1970s and early 1980s, this pattern has radically changed. The National Institute of Justice Drug Use Forecasting (DUF) system administers anonymous urine screens to adult female and male arrestees in twenty-three major U.S. cities. Since 1986 the DUF system has provided the United States with the first objective measure of drug use among arrestees in major urban centers, and its findings clearly show that the spread of serious drug use is greatest in neighborhoods in which crime, unemployment, and lack of education create a vulnerable population.[1]

Dramatic declines in drug use reported in both the High School Senior and National Household Surveys exclude those people most likely to be drug abusers. The High School Senior Survey is highly publicized—although 50 percent of all arrestees never complete high school. Similarly, the National Household Survey excludes not only the homeless but also all those who live in group quarters and institutions—including military installations, college dormitories, hotels, hospitals, jails, and prisons. DUF data further demonstrate that an "urban underclass" of drug-involved criminal arrestees in the sixty-one largest U.S. cities contains as many frequent users of cocaine (620,000 to 1.1 million) as are estimated to exist in the entire U.S. drug-using population as measured by the National Household Survey—which excludes this group.[2]

The tendency to underestimate the drug-using population prompts serious misperceptions within the public and may precipitate a premature victory celebration in the "war on drugs." At a time when raising taxes is politically unpopular, it may be tempting to turn away from disadvantaged drug abusers—the majority of whom belong to racial and ethnic minorities. To do this would leave these communities, already disadvantaged, with even fewer resources to combat the multitude of social ills that afflict them. Ignoring these problems over past decades has enabled poverty, illiteracy, infant mortality, teen pregnancy, child abuse, homicide, prostitution, and gang activity to grow to unprecedented proportions. Many of today's addicts are the children and grandchildren of those whose addiction and criminality were left unaddressed a generation ago.[3]

For these forgotten groups, it is inappropriate to think of drug "rehabilitation" programs. There is little in the experience of underclass addicts or of their communities that gives them a reference point for complying with middle-class norms. Social scientists are finding that the psychological profiles of inner-city U.S. children today are similar to those of children growing up in war-torn, Third World countries. The profiles reveal a lack of short-term memory, which, it is explained, is a psychological survival mechanism; the children learn to "erase" what is too painful to bear. Because drug abuse prevention, treatment, and research have focused on articulate white males, it is not surprising that U.S. officials find few weapons in the armory of models that have proven effective for unacculturated minority drug addicts—a population unaffected by the "just say no" campaigns of the 1980s. With few exceptions, drug treatment methods have not been developed for habili-tation but for rehabilitation (or for pharmacological intervention and stabilization, as in methadone maintenance).

Publicly funded interventions for drug users can be divided into three major categories: outpatient methadone, residential (including therapeutic communities), and outpatient drug free. To this should be added chemical dependency treatment, otherwise known as the Minnesota Model, which usually serves more advantaged addicts whose treatment is reimbursed by insurance. The two interventions used most frequently with underclass drug users are methadone maintenance and thera-peutic communities.

Methadone maintenance is designed for adults with long-standing dependence on heroin. Methadone treatment has the specific goal of reducing or eliminating the consumption of illicit drugs and concomitant predatory crime. In recent years it has also been applied to reducing needle use among heroin addicts, thus helping to reduce AIDS-HIV transmission. Extensive studies show that when properly administered, methadone is effective in achieving those goals—and it is inexpensive compared with residential care.[4] But methadone is a limited tool. It is not suggested even by its most zealous proponents to be appropriate for nonopiate drug users (now the largest proportion of addicts) or for the youthful (often subteen) addict. Nor does it promote individual psychological development or community integration; rather, it stabilizes individuals and reduces criminal behavior.

Therapeutic Communities

From its inception, therapeutic community methodology has addressed the needs of criminally involved addicts and has recognized the need for habilitation, not just rehabilitation. The self-help therapeutic community (TC) for substance abuse[5] originated in the United States through Charles Dederich, a former alcoholic and Alcoholics Anonymous (AA) zealot who in the 1950s inadvertently discovered that his brand of unorthodox and confrontational encounter groups caused some heroin addicts to stop using drugs. This discovery, coupled with an abundance of heroin addicts available to test the method, led to the establishment in 1958 of Synanon: a not-for-profit corporation that became the progenitor of therapeutic communities for drug addiction throughout the United States. Although Synanon's antipsychological stance and AA roots precluded scientific study of its members, it was soon clear that Synanon was having success in an area in which failure was the norm. At the time, conventional wisdom was "once an addict, always an addict." Synanon's claim that the most degraded and deviant members of society could live in a law-abiding, self-managed community and be the catalysts for their own recovery was—and remains—revolutionary.

Although acknowledging the absence of a medical "cure" for addiction, professionals showed little enthusiasm for Synanon's approach; they were especially skeptical of an addict's ability to reform without the benefit of trained psychiatric expertise. One exception to this thinking was Dr. Daniel Casriel (the first psychiatrist to visit Synanon), who proclaimed that there was now hope for those persons whose character disorders had made them the social outcasts of society.[6] The heroin crisis of the 1960s pushed public officials to provide funds for newly formed programs inspired by the Synanon Method.[7] Many such programs were started or staffed by ex-addicts who had been at Synanon, or by professionals such as Dr. Casriel of Daytop Village and Dr. Mitchell Rosenthal of Phoenix House.[8]

In the past thirty years, the therapeutic community has become a major element in the effort to ameliorate the effects of drug use in the most disadvantaged populations. It is important to note that modern TCs, although rooted in Synanon, vary considerably from the Synanon approach.

The Synanon Approach

Synanon was an AA offshoot that rejected professionals and the medical-psychological approach to addiction and counseled the power of "self-reliance" in a self-help community. Its methodology of empowerment taught addicts to help each other out of their addiction, criminality, and other antisocial behaviors.

Although Synanon began with alcoholics and became famous for its work with heroin addicts, it never focused on drug addiction as its primary purpose; nor did it ever accept the notion that addiction was a disease requiring a professional cure. Its declaration of purpose stated that it was formed to research and investigate the causes of personal alienation—including but not limited to alcoholism, other drug addiction, criminality, and delinquency.[9] Many different people with all manner of compulsive behavior (gambling, eating, and the like) went to Synanon for help, and all behavioral problems were met with the same self-help-in-community approach. In 1970, for example, as the surgeon general's pronouncements about the health consequences of tobacco use became more forceful, Synanon members quit smoking en masse. Synanon's claim was that addicts gave up drugs as a "by-product" of actively engaging in a health-promoting community.

Synanon never directly accepted public funds. Although donations of cash and goods were actively and effectively solicited, Synanon's main income came from its own businesses; these grew to over $20 million per year and were consistent with the self-reliance message. The only U.S. TCs to continue this approach are the Delancey Street Foundation in California and Habilitat in Hawaii.[10] All other U.S. TCs are part of the publicly funded behavioral health care system, although some supplement their funds with other activities.

Synanon proudly flaunted its antiestablishment posture. There were many publicized battles with city councils, zoning commissions, licensing commissions, and probation departments and with the drug czars of the day—who were often appalled by the arrogant, pugnacious, racially integrated group of outcasts living together. Synanon's economic independence permitted it to make scathing public criticisms of the medical, treatment, and correctional establishments of the day with impunity. But as with present-day TCs, it formed a physical and psychological bridge between deviant underclass norms and the acquisition of mainstream social norms and behavior. Synanon prided itself on teaching hard work, honesty, parental responsibility, marital stability, and conventional morality.

But unlike the TCs of today, Synanon saw its role as much larger than merely the transformation of the underclass into hard-working, middle-class citizens. Synanon styled itself as a "model society" that demonstrated to the racially torn United States of the 1960s how blacks, whites, and Hispanics could live together in community; how the lawless could live lawfully without criminal justice supervision; how the dependent could learn self-reliance; how the irresponsible could become the compulsively responsible. This eventually led Synanon to stop blessing the transition of its members back into mainstream society, which was seen as fundamentally unhealthy for those with addiction backgrounds.

The organization also purported to enable outcasts to speak with power brokers in a society in which social stratification prevented such contact. Many of the six thousand nonresident members were prominent professionals. All were involved in community outreach programs that used encounter groups between recovered ex-addicts and successful "squares" (nonaddicts) to promote a dialogue on morality and "right living." Dederich believed that reformed outcasts had a great deal to say to those in positions of power and privilege. Only when society accepted and integrated *all* its members, Dederich proclaimed, could it hope to achieve social health and social justice.

As with AA, there was no "staff" at Synanon. All were "members" who lived at the facilities, with varying degrees of status based on length of sobriety and achievement within the organization. Even fifteen years after its formation, with millions in assets, members drew no salary, but met their physical needs in a communal way. Dederich did not eschew U.S. capitalism—quite the contrary— maintaining a sense of community in which ex-addicts' therapeutic skills and community-building abilities were nurtured and respected. This differs from publicly funded TCs, in which staff are salaried and few, if any, live at the program site— thus introducing a "we" versus "they" distinction Synanon sought to avoid. This dichotomy is ameliorated somewhat by the regular recruitment of TC clients to become trainees and then staff members.

By the early 1970s, over 300 U.S. therapeutic community drug treatment programs could trace their origins to the Synanon approach. Synanon grew to have a residential membership of over 2,500 and a nonresidential membership of 6,000, with branches in nine U.S. cities and in Puerto Rico. Nonetheless Synanon began to decline in the mid-1970s and was out of business by the end of the decade.[11]

TC Development in the United States

The therapeutic model derived from Daytop, Phoenix House, Odyssey House, and Gateway developed prominent characteristics:

- an institutional bias toward the treatment of male opiate addicts
- rigidity in structure
- relatively uncompromising discipline for program violations
- separation of residents from family influences (considered to be "negative")
- "on-the-job" training of ex-addict staff members
- hierarchical structure that equated clinical progress with moving up the ladder of program responsibilities
- a twelve- to twenty-four–month expected length of stay, with implicit acceptance of a very high dropout rate
- an antipsychological, antimedical orientation toward drug abuse

By the mid-1970s these characteristics had begun to change. Many TCs were larger and better established, and became part of the public health care system in the northeastern United States. Some began to successfully apply prevention programs to a broader version of the model—reaching out to adolescent substance abusers, polydrug abusers, clients under criminal justice supervision, addicted women with children, and school-age youngsters. Many TCs now have extensive family programs that bring their clients' families and "significant others" into the treatment process. In recent years more effort has been devoted to reentry programs. In many of these, continuity of care has come full circle by urging TC participants to join AA or Narcotics Anonymous (NA) fellowships.

The most dramatic change, however, has been the introduction of public funding. With this funding came public scrutiny, audits, licensing by bureaucratic agencies, outside boards of directors, and constraints regarding who could be accepted for help. Public funding added the language of the medical and academic communities, in which the habilitative processes of community became translated into the medical terminology of drug abuse treatment. First "interpreted" by academics, psychologists, and physicians as a medical rather than a community approach, then controlled by the constraints of public funding, some of those involved with TCs became concerned about the loss of uniqueness and integrity. Some TC voices complained that the only model developed by the underclasses for the underclasses—the Synanon model—had been co-opted by the very groups that had been unsuccessful with addicts in the first place.

In general, TCs have come to emphasize group rather than individual therapeutic intervention. They stress firm behavioral norms with a system of clearly defined rewards and punishments within a communal economy of housework and other roles. They employ reality-oriented group and individual psychotherapy, which includes lengthy encounter sessions focusing on current living issues and deep-seated emotional problems. They impose a series of hierarchical responsibilities, privileges, and promotion of esteem through working up a "ladder" of tasks from admission to graduation—permitting some degree of mobility from client to staff member. Finally, they display an institutional bias toward underclass clients.[12]

Effectiveness of Treatment

Over the past quarter century, there have been two large-scale, federally sponsored treatment outcome studies: the Drug Abuse Reporting Program (DARP), a twelve-year follow-up study of a national admission sample cohort of clients from 1969 to 1971,[13] and the Treatment Outcome Prospective Study, a ten-thousand-person national cohort analysis of admissions to forty-one treatment programs between 1979 and 1981.[14] Another large study is currently in progress. Principal findings to date demonstrate that

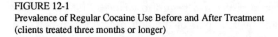

FIGURE 12-1
Prevalence of Regular Cocaine Use Before and After Treatment
(clients treated three months or longer)

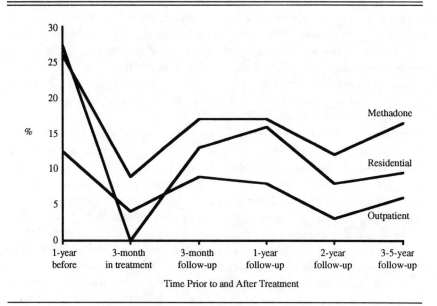

Note: Percent = percent of patients treated using cocaine regularly.

Source: Reprinted, by permission of the publisher, from *Drug Abuse Treatment: A National Study of Effectiveness,* by Robert L. Hubbard et al., copyright 1989, The University of North Carolina Press, 109.

- Treatment reduces drug consumption and other criminal behavior for a substantial number of people; most do best while in treatment and do worse after treatment but are demonstrably better than before they entered treatment.
- Treatment is effective in all modalities, but effectiveness varies considerably among programs.
- Length of time in treatment is almost universally correlated with posttreatment success. (In fact, time in a program may be regarded as the one finding that has been nearly incontrovertible in drug abuse treatment studies. No matter what the treatment modality, those adults who stay in treatment longer almost invariably do better on all measures of posttreatment performance.)
- Benefits outweigh costs.[15]

Treatment works and is cost-effective. However, "success" must take into consideration that relapse and several treatment episodes are often necessary to attain abstinence. A definition of success must also recognize that even when treatment does not achieve total abstinence, it often reduces drug consumption, criminality, and the social costs of addiction (see trend lines in Figure 12-1). If a hard-core criminal addict becomes a casual user, there has been relative success—especially if an addict with a lifetime history of criminality and criminal justice supervision never goes to prison again. One 1989 study projected a public-sector gain of $11.31 in benefits from each dollar spent on drug treatment.[16]

Therapeutic communities take more time and money than outpatient drug-free or methadone programs, but they realize greater long-term improvement when patients stay for at least a year. Even clients remaining three months show demonstrable gains. Not only is drug use substantially reduced but so is criminality—with dramatic improvements in psychological function, capacity for employment, stability of relationships, and community involvement.[17] This is consistent with the TC outlook that drug abuse is merely one part of the problem. As one expert has explained, TCs regard drug abuse as the result of impeded personality development or accumulated deficits resulting from socioeconomic disadvantage and dysfunctional family background.[18]

So few studies have been done of adolescents in TCs or other treatment modalities that results, although positive, are not authoritative. Generally, TCs have worked effectively with older adolescents whose admission profiles have not been substantially different from those of adults. Studies of women in TCs indicate that although most TCs have not been organized with women's needs as a priority, women have shown improvements during both treatment and posttreatment.[19]

Research has yet to determine client characteristics that predict success, but studies show that unlike methadone maintenance programs, TCs can effectively serve participants who use a variety of different drugs. In the late 1960s, TCs treated a small but significant proportion of those using barbiturates, methamphetamines, hallucinogens, and cocaine. Studies at the time showed outcomes comparable for all drug users, thus anticipating the successful adaptation of TCs to primary cocaine users in the 1980s.[20]

The major problem with TC treatment is retention. The DARP study showed that twelve months after admission, 71 percent of the clients had left treatment, although only 5 percent had completed their treatment plan.[21] Although much more attention has been given to retention in the last decade, it remains the cardinal issue for treatment improvement and cost-benefit increases for TCs.

Prison Drug Treatment

The United States had over one million incarcerated persons in 1989, as shown in Table 12-1, and more than four million under criminal justice supervision (probation and parole)—more than any other nation in the world. The vast majority of these are drug abusers.[22] The largest and most accessible population of addicts is in prisons and jails, and much of the demand for cocaine and other illegal drugs in the United States stems from the persons who are detained and supervised by the criminal justice system.[23] Retention is increased significantly when treatment is

TABLE 12-1
Federal and State Offenders Under Correctional Supervision, 1989

Type of Supervision	Number in 1985	Number in 1989	% Change 1985-1989	% of Total Under Supervision 1989
In the community				
Probation	1,968,712	2,520,479	28.0	62.2
Parole	300,203	456,797	52.2	11.3
Totals	2,268,915	2,977,276	31.2	73.4[a]
Incarcerated				
Jail	254,986	393,303	54.2	9.7
Prison	487,593	683,367	40.2	16.9
Totals	742,579	1,076,670	45.0	26.6
Total under correctional supervision	3,011,494	4,053,946	34.6	100.0

[a]Percentage figures do not add because of rounding.

Source: Based on data in L. Jankowski, "Probation and Parole 1989," *Bureau of Statistics Bulletin* NCJ-125833 (Washington, D.C.: Bureau of Justice Statistics, 1990), with adjustments in figures for total percentage changes 1985-1989.

initiated within an institution; compulsory treatment is as successful as voluntary treatment in most cases.[24]

"Shock incarceration" or "boot camp"–type programs, widely embraced as a miracle cure during the 1980s despite the lack of evidence of their efficacy, have not been shown to reduce recidivism.[25] This is consistent with other indications that programs lacking treatment elements do not reduce recidivism rates of drug-involved criminal offenders. Treatment programs within institutions, by contrast, often lead to continuation of drug treatment in the community postrelease.[26] Additionally, segregating prison drug treatment programs from the general prison population and using ex-addicts as counselors (as well as other recognized TC methods) have demonstrably improved both institutional management of inmates and posttreatment results.[27] For example, two prison-based TCs, Stay'n Out (in New York) and Cornerstone (in Oregon), show significant reductions in recidivism and improvements in parole outcomes for program participants compared with a control group of untreated inmates.[28]

It might be argued that the United States is the first industrialized country to attempt to incorporate incarceration as a bulwark in its approach to long-standing social problems.[29] Florida's Commission on Ethnic and Racial Bias projects that by 1994, 40 percent of all nonwhite males between ages eighteen and thirty-four will be incarcerated or under criminal justice supervision.[30] Prison populations will continue to grow for some time. Politicians are sensitive to the moods of the voting citizenry, and it is probably fair to say that no U.S. politician has lost an election in the past fifteen years by being "too tough" on criminals and drug abusers. Only when voting citizens begin to question the large expenditures and negligible results of the present approach will policy change.

Improving the TC: Amity Interventions

One current outgrowth of the TC movement is Amity, Inc.—a not-for-profit organization in Tucson, Arizona, that is a comprehensive therapeutic community model working with today's drug-using underclass. Amity operates facilities in three Arizona cities as well as a large prison-based TC in San Diego, California. Services include long-term adult and adolescent communities; adult and juvenile prison-based TCs; outreach, education, and prevention for youth, schools, and neighborhoods; AIDS prevention, education, and outreach; residential and vocational services for pregnant addicts and for addicted mothers and their children; and counseling and treatment for homeless substance abusers. Amity also has a nonresidential community center that serves as an alternative to prison for first-time offenders with drug histories and for probationers facing revocation because of drug involvement.

Organizational goals have been to respond to historically underserved populations and to develop pilot programs and community partnerships that apply the TC modality with other professionals involved with addicts (welfare, corrections, proba- tion, health departments, neighborhood improvement, homeless shelters, and similar groups).[31] We describe four interventions that have improved the effectiveness of the therapeutic community model.

Responding to the Needs of Women

At the inception of publicly funded drug treatment in the 1960s, programs were designed for and run by men. They did not take women clients into account— especially women convicts, drug-using prostitutes, or pregnant teenagers. Female addicts have been considered sicker, more resistant to drug treatment, and more difficult to deal with than their male counterparts—or any class or ethnic group.

In 1974 the National Institute on Drug Abuse (NIDA) established a program for women's concerns. In 1976 Public Law 94–371 granted priority consideration to funding women's treatment programs (although children of addicts were not included in this initiative). NIDA studies showed that 70 percent of addicted women had been raped or molested prior to addiction. Another study showed that among street prostitutes, as many as 70 percent had been sexually abused as children and repeatedly raped as adults.[32] Women drug users are disproportionately the victims of childhood sexual abuse, with estimates of sexual molestation as high as 60 percent (compared to 20 percent for men). Samples of treatment programs taken during the early 1980s indicated that the majority did not address issues of sexuality. In fact, drug-dependent women frequently reported sexual harassment within the program itself.[33]

U.S. drug policy is beginning to recognize the needs of women, largely through extensive media coverage of the plight of "crack babies" and their addicted mothers. The need for treatment of pregnant addicts becomes more apparent to policymakers when they consider that the cost of care for a crack baby can easily exceed $100,000 and that one year of special education for a drug-impaired third-grade child can cost $13,000.[34] "Only 12 female cocaine users sought treatment in Philadelphia 10 years ago," according to one newspaper account. "In 1989, there were more than 3,300. Today, nearly half the addicts in the city are women, and one in five babies born here last year had cocaine in their system."[35] Female intravenous drug users— many of them prostitutes—are at high risk of becoming infected with HIV and spreading that infection to their sexual partners, to their needle-sharing partners, and to children through perinatal transmission.

Many of the adult drug users in the system today are children whose mothers were ignored by the system two decades ago. "In New York City," for example, "there are over 125,000 women seeking treatment of chemical dependency and the drug related problems of their infants and children. The number of pregnant women using cocaine during pregnancy has more than quadrupled between 1985 and 1990."[36] The differences between treatment and prevention blur when intergenerational drug use and criminality become the norm, as they have in many underclass neighborhoods.

In 1981 Amity was a small (n=35) residential program with only one female resident. Although the planned duration of treatment was one year, the average length of stay for female residents had been forty-two days. Amity then introduced a series of changes:

- A female program director with ten years of TC experience was hired.
- Additional women staff members were hired until the ratio of female to male staff was 6:4.
- Special women's groups were held (as soon as there were enough women clients).
- Emphasis was placed both in the curricula and in daily activities on respect for women and on the importance of learning how to form nonsexual relationships.
- A small pilot project was started allowing women in duress to bring their children with them into the community.

Repeated surveys of women in treatment at Amity revealed that they averaged more than ten years of serious substance abuse over five years of prostitution and over two hundred sexual partners per year. Three-quarters had been molested or raped before age eighteen (the average number of rapes was six). For over half, Amity was the first attempt at drug treatment.

Results have been impressive. The proportion of women in treatment increased from 0.08 percent in 1981 to 32 percent by 1983. Length of stay increased for both women and men in spectacular fashion, as shown by Figure 12-2. The length of

FIGURE 12-2
Length of Stay at Amity, by Gender: 1974-1989

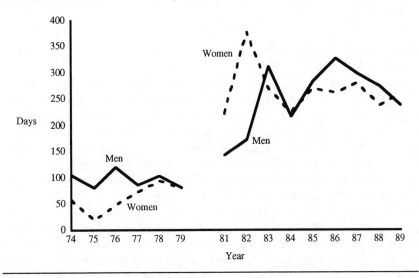

Note: Days = average length of stay, in number of days.

stay for the Amity adult TC is now roughly twice the national average for TC programs (which ranges from about 90 to 120 days). Women who were allowed to bring their children into the community successfully completed the program. Three years later, informal follow-ups showed that almost all were employed, that they were free from criminal activity or drug use, and that their children were functioning normally.[37]

The dramatic change in retention suggests that meeting women's needs has a beneficial effect on all community participants. Carol Gilligan has observed that women's path to maturity differs significantly from that of men: Women almost always have the formation and maintenance of relationships as primary tasks. Gilligan also suggested that when women are given equality in community, they balance the more hierarchical and separatist tendencies of typical male development.[38] The new model allowed women at Amity to feel physically and psychologically safe,[39] and their own self-disclosure encouraged men to take similar emotional risks. Addicted men began to reveal histories of sexual molestation they had promised to "take to the grave."

Having a woman (a former addict) as the program director with a predominantly female staff positively affected both men and women. Women reported inspiration for their own personal growth; men reported security, with less need to challenge authority. Children's participation in the community also appeared to have a beneficial effect on men, who began to take a greater interest in their own children.

Many said that the presence of children changed their perception from being patients in "just another program" to being responsible participants in an extended family setting.

Moving Toward Professionalism: New Methods of Staff Training

Drug treatment outcome studies have focused on client outcome, ignoring how staff—the most salient component of the treatment environment—affects retention, outcome, and perceptions of program participants. Substance abuse staff qualifications are moving rapidly toward academically trained and professionally certified counselors. There have been consistent efforts to develop a nationally recognized substance abuse credential. Over thirty states currently certify drug and alcohol abuse counselors. Often the credentialing of counselors is required for state licensing of programs; unlicensed programs cannot receive state funds.

Such training holds the promise of increased competency, reduced liability, professional advancement, and sophistication in the treatment of individuals with a diversity of problems and backgrounds. But little of the training offered in the field of substance abuse today helps staff members understand the constantly changing street culture. Even ex-addicts several years removed from the streets need to stay current with the acceleration of impairment. Available training does little to help academically trained and certified staff change perceptions by program participants that programs are just another institution populated by social workers making a living from the drug addict's misery.

Unfortunately, there is a tendency for professionals to see drug abusers as helpless victims. Low expectations are based on inadequate understanding. The original vitality of the TC approach depended on the perception of members that they had been accepted into a community—not a clinic. Living in the community were people whose life experiences, criminality, education, and racial and cultural characteristics were consistent with their own but who were behaving responsibly. High expectations were set by these credible role models, who knew the extent to which change was possible because they had changed themselves.

With publicly funded TCs the question becomes: Beyond recruiting and training former clients to become staff members, how can staff be trained to understand the community? How can "professionals" and ex-addicts become part of a community that recognizes the worth of each and develops shared values?

Amity introduced retreats for staff and residents in the mid-1980s. In addition to normal professional training activities, these eight-day retreats are held quarterly and usually include seventy-five to one hundred participants. All counseling staff participate in at least one retreat per year. Retreats are attended by staff (45 percent), residents (45 percent), and outside guests and program graduates (10 percent). Conducted by the most senior Amity staff, activities include encounter groups, outdoor experiences, art, family reconstruction workshops, and other experiential and didactic workshops. The participants are completely emerged in curricula for the entire period, with no outside activities. Staff and residents interact throughout. Retreats emphasize and reinforce a sense of community, reduce social distance between staff and residents, and accelerate the transmission of vital information—in particular, about norms and mores in the rapidly changing street culture. Both residents and staff members regard retreats as a crucial intervention that keeps Amity feeling more like a community and less like a fragmented organization. Amity's high retention rate may reflect this approach. Adaptations of this model may be useful particularly for those who work with diverse racial and ethnic populations.

Drug Treatment in Jails

A National Institute of Justice study determined that whereas the average cost of incarceration is about $25,000 per year, the average cost of crimes committed by each released inmate comes to $430,000 per year in victim losses, police costs, court work, private security expenses, and other expenses. The director of the National Institute of Justice used the study to draw a confounding conclusion: "Public debate has mistakenly focused on the cost of imprisonment compared to the cost of probation," he intoned, and went on to urge further construction of prison beds rather than the adoption of effective treatment efforts.[40]

Intensive drug interventions are scarce in federal prisons, but they are practically nonexistent in county or state jails. Of 1,687 jails participating in one survey, only 7 percent of the inmates were involved in some form of drug treatment—and that "treatment" might be as little as an occasional class with an overworked counselor or volunteer or a few videotapes. In fact, only 2 percent of the jails surveyed had more than ten hours per week of treatment activities—an effort that is completely inadequate for inmates who have extensive histories of serious drug abuse and assorted criminal problems. Information from the Drug Use Forecasting System indicates that at least 60 percent of inmates test positive for illicit drugs at the time of arrest.

Treatment in a jail or prison setting provides an important opportunity to engage offenders in a therapeutic environment with others who are experiencing similar difficulties. Many drug-involved offenders are unlikely to seek treatment on a voluntary basis and have a poor record of treatment participation. Incarceration is frequently the first lengthy period of abstention from drugs since initiation of regular drug use. Correctional treatment provides the opportunity to confront the inmate with the clear and unavoidable consequences of past drug use, to reduce the denial that often undermines involvement in treatment, and to develop life- and drug-coping skills in a structured and supportive milieu.[41]

Seeking to improve the situation in jails, Amity provided volunteer drug abuse services to inmates in the Pima County Jail for over five years. This project was designed by both organizations, each of which supplied senior staff members to jointly manage the project. Their supervisory team oversaw every aspect of the program—from selection of participants to disciplinary matters to joint supervision and training of both jail and correctional staff. The sheriff's department recognized the value of Amity's trained ex-addicts and ex-offenders. The program featured an intensive curriculum that included regular encounter groups, week-long workshops on specific recovery-oriented topics, the use of video playback, participants working together in the jail's food services department, and structured community responsibilities in which participants took day-to-day responsibility for helping to manage the program under staff guidance. The program also emphasized continuity of treatment: Many participants made a transition to Amity's long-term residential services, others to other local treatment providers, and some to regular encounter groups jointly sponsored by Amity and the local probation department. Eventually, the jail program included day services for female offenders in the same unit as males. As with other Amity adult programs, the inclusion of women appeared to improve the environment for men by increasing self-disclosure.

After three years of operation, over four hundred jail inmates have participated in the Amity–Pima County Jail Project. Psychosocial measures given at intake, release, and six-months postrelease demonstrate significant improvements ($p < .01$) in levels of depression, anxiety, and self-concept for both males and females. These measures are found in other studies to be associated with stable reductions in drug abuse and improvements in prosocial functioning. Further, recidivism rates to substance abuse and rearrest are around 36 percent, which is very low for a short-term intervention. (Normal recidivism exceeds 65 percent.) Ninety-five percent of those successfully released from the program sought some kind of continued substance abuse treatment (residential, outpatient, AA, NA, or Amity-sponsored groups in the community). For many of these chronic substance abusers, this was their first treatment experience, and their efforts to continue treatment demonstrate changes in attitude about themselves and their responsibilities.[42]

Addressing the Needs of Adolescent Addicts

Trends for adults are repeated with adolescents. Although relatively advantaged high-school seniors are turning away from drug abuse, there is evidence that abuse among the most disadvantaged may be increasing. More than adult treatment, adolescent treatment has been aimed at youth who are acculturated, verbal, and oriented toward middle-class society. Few public or private organizations have devoted sufficient resources to alienated, drug-involved, violent teens. With the turn toward harsh punishments for juvenile offenders in the 1980s, more teens were tried as adults and social services were proportionately less available. At the same time, the continued rapid decay of inner cities and the advent of crack left advocates completely unprepared for the underclass teen of today. Like adults, teens are disproportionately incarcerated and experience social bias: According to the Florida Supreme Court Racial and Ethnic Bias Study Commission, "Minority youth are treated differently at every step of the judicial process than similarly situated white youth."[43] Criminal justice intervention with teens is a predominant method of dealing with deviance, and habilitative resources are rarely available.[44]

Today's disadvantaged drug-using teenager is quite different from his or her peer of only ten years ago. Typically black or Hispanic, the contemporary teen is much more likely to come from a home in which one or both parents have substance abuse histories and involvement in the criminal justice system and in which the family is chaotic, poorly organized, impoverished, and abusive; the teen has probably been a victim of physical or sexual abuse in childhood and in all likelihood began using alcohol, drugs, or toxic vapors under ten years of age and became addicted by age thirteen. Girls are likely to have been sexually active before reaching puberty, to have been raped or molested, and to have had children or an abortion. Male or female, the teenager may have had experience as a prostitute (for sex, for drugs, for food and shelter, or for companionship), and if male, has probably been involved in several rapes—sometimes gang rapes. He or she has probably never had sex without being "high."

Often, the drug-abusing teenager began getting involved with the criminal justice system very early—perhaps before becoming a teen. The prospect of arrest, detention, or incarceration is not especially frightening; jail may be safer than the streets. Additionally, the teen is probably involved in gang activity and has been a drug distributor and drug dealer.[45]

The availability of crack cocaine has changed the street scene in ways few public officials understand. Overnight, poor and vulnerable children became victims of a drug that is inexpensive, easily available, ten times more potent than the heroin that created the heroin scare in New York in the early 1960s, and more addictive than any drug of modern times. In neighborhoods in which even $3 "rocks" of crack were too expensive, children continued to use gasoline, marijuana laced with PCP, spray paint, and other toxic substances. Despite the overwhelming media coverage of crack, few outside the immediate scene have any familiarity with the devastating violence and sexual promiscuity young women experience in crack houses in inner-city neighborhoods.[46]

Amity has worked closely with the Arizona Department of Juvenile Corrections since the mid-1980s to develop a comprehensive model for youth that begins in juvenile correctional institutions, moves to community-based residential care, then to transitional homes and aftercare. This intensive model is based on the premise that these teenagers are developmentally arrested and that they have not had the environment, circumstances, or encouragement to develop a less deviant value system. This model assumes that several months and perhaps years of a modified therapeutic community regime are necessary for teens to acquire the attitudes and skills that will enable them to live successfully. It further assumes that without successful intervention, these youth are the next generation of adult drug-using criminals—ready to spend their lives in and out of police stations, courts, jails, and prisons.[47]

Working with such youth requires discretion and sensitivity. They are physically mature, street smart, and hardened beyond their years. At the same time, they are emotionally immature—often illiterate, frightened, and naive about the world beyond the barrio and the detention center. As modified for the special needs of these youth, the TC provides an intensive 24-hours-per-day, 365-days-per-year holistic learning environment; a focus on family resources; and a curriculum that includes academic instruction at grade level, prevocational and vocational training, encounter groups and workshops to improve ability to express and control feelings, learning skills of cooperation with peers and adults, learning how to build and maintain positive peer networks, and supportive adult relationships. Transition homes, aftercare support, and relapse prevention help ensure that gains made in treatment are supported and strengthened after treatment. There is also a particularly rare opportunity for young women to participate in a community that includes both adolescent and adult addicts who are mothers learning to become effective and caring parents.

The development of this model is based on several years of cooperation between the Arizona Department of Juvenile Corrections and Amity. Evaluation of the program remains to be done, but the development of a working relationship between a private drug treatment agency and a public correctional agency is an important accomplishment. This joint venture targets youth who are 60 percent nonwhite and come from barrios, ghettos, and native American reservations in Arizona. The project offers an opportunity for these youths to learn skills and attitudes that can help them change their headlong rush toward criminality and continued incarceration as adults.

Whatever the final outcome of the Arizona-Amity program, the problems of youth pose a central challenge to U.S. society. As C. Ronald Huff has written:

> Youth gangs are symptomatic of many of the same social and economic problems as adult crime, mental illness, drug abuse, alcoholism, the surge in homelessness, and multi-generational "welfare families" living in hopelessness and despair. While we are justly concerned with the replacement of our physical infrastructure (roads, bridges, sewers), our human infrastructure may be crumbling as well. Our social, educational, and economic infrastructures are not meeting the needs of many children and adults. Increases in the numbers of women and children living in poverty (the "feminization" and "juvenilization" of poverty) are dramatic examples of this recent transformation.
>
> To compete with the seductive lure of drug profits and the grinding despair of poverty, we must reassess our priorities and reaffirm the importance of our neighborhoods by putting in place a number of programs that offer hope, education, job skills, and meaningful lives. It is worth the cost of rebuilding our human infrastructure since it is, after all, our children whose lives are being wasted and our cities in which the quality of life is being threatened.[48]

The decline in casual drug use can be the occasion for the United States to abandon its costly and generally ineffective efforts to use law enforcement and punishment as its bulwarks for demand reduction in the campaign against drug abuse. If the United States turns toward its underclass drug abusers, models that have been successful in the habilitation of such users should play an important role in building bridges out of the barrio and ghetto and into productive roles in society. This is not possible without addressing all the needs of these disadvantaged drug users. It makes little sense to provide drug abuse treatment for the impaired native American when, at the end of treatment, the oppressive poverty and hopelessness of the reservation remain. We will not be successful in intervening with the pregnant addict if there is no way for her to provide adequate shelter, nutrition, and health care for herself and her child or children during and after treatment. Nor is it effective to use methods that call for one-on-one interventions with underclass drug users. Instead, community and institutional intervention methods, such as adaptations of therapeutic communities, can be used to transform penal institutions into habilitative centers and underclass neighborhoods into healthy communities.

Implications for Latin America

Latin America, now addressing its own internal drug consumption and abuse problems, has much to learn from mistakes made in the United States. Rather than squandering limited economic and social resources on drug interdiction and relying on law enforcement to reduce demand, Latin America can begin to build effective programs and the social infrastructure for healthy communities. Latin America must not, like the United States, ignore its socially disadvantaged—including the millions of abandoned children and the poor who have turned to *basuco* and toxic inhalants. South American countries should not expect medically inspired models designed for less-pressing problems of middle- or upper-class educated clients to help those—as in U.S. urban areas—for whom addiction begins in childhood and who are poor, illiterate, hungry, and hopeless.

Using Models Applicable to Similar Populations

Underclass neighborhoods in Rio de Janeiro, Bogotá, or Lima may not be that dissimilar from the desolate ghettos of Newark, Philadelphia, and Chicago; the gang-controlled barrios of Los Angeles, Houston, or New York; or the impoverished and alcohol-devastated native American reservations of South Dakota and Arizona. In 1987, for example, 60 percent of female-headed families in the United States lived below the poverty line. Forty-five percent of all black children and 39 percent of all Hispanic children are living in poverty. Black men over age eighteen are the only group in the United States for whom life expectancy is consistently dropping, with murder being the most frequent cause of death.[49] In the United States, children are more likely to live in poverty than any other social group.

Treatment methods that are effective in devastated and penurious environments in the United States may have the greatest promise for successful adaptation for similar populations in Latin America. Latin American countries need to understand that the TC model can be applied in a much broader manner than it has been in the United States, where it is identified with adult hard-core drug addicts. The model can be adapted to serve pregnant addicts, provide a habilitative community for abandoned children, serve the homeless, and work in the criminal justice system with drug-using offenders. Furthermore, origins of the model show that it need not be limited by exclusive reliance on public funds. Therapeutic community interventions can develop their own self-supporting (or self-supplementing) economic enterprises, which make them less expensive and more replicable. Adaptations of these types of economically self-reliant TCs can be found throughout the world, including both agricultural and industrial TCs in Scandinavia and Europe.

The family structure of Latin American countries may be more amenable to involvement in drug abuse treatment. Such is the case in Italy, where adaptations of the U.S.-born therapeutic community have a pretreatment phase involving the entire family. During treatment family members participate actively, and retention is as high as 80 percent. Treatment programs and community mobilization efforts in Latin America should explore whether the needs of women are being met. Meeting these needs may improve the ability of an organization to become a real community, which is the environment most restorative of human values. Modifications of this model may have some relevance for jurisdictions in South America in which abandoned children left to their own devices are increasing in number and in deviance. The use of therapeutic community methodology to build communities where children can live in a stable environment that provides safety, shelter, food, and the conditions for normal development can be a cost-effective method for addressing these problems.

Avoid Punishment as the Paramount Solution

Latin America must not rely on criminal justice sanctions to solve drug demand. These countries cannot afford the folly engaged in over the past decade in the United States with its massive prison construction campaign to incarcerate drug-abusing criminals. Social deviance must be attacked at its roots in the disenfranchised and impoverished communities that are outside the social and economic life of the society. Beyond rebuilding the social and economic infrastructures of these communities, attention should be given to habilitative programs and community efforts that address the developmental and social deficits of underclass drug users. For those who have become criminally involved, the U.S. experience teaches that incarceration alone does not reduce drug abuse and its attendant criminality. Only intensive long-term interventions with criminal addicts in highly structured community-based programs or while incarcerated will reduce criminal recidivism.

Final Thoughts: Drug Users as Toxic Waste

Criminality and drug abuse are as much by-products of modern U.S. social practices as toxic waste is an expected by-product of modern industry. Postindustrial society is synonymous with the breakdown of community, neighborhood, and family. This has led to the disintegration of the crucible in which the values we recognize as human are formed. We have reached a point in the United States where the term "underclass" is acceptable; we have large numbers of people who do not feel part of society, who take no responsibility for that society, and who are harmful, or "toxic," to it.

For years, we dumped our industrial toxic waste and ignored any possible consequences; rivers were poisoned, ground polluted, air saturated with toxins. When there were major and visible accidents—Love Canal, the Exxon spill—we paused and moved briefly beyond the veil of denial and acknowledged the real cost. Many areas will never be restored to their original purity, yet pollution continues. It is considered too expensive to take steps to control pollutants. When the garbage is not visible, society is not concerned.

As with toxic waste, drug users attract little community attention when they are out of sight. Whether through incarceration, homelessness, or lack of advocacy, they are forgotten until their toxic properties begin to cause harm. The majority of those incarcerated come back into society; homeless children grow into gang members then become violent adults; intravenous drug users spread AIDS—as with toxic waste, they all bring harm. We begin to comprehend the true cost when we follow drug users through their wasted lives; through their criminal activities, their lost productivity; their arrests, trials, and incarcerations; their illegitimate, abandoned, and abused children. Like the ports that refused entry to the infamous garbage barge from New York City, no neighborhood or community wants drug addicts or offenders of any age near it whether they are actively addicted, in prison, or in a treatment setting. They are considered toxic—like garbage, never to be brought back into the home.

For decades the United States has not demonstrably changed its methods with its "toxic" population. The pollution spreads, causing heretofore unheard-of mutations. What has been the cost of not investing in breaking the cycle of addiction? Can we afford that price? Treatment begins the process of change from being toxic to inert and, at best, useful. Buckminster Fuller once stated that the problem with smog was that it represented energy in the wrong place; Ralph Waldo Emerson observed that a weed was a plant whose virtue had not yet been discovered. Both analogies are applicable. The most powerful and seasoned warriors in the so-called drug war may be the recovered wounded. Lewis Yablonsky views TC graduates as assets that in a sense are antibodies in the overall social system who have been immunized against substance abuse. They provide a kind of social vaccine for the overall social system. The explosive development of therapeutic communities has produced a social vaccine that if properly applied, increasingly can significantly reduce the international substance abuse problem.[50] TC graduates, who have addressed addiction through whole-person education, have addressed their own toxicity—their own problems with violence, irresponsible parenting, unhealthy relationships. If each graduate could successfully "inoculate" five afflicted individuals, we could witness large-scale community recovery. Let us not discard this population as a toxic waste. Let us regard its presence as a resource and an opportunity.

Notes

1. Eric Wish, "U.S. Drug Policy in the 1990s: Insights from New Data from Arrestees," *International Journal of the Addictions* 25, no. 3A (1990): 377–409.

2. Wish, "U.S. Drug Policy."

3. In the 1965–1975 period, federal support boosted the development of the publicly funded tier of drug treatment, but during the following decade federal support was drastically reduced. Although individual states were expected to pick up the costs of programs, overall support dropped. When public attention again focused on drug abuse in the mid-1980s, newly appropriated funds were directed mainly toward drug traffickers and prevention among nonuser groups.

4. M. Douglas Anglin, M. L. Brecht, and E. Maddahian, "Pretreatment Characteristics and Treatment Performance of Legally Coerced Versus Voluntary Methadone Maintenance Admissions," *Criminology* 27, no. 3 (1986): 537–557; M. D. Anglin, G. R. Speckart, M. W. Booth, and T. M. Ryan, "Consequences and Costs of Shutting Off Methadone," *Addictive Behaviors* 14 (1989): 307–326; Dean Gerstein and Henrick Harwood, *Treating Drug Problems: A Study of the Evolution, Effectiveness, and Financing of Public and Private Drug Treatment Systems*, vol. 1 (Washington, D.C.: National Academy Press, 1990), 151–155; Robert Hubbard, Mary Ellen Marsden, J. Valley Rachal, Henrick Harwood, Elizabeth Cavanaugh, and Harold Ginzburg, *Drug Abuse Treatment: A National Study of Effectiveness* (Chapel Hill: University of North Carolina Press, 1989), 159–160.

5. Because the term *therapeutic community* is almost universally misused and misunderstood, it is important to distinguish this type of therapeutic community from the totally independent and very efficient programs (pioneered by Maxwell Jones) that democratized mental hospitals in England. Jones's therapeutic communities have had a wide influence in mental health treatment and to some extent have influenced substance abuse treatment, particularly in Europe.

6. Daniel Casriel, *So Fair a House: The Synanon Story* (Beverly Hills, Calif.: Book Company of America, 1965), 457–473.

7. Lewis Yablonsky, *Synanon: The Tunnel Back* (Baltimore: Penguin, 1965), 3–25.

8. Lewis Yablonsky, *The Therapeutic Community: A Successful Approach for Treating Substance Abusers* (New York: Gardner, 1989), 36–41.

9. Yablonsky, *Synanon*, 3–25.

10. Unlike Synanon (which stopped having graduates from its programs in 1967), Delancey does have program graduates. Its recommended length of treatment exceeds that of other publicly funded TC programs.

11. Synanon began to define itself by the late 1960s as an alternative model society that would show the world how to solve the problems of drug addiction, racism, family disintegration, and the like. However, Synanon's ex-alcoholic founder Charles Dederich began drinking again in the mid-1970s and was subsequently charged with and convicted of deadly assault against an attorney who was suing Synanon. Synanon stopped working with addicts, declared itself a new religion, became widely discredited as a cult, and lost its tax-exempt status; it no longer exists.

12. Gerstein and Harwood, *Treating Drug Problems*, 154–156.

13. S. B. Sells and D. D. Simpson, "Evaluation of Treatment Outcome for Youth in the Drug Abuse Reporting Group (DARP): A Follow-up Study," in G. M. Beschner and A. S. Friedman, eds., *Youth Drug Abuse: Problems, Issues, and Treatment* (Lexington, Mass.: D.C. Health, 1979), 1–14.

14. Hubbard et al., *Drug Abuse Treatment*, 43–55.

15. Gerstein and Harwood, *Treating Drug Problems*, 134–136.

16. *Treatment Works: The Tragic Cost of Undervaluing Treatment in the "Drug War": Executive Summary and Highlights* (Washington, D.C.: National Association of State Alcohol and Drug Abuse Directors, 1989), 1–5.

17. W. S. Condelli, "Client Evaluations of Therapeutic Communities and Retention," in George DeLeon and J. T. Ziegenfuss, eds., *Therapeutic Communities for Addictions* (Springfield, Ill.: Charles C. Thomas, 1987), 131–139; George DeLeon and Nancy Jainchill, "Male and Female Drug Abusers: Social and Psychological Status 2 Years After Treatment in a Therapeutic Community," *American Journal of Drug Abuse* 8, no. 4 (1981–1982): 465–497; George DeLeon, *The Therapeutic Community: Study of Effectiveness* (Rockville, Md.: National Institute on Drug Abuse, 1984), 21–29; George DeLeon, "The Therapeutic Community for Substance Abuse: Perspective and Approach," in DeLeon and Ziegenfuss, *Therapeutic Communities for Addictions*, 5–18; George DeLeon, "Psychopathology and Substance Abuse: What Is Being Learned from Research in Therapeutic Communities," *Journal of Psychoactive Drugs* 21, no. 2 (1989): 177–188.

18. DeLeon and Jainchill, "Male and Female Drug Abusers."

19. DeLeon and Jainchill, "Male and Female Drug Abusers."

20. George DeLeon, Harry Wexler, and Nancy Jainchill, "The Therapeutic Community: Success and Improvement Rates 5 Years After Treatment," *International Journal of the Addictions* 17, no. 4 (1982): 703–747; and Hubbard et al., *Drug Abuse Treatment*, 152–177.

21. Sells and Simpson, "Evaluation of Treatment Outcome."

22. L. Riechers, "An Overview of Drug Treatment Programs in Prison," *Criminal Justice Policy Council: Research Analysis* 12 (February 1991): 1–4.

23. Wish, "U.S. Drug Policy."

24. C. G. Leukfeld and F. M. Tims, eds., *Compulsory Treatment of Drug Abuse: Research and Clinical Practice* (Rockville, Md.: National Institute on Drug Abuse, 1988).

25. D. G. Parent, *Shock Incarceration: An Overview of Existing Programs* (Washington, D.C.: U.S. Department of Justice, 1989), 35–42.

26. Peggy Glider, Rod Mullen, Cathy Davis, and Mary Ker, "Substance Abuse Treatment in a Jail Setting: A Therapeutic Community Model," unpublished manuscript (Tucson, Ariz., 1991).

27. Marsha Chaiken, "In-Prison Programs for Drug-Involved Offenders," *Issues and Practices* (July 1989): 41–63; D. S. Lipton and Harry K. Wexler, *The Drug-Crime Connection Invests Correctional Rehabilitation with New Life* (New York: Narcotic and Drug Research, Inc., 1988), 1–11.

28. G. Field, "The Cornerstone Program: A Client Outcome Study," *Federal Probation* 50 (1984): 50–55; M. K. Wexler, G. P. Falkin, and D. S. Lipton, *A Model Prison Rehabilitation Program: An Evaluation of the Stay'n Out Therapeutic Community* (New York: Narcotic and Drug Research, Inc., 1988), 17–25.

29. Mark Mauer, "Americans Behind Bars: A Comparison of International Rates of Incarceration," *The Sentencing Report* (January 1991).

30. Report and Recommendations of the Florida Supreme Court Ethnic and Racial Bias Study Commission, "Where the Injured Fly for Justice" (Tallahassee, December 11, 1990).

31. "Amity Mission Statement" (Tucson, Ariz.: Amity, Inc., 1986–1991).

32. Mimmie H. Silbert, A. M. Pines, and T. Lynch, "Substance Abuse and Prostitution," *Journal of Psychoactive Drugs* 14, no. 3 (1982): 193–197.

33. "Proceedings and Debates of the 101st Congress, Second Session," *Congressional Record* 119 (Washington, D.C.: U.S. Government Printing Office, September 24, 1990).

34. A. Toufexis, "Innocent Victims," *Time* (May 13, 1991): 55–60.

35. R. Palley, "Women Fighting Addiction: New Images Make New Life Possible," *Philadelphia Daily News*, February 6, 1991, 6.

36. S. Sofer, "The Family Center Program: Breaking the Cycle," unpublished manuscript (1991).

37. Sally Stevens and Peggy Glider, *Therapeutic Communities: Substance Abuse Treatment for Women* (Rockville, Md.: National Institute on Drug Abuse, forthcoming); S. Stevens, N. Arbiter, and P. Glider, "Women Residents: Expanding Their Role to Increase Treatment Effectiveness in Substance Abuse Programs," *International Journal of the Addictions* 24, no. 5 (1989): 425–434.

38. Carol Gilligan, *In a Different Voice* (Cambridge, Mass.: Harvard University Press, 1982), 24–63.

39. Although Amity has never achieved a numerical balance between men and women, it is nonetheless possible to construct a psychological environment—even with males in the majority—that is not male dominated and in which women feel safe.

40. E. W. Zedlewski, *Making Confinement Decisions* (Washington, D.C.: U.S. Department of Justice–National Institute of Justice, 1989).

41. Robert L. May et al., "The Extent of Drug Treatment Programs in Jails: A Summary Report," *American Jails* (September-October 1990): 32–34.

42. Glider et al., "Substance Abuse Treatment in a Jail Setting."

43. Florida Supreme Court Ethnic and Racial Bias Study Commission, "Where the Injured Fly for Justice."

44. Rod Mullen, Naya Arbiter, and Peggy Glider, "A Comprehensive Therapeutic Community Approach for Chronic Substance-Abusing Juvenile Offenders: The Amity Model," in Troy Armstrong, ed., *Intensive Interventions with High-Risk Youths: Promising Approaches in Juvenile Probation and Parole* (Monsey, N.Y.: Willow Tree Press, Inc., 1991), 211–243.

45. Mullen, Arbiter, and Glider, "A Comprehensive Therapeutic Community Approach."

46. James Inciardi, "Kingrats, Chicken Heads, Slow Necks, Freaks, and Blood Suckers: A Glimpse at the Miami Sex for Crack Market," unpublished 1991 report to Birch & Davis International, Inc. (under contract to NIDA).

47. Richard Dembo, M. Dertke, L. LaVoie, S. Borders, M. Washburn, and J. Schmeidler, "Physical Abuse, Sexual Victimization, and Illicit Drug Use: Replication of a Structural Analysis Among a New Sample of High-Risk Youths," *Violence and Victims* 4, no. 2 (1987): 131–138.

48. C. Ronald Huff, "Youth Gangs and Public Policy," *Crime and Delinquency* 35, no. 6 (October 1989): 524–537.

49. "U.S. Children and Their Families: Current Conditions and Recent Trends, 1989," U.S. House of Representatives, 101st Congress, 1st Session (Washington, D.C.: U.S. Government Printing Office, 1989).

50. Yablonsky, *The Therapeutic Community*, 36–41.

13

Community Mobilization and Human Technology Skills

Michael C. Hoffmann

Prevention begins with communities. Community mobilization incorporates the principle that individuals in the community must recognize that they have problems in order to solve those community problems. One of the most overlooked aspects of the prevention effort is that it must be a *proactive* process, not a *reactive* one. Too much attention has been devoted to treating the symptoms of dysfunctional behaviors associated with substance abuse. Only a handful of programs in the United States and abroad emphasize what all prevention programs should be emphasizing: the creation of an environment that promotes the health and well-being of the people in the community. As William Lofquist has explained:

> Designing separate systems for remedial work may make some sense, but addressing the common conditions which promote those symptoms calls for a different approach. If we can get beyond the notion that prevention is only "stopping something from happening" to a more positive approach that creates conditions which promote the well-being of people, we can build communities that are relatively free of the symptoms we have designed our services around. This may sound utopian and idealistic, but it is not. It is a practical matter of people becoming responsible at many levels. A generic approach to prevention which does not get caught up in remedial thought processes as has happened so much in the past frees us to use our resources more creatively and effectively.[1]

Since 1971 the U.S. Department of Education has developed approaches in the human technology field to explore the most effective means for mobilizing communities. Research so far has demonstrated that local people can best solve local problems (when trained in basic skills), usually with local resources; that people support and take ownership in what they help create; and that problems and solutions differ with location. Findings also show that teams of people are much more effective than individuals in solving problems. A diversity of prevention strategies must be developed to address the multiple causes of alcohol and drug abuse. Finally, it is necessary to mobilize the entire community—including school personnel, students, parents, law enforcement agencies, and civic and governmental organizations—to address local alcohol and drug-related problems.[2]

Policymakers and specialists must move beyond a "doing for" to a "doing with." Prevention systems should attempt to reach 100 percent of the people, and they must be sensitive to all ethnic constituencies within the community.[3]

The community must agree that in fact there is a problem. If the problem is not visible, the community will not support measures to resolve it. Ownership of the problem is primary to its resolution, and our experiences have shown that the most successful prevention efforts are those that facilitate this act of ownership. Individuals, institutions, and communities should avoid dependence on outside professionals or programs; otherwise, the community might regress after the outsiders leave. The role of the professional in prevention programming should be to facilitate the transfer of knowledge, abilities, and resource identification to the communities in order to establish a relationship that reflects, again, a doing with instead of a doing for or to. One quote frequently heard in training circles clearly brings home this point: "Be a guide on the side, not a sage on the stage." Although research confirms that communities can sometimes get involved in the search for solutions through the efforts of a charismatic individual, we must be extremely cautious about the creation of personality cults.

Community mobilization is a process, not an event. Planned social change involves several identifiable phases. First is denial: People refuse to accept the idea that there is a problem. They refuse to participate in planned activities, and they accuse preventionists of giving their community a bad name. Second, community members come to recognize the existence of a problem in their community and begin the learning process. This transition can occur for a variety of reasons: a watershed event (such as the death of a teen due to overdose or driving under the influence), a seizure of illegal drugs, or the involvement of a charismatic individual.[4] Third, community members enter a deeper study of the problems associated with substance abuse: They learn about effective prevention techniques and begin to see possibilities for application. Fourth, the community makes a decision and participates in training that includes in-depth information-giving, intrapersonal and interpersonal prevention techniques, analysis of social policy, analysis of community-sector partic-ipation, and planning for practical action. Fifth comes understanding of the social implications of and societal response to the strategic plan to bring about community change. (For example, the depiction of alcohol use or abuse as a negative social norm could cause discomfort or rejection by the community as a whole. This may be demonstrated by loud protests by the beer and wine industry, by local taverns or cocktail lounges, or by individuals.) Sixth is adoption of the strategy itself: The community begins to develop positive social norms and accept new attitudes toward the use or abuse of alcohol and other drugs. Seventh and last is a long-term commitment. The community maintains the momentum, expands the participation of all the sectors of the community, promotes cooperation with formal and informal leadership structures, deflects individual and organizational egoism, and promotes a well-defined policy regarding the use and abuse of alcohol and other drugs. The collective prevention effort continues to train new community teams and evaluate their efforts on an ongoing basis and reinforces the community prevention system framework.[5]

One example of this general model is the smoking cessation campaign initiated by the U.S. Surgeon General in the early 1960s. It has taken decades for specific changes in cigarette smoking habits to be noted. As a result, we now have separate smoking sections in public places, indoor clean air acts passed by city councils and state legislatures, and a reduction of smoking rates from 40 percent of the U.S. adult population in 1965 to 29 percent in 1987. Nearly half of all living adults who have smoked have quit.[6]

Human Technological Skills

How do we "empower" communities to take ownership? How do individuals commit to working together in harmony? How do they resolve conflicts? What makes teams of people more effective than individuals? How do we transfer assessment and planning skills?

In the early 1970s, the U.S. Department of Education, through its Regional Training Center Network, created the School Team Approach. Placing great emphasis on teamwork, this method forms small groups of faculty and others and provides them with vital, pertinent, and state-of-the-art information regarding effective prevention methodology. The teams form their own action plans without interference from any outside professional.

From 1981 to 1987, the U.S. Department of Education conducted an intense evaluation of the School Team Approach. Based on a large-scale questionnaire, Table 13-1 reveals a clear point: Overall, the longer the teams exist, the greater the decline in substance use.

Approximately two-thirds of all state departments of education have adopted this model on a permanent basis and continue to seek better results. Moreover, the model promotes capacity-building: Once the prime players have been trained, the model can be replicated and multiplied—alleviating the need for constant training by the main service providers. Internationally, the model has been applied and implemented in Australia, Italy, and Brazil.

In view of these results, the Southwest Regional Center for Drug-Free Schools and Communities (established at the University of Oklahoma) built on the success of the School Team Approach by creating a training model to mobilize entire communities. If the School Team Approach is so successful, we asked, how can we develop a model for community teams to mobilize all sectors of the community? How can we take the theories of planned social change and transfer them to a practical model to bring about planned social change?

Since 1988 the Southwest Regional Center for Drug-Free Schools and Communities has created 263 community teams in the southwestern United States.

TABLE 13-1
Impact of School Team Approach

Grade Level	Substance	Reported % Change in Substance Use[a]	
		Teams Active 1 to 2 Years	Teams Active 3 or More Years
High school	Tobacco	+ 6	-14
	Alcohol	-21	-38
	Marijuana	-31	-33
	Other drugs	-54	- 1
Junior high school	Tobacco	-16	-24
	Alcohol	-10	-18
	Marijuana	-19	-12
	Other drugs	-38	-22

[a]Positive sign means increase in use, negative sign means decrease in use.

Source: Based on data in Ralph Earle, *Executive Summary Report, National Data Base and Program Suppport Project* (Amherst: University of Massachusetts, 1987).

Qualitative and quantitative data about their impact on social change and prevention in general are being collected and analyzed. However, initial reports have indicated very positive results in community-wide prevention awareness and participation and in the formation of a strong coalition for prevention activities.

International Applications

In 1989 the Inter-American Drug Abuse Control Commission of the Organization of American States (CICAD) sponsored regional workshops on education for drug abuse prevention. I was then at the University of Oklahoma and was invited to present the community mobilization model to the assembled delegates. As a result, the University of Oklahoma offered to assist member nations in training specialized teams to adopt and implement the model in their respective nations.

In response to a request from the government of Argentina, the first hemispheric project for community mobilization was initiated by CICAD and the University of Oklahoma in collaboration with the Secretaría para la Prevención de la Drogadicción y la Lucha contra el Narcotráfico. The project has several phases: formation of a team, training the team in the United States (at a session sponsored by the Southwest Regional Center for Drug-Free Schools and Communities), and diffusion of ideas to additional teams in Argentina (to provide internalization of the training process on the part of the Argentine Training Team and a "transference" of relevant training skills).

Nearly 70 percent of the participants reported that the training was "very useful," and approximately 30 percent reported the training as "average" in usefulness; less than 2 percent reported the training as "not useful." The Argentine teams have since been preparing for follow-up events. Many participants indicated that this training empowered and motivated them as no other training experience had. "You did not come in like you were the experts," they often said, "and tell us what to do in our communities and how to do it." Most of the teams have reported high activity in the implementation of existing or new action plans.

A fourth and final phase will include continued technical assistance by the Argentine Training Team as requested by individual community teams as well as an organized evaluation of the teams' impact in the communities. A twelve- to fourteen-month follow-up with all the teams will take place to analyze what worked, what did not work, and how things might be improved.

In general, we must be very cautious about the designs of key policymakers whose principal agenda is self-promotion and aggrandizement. As prevention specialists, we must take decisive stands against dilettantes and bureaucrats whose political ambitions are more grand than the objective of drug-free communities. In many ways the self-serving activities of these individuals are as harmful as drug trafficking itself. The task of helping people regain their health should be an act of humility, wisdom, and love.

Notes

1. William Lofquist, *Discovering the Meaning of Prevention: A Practical Approach to Positive Change* (Tucson: Associates for Youth Development, 1989), vi–vii.

2. Alcohol and Drug Abuse Education Project Program, *An Overview of the School Team Approach, Alcohol and Drug Abuse Education Program* (Washington, D.C.: U.S. Department of Education, 1987).

3. U.S. Department of Health and Human Services, Office of Substance Abuse Prevention, *Community Prevention System Framework for Alcohol and Other Drug Prevention: The Future by Design* (Washington, D.C.: The Circle, Inc., 1990).

4. Office of Substance Abuse Prevention, *Community Prevention System Framework*.

5. Michael C. Hoffmann, "Phases in Community Planned Social Change," in Everett Rogers, ed., *Diffusion of Innovation* (Norman: University of Oklahoma Press, 1983).

6. *U.S. Surgeon General's Report* (Washington, D.C.: U.S. Government Printing Office, 1989).

14

Drug Abuse Prevention
in Latin America

Roberto Lerner

Over the past fifteen years, and especially since the late 1980s, there has been mounting concern about the use and abuse of drugs in most countries of Latin America. The consumption of drugs has become both a social problem and a public issue throughout the region. As in other Western societies,[1] popular attitudes toward drugs in Latin America have entailed more than preoccupations with public health. Public opinion and official policies have frequently been shaped by ideological, geopolitical, and even ethnic considerations.[2] As a result, drugs and social representations of them seem to follow cyclical patterns of idealization and satanization.

Stripped to its essentials, drug prevention can be viewed as an array of actions that have as their final purpose the creation of negative attitudes toward drug use, or at least toward the use of certain drugs. When that purpose is attained among mainstream groups within society—that is, among the middle classes—significant decreases in drug use can be and have been achieved for significant periods of time without a change in the levels of availability.[3] The consumption of drugs (or at least some drugs) ceases to be a central social issue—which does not mean it ceases to be a social problem.

This chapter surveys and analyzes the main preventative methodologies and actions in use in Latin America for substance abuse. It also offers some reflections on the nature of prevention and its targets, especially in the context of Andean societies.

Principles for Prevention

There is no reason to expect that an original model for drug abuse prevention will emerge from Latin America. Most efforts in the region follow general models that have predominated elsewhere.[4] In this sense, we can identify four basic approaches.

- *The public health model*—Drugs are regarded as the equivalent of pathogenic agents. The goal of prevention is to avoid exposure to these agents, either through the manipulation of the environment or through the reinforcement of individuals and their natural defenses.

- *The sociocultural model*—Drug-related behaviors, like other behaviors, are seen as the object of formal and informal social controls whose broad purpose is to minimize risks for the group as a whole. Abuse and addiction are interpreted as extreme and unacceptable deviations from the societal norm (the nature of which tends to be taken as a given). The overall purpose of intervention is to minimize social harm.
- *The distribution control model*—The number of problematic drug users depends on the total amount of drugs consumed in a given group, most of it by nonproblematic users. The strategy is to increase the price—literally and figuratively—of drug use through fiscal, legal, repressive, and educational measures. The central idea is to make reduced or nonexistent drug use a matter of social responsibility in the face of formal regulations. Individuals are to be held accountable for infringement of these norms.
- *The proscriptive model*—Any involvement with psychoactive substances is considered unacceptable. Abstinence is prescribed for all. This is to be enforced through legal repression and through social controls based on fear.

These models provide conceptual coherence for programs that might share some or all of their traits. In practice, actual preventive methodologies can employ features of more than one model.

Recently there has developed a quest for integral models that focus more on the social processes that lead to reduced drug use than on broad philosophical principles. In Latin America, this quest has taken the form of concerns with community involvement, living conditions, health and education, and related matters. As we will see, however, most of the specific interventions that fall under this rubric hardly refer to these concepts.

The Roles of Research

Most institutions dedicated to the prevention of drug abuse in Latin America claim that their programs are based on scientific research or that their efforts are evaluated in a systematic way. Research itself does not constitute preventive action, but the generation of knowledge about psychoactive substances and their impacts on society is essential to the design and implementation of preventive interventions. Several types of investigation are currently under way in Latin America.

Most biomedical research is done in universities. Because of budgetary limitations, however, studies of addiction are few and far between. Some institutions—such as the Center for Information and Education for the Prevention of Drug Abuse (CEDRO) in Peru, the Fundación Nuestros Jóvenes in Ecuador, and the Centros de Integración Juvenil in Mexico—promote research through contests for university students.

Socioeconomic research usually attempts to establish the relationships among elements of the drug problem and such broad factors as macro- and microeconomic indicators, migratory flows, use of natural resources, and the maintenance or disruption of ecological and social equilibria. Understandably, these studies are more common in countries in which drug production and trafficking have been accompanied by demographic displacements, economic distortions, political conflicts, and institutional instabilities. In Peru and Bolivia, for example, research of this type purports to show the relationship between drug availability and drug use and the connections between the production of coca leaf for traditional use and the manufacture of illicit drugs.

Epidemiological research seeks to measure the use of psychoactive substances and then relate this degree of use to demographic, socioeconomic, and regional variables to determine patterns of drug use among specific populations. When carried out on a periodic basis, such studies can help identify high-risk populations and areas, target substances, and ultimately evaluate the medium- and long-term results of overall prevention efforts. Investigations of this type can focus on groups including households, for which the basic goal is to obtain information from a random or systematic sample that can be projected to the general population at large. As María Elena Medina-Mora and María del Carmen Mariño have shown in Chapter 3, only a handful of Latin American countries have conducted research of this type.

Alternatively, research may concentrate on target populations, such as high-school students, prison inmates, and the like. Mexico and to a lesser extent Brazil have some experience with this approach; in Peru, the Ministry of Education conducted a survey of high-school students in 1989.[5]

Qualitative research focuses on the interaction between researchers and subjects during the course of specific interventions. Workshops on applied investigation and participative research have been carried out in Argentina, and there have been studies of community interventions in Mexico, Bolivia, Colombia, and Brazil. Longitudinal research follows a group of subjects through time, so as to establish causal links and changes in variables related to the use of psychoactive substances. In Latin America, this type of study has been carried out mostly by clinicians. The relevance for prevention is just now being recognized, and follow-up on high-risk groups on the basis of nationwide studies is in its early stages.[6]

Studies of social representations, by comparison, explore popular perceptions about drug-related matters. This is especially important for programs for prevention, because they allow both planning and long-term evaluation of public awareness campaigns. Such work is also crucial to decision makers and those who try to influence them. Often conducted in countries in which drug production is a problem, many of these studies have clearly political objectives. The only nationwide studies of both the general public and opinion leaders appear to have been done in Peru.[7]

Finally, almost all institutions and organizations involved in prevention at the public or private level proclaim their adherence to evaluation studies: internal evaluations, qualitative evaluations, process evaluations, and so on. The conspicuous absence of rigorous methodology seems to be commonplace around the world, especially in Latin America. Sometimes institutions are evaluated by the funding organizations but more with an eye toward administrative efficiency than preventive success. There have also been some pre- and post-tests for massive television campaigns in Bolivia, Brazil, and Peru. But in general, serious evaluations of policy outcomes are virtually nonexistent.

Types of Preventative Action

In spite of the theoretical importance of research on psychoactive substances, actual investigations are uneven throughout the region. Yet preventative actions abound. There are two general types of campaigns: One deals with public awareness of the issue, the other with the development of effective agents for prevention.

Public Involvement and Awareness

This category includes actions designed achieve qualitative changes in the community's attitudes about drugs and their impact on society and individuals. The stress is on community participation and the generation of a collective consciousness about the necessity for strong social responses on three distinct levels:

- Opinion leaders—to affect people who have influence on the formation of social representations.
- Institutions—to prepare organizations to include within their activities a prevention component, to receive technical information, and eventually to design prevention interventions wherever they work. In Latin America, we find vast networks of organizations more or less coordinated by governmental agencies (as in Bolivia and Brazil) and nongovernmental entities (such as CEDRO in Peru and the Centros de Integración Juvenil in Mexico).
- Public opinion—to motivate the general population (or certain sectors of it) to take part in drug prevention activities or to raise collective expectations about community and social development. This kind of campaign has become widespread in Latin America through the mass media (especially effective in reaching the poor), through contests (for journalists, artists, students), and through general events (such as "smokeless days," marathons, and other sporting events).

In one way or another, every Latin American institution involved in prevention makes an active effort to engage the support and participation of the community with which it works. Social mobilization clearly has an essential role in successful prevention campaigns—especially in the formation, maintenance, and dissemination of social attitudes against the use of psychoactive substances. But when it is done without serious planning—more to display evidence of activity than in response to objective conditions—social mobilization can be counterproductive. It can lead to the creation of a public hysteria that runs contrary to the ways of an open society, to the saturation of the media, and to the debilitation of preventive agents in the community.

In Latin America, as we will see, prevention campaigns have often responded to geopolitical agendas—especially in drug-producing countries. Unfettered social activism could cause problems in the future.

Diffusion of Knowledge and Capacity

Virtually every institution engaged in drug prevention in Latin America (and probably elsewhere) stresses the importance of information and education. These are somewhat different activities: It is one thing to present data and facts and another to promote the understanding and internalization of concepts. Most institutions in Latin America propose dynamic educational processes, although with differing degrees of public participation.

One kind of effort entails the dissemination of information that is directly related to psychoactive substances, their effects on individuals and groups, and the types of individual and collective responses necessary to decrease or eliminate their abuse. There are documentation centers that offer specialized information, such as scientific knowledge, to a variety of audiences. Some centers (in Argentina, Brazil, Colombia, Mexico, and Peru) subscribe to scientific data bases (such as Medline and Adline) in developed countries and also produce scientific journals about drug issues and community psychology. There are efforts to reach the public at large through readily accessible printed or audiovisual materials. Research centers in the Andean countries also produce publications that focus on the political and socioeconomic dimensions of drug production and traffic. In some cases, we find a daily follow-up by the local press on matters related to drugs and psychoactive substances. These documentation centers not only serve academicians, scientists, politicians, and journalists; in many cases they provide essential resources for active prevention programs and constitute the core of informal think tanks.

Capacitation, or training, is another essential activity. Here the idea is to increase the level of information individuals have about drugs, about the impact of drugs on society, and about the range of effective responses. Ultimately, the objective is not only to transmit information; it is to train effective agents whose efforts will be multiplied within their own communities. Participants in training programs thus become preventive agents.

Typically, capacitation comes through lectures and presentations to a wide range of audiences. Despite widespread skepticism about this form of training, the sense of social urgency creates considerable demand for these services. Training courses for specific groups—such as health workers, social workers, judges, teachers, and so on—are gaining currency throughout the region. Finally, some institutions of higher learning are beginning to offer curricula and degrees in these subject areas; Argentina has acquired considerable experience in interdisciplinary education for professionals interested in psychoactive substances.

A third activity involves technical assistance because a number of institutions serve as consultants in the field of prevention. They give support to other institutions that are willing to begin preventative programs in their own communities. The process involves diagnosing the community problem with respect to drugs and then helping local leaders design a prevention campaign as well as procedures for implementation and evaluation.

Throughout Latin America, documentation centers try to work closely with the mass media to maintain a flow of information about psychoactive substances. This can be done through intensive short-term campaigns or through permanent columns in newspapers or spots on TV and radio. This is a difficult area, however, due partly to the cost of mass-media advertising and partly to the absence of a tradition of public service advertising.

Finally, some centers offer services for secondary or tertiary prevention—that is, they attempt to deal with the consequences of drug use and abuse rather than concentrating only on "primary prevention" of drug consumption itself. Hot lines are now quite common in Latin America. There are also some counseling services that prepare drug abusers and their families for treatment.

A second broad effort throughout Latin America deals with general societal matters rather than with psychoactive substances alone. One of the most important criticisms of traditional prevention methods, especially those that borrow from infectious disease models, is that they focus almost entirely on cognitive learning at the expense of socioemotional development. According to the critique, people use and abuse drugs not because of ignorance but because of social and emotional needs. Drug consumption thus responds to broad societal processes (such as curiosity or peer pressure) and pertains to a general category of risky or problematic behaviors. Consequently, according to this view, prevention should reinforce individual abilities, support healthier life-styles and environments, and focus on the processes at work— not merely on drugs alone. In Latin America, in fact, most of the people and organizations that work on prevention tend to stress this broad societal approach. Of course, ideological discourse and stated intentions can sometimes be removed from actual practice.

Some of the practical methodologies used in the name of drug abuse prevention include workshops for parenting skills—regularly held in Argentina, Bolivia, and Chile—especially in regard to critical moments in the life cycles of adolescents. Other activities focus on life skills—such as interpersonal problem solving, tolerance for frustration, consequential thinking, and perspective-taking. Some school programs work on these skills in the belief that they will retard or reduce the initiation of drug use.

The alternative use of free time often receives special attention. Many programs tend to stress negative messages of the "just say no" variety, which at best are incomplete. This counsel is being generated and transmitted in societies in which immediate gratification tends to be the rule. It is therefore essential when focusing on basically deprived populations to offer them positive alternatives to drug use—especially for younger populations. Many institutions in Latin America emphasize the importance of community activities that reinforce solidarity, sharing, and social participation.

Peer-group leaders can provide a crucial resource. Some capacitation programs make explicit efforts to identify natural leaders and then reinforce their position and authority through the training process. Once selected by their peers, they receive training in group dynamics, conflict management, developmental psychology, and so on. The leaders thus are enabled in early phases to manage conflicts and transgressions against the norms of the group, and they acquire sufficient influence to promote alternative activities and healthy life-styles. This reliance on natural leadership is extremely promising; and it has been used to good effect in Mexico, Peru, and Bolivia. It is especially useful in cultural contexts with strong community traditions.

One of the most imposing obstacles for prevention programs in Latin America is the fact that psychoactive substances seem to be correlated, in either production or consumption, with deteriorating living conditions—in particular, with the scarcity of employment opportunities for youth. In recognition of this reality, preventive programs have recently begun to stress the importance of income generation, especially among socially and economically disadvantaged sectors. In Lima, Bogotá, La Paz, and São Paulo, for example, there are programs for street children who use inhalants. The goal is to involve them in a noninstitutional resocialization scheme through street educators who set up a haven where young people can keep their working material, learn further skills, receive medical attention, and so on. In many countries there are also programs that try to organize youngsters living in high-risk areas for the purpose of creating small-scale businesses.

Yet another approach for working with communities is through encounter groups. In this case, preventive teams collaborate within a community and offer its members the possibility of reflection, discussion, and attitudinal change about the problems that beset it. The goal is to help the communities help themselves.

Conclusion

This typology of preventive actions in Latin America yields several general conclusions. First, Latin America has a wide range of programs that includes virtually all the types and styles found elsewhere around the world. Every nation in the region (with the exception of Panama until 1988) has legal instruments that define the role of prevention and drug-related matters in general. Drug legislation has created governmental agencies that determine policies and, in many cases, national plans for combatting drug use and abuse. Most of this legislation is fairly recent—it began in the late 1970s and accelerated in the 1980s, just as the cocaine cycle and antidrug offensive were gaining prominence in U.S. society. Development of this legislation occurred especially in the Andean countries.

Prevention efforts are carried on by both governmental and nongovernmental organizations (NGOs). Official agencies seem to have great weight in Mexico, Brazil, and Costa Rica, where even NGOs are financed by public funds. NGOs, which are usually financed by international or foreign national cooperation agencies, are especially active in the Andean countries.

Most of the preventive programs in Latin America tend toward a "demedicalization" of the intervention process, stressing integral education schemes and community participation. The ideology of prevention seeks to go beyond negative messages to promote the overall development of groups and individuals. This kind of strategy is of utmost importance when working with deprived communities—such as those found throughout the region—in which prevention must be accompanied by improved survival techniques and living conditions. In practice, however, these preventive programs often resemble political platforms, and one has to wonder whether such broad promises of social salvation have not interfered with the realization of more concrete but less ambitious actions.

The kind of preventive intervention implied by the integral model is difficult to reconcile with the funding priorities of international agencies and the urgencies of geopolitical agendas, especially in countries in which drug production and trafficking are at center stage. In contrast to the current emphasis on the short term, these strategies require a long-term and rational context.

The practical programs of most preventive organizations, on the other hand, tend to focus on capacitation, the diffusion of specific knowledge, and public awareness. The latter has caused some interesting psychosocial phenomena in the Andean world, where cocaine completely dominates public perceptions. When asked which drug is the most widely consumed in Peru, for instance, the majority of the general population and opinion leaders automatically answer "coca paste." This substance is not the most frequently consumed drug or even the most frequently consumed illicit drug. But the semantic knot "coca-paste–cocaine," so to speak, has absorbed all meanings of the word "drug."[8]

Especially conspicuous is the relative absence of research—or, to put it a slightly different way, the absence of a clear relationship between research on the reality of psychoactive substances in Latin America and preventive practice throughout the region. Most programs seem to respond to ideological stimuli that are determined by realities other than concrete local or regional conditions.

This is not to advocate the creation of a Latin American model of drug prevention. The emphasis on Latin America's singularity has been a recurrent feature of the region's relationship with the developed world, resting on the dubious belief that Latin Americans have little in common with the rest of humankind. I contend that the opportunity for implementation of preventive actions in the region (rather than the models or methodologies) has been determined by contemporary conditions outside Latin America.

Most preventive efforts in the developed world, especially in the United States, have been designed to address the spread of illegal drug use by the middle classes. Leaving aside the inflated and often ridiculous rhetoric of the "war on drugs," U.S. society has been responding to the existence of a genuine problem. Even so, this specific concern has been imposed on other countries more because of the fact that they are production and trafficking sources than because of epidemiological realities. To be sure, a public convinced that a country is on the verge of being overcome by any given drug will be more susceptible to radical and simplistic solutions. This is a political matter.

But this kind of propaganda could have an unexpected effect on the prevention front. We cannot yet anticipate the consequence of prevention programs centered on a specific drug—for example, cocaine in the Andean countries—in a context of both high availability and low consumption. We may merely be reinforcing an already strong predilection toward abstinence. But if availability increases (as seems likely) and usage begins to climb, it could also be that these programs will have weakened or even paralyzed natural preventive dispositions toward the drug in question. In short, we will have created a self-fulfilling prophecy.

Drug prevention in Latin America is rich and complex. It has to be considered a long-term task and must be removed from the geopolitical context it has acquired in recent years. It should establish its pace and its targets on the basis of objective scientific research. Only then will it be possible to have the peoples of Latin America, according to their own experience and aspirations, accept social and legal responsibility for their behavior with regard to drug use and abuse.

Notes

1. See David F. Musto, *The American Disease: Origins of Narcotic Control* (New Haven: Yale University Press, 1973); Charles Bachman and A. Coppel, *Le dragon domestique: Deux siècles de relations étranges entre l'occident et la drogue* (Paris: Michel Albin, 1989); Antonio Escohotado, *Historia de las drogas* (Madrid: Alianza Editorial, 1989); and for Latin America, Roberto Lerner and Delicia Ferrando, "El consumo de drogas en occidente y su impacto en el Perú," in Diego Garcia-Sayan, ed., *Coca, cocaína y narcotráfico: Laberinto en los Andes* (Lima: Comisión Andina de Juristas, 1989), 51–89; and Roberto Lerner, *Drugs in Peru: Reality and Representations* (Amsterdam: Catholic University of Nijmegen, 1991).

2. See W. J. Cloyd, *Drogas y control de información: El rol del hombre en la manipulación y el control del tráfico de drogas* (Buenos Aires: Ediciones Tres Tiempos, 1986); Jean-Charles Sournia, *A History of Alcoholism* (Cambridge: Basil Blackwell, 1990); J. P. Hoffmann, "The Historical Shift in the Perception of Opiates: From Medicine to Social Menace," *Journal of Psychoactive Drugs* 22, no. 1 (1990): 53–62.

3. See Lloyd D. Johnston, G. J. Bachman, and P. M. O'Malley, "Exploring the Recent Decline in Cocaine Use Among Young Adults: Further Evidence That Perceived Risks and

Disapproval Lead to Reduced Drug Use," *Journal of Health and Social Behavior* 31, no. 2 (1990): 173–184.

4. See J. Skirrow and E. Sanka, "Alcohol and Drug Use Prevention Strategies: An Overview," *Contemporary Drug Problems: An Interdisciplinary Quarterly* 14 (1987): 147–241.

5. R. Federico León, Nelly Ugarriza, and R. Mercedes Villanueva, "La iniciación y el uso intenso de sustancias psicoactivas: Un análisis de datos en una muestra nacional de colegios" (Convenio Peru/Agency for International Development: Ministerio de Educación, 1989); and Sournia, *A History of Alcoholism.*

6. Lerner, *Drugs in Peru.*

7. Delicia Ferrando, *Estudio de percepciones sobre drogas en la población urban del Perú: Una investigación de opinión pública* (Lima: CEDRO, 1989); Delicia Ferrando, "Segunda encuesta de opinión pública sobre drogas: Principales resultados," *Psicoactiva* 2, no. 2 (1989): 5–55; and Delicia Ferrando, "Opiniones y actitudes de los líderes de opinión peruanos sobre drogas," in press.

8. Lerner, *Drugs in Peru.*

15

Policies and Prospects
for Demand Reduction

Mathea Falco

Drug abuse has been a major problem in the United States for many years. During the last two decades, at least 40 million Americans have tried illicit drugs, and several million are heavy users. In recent years, drug abuse has also become a problem in many of the Latin American countries in which illicit drugs are produced. What was long viewed as a peculiarly U.S. disease is now an international concern, affecting both producer and consumer countries.

Foundations of U.S. Policy

The primary U.S. policy response to its domestic drug abuse problem has been to attempt to reduce foreign drug supplies through interdiction, law enforcement, and international cooperation. The theory is that curtailment of drug supplies will drive up retail prices, thereby reducing the numbers of users who can afford to buy drugs. In other words, reduced supplies will lead to reduced demand. Unfortunately, the theory has not worked well in practice. Despite billions of dollars expended on interdiction over the past decade, drug prices have remained low. In fact, in New York a dose of crack cocaine is now cheaper than the price of admission to a movie.

Despite low prices and widespread availability, however, illicit drug use is declining across the United States—particularly among more affluent, educated groups. The central reason for this decline is concern about health: More Americans now understand the real dangers many drugs present and have consequently turned away from them.

This drop in demand reflects the impact of intensive public education campaigns as well as changing social values that no longer view even occasional drug use as desirable, "glamorous" behavior. These attitudes are conveyed throughout society, as the campaign against cigarette smoking dramatically illustrates. Despite advertising expenditures of several billion dollars a year, the tobacco industry has not been able to reverse the sharp downward trend of smoking in the United States. Marijuana and cocaine, which have been tried by tens of millions of Americans, have suffered a similar deglamorization. Recent NIDA surveys report that casual use of these drugs dropped by nearly half in the late 1980s and early 1990s.

But these encouraging trends do not extend to chronic, addictive use of cocaine, crack, and heroin—the hard core of the U.S. drug problem that has not been affected by changes in public attitude. Several million Americans are addicts desperately in need of treatment and structured aftercare. Their children—and millions more children of alcoholics—are at very high risk of becoming substance abusers themselves. Yet, despite recent large increases in federal drug abuse funding, treatment is not yet available for all those who need it.

Only recently has the importance of reducing demand through education, prevention, and treatment programs gained widespread recognition in the United States. During the past decade, supply-reduction efforts dominated 80 percent of federal antidrug funding. Prevention, the heart of any demand-reduction strategy, received only 1 percent of total drug funding from 1982 to 1986. By 1986 President Ronald Reagan acknowledged that "all the law enforcement in the world" would not stop the scourge. The U.S. Congress adopted two major new drug laws in 1986 and 1988 intended to increase the focus on prevention and treatment. George Bush pledged to be the "education president" and to fight drugs with stronger efforts to reduce demand at home. Nonetheless, even today demand reduction receives only 30 percent of federal drug dollars—10 percent more than during the eight-year Reagan administration.

Because of the long neglect of demand reduction, research into promising approaches to prevention and treatment has been very limited. As a result, the cocaine-crack crisis that developed in the mid-1980s caught the United States unprepared: Little was known about how to reduce demand. In the past few years, however, new studies have found a number of promising models both for prevention and treatment. Although there is no single magic solution to this complex problem, research shows that programs exist that can have a significant impact in reducing drug abuse. The lack of simple answers can no longer be used as an excuse for national policies that ignore the central importance of demand reduction.

The United States has traditionally viewed drug abuse as a foreign problem, crossing its borders from other countries. As a result, the focus of U.S. cooperative efforts has been on reducing the supply of drugs produced by its neighbors in the Western Hemisphere. Only recently has drug abuse become a critical problem in these countries, erasing the historical distinction between consumer and producer nations. Government strategies must now reflect the complex interaction of supply and demand within individual countries as well as across national boundaries.

Contributions to this book provide a diverse array of perspectives on key issues of demand reduction; they also reflect fundamental differences that inevitably arise between consumer countries—notably the United States—and producer countries in Latin America. A striking example, which grows out of historical differences, is the way drug users and abusers are viewed. In the United States, user accountability is the new watchword, bringing with it tougher penalties that involve civil as well as criminal sanctions. In Latin America, as Roberto Lerner points out in Chapter 14, the user is viewed more as a victim of either the international cartels or geopolitical forces.

Some of these differences reflect not only contrasting economic roles—as producer and consumer—but also profoundly divergent historical development. In the early decades of this century, the United States passed laws to restrict and eventually prohibit heroin, cocaine, and marijuana—drugs largely produced outside its borders. Through these laws, Americans defined their drug problem not only as criminal but also as something foreign in origin. As David Musto points out in Chapter 2, certain drugs came to be associated with specific immigrant and minority groups: marijuana with Mexicans, opium and heroin with Chinese, and cocaine with African-Americans. Early in the twentieth century, these groups were viewed with suspicion by the dominantly European population. Whatever humanitarian goals the drug laws may have had in protecting the public health, they also reflected a certain xenophobia—an attempt to keep out so-called harmful influences.

As a result of this historical development, U.S. drug policy during much of this century has focused on supply reduction, especially of drugs produced abroad. The United States has tended to blame other countries for its own domestic problem and to seek solutions aimed at eradicating foreign production. In the past decade, this focus has intensified so that drug control now dominates the U.S. foreign policy agenda with numerous Asian, Southeast Asian, and Latin American countries.

The Problem in Latin America

In Latin America, the historical development of drug policy has been very different from that in the United States. Indigenous use of coca throughout the Andean region is an intrinsic part of both the ancient and modern cultures. In other regions, marijuana and peyote have been used in traditional religious practices. Until very recently, drug abuse as experienced in North America was extremely rare. As a result, governments did not adopt restrictive drug legislation.

However, governments generally prohibited drug production beyond that required for traditional and cultural uses, largely in response to U.S. pressure to curtail supplies. The UN 1961 Single Convention on Narcotic Drugs also required that countries restrict drug production to medicinal and legitimate commercial needs. Enforcing these restrictions has created serious political problems in Peru and Bolivia, where illicit production fuels an increasingly powerful underground economy. In 1990 President Alberto Fujimori of Peru suspended U.S.-supported anticoca enforcement efforts for fear that they would further strengthen the guerrilla insurgency led by the Shining Path.

The United States has also had limited success in eradicating domestic illicit drug production; marijuana remains a leading cash crop—particularly in the western states—notwithstanding periodic law enforcement efforts to destroy large fields. Nonetheless, for the past decade the United States has been urging Andean countries to eradicate coca, despite continuing difficulties in identifying an effective and environmentally safe herbicide for aerial eradication. Apart from the unresolved practical question of how to eradicate coca, political resistance has been enormous, as José Guillermo Justiniano explains in Chapter 7. Consequently, eradication has occurred in relatively small areas, generally by manual methods. Meanwhile, illicit coca production has grown exponentially, particularly in Peru.

Even with coca easily available and widely tolerated by society, drug abuse has only recently emerged as a significant problem in Latin America. Initially, drug use was thought to be restricted largely to the rich, who traveled abroad and adopted the "jet-set" fascination with cocaine. However, as María Elena Medina-Mora and María del Carmen Mariño clearly show in Chapter 3, drug abuse is also increasing among the poor—particularly among the most vulnerable groups, such as homeless children. This development surprised many observers, who believed the long cultural tradition of controlled drug use would limit abuse.

There is a multitude of sociological, economic, and individual reasons for the growth of drug abuse in Latin America. One intriguing theory is that excessive supplies of coca, a by-product of the explosion in U.S. demand in the 1980s, helped create a new domestic market in the producer countries. In contrast to the United States, where drug supplies rush in to meet demand, the root of the problem in Latin America appears to be the reverse: that increasingly cheap, easily available drugs led to new consumption.

U.S. drug control policies may unwittingly have contributed to this development. In 1981 the recently elected Reagan administration radically shifted the focus of U.S. drug policy toward border interdiction, attacking all illicit drugs equally. Many foreign traffickers turned from marijuana to the far less bulky cocaine, which at that time was also substantially more profitable. Coca production expanded rapidly, doubling between 1982 and 1985. Prices dropped precipitously, falling from $60,000 a kilogram (wholesale in Miami) in 1981 to about $20,000 four years later. The excess supplies of coca set the stage for the development of crack, a refining breakthrough that both multiplied cocaine profits for street-level dealers and created a new group of addicts.

Yet, even the emergence of the crack epidemic in the United States in the mid-1980s did not absorb the still-expanding supplies of coca and cocaine. Consequently, traffickers looked to Europe to develop new markets. As prices fell, they also began to market *basuco* (smokable cocaine paste) as well as the more expensive refined cocaine in the producing countries themselves. Today, with demand for cocaine declining in the United States, these alternative markets are growing in importance. The tragic result is increasing cocaine abuse.

Future Directions

Drug abuse has become a truly global problem; thus, international cooperation has become of paramount importance. Although law enforcement still predominates as the primary strategy for cooperation, collaboration on prevention, education, and treatment has grown in recent years. Unfortunately, the United States has a long history of drug abuse; in the past decade, much has been learned about programs that have an impact in reducing drug abuse. It is important to explore how some of the models that show promise in reducing U.S. demand might also be relevant in other countries.

Yet, as illicit drug use in the United States declines—as it has quite substantially in the past four years—U.S. interest in international cooperation may also decline. It is also possible that patterns of U.S. drug use will shift to new products such as "ice," a powerful synthetic methamphetamine that can be easily produced at home from readily available chemicals. Either scenario—a continuing decline in demand or a switch to domestically produced drugs—will mean that the producer countries will lose much of their current importance for the United States.

Unfortunately for long-term policy implications, U.S. foreign assistance to the Andean countries concentrates primarily on drug eradication and interdiction. Given the severe budget constraints the United States is facing in the next decade—and congressionally mandated spending limitations—it is unlikely that substantial levels of assistance will be sustained if cocaine is no longer perceived to be a major threat within the United States.

This is particularly tragic in view of the expanding drug abuse problems within many of the producer countries. Prevention and treatment programs there are still in the beginning stages; finding adequate financial support for these efforts is already a major challenge. Although U.S. narcotics control assistance to the producer countries has included some funding for epidemiological studies and education programs, it has been extremely limited. In addition to humanitarian concerns, this assistance was intended to strengthen the resolve of governments to fight drug production by showing them that their countries also had drug abuse problems.

In view of the problems the United States is having in adequately funding its own prevention and treatment programs, it will probably not expand its support for Latin American demand-reduction efforts—particularly if U.S. demand declines further. Some Latin American critics have noted that in fact, expanded drug consumption by other countries may serve U.S. interests by diverting supplies elsewhere. Nonetheless, current levels of coca production are so high that even if substantial amounts are diverted to Europe, relatively cheap supplies will still be available for the United States.

As argued by the Inter-American Commission on Drug Policy, the Andean countries should consider creating a regional forum for cooperation on demand reduction. Such cooperation would allow governments to enhance the opportunities arising from successful law enforcement efforts against refining and trafficking. The disruption of the Medellín cartel in Colombia in 1989–1990, for example, caused an immediate rise in local cocaine prices in the Andean countries as well as a precipitous drop in coca leaf prices in Peru and Bolivia. In practical terms, this meant local users were faced with much higher prices, driving at least some of them away from coca paste and cocaine and preventing others from becoming users. It also meant coca farmers would be more willing to turn to alternative crops that would pay them as well as or better than coca. Improved cooperation within the region would increase the possibility that these windows of opportunity are used to reduce coca-cocaine use and production. Of course, without adequate resources to support these efforts, the impact of law enforcement will be short-term—even at the local level.

This volume eloquently demonstrates the central role demand reduction must play in long-term strategies to combat drug abuse. For the past decade, U.S. drug policy has concentrated primarily on supply reduction through interdiction and law enforcement. In relations with Latin American producing countries, the dominant U.S. interest has been to curtail production and trafficking. Law enforcement officials are now among the first to point out the failure of this approach. Illicit drugs are cheap and easily available; decreases in drug use have been achieved because of health concerns and antidrug social attitudes. Yet, the critical importance of demand reduction has not yet been fully recognized by U.S. officials, and it plays virtually no role in U.S. international drug control policy. Perhaps the so-called "supplier" countries in Latin America will be the ones to lead the way to a more effective regional and hemispheric policy based on the importance of demand reduction.

16

Taxes, Regulations, and Prohibitions: Reformulating the Legalization Debate

Mark A.R. Kleiman and Aaron Saiger

Drug legalization has emerged from the shadows of the discourse over U.S. drug policy. Repeal has been debated by the readers of advice columnist Ann Landers, formally denounced by both Congress and the executive branch, and debated at considerable length in the letters and op-ed pages of U.S. newspapers. A parallel debate—similar in substance if not in tone—has taken place in the pages of learned journals, where advocates of the status quo have been challenged by some tired veterans of the drug wars—judges, prosecutors, probation and juvenile officers, and a small number of elected officials—and by a handful of academics, economists, lawyers, and physicians.[1]

The current legalization debate—at both the popular and the scholarly levels— is surprisingly muddled. Even such basic details of legalization proposals as which drugs should be covered and how regulation would replace prohibition are rarely specified, leaving both sides arguing in the dark. The debate often blurs even the elementary distinction between the effects of drugs and the effects of drug control policies.

This chapter seeks to clarify some of these confusions. The first section surveys the current debate about drugs in the abstract. It is followed by discussion of three drugs: alcohol, marijuana, and cocaine. These case studies are meant to illustrate the types of considerations that ought to govern rational debate over the drug laws.

Arguing About Legalization

Ethan Nadelmann, in arguing for legalization, asks his readers to compare today's commerce in licit tobacco to the state of the world if the production, sale, and use of tobacco were made illegal. As millions of newly criminal nicotine addicts searched for ways to feed their addiction, black market dealers would take over. Revenue that

This chapter is based partly on our previous paper, Mark A.R. Kleiman & Aaron J. Saiger, *Drug Legalization: The Importance of Asking the Right Question*, 18 HOFSTRA L. REV. 527 (1990). Reprinted by permission.

now flows to the states as cigarette excise taxes would instead feed the coffers of criminal organizations. A large, expensive, and corruptible Tobacco Enforcement Administration would need to be created. Courts would be clogged with users caught with tobacco and with the dealers caught selling it. The nation would suddenly confront a daunting, dangerous, and expensive tobacco problem.[2]

Along with other proponents of drug legalization, Nadelmann argues that this fantasy about illicit tobacco reflects the reality of the currently illicit drugs. The basic claim of these proponents is simple: Prohibition and enforcing prohibition impose social costs that exceed the value of the goals prohibition achieves (the social costs it avoids).[3] In particular, making drugs illegal creates a menacing and costly black market without significantly diminishing the quantity of drugs consumed. In this view, legalization would make the streets safer, put the black market dealers out of business, and focus attention on the medical problem of addiction rather than the legal problem of drug dealing.[4]

In reply, supporters of the status quo contend that the benefits of prohibition justify its costs.[5] Some of these supporters claim that safer neighborhoods and lower law enforcement budgets would not balance the damage to the public health and well-being that increased consumption of legalized drugs would create. Others hold that the damage done by prohibition is not as significant as legalization advocates assert.[6]

The debate between these two camps has proven curiously unamenable to resolution. Since the basic arguments were first framed, they have been repeated in various permutations and with varying degrees of rancor; but the repetitions have made little progress toward either sharpening the questions or determining who is right. In part, this is because of the necessarily speculative nature of the discussion. Almost no data are available on which to base conclusions; the few historical models are so far distant from current U.S. conditions that they shed little light. But a few conceptual clarifications seem in order.

Arguments That Apply to the Legalization of One Drug Need Not—and Often Do Not—Apply to Others. Much of the popular and scholarly debate on both sides of the legalization question, as with much of the drug policy literature in general, treats the nation's drug problem as if it were due to some singular, indivisible "drug" and were susceptible to an equally uniform response. In fact, each drug has its own consumption problem; each harms users and others in different ways and to different degrees; and each has its own supply system, market structure, and demand patterns—making it susceptible to different interventions.[7]

The Details of a Legalization Regime Are Crucial Determinants of Its Outcome; Such Details Should Not Be Left Undefined. Legalization, like prohibition, does not indicate a unique strategy. Perhaps the most prominent inadequacy of current legalization arguments is their failure to specify what is meant by legalization. Current drug policy provides an illustration of this diversity of application. Heroin and marijuana are completely prohibited, but cocaine can be used in rigidly defined medical contexts (not including any in which the drug's psychoactive properties are exercised).[8] A wide range of painkillers, sleep inducers, stimulants, tranquilizers, and sedatives can be obtained and used with a doctor's prescription for their psychoactive effects;[9] weaker preparations of some of these drugs are items of ordinary commerce. Alcohol and tobacco are available for recreational use but are subject to an array of controls including excise taxation, age minimums, curbs on advertising, warning label requirements, retail licensing, and bans on use in some public places.

Drug legalization therefore can be thought of as moving drugs along a spectrum of regulated statuses in the direction of increased availability. However, although legalization advocates do not deny that some sort of controls will be required, their proposals rarely address the questions of how far on the spectrum a given drug should be moved or how to accomplish such a movement. This is unfortunate because the consequences of legalization depend heavily on the details of the regulatory regime that accompanies legal change. The price and conditions of availability of a newly legal drug will be more powerful in shaping its consumption than the fact that the drug is legal. Rules about advertising, place and time of consumption, and availability to minors help determine whether important aspects of the drug problem get better or worse. The amount of regulatory apparatus required and the way in which it is implemented will determine how much budget reduction can be realized from dismantling current enforcement efforts. Such details should not be dismissed as easily determined or postponed as a problem requiring future thought.[10]

The Effect of Prohibition on Current Consumption Levels Should Not Be Underestimated. For many legalization advocates, the discovery that drug prohibition has significant costs appears to have obscured its possible benefits.[11] Some advocates of legalization simply assume that prohibition has no effect on consumption and thus that legalization can shrink the drug problem at a stroke by legislating away an entire category of costs.[12] Other, more sophisticated accounts choose simply to minimize prohibition's effects.[13]

However, these assertions fly in the face of research and experience. Prohibition and enforcement make the currently illicit drugs more expensive and less available.[14] Black market cocaine costs nearly twenty times as much as legal, "free market" cocaine;[15] and it is implausible that a twentyfold change in a drug's price would have only a trivial effect on volume. It is also unlikely that even holding price constant, the convenience and safety of a licit purchase would fail to attract new customers (or to increase the volume consumed by existing ones). As an illustration, consider the history of alcohol criminalization: Prohibition clearly decreased alcohol consumption, and Repeal just as clearly increased it—by substantial amounts.[16]

Legalization advocates emphasize the heavy load of damage associated with the currently licit drugs—alcohol and tobacco—to highlight the arbitrariness, even irrationality, of the current categorization of drugs into forbidden and permitted.[17] But unless one thinks drug policies are made under Murphy's Law, the fact that the licit substances cause more health damage than the currently forbidden ones suggests that on balance, prohibition tends to protect health. Making the cocaine problem more like the current alcohol or tobacco problem would be a major public health disaster. Yet, it is far from clear that legal cocaine would be less attractive or less harmful to users' health than alcohol and tobacco. The cases of alcohol and tobacco are indeed instructive, but they make a point opposite to the one legalization's advocates intend: They demonstrate that legal availability can carry costs at least as significant as those of prohibition.

Legal Regimes Should Not Be Considered in Isolation from the Problems of Implementation and Enforcement. Some legalization advocates concede that legalization has potential costs, but urge that it be implemented because potential benefits are great and the risks containable.[18] A more lively appreciation of legalization's pitfalls and of the high costs of the problems that do occur might reduce the enthusiasm of the legalization camp. Consider the prohibition of illicit drugs to minors. If completely effective, it would ameliorate many of the consumption-related costs of legalization. But current tobacco and alcohol policy—both drugs are nominally forbidden to minors but are widely available to and used by adolescents— is far from encouraging on that score.

The oft-heard plea for legalization "experiments" is similarly remote from the world of practice.[19] Reprohibition after any failed wholesale legalization experiment would prove extremely costly. The increase in costs would be directly proportional to the increase in market size that results from legalization.[20] In the circumstance in which reversal would be most called for—an explosion in consumption— enforcement costs would be the greatest and the probability of a failed reprohibition highest. As the genie explained to the fisherman, not all processes are reversible. Although irreversibility is not itself an argument for the status quo, it is an argument for caution.

Arguments About Consequences Should Be Distinguished from Arguments About Morals. Arguments over legalization involve different predictions about the results of alternative policies and different value-weighing of those results. For example, legalizers are likely to stress crime reduction, whereas prohibitionists tend to emphasize users' health.[21] But both sides in the debate as we have presented it agree that policies are to be judged by their predictable consequences and that the balance of advantage ought to determine the choice.

But this debate about the consequences of alternative drug policies is not the only legalization debate now taking place. Legalization is also urged and deplored for reasons of principle not directly reducible to results by those who see themselves as guardians of liberty on one hand and of virtue (or "traditional values") on the other. The "libertarian" position holds that the use of mind-altering drugs is never a proper subject of public policy and should always be left to individual choice; it is the right of each adult to make that choice, and it is unjust for the state to interfere.[22] Their opponents, the "cultural conservatives," consider the use of the currently prohibited drugs as a vice that must be forbidden, even if it cannot be suppressed, to express social repudiation of that which degrades human life.[23] From the cultural conservative viewpoint, black market crime and official corruption are unfortunate side effects of a duty the government is nonetheless obligated to discharge. To use such side effects as an excuse for avoiding drug control would be to sidestep the obligations the state owes its citizenry.[24]

As with the debate about consequences, the debate about principles that is carried on between libertarians and cultural conservatives contributes to our understanding of what is at stake in formulating and enforcing drug policy. However, in the contention over legalization, the two debates are being waged simultaneously—often in the same forums—and are poorly distinguished from one another.

This confusion helps account for the peculiar fury that has attached itself to the legalization question. A purely consequentialist debate over legalization—over the plausibility of alternative predictions and the weights to be assigned to competing goals—could be conducted with no more passion than the debate over any other comparably complex social policy question. In a debate over principle, however, any assertion that a particular course of action has an advantage is often taken to be the equivalent of an endorsement of that position. Whoever asserts that free legal availability of cocaine would likely increase the number of chronic heavy cocaine users is likely to find himself or herself attacked by libertarian proponents of legalization as favoring a police state.[25] By the same token, to point out that drug prohibition tends to increase the rate of predatory crime is to risk being branded by cultural conservative opponents of legalization as indifferent to the personal and social degradation of a life spent "under the influence."[26]

Legal Alcohol?

Drugs that are currently legal provide a convenient set of models for the legalization debate. Examining licit drug control allows us to consider real-life, working, regulatory regimes rather than the artists' sketches now passing for legalization proposals. Alcohol provides a superb example of legalization gone awry. Regulations governing alcohol, the nation's premier recreational psychoactive, are fantastically permissive when measured against either the rules for other drugs or benefit-cost criteria.

Alcohol is a very dangerous drug. Had Congress failed to exempt it specifically from the provisions of the Controlled Substances Act, it could be placed in Schedule I along with marijuana and heroin as a psychoactive drug with no accepted medical use and great potential for harm. Indeed, as a product unsafe in its intended use, alcohol could perhaps be vulnerable to challenge under the Consumer Product Safety Act. Casual or experimental alcohol users are at risk of progressing to heavy, chronic use or to alcohol binges comparable to the abuse-capture risks of marijuana or powder cocaine.[27] An estimated 18 million Americans in 1987, out of 140 million total drinkers, had significant drinking problems.[28] Many of these "problem" drinkers find that their alcohol use is no longer fully under their deliberate control, and some are the victims of a physical dependency that makes them actively ill if they do not get a daily ration of their drug.[29]

Heavy chronic alcohol use is associated with a wide variety of diseases, and alcohol has been estimated to cause approximately twenty thousand excess disease deaths per year.[30] More than one-third of all crime leading to state prison sentences in 1986 was committed under the influence of alcohol,[31] as has been an even greater proportion of domestic assault, sexual assault, and the physical and sexual abuse of children—all of which are underreported and underpunished.[32] Tens of thousands die annually and many more are maimed in alcohol-related traffic accidents, drownings, and fires—including thousands of people who were not drinking themselves.[33] Alcohol's contribution to industrial accidents and decreased economic productivity is unknown.

One possible conclusion to be drawn from this catalog of catastrophes would be that alcohol should be assigned its rightful place in Schedule I of the Controlled Substances Act. This is a conclusion with some appeal. But just as the costs of controlling illicit drugs do not of themselves justify legalization, the extensive damage done by alcohol is not sufficient to justify reprohibition. The costs of criminalizing alcohol would be high; there are other means of reducing alcohol-related damage; and not all alcohol users incur or cause harm related to their drug use. Many users testify that they derive pleasure and relaxation from drinking, that it contributes to sociability, and that their drinking habits cause no harm to others or to themselves more serious than an occasional hangover.[34]

This testimony need not be taken at face value. Drug users can and do deceive themselves about the damage they incur and the damage they do to others. Nor should such testimony be ignored. Benefits are an essential part of a cost-benefit calculation, and consumers—even drug consumers—have information about benefits that is too often disregarded in the legalization debate.

Even if the total benefits of alcohol availability were exceeded by its total costs, that alone would not establish the case for reprohibition. It would still have to be shown that the excess of costs over benefits (including black market and enforcement costs) would be less under some practicable form of prohibition than it is now. The size of the existing alcohol market makes these added costs of prohibition likely to be substantial. One can regret Repeal without wishing to reverse it.

But consider those other means of reducing the costs alcohol imposes on drinkers and on others. What are they? To what extent can they reduce costs while preserving benefits? Education in schools and communities is an attractive option, but the evaluation literature is mixed.[35] The most hopeful result is from a Kansas City study that found that alcohol use among sixth and seventh graders was reduced by half as the result of an integrated (and expensive) drug education program.[36] If those reduced rates of early use (delayed ages of onset) translate into a lower incidence of later heavy use, this result would be very significant. Longitudinal studies, however, have yet to be done.

Although hard liquor advertisements are banned from the broadcast media, liquor is advertised freely in magazines and newspapers. Beer and wine advertising is essentially unrestricted. Much of this advertising appears to be directed at adolescents; legislation and regulation have limited potential to alter this unfortunate fact. More comprehensive advertising bans would be of doubtful value in reducing consumption; they might also deprive consumers of price information, solidifying current market shares and reducing competition to the detriment of consumers. There are also forms of promotion—such as sporting event sponsorship, coupons, and free samples—that a mass-media advertising ban does not reach.

More promising is negative advertising, which should be directed at all the costs of alcohol use and not just drunken driving. In 1970—when advertisements for cigarettes were banned from radio and television, taking the rare but powerful antismoking advertisements with them—cigarette consumption actually increased.[37]

Another way to reduce alcohol-related damage is to offer treatment services to those who want to quit. But the extensive evaluation literature fails to identify systematic advantages of even quite rigorous treatment over voluntary self-help through Alcoholics Anonymous (or its spin-off, Rational Recovery). Environmental and demographic factors predict success much more strongly than does type of treatment.[38]

Mechanisms for seller liability, although perhaps attractive on moral grounds, are similarly limited in their likely practical effects. Nor could more restrictions on the time and place of retail sale be expected to change significantly patterns of use and abuse.

There may be more promise on the user accountability side. It might help if courts and informal mechanisms of social control began to treat alcohol intoxication as an exacerbating rather than a mitigating circumstance in cases of unpleasant or criminal behavior. One possible sanction for alcohol-related misbehavior—violent crime, drunken driving, or disorderly conduct—would be a personal drinking ban enforced by routine chemical monitoring.[39] This approach has real promise for alcohol—as it does for illicit drugs—but at present there is no movement to advocate its implementation.

The current alcohol control regime purports to ban alcohol use by children. However, in the absence of vigorous enforcement measures, "leakage" from older to younger drinkers has made this ban a paper blockade. Heavy drinking is more common among adolescents, to whom it is forbidden, than among adults.[40] Part of this failure lies in enforcement: Giving alcohol to minors is not treated, by law or custom, with the harshness ordinarily associated with dealing drugs to children. But even aggressive enforcement cannot change the fact that a drug that is legal for adults is likely to be available to minors. Every adult is a potential source of alcohol for children, and the attractions of the drug are increased by its identification with being grown-up. Moreover, age restrictions are not only arbitrary; they are *obviously* arbitrary—selling beer to a twenty-year-old is a crime but selling it to him or her three months later is licit commerce. This matters because a drinking age, unlike a minimum age for a driver's license, is not self-enforcing. Unless a punishment is designed for reselling alcohol to minors that is severe enough to deter adults, not so severe as to tie up the courts with trials and appeals, and obviously appropriate to the crime, heavy leakage across the age barrier will no doubt continue.

The only regulatory institution now in force that has significant potential to control alcohol abuse is alcohol taxation, which discourages consumption by making the drug more expensive. Yet, U.S. alcohol taxes have been declining in real terms since the Korean War.[41] Even if the social costs of crime and costs to drinkers are excluded, alcohol taxes fall markedly short of the costs of alcohol consumption to society. One study estimated the average external social cost of an ounce of alcohol at forty-eight cents—even ignoring the cost of drunken crimes—whereas the average sale and excise taxes (federal and state) add up to only twenty-three cents per ounce.[42] Beer—the alcohol product most widely used by adolescents—is particularly undertaxed, with the result that cheap beer is sometimes less expensive at the retail level than name-brand soft drinks.

Alcohol taxes should be significantly higher, and the alcohol in beer should be taxed as heavily as the alcohol in liquor.[43] Fixing the magnitude of an increase is complex, however. The costs of raising taxes include lost consumers' surplus, some redistribution of the total tax burden toward the poor, and further impoverishment of those who cannot or do not quit heavy drinking. A very steep tax increase might also lead to the development of a black market in untaxed alcohol—with attendant costs of enforcement, adulteration, and violence.

It would be best to tax every drink according to its social costs. Some drinks do no harm and therefore should not be taxed; other drinks impose extraordinary costs and should therefore be taxed heavily. Yet, taxation by nature is undiscriminating. Since the theoretical and practical barriers to multiple levels of taxation are insurmountable, taxation—set to cover average social cost—is sure to put too high a price on most use and not enough on some. Another mechanism is therefore required.

The obvious solution is to prohibit drinking entirely by persons whose drinking carries social costs far above the level set by taxation. Youthful drinking is not the only type of drinking that causes disproportionate harm. Heavy drinking by anyone, drinking by "compulsive" users (those whose drinking is no longer under their deliberate self-control), and drinking by those who commit crimes or act recklessly while intoxicated all fall into this category and could be prohibited. The ban on purchase of alcohol by minors could be extended to adults whose use has led to crime or reckless behavior, and an absolute ceiling could be set on the quantity of alcohol anyone could purchase within a given period. A central data base of ineligible purchasers could be maintained, or if that proved costly or infeasible, all persons could be licensed to purchase alcohol as they are to drive—with licenses revocable for alcohol-related offenses, including resale to unlicensed individuals.

Such "positive" licensure is an attractive strategy. It could be conditioned on passing a written test on drinking safety, as is now done for driving. Drinkers' licenses might even be issued in conjunction with drivers' licenses, or drinking licensure could be indicated on the driver's license. Licensure would allow relatively easy enforcement of personal quantity limits by a system similar to that used to keep credit card holders within their credit limits. It could also allow teetotalers to identify themselves—and thus perhaps to make themselves eligible for lower auto, life, and health insurance premiums—and it could allow those who wish to stop drinking the crutch of tearing up their drinkers' licenses.

Licensure would have its costs. A number of practical problems, some more difficult than others, suggest themselves immediately. A national system might be required because differences in state standards might lead to jurisdiction-hopping. The administration of quantity limits would require a central computer and the development of privacy safeguards. Everyone, not just young adults, would need to be "carded" in bars and liquor stores and at social functions at which alcohol was distributed without charge.

Parties in private homes raise complex regulatory issues. For example, hosts of such parties would need either to card their guests or to know their legal status, and they would need some waiver of quantity limits to buy enough alcohol for their guests. Employment discrimination against drinkers would also require regulation or perhaps be forbidden in most occupations and mandated for a few. Perhaps the most intractable questions involve alcohol use by pregnant women. Both of the available regulatory choices—allowing pregnant women their ordinary alcohol allotment or denying them the drinking rights enjoyed by others—are unappealing, for different reasons.[44]

Finally, licensure would involve significant enforcement costs, especially because in some cases it makes access to alcohol inversely proportional to the motivation for obtaining it. Leakage is sure to be significant, although its specific features depend on the regulatory details. For example, if personal alcohol limits were high, light drinkers would have a strong incentive to sell their excess to others at a profit; if the limits were low, much harmless drinking would be curtailed and a black market encouraged.

Despite these problems, a regime consisting of higher taxation and positive licensure has strong potential to control the costs of alcohol use, including the costs of its own enforcement, while maintaining most of the benefits of legal availability. This regime would depart from the dichotomy that currently governs U.S. drug control: prohibition or free commerce. It concedes that the social costs of a flat ban are too great to justify prohibition; but rather than replacing prohibition with free drug commerce, it suggests a middle option—one that might be called "grudging toleration"—with strict controls to decrease consumption and minimize harms.

If the category of "grudgingly tolerated vice" could be successfully institutionalized, over time it might provide a framework for the control of other drugs—some now licit and some now illicit. With a working alcohol control regime in place, the alcohol problem would be considerably smaller, at which time a proposal to make our marijuana or cocaine problem more like our alcohol problem might sound more attractive than it does now.

But at the moment, there is no working model of grudging toleration. It does not even exist as a social category. Under such circumstances, new legalization regimes are likely to tend toward the relatively unrestricted availability that characterizes alcohol. The costs of such availability suggest that those who advocate the legalization of now-illicit drugs might best begin the process of drug control reform by proposing and testing reforms of current alcohol policy.

Legal Marijuana?

If one of the currently illicit drugs had to be chosen for legalization, marijuana would be the obvious candidate. For this reason, marijuana is the favorite example of those who advocate legalization of drugs,[45] whereas opponents concentrate their fire on heroin and cocaine.

Several facts make marijuana prohibition look like a questionable bargain. First, marijuana is the most widely used illicit drug.[46] An estimated 66 million Americans have tried marijuana at least once, and in 1988, 6.6 million people in this country reported using the drug once a week or more.[47] Users also report that marijuana is easy to obtain. Although there is some evidence of short-term shortages of low-potency marijuana, 85 percent of high-school seniors continue to report that they could get the drug when and if they wanted it.[48] Therefore, a substantial proportion of those who would use marijuana if it were legal are probably already using it.

Marijuana has by far the lowest ratio of measured harm to total use of all the illicit drugs. Although a noticeable proportion of all regular marijuana users become at least daily users for some period of time, this becomes a chronic condition for relatively few.[49] Even so, the absolute number of heavy daily users of marijuana—people who spend most of their waking hours under the influence—is distressingly large: a few million Americans at any given time.[50] But even the existence of this rather obvious "problem" population must be inferred from data about drug markets rather than directly observed in the form of deaths, injuries, crimes, or skid row personal collapses.[51] Even if prohibition and enforcement were very successful in reducing marijuana consumption, questions could still be raised about the benefits of that reduction.

Finally, marijuana prohibition is expensive; calculations suggest that marijuana enforcement at the federal level alone cost nearly a billion dollars in 1988.[52] These costs seem high, both relative to the large numbers of persons who continue to use the drug and to the degree of severity of the consequences their use seems to impose.

It is therefore no wonder that the legalization of marijuana is offered as an obvious and relatively risk-free first step toward drug legalization.[53] Nevertheless, our experience with alcohol should make us doubt that any drug control proposal is risk free. Even the best control regimes have significant costs.

The actual risks of marijuana legalization become clear when the particulars of control regimes are considered. Two very different regimes have been proposed:

marijuana decriminalization, which makes marijuana use legal but continues to ban marijuana commerce; and true legalization, which allows free commerce in the drug. The likely impacts of these two proposals are widely disparate, but few legalization proponents devote much attention to this range of possible results. The debate over marijuana laws is a textbook case of the necessity of detailed regulatory proposals for sensible discussion.

Decriminalization would make marijuana possession legal or, as with traffic violations, only mildly punishable. Import, processing, and distribution of the drug would remain illicit. Such a regime—under which dealers are targeted but users are not—is essentially that of the Eighteenth Amendment, under which alcohol could be legally owned but not sold. Marijuana decriminalization has been instituted in a number of states and in the Netherlands and has been endorsed by a wide variety of national organizations and, in a 1988 *National Law Journal* survey, by a surprising proportion of longtime prosecutors.[54]

The aim of decriminalization is to create enforcement savings without any great increase in consumption costs. The potential savings are obvious. The 327,000 people arrested for marijuana possession in 1988 would once again be on the right side of the law, and the extensive investigative and punishment resources now applied to them—mostly by local jurisdictions—could be used elsewhere.[55]

It appears unlikely that decriminalization would lead to large increases in marijuana consumption. Survey evidence and the experience of decriminalized states suggest that fear of arrest plays little role in discouraging marijuana use.[56] Because commerce in the drug would remain forbidden, there would be no reason to expect major changes in availability or public attitudes. If use were not punishable, it might be possible to reduce marijuana's most well-documented health hazard— lung damage—by carrying out public service campaigns to encourage the use of water-filtered smoking devices to replace the ubiquitous "joint."

Decriminalization would also have costs. A policy that eliminates one of the deterrents to drug use should be expected to increase consumption at least minimally. By leaving the black market untouched but increasing consumption, decriminalization benefits black market marijuana dealers. Rational marijuana traffickers ought to fear legalization above all things but should regard decriminalization as an entirely good idea. An ingenious middle course, in effect in Alaska until recently, allowed the growth and consumption of small quantities at home for personal use.[57] This presumably reduced the size of the commercial black market while preserving most of the potential benefits of decriminalization. In effect, decriminalization is a proposal for a redistribution of enforcement costs: It makes user-associated problems smaller and dealer-associated problems bigger. The balance of advantage is not self-evident.

Allowing licit commerce would be a vastly different proposal. Such a regime could tax marijuana, license users, limit quantity, restrict potency, and so on. It is plausible that such a regime—constructed on the model of grudging toleration— would vastly reduce the enforcement problem, although the size of this potential benefit is reduced by the fact that marijuana use is so prevalent among youth, for whom use would presumably remain illegal. Additionally, some heavy users who now pay for their own marijuana from their earnings as marijuana dealers might turn to property crime instead.[58] However, several billion dollars in annual revenue would become available to various levels of government—most of it transferred from the revenues of illicit enterprises.

Legalization, however, could lead to dramatic increases in consumption. Under prohibition, marijuana is available to a determined buyer but is still far less easy to find and of a less consistent quality than most legal commodities. Under a regulatory regime, it would become vastly more available. Buying marijuana would be as quick and easy as buying a chocolate bar, for example.

How much damage would this consumption increase do? As with occasional and moderate drinking, occasional and moderate marijuana use does not cause evident harm. However, two sorts of marijuana consumption have significant social costs: very heavy use and use by children. Preventing growth of either of these user populations must be a design criterion for any legalization strategy. Effective prevention would require taxation, licensing, and quantity restrictions similar to those we have described for alcohol—with all their associated problems. In particular, there would be laws proscribing sale to minors, who now make up a large minority of marijuana users.[59] If enforcement of this law were lax, youthful consumption would grow; if it were severe, enforcement levels might decrease little from the current regime.

Some other details of marijuana regulation might differ from regulation of alcohol. Because marijuana is so much more compact than alcohol, marijuana leakage from adults to children and other ineligible users could become more of an illicit enterprise than the leakage of alcohol.[60] Because marijuana legalization involves a change in the drug's social status, it would also have important social effects—including use by role models. Such social acceptability may make marijuana use no worse a problem than cigarette smoking, but making marijuana smoking more like cigarette smoking is not a desideratum.

Marijuana potency varies widely. The concentrations of tetrahydrocannabinol (THC), the major psychoactive agent in marijuana offered for sale, vary from less than 3 to more than 10 percent.[61] There is reason to think that the more potent product may pose greater risks of overintoxication, although less potent varieties impose greater lung damage for the same drug experience. Marijuana users believe the subjective effects of the high-potency connoisseur grade are qualitatively different from the commercial product.[62] This raises another policy design problem: Should there be limits, beyond labeling requirements, on marijuana potency? If so, a black market might develop in illegal high-potency marijuana; if not, the newly legal marijuana industry might compete to provide more potent (and therefore possibly more dangerous) forms of the drug. Perhaps tax rates could be adjusted to discourage very high-potency marijuana without flatly forbidding it.

Setting tax rates poses a difficult problem. Untaxed or lightly taxed marijuana would be significantly cheaper than it is on the current black market; a prerolled "joint" might cost a few cents, like a tobacco cigarette or a tea bag. Significant increases in consumption could be expected to result from such a sharp decline in price. Heavy taxation, however, risks the possibility that the black market could continue to profit from selling untaxed marijuana. At best, heavy taxation would require serious enforcement efforts.

Marijuana legalization, then, has the potential to make some things better and others worse. The magnitude of these changes under any specific regulatory regime is a matter for further conjecture and analysis; whether the changes add up to a good or bad trade depends on what is likely to happen and on what weights are assigned to different aspects of the problem. But the spectrum of the possible results of marijuana legalization is much broader than some of its proponents seem to believe. Low-tax, high-potency legal marijuana could lead to severe social costs within user populations of the greatest concern; high-tax, low-potency marijuana could maintain black markets and their associated costs while increasing consumption more modestly. Decriminalized marijuana could lead simultaneously to lower law enforcement expenditures and increased criminal wealth and power.

If legalizing marijuana were to lead to modest increases in heavy drug use and drug use by minors (say, 10 percent), it could reasonably be considered a dramatic success. If instead those levels were to triple and marijuana potency were to rise, it would have to be counted an expensive and difficult-to-reverse failure. In the absence of any quantitative estimate of the probabilities of these two outcomes, legalizing marijuana has to be rated a high-stakes gamble.

Legal Cocaine?

Just as proponents of legalization often speak as if all drugs were like marijuana, supporters of the legal status quo seem to view all currently illicit drugs as if they were cocaine. Their specific arguments against cocaine legalization, however, are especially effective given the emergence of "crack" cocaine. The smokable form of cocaine provides a powerful but short-lived drug experience for a few dollars per dose. Its unpleasant aftereffects, relieved by more smoking, keep some users coming back for more for as long as their money lasts.[63] The spread of violence related to crack dealing and of crack-related law enforcement costs[64] has fueled the drive for legalization. But the invention of crack makes the legalization of cocaine a less plausible rather than a more plausible strategy. Crack makes cocaine a drug peculiarly ill-suited to legalization.

In the 1970s cocaine was fairly expensive.[65] Taken intranasally in the form of powder, the effects of a small dose were sufficiently subtle that experienced users could not reliably tell whether they were taking cocaine or a placebo in double-blind trials.[66] Its user base was relatively small and mostly affluent.[67] It was possible to argue that powder cocaine, a problem of the rich, did not merit particularly vigorous social intervention; drug use by the rich has fewer external costs than use by the poor because rich users have private resources with which to absorb the costs of their use.

Three things happened in the late 1970s and early 1980s to shatter this relatively serene picture. The first was a technical innovation. Users learned how to "free-base"—to convert cocaine to a smokable form—which gave a far more intense and short-lived drug experience.[68] The second was a marketing innovation. Dealers learned to make the conversion from powder to "base" and to package single-dose units as crack.[69] The third was a collapse in black market prices, due in part to a concentration of federal enforcement resources on markedly unsuccessful interdiction efforts and in part to the failure of the overall enforcement effort to grow fast enough to keep pace with the growing market.[70] These three transformations spread the use of cocaine across the socioeconomic spectrum and across the country.

Economist Milton Friedman has suggested that the invention of crack was a consequence of the illegality of cocaine.[71] But it is more plausible to think that competing cocaine companies—which would have the same economic incentives as traffickers but which would also enjoy access to licit product research, marketing, and distribution systems—would have orchestrated an even more rapid diffusion of new technology than actually occurred.[72]

Legalizing cocaine in a world in which it will be converted into crack has costs and benefits very different from legalizing cocaine that will be snorted as powder. The potential benefits are great because the illegality of crack is clearly responsible for many of its most significant costs. Crack dealers trade gunshots on the streets of urban neighborhoods.[73] Crack dealing is also a lucrative business, able to offer financial opportunity in areas in which little licit opportunity exists.[74]

Turning crack into a regulated and legal commodity would separate economically motivated lawlessness from the demand for an inexpensive high. The illegal crack distribution industry would shrink, much to the relief of neighborhoods now held captive by street drug markets. Youth gangs and criminal groups would lose influence. Removing the financial incentives the crack business offers youth would help restore families and schools.

The question nonetheless remains: What would happen to consumption and to the death, disease, damage, and crime caused by the drug itself? Crack did not become popular because it was illegal but because the demand for the cheap, intense high it provides is great—perhaps especially great in poor, urban areas. Speculation about why this is the case—lack of financial opportunity, single-parent families, racism—does not change this fact.

Many of the effects of crack remain unclear; its recent introduction means that available knowledge is scant, unreliable, and unusually dependent on investigations by the popular press. However, a number of factors suggest that the costs of legalization in the form of increased drug abuse would be substantial.

The crack-using population is much smaller than that using marijuana; there are still areas in which crack is relatively difficult to get, although it is becoming more widely available. Legalizing crack would therefore create new access to a drug in a way marijuana legalization would not. Crack generates compulsive use in a way very different from depressants such as heroin and alcohol. An estimated one crack user in three becomes a repeat binge user. This ratio is about as bad as it could be—high enough to mean that widespread use will generate widespread destruction but low enough that many adolescents are exposed to crack users who are using "successfully."

The harm done by crack use is orders of magnitude greater than that done by marijuana. Crack is a much more potent psychoactive. It imposes significant physiological damage and is especially debilitating to fetuses in utero.[75] The psychological effects of the drug are strong enough to detach many users from their neighborhoods, jobs, schools, and families. Long-term use may lead to a particularly antisocial condition known as stimulant psychosis, characterized by aggressive behavior.[76]

Nor is it clear that on balance, legalization would even decrease predatory crime. Surely, crime by dealers would fall, but crime by users is another story. If the legal price were high (say, ten dollars per dose) and increased availability led to a substantial increase in the number of compulsive users, the result presumably would be an increase in income-producing crime to pay for crack—with licensed sellers replacing street dealers as the recipients of the proceeds of burglary. This would be compounded by the fact that those crack users who now support their habits by dealing would find themselves out of business and in need of a new source of income.

If, on the other hand, the legal price were low (near the pharmaceutical price of five dollars per gram, or about twenty-five cents per dose), one can only imagine the resulting increase in drug abuse damage and in pharmacologically generated violent crime. Perhaps user licensure and quantity restrictions could limit the health costs of a low-tax legalization regime. However, it is hard to imagine how they would do so, given the strong compulsion generated by crack in some of its users, without simply re-creating the current black market with an expanded customer base created by legal experimentation.

In sum, now that crack is here, both high- and low-tax legal cocaine would likely leave us with a worse cocaine problem than we have now. The attention now given to abandoning prohibition should be focused instead on ways to make the enforcement of that prohibition less costly and more effective.

Legalization and Drug Abuse Control

The pragmatic question about drug control is how to manage the availability of a wide range of existing and potential psychoactives to get the best mix of costs and benefits. Changing the legal status of drugs is only one of many possible interventions that can affect that mix. Less dramatic proposals, which offer the potential for real progress with smaller risks, deserve at least equal attention.

Without changing the legal status of alcohol and tobacco, we could create new regulatory regimes that would reduce both the prevalence of their use and the resulting crime, death, and injury. Without changing the legal status of marijuana, we could dramatically reduce enforcement costs with little or no increase in abuse. Changing the legal status of cocaine is ill-advised, but this does not imply that current enforcement practices could not use dramatic reform.

The challenge of drug policy is to find least-cost solutions to the problems created by the age-old fact that some human beings take more of various mind-altering substances than is good for them and their neighbors and by the modern fact that the variety of available psychoactives is rapidly increasing. To concentrate on changing labels from legal to illegal is to miss all of the hard work and most of the social importance that accompany this challenge.

Notes

1. Marcia Coyle, "Prosecutors Admit: No Victory in Sight," *National Law Journal* 10, no. 40 (August 8, 1988): S2–S3; Milton Friedman, "An Open Letter to Bill Bennett," *Wall Street Journal*, September 7, 1989, A16; Kurt Schmoke, "An Argument in Favor of Decriminalization," *Hofstra Law Review* 18 (1990): 501; Ethan Nadelmann, "The Case for Legalization," *Public Interest* 92, no. 3 (Summer 1988): 3–31.

2. Nadelmann, "The Case for Legalization," 12–13.

3. Nadelmann, "The Case for Legalization," 11–29.

4. Schmoke, "An Argument in Favor of Decriminalization," 505.

5. James Q. Wilson and John DiIulio, "Crackdown: Treating the Symptoms of the Drug Problem," *New Republic*, July 10, 1989, 21–22.

6. Mark Moore, "Actually, Prohibition Was a Success," *New York Times*, October 6, 1989, A21.

7. Of particular importance are the price elasticities of demand for various drugs and the relations of complementarity or substitutability among them. See Peter Reuter and Mark Kleiman, "Risks and Prices: An Economic Analysis of Drug Enforcement," in Michael Tonry and Norval Morris, eds., *Crime and Justice: An Annual Review of Research* (Chicago: University of Chicago Press, 1986), 289–310; John Dinardo, *Are Marijuana and Alcohol Substitutes? The Effect of State Drinking Age Laws on the Marijuana Consumption of High School Seniors* (Santa Monica, Calif.: The RAND Corporation, 1991); Mark A.R. Kleiman, *Marijuana: Cost of Abuse of Control* (New York: Greenwood Press, 1989), 93–95; I. Ornstein, "Control of Alcohol Consumption Through Price Increases," *Journal of Studies on Alcohol* 41, no. 9 (September 1981): 807–818; Karen E. Model, *The Effect of Marijuana Decriminalization on Hospital Emergency Room Drug Episodes: 1975–1978* (Cambridge, Mass.: National Bureau of Economic Research, 1991).

8. 21 United States Code, sections 812, 829(a), 841–858 (1988).

9. Controlled Substances Act, Public Law no. 91–513 (1970).

10. Nadelmann, "The Case for Legalization," 6–7.

11. As John Kaplan has noted, "There is considerable temptation to conclude without any . . . examination that our present policy is so costly that free availability just has to be better."

John Kaplan, *The Hardest Drug: Heroin and Public Policy* (Chicago: University of Chicago Press, 1983), 110.

12. See Friedman, "An Open Letter to Bill Bennett," A14.

13. Mathea Falco, "The Bush Drug Plan: Nothing New," *New York Times*, September 5, 1989, A19; Peter Kerr, "The Unspeakable Is Debated: Should Drugs be Legalized?" *New York Times*, May 15, 1988, A1.

14. Reuter and Kleiman, "Risks and Prices."

15. Office of National Drug Control Policy, *National Drug Control Strategy* 1 (Washington, D.C.: U.S. Government Printing Office, 1989), 6.

16. M. Moore and D. Gerstein, eds., *Alcohol and Public Policy: Beyond the Shadow of Prohibition* (Washington, D.C.: National Academy Press, 1981), 62–63.

17. Ethan Nadelmann, "Drug Prohibition in the United States: Costs, Consequences, and Alternatives," *Science* 245 (1989): 943; Rufus King, "A Worthless Crusade," *Newsweek* (January 1, 1990): 4–5.

18. Nadelmann, "Drug Prohibition in the United States," 946.

19. Daniel Koshland, "The War? Problem? Experiment? on Drugs," *Science* 245 (1989): 1,309.

20. Nadelmann's scenario for illegal tobacco, for example, fails to note that a newly created tobacco black market would begin with an established consumer base in the tens of millions; current users of heroin, by contrast, number only in the hundreds of thousands.

21. See, for example, Peter Hammill, "The Great American Drug Muddle," *Lear's* (March 1990): 156–162; John Kaplan, "Taking Drugs Seriously," *Public Interest* 92 (1988): 32, 34.

22. The most consistent statement of this position is Thomas Szasz, *Ceremonial Chemistry: The Ritual Persecution of Drugs, Addicts, and Pushers*, rev. ed. (Holmes Beach, Fla.: Learning Publications, 1985).

23. See *National Drug Control Strategy* 1; James Q. Wilson, "Against the Legalization of Drugs," *Commentary* 89, no. 2 (February 1990): 21–28.

24. Wilson and DiIulio, "Crackdown," 21–22.

25. Hammill, "The Great American Drug Muddle," 162, predicts that maintaining drug prohibition "will lead inevitably to the creation of a vast archipelago of drug gulags . . . and more and more young people firing machine guns from the heart of darkness."

26. Wilson and DiIulio, "Crackdown," 22.

27. See results of Partnership Attitude Tracking Studies as reported by Partnership for a Drug Free America, *Newsletter* 4, no. 3 (Fall 1990).

28. Secretary of Health and Human Services, *Sixth Special Report to the U.S. Congress on Alcohol and Health* (Washington, D.C.: U.S. Government Printing Office, 1987), 11.

29. For a discussion of the logical structure of problem drinking and other compulsive behavior, see Thomas Schelling, "The Intimate Contest for Self-Command," *Public Interest* 60 (Summer 1980): 94. A discussion of alcohol particularly can be found in Herbert Fingarette, *Heavy Drinking: The Myth of Alcoholism as a Disease* (Berkeley: University of California Press, 1988).

30. Secretary of Health and Human Services, *Sixth Special Report*, 11.

31. Bureau of Justice Statistics, *Correctional Populations in the United States* (Washington, D.C.: U.S. Government Printing Office, 1986), 39.

32. Clare Jo Hamilton and James J. Collins, Jr., "The Role of Alcohol in Wife Beating and Child Abuse: A Review of the Literature," in James J. Collins, Jr., ed., *Drinking and*

Crime: Perspectives on the Relationships Between Alcohol Consumption and Criminal Behavior (New York: Guilford Press, 1981), 253–267.

33. National Highway Traffic Safety Administration, *Fatal Accident Report System* (Washington, D.C.: U.S. Government Printing Office, 1986).

34. U.S. Departments of the Treasury and of Health and Human Services, *Report to the President and the Congress on Health Hazards Associated with Alcohol and Methods to Inform the General Public of These Hazards* (Washington, D.C.: Departments of Treasury and HHS, 1980), i.

35. *National Drug Control Strategy* 1, 49–53; Kaplan, "Taking Drugs Seriously," 42–43.

36. Mary Ann Pentz et al., "A Multicommunity Trial for Primary Prevention of Adolescent Drug Abuse," *Journal of American Medical Association* 261, no. 22 (June 9, 1989): 3,259–3,266.

37. James L. Hamilton, "The Demand for Cigarettes: Advertising, the Health Scare, and the Cigarette Advertising Ban," *Review of Economic Statistics* 54 (1972): 401, 411.

38. Fingarette, *Heavy Drinking*, 76–80.

39. Such monitoring presents some technical problems, because alcohol's simple chemistry leaves no distinctive metabolites that can be detected in urine.

40. Williams and Vejnoska, "Alcohol and Youth: State Prevention Approaches," in C. M. Felsted, ed., *Youth and Alcohol Abuse: Readings and Resources* (Phoenix, Ariz.: Oryx Press, 1986).

41. Moore and Gerstein, *Alcohol and Public Policy*, 71.

42. W. G. Manning, E. B. Keeler, J. P. Newhouse, E. M. Sloss et al., "The Taxes of Sin: Do Smokers and Drinkers Pay Their Way?" *Journal of the American Medical Association* 261, no. 11 (March 17, 1989): 1,604, 1,608.

43. Thomas Schelling makes a vigorous counterargument on the beer-versus-liquor point: Because drunkenness is far more likely to result from imbibing alcohol in concentrated form, tax discrimination against distilled spirits is rational. Against this argument must be weighed the role of beer and wine (particularly wine coolers) in initiating adolescents and even children to drug use.

44. See "Case Against Pregnant Woman Is Dismissed," *New York Times*, February 3, 1990, 10.

45. Nadelmann, "The Case for Legalization," 25–26.

46. National Institute on Drug Abuse, *Overview of the National Household Survey on Drug Abuse* (Washington, D.C.: U.S. Government Printing Office, 1989), 2–4.

47. National Institute on Drug Abuse, *Overview*, 3.

48. Joseph B. Treaster, "Costly and Scarce, Marijuana Is a High More Are Rejecting," *New York Times*, October 29, 1991, A1; National Institute on Drug Abuse, *Drug Use, Drinking, and Smoking: National Survey Results from High School, College, and Young Adult Populations 1972–1988* (Washington, D.C.: U.S. Government Printing Office, 1989), 154.

49. Gordon Black Survey; National Institute on Drug Abuse, *Drug Use*, 31–33.

50. Mark A.R. Kleiman, *Marijuana: Costs of Abuse, Costs of Control* (New York: Greenwood Press, 1989), 16–17.

51. Kleiman, *Marijuana: Costs of Abuse*, 16–17.

52. For similar calculations, see Kleiman, *Marijuana: Costs of Abuse*, 156.

53. Nadelmann, "Drug Prohibition in the United States," 945.

54. Nadelmann, "The Case for Legalization," 29; Coyle, "Prosecutors Admit," S2. As of mid-1991, various forms of decriminalization were in effect in California, Colorado, Maine, Minnesota, Mississippi, Nebraska, New York, North Carolina, Ohio, and Oregon.

55. Federal Bureau of Investigation, *Crime in the United States 1988* (Washington, D.C.: U.S. Government Printing Office, 1989), 167–168.

56. Maloff, "A Review of the Effect of the Decriminalization of Marijuana," *Journal of Contemporary Drug Problems* 10 (1981): 307.

57. Bonnie, "The Meaning of 'Decriminalization': A Review of the Law," *Journal of Contemporary Drug Problems* 10 (1981): 277.

58. This potentially dangerous result is more relevant to heroin or cocaine, where economically motivated user crime is a major feature of the current illicit market, than to marijuana.

59. National Institute on Drug Abuse, *Drug Use.*

60. Kaplan, "Taking Drugs Seriously," 39.

61. E. Brecher and the editors of *Consumer Reports, Licit and Illicit Drugs* (Boston: Little, Brown, 1972), 404–405; William Novak, *High Culture: Marijuana in the Lives of Americans* (New York: Knopf, 1980), 177–180.

62. Novak, *High Culture,* 187–195.

63. Jefferson Morley, "What Crack Is Like," *New Republic* 201, no. 14 (October 2, 1989): 12–13.

64. "A Tide of Drug Killing," *Newsweek* (January 16, 1989): 44–45; "Another Bloody Year," *Time* (January 8, 1990): 53.

65. Wilson and DiIulio, "Crackdown," 22–23.

66. Craig Van Dyke and Robert Byck, "Cocaine," *Scientific American* 246 (1982): 128, 139.

67. Wilson and DiIulio, "Crackdown," 22.

68. A. Washton and M. Gold, eds., *Cocaine: A Clinicians' Handbook* (New York: Guilford Press, 1987), 176–177.

69. Washton and Gold, *Cocaine,* 177.

70. Peter Reuter et al., *Sealing the Borders: The Effects of Increased Military Participation in Drug Interdiction* (Santa Monica, Calif.: RAND Corporation, 1988).

71. Friedman, "An Open Letter to Bill Bennett," A16.

72. Mark Kleiman, "Letter to the Editor," *Wall Street Journal*, September 29, 1989, A15.

73. Wilson and DiIulio, "Crackdown," 21.

74. Terry Williams, *The Cocaine Kids: The Inside Story of a Teenage Drug Ring* (Reading, Mass.: Addison-Wesley, 1989), 8.

75. Barry Zuckerman et al., "Effects of Maternal Marijuana and Cocaine Use on Fetal Growth," *New England Journal of Medicine* 320 (1989): 762.

76. Estroff, "Medical and Biological Consequences of Cocaine Abuse." In Washton and Gold, eds., *Cocaine,* 28–29.

PART THREE

Exploring International Cooperation

A central theme throughout this book concerns the desirability and feasibility of international collaboration against drug abuse and trafficking. Parts One and Two have emphasized the crucial importance of defining common goals and strategies—through supply control, demand reduction, or some sort of combination of the two. Assessing convergence and divergence in national interests, contributions in Part Three shed additional light on possibilities for multilateral cooperation.

Chapters 17–22 explore questions of means as well as ends. What might be the most appropriate *form* for international coordination? Theoretically, several options are at hand:

- Given the worldwide nature of the drug industry, participant countries could rely on global organizations, most notably the United Nations.
- Given the importance of production and consumption within the Western Hemisphere, countries of the region could turn to formal institutions of their own, such as the Organization of American States.
- Given the difficulties inherent in bureaucratic organizations, countries might instead choose to work through informal regional arrangements, such as the Cartagena accords of February 1990.
- Given the need for swift and decisive action and the complexity of multilateral negotiations, countries of the hemisphere might decide to concentrate on bilateral strategies and understandings.
- Given the force of domestic political pressure as well as the limitations of diplomacy, nations may abandon efforts at international collaboration and resort to unilateral action.

What approach is likely to be most effective? For what purpose? Under what conditions?

Lisa L. Martin initiates this inquiry by searching out conceptual bases for effective international cooperation on drugs. In a sweeping comparative synthesis, she examines the history and logic of international agreement in three distinct issue-areas: security arrangements (military alliances and arms control), economic agreements (especially on trade and monetary policy), and social concerns (including human rights and environmental protection). And as a result, she finds that several elements for collaboration are absolutely central. One is the "shadow of the future," which encourages nations to ponder long-term implications and interests; another is accurate information (about the actions of other countries); yet another, of special relevance to health questions, is the achievement of a "scientific" consensus on the causes and character of the malady—in this case, drug addiction and abuse.

Equally important, in Martin's view, is the articulation of a common interest. Both partners in a cooperative agreement must anticipate meaningful benefits:

"Governments will cooperate only if their perceived benefits exceed the costs they will have to bear." Abstract promises about high-minded benefits for the world community as a whole are insufficient and irrelevant. "In order for cooperation to be stable," Martin writes, "every state involved must feel that it benefits from ongoing cooperation." As this book clearly shows, that has not always been the case in antidrug policy.

In demonstration of this point, William O. Walker III offers an incisive review of the historical record. Unilateral efforts ranging from prohibition in the Philippines to governmental monopolies in Asia to incarceration in the United States have met with only partial success: In Walker's judgment, "coercive unilateral efforts in themselves cannot seriously affect drug production, trafficking, and consumption." Nor have bilateral or multilateral approaches yielded lasting and meaningful results. Ultimately, in Walker's view, the challenge is more political than institutional: "Can drug control ever become a domestic and foreign policy goal of the first order?"

From a multilateral perspective, Jack Donnelly reviews the evolution of antidrug efforts from the Shanghai conference of 1909 through the present programs of the United Nations. The United Nations, in his estimation, has been "remarkably successful" in the articulation of international norms and the supervision of licit commerce in drugs and has considerable potential for the dissemination of knowledge and information; but the United Nations has only a marginal role in the actual implementation of global policy and is "likely to play a particularly peripheral role in the Americas." One recent achievement of the United Nations has been the development of an integrated approach to drug problems, including concerns about demand as well as supply, in the 1988 Convention Against Illicit Traffic in Narcotic Drugs and Psychotropic Substances. One persisting weakness, however, comes from funding limitations. "The real issue," as Donnelly writes, "is how deep the normative commitment to an intensified war on drugs really extends—that is, how much states are willing to pay to back their fine-sounding words."

Reflecting on a key point in Donnelly's interpretation, Abraham F. Lowenthal suggests that the Organization of American States (OAS) might provide effective coordination for multilateral antidrug policy at the regional level. Created in the late 1940s as an instrument of the cold war, the OAS showed signs of atrophy by the 1960s and weakened continually through the 1970s and 1980s. The end of the cold war offers new opportunities, however, and the OAS has gained strong leadership in quest of a new institutional mission. In light of these trends, Lowenthal offers a series of positive steps for the OAS to take in the development and enhancement of its antidrug role.

Focusing on the implications of bilateral and unilateral approaches, María Celia Toro presents a Mexican perspective on the evolution of U.S.-Mexican relations. Unilateral antidrug policies, in Toro's estimation, have suffered from inherent limitations: They have been assigned unattainable goals, have attempted to coordinate law enforcement ("by definition a national prerogative"), and have failed to recognize differences in national interests. The principal U.S. national interest resides in the reduction of trafficking and of demand; the principal national interest of Mexico and of other Latin American countries is the preservation of governmental authority. Crop eradication and interdiction of shipments, tactics promoted by the United States, moreover could lead traffickers to stockpile inventories and develop a consumer market within Mexico: "In this fashion, current policy could have a counterproductive effect on public health in Mexico." Nonetheless, assuming that Mexico would or should concur with U.S. goals and priorities, the United States has frequently (and counterproductively) attempted to impose its will on the Mexican government. More promising are coordinated bilateral efforts, such as Operation Condor of the 1970s, but these face technical and political limitations—including corruption and the "structural weakness of criminal justice systems throughout the continent." The presence of DEA agents on Mexican territory has been a continuing source of resentment. And on the basis of past experience, Toro expresses considerable skepticism about prospects for genuine reciprocity between partners with unequal power positions.

Concluding the analysis, David R. Mares employs game-theoretic models of strategic interaction to unravel the logical structure of inter-American efforts against drugs. Supply-control policies—dominant through the 1980s—produce a highly skewed distribution of payoffs, with the United States receiving the most benefit and paying the least cost. This corresponds to a game known as Bully, in which one player-country (in this case, the United States) will achieve a satisfactory outcome no matter what player B (Latin America) does. But this appears to be changing because domestic demands from U.S. citizens for more effective drug policies could erode support for supply-control policies. In this case, a more complex (two-level) game is likely to shift from Bully to Deadlock, according to Mares, in which neither the United States nor Latin America would have a logical incentive to cooperate with the other.

Emphasis on demand reduction, advocated by the Inter-American Commission on Drug Policy, would yield yet another circumstance: a U.S. commitment to pursue its course with or without Latin American cooperation, leaving Latin America with ample room for maneuver. The Bully game would thus be reversed. Future policy may represent a complicated combination of supply-control and demand-reduction strategies, in Mares's judgment, but his analysis ends with a sobering note: "We must be careful . . . not to believe the United States can produce cooperation merely by recognizing that demand factors are the principal determinants of the problem. If U.S. domestic groups simply focus on U.S. demand and ignore foreign-supply issues, Latin American negotiators may find themselves in an unaccustomed role: that of the Bully."

Chapters in Part Three raise two central issues. One is the desirability of "linkage." William Walker surmises that linking antidrug concerns with other, presumably more important foreign policy goals might provide the bases for common action within the Western Hemisphere. Examining a U.S.-German decision on macroeconomic policy, Lisa Martin likewise observes that packaging of issues "allowed the governments to find a set of agreements that left all better off than the status quo, whereas none of the individual agreements would probably have been adopted on its own." From a Mexican perspective, however, María Celia Toro expresses apprehension that drug policy under linkage will be used as a weapon, not as an inducement. For example, the U.S. process of "certification" for antidrug efforts threatens Mexico and other countries with strict economic sanctions. This is a highly negative version of linkage. The question, of course, is what gets linked with what and how.

A second issue concerns the age-old question of sovereignty. Walker declares that effective inter-American cooperation on drugs in the long run will require modification and relaxation of traditional concepts of sovereignty. But as others point out, law enforcement and police powers are fundamental attributes of nationhood. On the prospect of relinquishing or sharing control in this area, Jack Donnelly is blunt: "Virtually no state is likely to find this acceptable, given the centrality of the police power to the very idea of sovereignty." Toro is equally pointed: For Latin America, she writes, the potential intrusion of U.S. law enforcement agents "represents as important a threat as losing the war against the traffickers themselves. It represents the loss of state control." We are left with continuing questions: Will sovereignty pose an insuperable obstacle to constructive cooperation on drugs? Is the international system of nation-states capable of confronting global threats of drug trafficking?

17

Foundations for International Cooperation

Lisa L. Martin

States have attempted to cooperate to solve a wide range of common problems. This chapter presents a summary of generalizations about the problems of international cooperation and the conditions that facilitate solutions. I illustrate these generalizations with brief discussions of efforts to cooperate in different issue-areas. Using this comparative perspective, we can begin to generate lessons about the feasibility of various strategies for hemispheric cooperation on the drug issue while highlighting the types of problems states will face as they pursue cooperative strategies.

This chapter begins by drawing on the political science literature on international cooperation. Over the last decade, studies of international cooperation have proliferated, leading to a number of significant theoretical insights. I summarize the relevant findings of this theoretical enterprise. Analysis of problems of strategic interaction has led to expectations about the conditions and strategies that are conducive to international cooperation while recognizing the inherent difficulties of coordination of sovereign states' policies.

I focus on a specific type of strategy for facilitating cooperation: the use of international institutions. The perceived failure of some global institutions, such as the League of Nations, to achieve their stated goals led to a temporary rejection of such organizations for purposes of resolving international conflicts. Over the last two decades, however, we have seen renewed theoretical and practical interest in the role international institutions might play. Although rejecting the "idealist" assumptions of previous theorists, new approaches to the problem of international cooperation specify ways in which institutions allow states to overcome collective action problems, thus allowing states to achieve their desired goals at lower costs than unilateral action would entail.

The rest of this chapter moves from theoretical generalizations to practical considerations by examining efforts at international cooperation in a number of issue-areas. The three types of issues I consider are security, economic, and social. Conventional theories of international politics suggest that cooperation on security issues is more difficult than cooperation on economic issues. Nevertheless, we can find significant efforts to cooperate in the security area, such as military alliances and arms control regimes.

Much attention has been given to international cooperation on economic issues such as international trade or macroeconomic policies. We find a high level of variance in the success of these efforts to cooperate.

Finally, I turn to social issues such as human rights or protection of the environment. Again we find a mixed record of cooperation. In some cases, we find only perfunctory attempts to cooperate, which amount to little more than the creation of a forum for abstract discussions. On the other hand, issues such as public health show the possibility for extensive and effective international cooperation. I conclude with a summary of the lessons we might extract from this survey that are applicable to the problem of hemispheric cooperation to control drug abuse and trafficking.

Facilitating International Cooperation

Although many politicians and scholars use the term *international cooperation*, not all agree on its meaning. In the political science literature, Robert O. Keohane has offered a useful definition: He distinguishes between cooperation and "harmony." In a situation of harmony, actors confront no conflict of interest and there is no need for cooperation. Pursuit of their own self-interest "automatically facilitates the attainment of others' goals." In contrast, in a situation of discord, pursuit of individual self-interest can leave all actors dissatisfied with the outcome. Cooperation, according to Keohane's definition, can only arise from a situation of discord. Thus, cooperation refers to a process of mutual policy adjustment in which governments coordinate their policies to facilitate attainment of their goals.[1]

Much deductive and inductive research has gone into specifying the conditions that facilitate cooperation, or mutual policy adjustment, in the face of conflicts of interest among states. Much of this work draws on game theory, which considers an abstract world of strategic, rational actors with specified preferences. An influential work in this tradition is Robert Axelrod's *The Evolution of Cooperation*.[2] He considers a well-known game, the Prisoners' Dilemma, in which both players have strong temptations to "defect" but can benefit from mutual cooperation. Each wants to avoid being taken for a sucker, and gets his or her highest payoff from "suckering" the other. However, long-run payoffs are highest when players resist these temptations and settle into a pattern of mutual cooperation rather than mutual defection.

Axelrod looks for conditions that allow players to achieve the outcome of mutual cooperation. Importantly, he finds that the "shadow of the future" is a key variable. Actors that care about the future and anticipate gaining benefits from future cooperation may avoid the temptation to defect to gain short-term benefits. Alternatively, actors that, for whatever reason, care only about the short term will have little incentive to forego immediate benefits for the promise of future gains. In the jargon of game theory, this condition is called *iteration*; a more highly iterated game is often conducive to the establishment of cooperation relative to a one-shot interaction.

Axelrod has two other insights that are relevant to drug control. One is the importance of having good information. If players are not sure whether their adversaries cooperated or defected in the past or are afraid of possible undetected cheating, cooperation will be more difficult to sustain. Under conditions of imperfect information, actors may be tempted to cheat either because they may be able to do so without being detected or as a defensive maneuver because they fear unobserved defection by others. Thus, mechanisms that increase the level of information available to players will facilitate cooperation.

Axelrod also notes that the payoffs attached to various outcomes will influence the probability of cooperation. In other words, the higher the level of common interest, the higher the likelihood of cooperation. In particular, raising the payoff for mutual cooperation or reducing the payoff for mutual defection can encourage cooperative strategies. If the players perceive potential large gains from mutual cooperation, they have higher incentives to avoid the temptation to take advantage of one another. Similarly, reducing the payoff for unilateral defection or reducing the cost of unilateral cooperation can encourage cooperation. When the potential costs of a cooperative strategy are minimized, players will be more willing to take the necessary risks to achieve mutual cooperation. Thus, the degree of common interest among actors is an important determinant of successful cooperation.

A number of studies have attempted to apply these insights to cases of attempted international cooperation. After a review of case studies in both economic and security affairs, the editor of one influential volume agrees that Axelrod's emphasis on the degree of common interest and on the shadow of the future contributes significantly to our understanding of the practice of international cooperation.[3] And he points to an additional consideration: the number of actors. Axelrod's work concerned a series of bilateral (two-player) interactions, but many—if not most—situations in international politics involve more than two players. These multilateral situations present even more challenges for cooperation than bilateral cases. As the number of actors increases, the chances for undetected defection increase, assuring that all actors have common interests becomes harder, and enforcement of any agreement is more problematic. Thus, we might expect that cooperation becomes less likely as more states become involved.

A complementary approach to understanding international cooperation emphasizes the role international institutions or regimes can play in creating the necessary conditions for cooperation. The institutionalization of agreements—embedding them in mutually recognized norms, rules, and decision-making procedures—can improve the chances for cooperation by enhancing the conditions necessary for cooperative activity. Thus, regimes can act as an intervening variable between national self-interest and state behavior, encouraging cooperation.[4] Institutions enhance the chances of cooperation by providing information about members' behavior and preferences, thus decreasing the possibility of undetected cheating. They also extend the shadow of the future by establishing a stable framework for cooperation through assuring an ongoing relationship among specified states. Greater information and the expectation of future interactions with the same partners encourage states to pursue cooperative strategies.

In addition, institutions reduce transaction costs. As the name implies, these are the costs associated with carrying out transactions. These are considered separate from the inherent, substantive costs of carrying out particular policies. Transaction costs include such factors as the cost of negotiations, monitoring costs, and enforcement costs. All of these can be high in the anarchic international system, which has no supranational government to provide the infrastructure. However, international regimes or formal institutions can provide this infrastructure in particular issue-areas, thus reducing the friction normally involved in international cooperation.

One further theory of international cooperation deserves mention. This is the hegemonic stability theory, originally presented by economists as an explanation of patterns of international economic cooperation.[5] Since then, political scientists have applied this approach to many instances of attempted cooperation. Hegemonic stability theory suggests that international cooperation is stable only when it is supported by a single, dominant power, or hegemon. Great Britain in the nineteenth century and the United States in the decades after World War II acted as hegemons. Their disproportionate power gave them both the willingness and the wherewithal to promote multilateral cooperation. They bore many of the costs of monitoring and enforcement, according to this theory, and thus sustained cooperation. However, as their power declined, the benefits they derived from acting as hegemons decreased, as did their ability to enforce cooperation on other states. Thus, without a single, dominant power to guide the system, international cooperation broke down—in the 1920s and 1930s and perhaps again in the last decade or so. I discuss applications of hegemonic stability theory in more detail below.

These approaches to international cooperation all assume that states are rational actors, basing decisions about cooperation on calculations of the costs and benefits of alternative strategies. The core assumption is that governments will only cooperate if their perceived benefits exceed the costs they will have to bear. Although this is a straightforward and simple proposition, it highlights the necessity of considering cooperation from the viewpoint of individual states, not of the international system as a whole. In order for cooperation to be stable, every state involved must feel it benefits from ongoing cooperation. If all the benefits accrue to one state, while others bear high costs and gain few benefits, there is no rational reason for these others to cooperate. In this kind of asymmetrical situation, mechanisms must be found to redistribute the gains from cooperation so that every party benefits, not just one. Such mechanisms may involve issue linkage or side payments to the party bearing the primary costs of cooperation. In the case of drug policy, the distribution of costs and benefits is highly asymmetrical, implying the need for some form of redistribution to maintain cooperation.

Overall, political scientists offer a number of hypotheses about the conditions under which states are likely to cooperate. The most important of these include a long shadow of the future, good information, and a high degree of common interest.

In addition, reducing the number of actors involved and reducing transaction costs can facilitate cooperation. International institutions can help provide these conditions by providing a stable set of expectations about others' behavior. Another perspective on international cooperation focuses not on strategic variables but on the concentration of power. Hegemonic stability theory suggests that power concentrated in the hands of a single state leads to cooperation, whereas dispersed distributions of power lead to instability.

Cooperation in Security Affairs

Numerous analysts have argued that international cooperation on security affairs falls far short of what states have achieved on economic issues. This assumption is reflected in case studies of international cooperation, where much research has focused on economic issues with relatively little examination of state efforts to coordinate policies on issues directly affecting national security. However, I argue in this section that we can identify successful instances of cooperation on security affairs.

Theorists have presented a number of arguments to account for the supposedly low level of cooperation in this issue-area. Charles Lipson, for example, focuses on the short time horizon states are forced to adopt when confronted with threats to their national security.[6] When a nation's physical survival is at stake, it is forced to put a very strong value on the immediate horizon—leading to a short shadow of the future. As discussed above, this leads to strong temptations to defect from cooperative arrangements. The expectation of future benefits from cooperation cannot encourage states to run short-term risks by pursuing a "nice" policy. Because the immediate costs of such action may be disastrous, governments need to think about the short term—thus decreasing the likelihood of sustained cooperative activity relative to that on economic issues.

Robert Jervis basically agrees with Lipson's analysis while providing a number of additional arguments supporting the distinction between economic and security affairs. His analysis of the "security dilemma" is a classic portrayal of the structural conditions that plague efforts to cooperate when state survival is at stake.[7] States find themselves in a security dilemma when efforts to protect one state automatically threaten other states. This unfortunate characteristic of security interactions leads to a situation of extreme insecurity and instability, thus making sustained cooperation difficult to achieve even as it has potentially enormous payoffs. Jervis identifies four key differences between cooperation problems in the economic and security realms— greater competitiveness in security issues, greater difficulty in ascertaining the goals of state actions, higher stakes in security issues, and greater problems of detection and monitoring.[8]

In general, these difficulties do make security cooperation somewhat less frequent than economic cooperation. However, similar problems sometimes confront economic regimes, whereas some security regimes manage to escape this dismal pattern of confrontation. Jervis notes the necessary conditions for the formation of security regimes: The great powers must be reasonably satisfied with the status quo; there must be general confidence that all states place a high value on mutual security and cooperation; no states can believe their needs are best met by expansion; and clearly, war must be seen as costly.[9] To illustrate these theoretical points, Jervis analyzes the Concert of Europe—at its strongest in 1815–1823—as "the best example of a security regime."[10] The stringent conditions for cooperation were met among the great powers in Europe during this period, and the international regime had strong moderating influences on state behavior. When the Concert broke down, states reverted to more aggressive, less cooperative policies. Two important causes of the regime's breakdown were fading memories of the Napoleonic Wars and the fear of domestic unrest. As governments lost the historical memory of the ravages of the Napoleonic Wars, the perceived costs of mutual defection fell.[11]

This brings us to a common theme in analyses of security regimes. As the perception of a common threat falls, the incentives to cooperate fall as well. Thus, identification of and common agreement on an external threat are factors that create common interests and encourage cooperation. One version of this argument uses the concept of *balance of threat* to explain the formation of military alliances.[12] The perceived threat presented by other states, which is based on a combination of their national power and aggressive intentions, creates incentives that explain how and why military alliances form. One study applies this theory to alliance patterns in southern Asia, where it appears to fit the empirical evidence quite well. We could also consider how this theory helps explain current changes in alliances. As the Soviet threat has faded, the North Atlantic Treaty Organization (NATO) has found it necessary to identify new sources of potential danger in order to justify its continued existence and maintain its coherence. Examination of military alliances suggests that the strength of external threats is an important determinant of the level of cooperation among alliance members.

This conclusion can be extended to types of security cooperation that go beyond purely military agreements. One example is the control of technology transfer. For years, the Western Alliance controlled the flow of technology to the Soviet bloc. Efforts to cooperate to control technology exports began soon after World War II. However, in spite of overwhelming U.S. power, Washington achieved only minimal cooperation from its allies until the outbreak of the Korean War.[13] In this case, the perception of an external threat appears to be a better predictor of cooperation than hegemonic stability theory. Only after the Korean War revealed that the Soviets had aggressive intentions (according to contemporaneous analyses) and that imported technology contributed significantly to the Soviet ability to behave aggressively did European allies become willing to cooperate to control exports. Previously, they believed the costs of such controls outweighed the benefits and resisted U.S. efforts to coordinate export control policies. Recently, as the Soviet threat has declined, export controls have been reduced. This explanation of NATO export control policy can be extended to other instances of economic statecraft.[14]

One final type of security cooperation that deserves brief comment here is arms control. How and when do states manage to break out of arms races, to mutually agree to reduce or at least limit the growth of their military stockpiles? Analyses of arms races appear to support the general arguments already outlined. First, states often find themselves in a security dilemma in which purely defensive measures appear offensive to potential antagonists. This can easily lead to a complete breakdown of cooperation and hence to arms races. However, when the costs of an arms race are high, states see benefits in finding ways to break the cycle and end the race. Thus, we can identify factors that help explain when states will cooperate to control or end an arms race.

Studies have shown that two factors, information and control, are essential to successful cooperation.[15] If states are uncertain about others' capabilities or intentions, they will find it necessary to protect themselves from possible defection by others and thus find it difficult to cooperate. Mechanisms that can increase the level of reliable information available to both sides are essential to maintaining cooperation—hence the emphasis on verification in arms control agreements. Second, governments need to be assured that their counterparts have effective control over policy and can enforce arms control agreements. If a government is worried, for example, that its partner is not in control of its military establishment, the incentives to act defensively and to refuse to cooperate rise quickly. The ability to commit credibly to carrying out agreed policies is a necessary condition for sustained cooperation.

In conclusion, studies of international cooperation on security affairs suggest that it is more difficult for states to cooperate in this issue-area than on economic issues. However, this does not imply that all efforts are doomed to failure. The identification of a common threat enhances states' incentives to cooperate because the perceived benefits of unilateral policies decline. In addition, access to reliable information and government control over military activities are necessary conditions for cooperation on security affairs.

Cooperation in Economic Affairs

In contrast to the paucity of studies on security cooperation, political scientists have produced an extensive array of studies of cooperation on economic issues. States have attempted to coordinate their policies on a broad range of economic issues including trade, monetary affairs, and macroeconomic policies. Their efforts have met with varying levels of success. In this section I examine several examples of economic cooperation.

Throughout history, states and other political entities have engaged in trade with one another. Although the benefits of cooperating to allow the free flow of goods among regions are high, the temptations to control such trade in order to reap short-term benefits are also high. Thus, states have often engaged in trade wars, in which a pattern of retaliatory tariffs and other restrictions on trade lead to reduced levels of international commerce.[16] How can we explain the observed level of variation in the degree of cooperation on international trade?

One persuasive explanation relies on the historical experience of the United States and its major trading partners in the twentieth century. During the 1930s, international trade collapsed under the weight of the Great Depression. International trade did not recover until after World War II. However, when it did recover it made dramatic gains, with the level of trade increasing rapidly from 1945 until the present. The level of tariffs, which presented the major impediment to trade before World War II, rapidly declined until tariffs became only a minor hindrance to trade for most countries.

However, in the 1970s a number of analysts began to note new threats to the international trading system. Although tariffs remained low, nontariff barriers such as voluntary export restraints and other quantitative restrictions on trade seemed to proliferate. Today, some authors warn that the global trading system is on the verge of splitting into a number of regional blocs. Problems during the Uruguay round of the General Agreement on Tariffs and Trade (GATT) symbolize and may exacerbate this trend. The primary theory that has been offered to explain these tensions over trade is hegemonic stability theory. When no single powerful country exercised leadership in the 1930s, international cooperation on trade collapsed. When the United States played a leadership role after World War II, multilateral cooperation expanded. However, the decline of U.S. power relative to that of other states, according to this perspective, weakened the system beginning in the 1970s.

How well does hegemonic stability theory conform to the facts of cooperation on international trade? Although it appears to conform to the broad outlines of surges and recessions in cooperation, it is not sufficient. Whereas the "new protectionism" may threaten international trade today, trade nevertheless remains at historically high and increasing levels. The decline in cooperation today is much less obvious than in the 1930s. What explains continued cooperation in spite of threats to the system? Much of the explanation may lie in the factors noted above as conducive to cooperation in general.

First, all states recognize a high level of common interest in maintaining relatively free trade. Levels of economic interdependence are exceptionally high today, and the costs of cutting ties to other countries are immense. Thus, although the United States and Japan may snipe continually at one another, neither has been willing to bear the costs of an all-out trade war. Second, the shadow of the future is long. Governments perceive that their actions lead to responses from other countries and anticipate that actions to restrict trade will lead to harm to their domestic exporters in the future as others retaliate. In contrast to security crises, where the survival of the state is at stake, in economic issues it is possible for governments to take the future—not just the immediate present—into account when formulating trade policies.

A third factor facilitating continued cooperation on trade is the relatively high level of institutionalization in this issue-area. The GATT, although designed as a temporary measure, has been highly successful in formulating explicit rules and decision-making procedures for international trade in manufactures. Although the level of information about governments' economic policies is generally higher than that about security policies, the GATT has further increased access to information and certainty about the rules of the game. In addition to providing information, the GATT helps extend the shadow of the future by tying states into an ongoing series of negotiations and reduces transaction costs by providing a forum and rules of the game for these negotiations.

In trade, the major threat to cooperation comes from domestic politics. Loss of control over trade policy—for example, by the executive branch of the U.S. government to the legislative branch—could lead to defection. Thus far, the executive branch has been able to fend off congressional demands for protection, but an assertion of congressional authority in this issue-area could lead to tighter restrictions on trade. In 1934 the Reciprocal Trade Agreements Act marked a key domestic shift in U.S. trade policy because Congress delegated significant authority for setting tariffs to the president.[17] Multilateral mechanisms can help foster cooperation in international trade, but cooperation also requires domestic settings that allow politicians to hold off demands for protection.

In addition to cooperation on commerce, states have attempted to cooperate in monetary affairs. The general outlines of patterns in international cooperation follow those just discussed for commerce. Monetary cooperation, which in the nineteenth century was defined as maintenance of the gold standard, collapsed during the 1930s.[18] The fundamental problem leading to this failure was changes in the international economic system that led to the destruction of common interests in any type of monetary order. Domestic economic problems and misaligned exchange rates, along with other factors, meant governments perceived little benefit from cooperation; at the same time, the lack of a hegemonic power meant no powerful state attempted to "enforce" cooperation. Monetary cooperation resumed on a limited scale when Nazi Germany was seen as a threat on the horizon. Once again, perception of an external threat raised the perceived benefits of cooperation and in this case led to some coordination of policies among the United States, Great Britain, and France.

After World War II, the United States played a central role in establishing a new monetary regime. This regime, known as the Bretton Woods System, established pegged exchange rates and provided mechanisms to inject liquidity into the monetary system in order to allow states to overcome balance-of-payments difficulties.[19] However, the system could not function as planned until the 1950s, when European economies recovered from wartime destruction. After recovery, although the system never operated exactly as planned, high levels of international cooperation persisted until 1971. At this time, the Nixon administration brought the Bretton Woods System to an abrupt halt by declaring that the dollar was no longer convertible into gold at $40 an ounce, which had been a central element of the regime. Once again, hegemonic stability theory seems to perform well in explaining general patterns in the rise and decline of cooperation, although it leaves unanswered a number of important questions.[20]

Since 1971 no formally institutionalized monetary order has emerged to replace Bretton Woods. After a difficult transition period, however, we now find significant levels of cooperation among states regarding exchange rates. Although no international organization exists for this purpose, coordination of exchange rate policies often takes place through summit meetings of the leaders and finance ministers of the industrialized countries.[21] Without an institution to provide oversight and establish standards, however, these agreements are often short-lived. The most significant international cooperation to coordinate exchange rates now occurs at the regional level, particularly within Europe. The Exchange Rate Mechanism of the European Monetary System is quickly becoming a strong, centralized tool for maintenance of fixed exchange rates among most members of the European Community (EC). Europeans have been pushed in this direction by the pressures of international economic competition with the United States and Japan, again highlighting the incentives created by an external threat—in this case, an economic threat. In addition, the coordinating mechanisms within the EC allowed this process to take place much more rapidly than it could have without the facilitating structure of a regional organization.

International cooperation on domestic macroeconomic policies has been less successful than in the other two economic issue-areas discussed here. In the last two decades, the governments of many Organization for Economic Cooperation and Development countries have come to believe they could more easily pursue their domestic economic goals if their macroeconomic policies were coordinated to some extent. Pursuit of widely divergent macroeconomic policies can doom government efforts to control inflation or encourage growth. However, governments still believe macroeconomic policy is primarily a domestic issue, and they have been unwilling to cede any significant level of sovereignty on these policies to international decision making. Instead we find occasional efforts, again often formalized at summit meetings, to find agreement on these issues.

Although typically the agreements reached during these summits are minimal, an important exception came during the Bonn Summit of 1978. At this time the United States and Germany reached significant agreement on coordination of macroeconomic policies and modified their domestic policies in response.[22] One factor that allowed this high level of policy coordination was a "synergistic" linkage across issues because agreements on energy and trade policies were tied into the overall agreement. This packaging allowed the governments to find a set of agreements that left both countries better off than the status quo, whereas none of the individual agreements would probably have been adopted on its own. Governments were willing to compromise on issues that were less vital for themselves in exchange for concessions on the issues they cared the most about. In addition to linkage, the presence of influential domestic factions that favored international cooperation helps explain the unusual success of this attempt at macroeconomic cooperation.

Although this discussion of international economic cooperation is far from exhaustive, it illustrates the types of problems governments must overcome in order to cooperate and the conditions that are conducive to surmounting barriers to cooperation. One generalization is that the ability to cooperate is dependent on favorable domestic conditions. If domestic structures allow factions opposed to cooperative policies to determine government strategy, the chances for cooperation are low. Sometimes domestic reorganization must precede international efforts to cooperate, as with the U.S. delegation of trade policy to the executive branch in 1934. Second, as in the survey of security cooperation, it appears that the perception of an external threat is often the key factor that raises the benefits of cooperation sufficiently to overcome resistance. Finally, the creation of formal institutions in which negotiation and coordination of policies can take place facilitates cooperation. Although international institutions cannot substitute for common interests, they can encourage issue linkage, extend the shadow of the future, and provide information that allows states to work together to achieve those common interests. Ad hoc cooperation outside of institutions is often unstable because it lacks these dimensions.

Cooperation on Social Issues

A number of significant attempts at international cooperation do not fall neatly into either the security or economic category. For lack of a better term, this diverse group is categorized loosely as social issues. These run from the purely technical, such as coordination of postal policies, to highly conflictual issues, such as human rights and the environment. In this section I seek to ascertain whether patterns in these efforts at international cooperation resemble those for economic and security issues.

Under the auspices of the United Nations, many agencies operate to provide governments with information and support for different types of policy issues such as airline safety, international postal agreements, shipping, and the like. Many of these agencies operate quietly, with little attention either from publics or high levels of government. They simply provide necessary information and services to allow governments to perform their functions. In this respect, some apparently successful efforts at international cooperation do not meet the definition given above. In these cases, mutual accommodation of policies in order to overcome conflicts of interest is not evident. Instead, these agencies carry out primarily technical functions, allowing governments to perform more effectively and efficiently than they otherwise would. These organizations often operate under conditions that more closely approximate harmony than discord.

When fundamental conflicts of interest between states disappear, explaining "cooperative" activities in the loose sense of the term is not a challenge. These technical agencies in no sense threaten the sovereignty of governments or require them to take actions that open themselves up to cheating or exploitation by other states. However, the process by which political, conflictual issues become transformed into technical issues is sometimes interesting. Early theorists of international coop-eration were often criticized as being idealists because they assumed that all or at least most political issues could be transformed into purely technical affairs.[23] The innovation of more recent theories of international cooperation, as discussed above, is to ask about when cooperation can be achieved in spite of conflicts of interest rather than assuming that these conflicts are ephemeral.

One interesting case study of the transformation of an issue from a profoundly political affair into a primarily technical one involves public health. In a study of the evolution of international public health policies, Richard N. Cooper shows how state interests changed in the face of scientific advances.[24] Prior to accepted scientific understanding of the causes of diseases such as yellow fever and the plague, governments favored "solutions" to these problems that fit well with their economic self-interest. For example, trading states such as Great Britain recommended mea-sures that would make cities cleaner as the appropriate international response to the plague, whereas Italy—which did not depend so heavily on trade but was highly urban—favored quarantine of incoming ships. Only after scientific knowledge advanced to the point where there could be little disagreement about the effectiveness of various measures in combatting disease did states agree to cooperate at significant levels. Today, much international cooperation on control of disease (at least for well-understood diseases) does look like a technical affair, with little conflict of interest.

Cooper suggests that the state of knowledge about cause-and-effect relationships may explain the relatively low level of cooperation on macroeconomic policy. Until governments understand and agree on the effectiveness of particular policy tools in achieving their goals, they will find it difficult to coordinate their policies. This suggests a lesson for cooperation to control drug abuse and trafficking. Current efforts are hampered by disagreement about the most effective policies for combatting various aspects of the drug problem. Moving toward consensus on these issues through scientific research may eventually reduce, but will probably not eliminate, the current level of conflict of interest.

Other social issues do not show the movement toward transformation into technical issues that is evident in public health. Currently, many states are directing their attention to international cooperation to control various forms of pollution, save the rain forests, and conserve other natural resources. Although a number of agreements have been negotiated and in some cases ratified, thus far for the most part these agreements have not had major impacts on government policy. The United States in particular has been resistant to committing itself to multilateral environmental accords and has not taken the lead in pushing for negotiations. In addition, intense conflicts of interest between industrialized and industrializing countries inhibit efforts to find mutually acceptable solutions.

In spite of slow progress on the global level, some regional environmental regimes have been created and function quite effectively. The Antarctic has been protected since 1959 by a regime codified in a treaty that was recently renegotiated.[25] The heavily polluted Mediterranean Sea now receives some protection through the Mediterranean Action Plan, which has had an impact on government policies in the region.[26] In the environment, as in public health, the state of scientific knowledge is essential to explaining variations in the level of international cooperation. Until the causes of pollution, its effects on human beings, and the most effective means to control it are identified, reaching international agreement remains an elusive goal.

An additional social issue worth noting for efforts at international cooperation is human rights. This issue differs from many of the others discussed here in that human rights is not typically conceived of as a collective action problem. Pollution has obvious negative externalities because its effects are not limited to the producing country but spread regionally or globally. A government's treatment of its citizens— protecting them from violations of basic human rights including the rights to life, liberty, and the integrity of the person—is more commonly seen as an issue with primarily domestic effects. Although citizens of other countries may empathize with the plight of those overseas, the automatic interdependence seen in the environmental issue-area is not evident in the case of human rights.

This has led to a different pattern of cooperation on human rights issues internationally. The primary functions of global or regional cooperation on this issue have been to set standards and to provide forums for investigating and publicizing alleged violations of human rights.[27] The United Nations and some of its agencies have played leading roles in establishing standards for the respect of human rights and sometimes in undertaking investigations. Two regional systems to protect human rights have developed quite extensively, one in Europe and another in the Americas. Although some observers feel the European system is more highly developed, it has not had to confront the levels of conflict that characterize the situation in the Americas. The Organization of American States, through the Inter-American Commission on Human Rights (IACHR), has been active in promoting human rights in the hemisphere. Although the level of cooperation in this issue-area falls short of that in international trade, for example, the IACHR has publicized violations of human rights and thus has occasionally had an impact on government policies. However, the level of conflict of interest among states remains high, and many governments continue to insist that this is primarily a domestic issue.

This examination of cooperation on social issues has introduced an additional factor that may help account for patterns of international cooperation: the state of scientific knowledge in an issue-area. When no consensus exists on the causes of an international problem or on the most effective means to solve it, international cooperative efforts are hampered. In cases such as public health, increasing scientific knowledge has led to a decrease in the level of conflict of interest and thus to greater cooperation. However, we should be cautious in assuming that this is a necessary pattern: Increased knowledge may reveal conflicts as well as commonalities of interest.

Conclusion: Lessons for International Cooperation

This chapter has suggested general lessons about international cooperation that might have applications to the drug problem in the Western Hemisphere. Although each case of international cooperation is in some sense unique, patterns suggest generalizations about the conditions and strategies that promote international cooperation.

The first condition for successful multilateral cooperation is some degree of common interest. Although conflicts of interest always exist, states can sometimes overcome them if they perceive mutual benefits—that is, net benefits for every participant—from cooperation. However, identification of these common interests is not always easy. In examining a sample of security and economic cases, it appears that often the perception of a common threat is necessary in order to find a common interest in confronting it. This insight applies to military alliances as well as monetary coordination in the 1930s.

Another significant factor is the shadow of the future. The more states care about future benefits relative to the present, the more they are willing to forego immediate temptations to defect. In addition, states require good information about the preferences and behavior of others. International institutions can help fulfill both these conditions by providing a stable framework for cooperation and undertaking monitoring activities.

A number of other factors conducive to cooperation arose in my examination of actual cases. Although hegemonic stability theory did receive some support, hegemony does not appear to be a necessary condition for cooperation. The assurance of control is important—governments must be able to assure their counterparts that they have the necessary domestic power to carry through with agreements. In addition, an examination of cooperation on issues such as public health and the environment suggested that the state of scientific knowledge matters for cooperation. States find it difficult to cooperate when there is no consensus on the causes of and solutions to the problems they face. All of these insights may have applicability to the drug problem, to varying degrees. They suggest international, domestic, and social approaches necessary to move toward international cooperation.

Notes

1. Robert O. Keohane, *After Hegemony: Cooperation and Discord in the World Political Economy* (Princeton: Princeton University Press, 1984), 51–54.

2. Robert Axelrod, *The Evolution of Cooperation* (New York: Basic Books, 1984).

3. Kenneth A. Oye, "Explaining Cooperation Under Anarchy: Hypotheses and Strategies," in Kenneth A. Oye, ed., *Cooperation Under Anarchy* (Princeton: Princeton University Press, 1986), 1–24.

4. Stephen D. Krasner, "Regimes and the Limits of Realism: Regimes as Autonomous Variables," in Stephen D. Krasner, ed., *International Regimes* (Ithaca: Cornell University Press, 1983), 355–368.

5. Charles Kindleberger, *The World in Depression, 1929–1939* (Berkeley: University of California Press, 1973).

6. Charles Lipson, "International Cooperation in Economic and Security Affairs," *World Politics* 37, no. 1 (October 1984): 1–23. Lipson also notes other factors that differentiate security from economic affairs, including the availability of information.

7. Robert Jervis, "Cooperation Under the Security Dilemma," *World Politics* 30, no. 2 (January 1978): 167–214.

8. Robert Jervis, "Security Regimes," in Krasner, *International Regimes*, 173–194.

9. Jervis, "Security Regimes," 176–178.

10. Jervis, "Security Regimes," 178.

11. Robert Jervis, "From Balance to Concert: A Study of International Security Cooperation," in Oye, *Cooperation Under Anarchy*, 58–79.

12. Stephen M. Walt, *The Origin of Alliances* (Ithaca: Cornell University Press, 1987).

13. Michael Mastanduno, "Trade as a Strategic Weapon: American and Alliance Export Control Policy in the Early Postwar Period," *International Organization* 42, no. 1 (Winter 1988): 121–150.

14. Lisa L. Martin, *Coercive Cooperation: Explaining Multilateral Economic Sanctions* (Princeton: Princeton University Press, 1992).

15. George W. Downs, David M. Rocke, and Randolph M. Siverson, "Arms Races and Cooperation," in Oye, *Cooperation Under Anarchy*, 118–146.

16. John A.C. Conybeare, *Trade Wars: The Theory and Practice of International Commercial Rivalry* (New York: Columbia University Press, 1987).

17. Stephan Haggard, "The Institutional Foundations of Hegemony: Explaining the Reciprocal Trade Agreements Act of 1934," *International Organization* 42, no. 1 (Winter 1988): 91–120.

18. Kenneth A. Oye, "The Sterling-Dollar-Franc Triangle: Monetary Diplomacy 1929–1937," in Oye, *Cooperation Under Anarchy*, 173–199.

19. Benjamin J. Cohen, "Balance-of-Payments Financing: Evolution of a Regime," in Krasner, *International Regimes*, 315–336.

20. Barry Eichengreen, "Hegemonic Stability Theories of the International Monetary System," in Richard N. Cooper et al., eds., *Can Nations Agree? Issues in International Economic Cooperation* (Washington, D.C.: Brookings Institution, 1989), 255–297.

21. Robert D. Putnam and Nicholas Bayne, *Hanging Together: The Seven-Power Summits* (Cambridge: Harvard University Press, 1984).

22. Robert D. Putnam and C. Randall Henning, "The Bonn Summit of 1978: A Case Study in Coordination," in Cooper et al., *Can Nations Agree?* 12–140.

23. The schools of thought known as functionalism and neofunctionalism have been subject to this criticism. For examples, see David Mitrany, *A Working Peace System* (Chicago: Quadrangle, 1966); and Ernst B. Haas, *Beyond the Nation-State: Functionalism and International Organization* (Stanford: Stanford University Press, 1964).

24. Richard N. Cooper, "International Cooperation in Public Health as a Prologue to Macroeconomic Cooperation," in Cooper et al., *Can Nations Agree?* 178–254.

25. Oran R. Young, *International Cooperation: Building Regimes for Natural Resources and the Environment* (Ithaca: Cornell University Press, 1989), 55.

26. Peter Haas, "Do Regimes Matter? A Study of Evolving Pollution Control Policies for the Mediterranean Sea," paper presented at the 1987 annual meeting of the International Studies Association.

27. Jack Donnelly, *Universal Human Rights in Theory and Practice* (Ithaca: Cornell University Press, 1989).

18

International Collaboration
in Historical Perspective

William O. Walker III

The drug problem continues to plague the Americas in the early 1990s. The production of coca leaf, marijuana, and opium poppy continues to underwrite the well-being of untold thousands of persons—rich and poor—throughout Latin America and the United States. At the same time, extensive and innovative efforts to interdict the illegal trade in drugs have largely proved unavailing. What might be done to promote more effective cooperation in the struggle against drugs?

By February 1990 it appeared as though an answer to that perplexing query might be forthcoming. At the conclusion of a brief summit meeting held at Cartagena, Colombia, the presidents of Bolivia, Colombia, Peru, and the United States pledged consultation and collaboration in the war on drugs—especially cocaine.[1] Cartagena offered hope in at least four respects. First and most obvious, the very fact that an antidrug summit was held—outside the United States, no less—indicated that American governments were more prepared than ever before to undertake concerted action against drugs. Second, the Cartagena statements indicated a recognition of the mutuality of drug problems; drug production, trafficking, and demand constitute serious threats to the existing economic order in all four countries and carry unacceptable social costs as well. Third, for the first time in such an important forum, the United States acknowledged the benefits of efforts to reduce demand as well as of campaigns to suppress supply. Finally and most broadly, the ostensible flexibility in Washington's position intimated that coping with the drug problem might open the door to a real reciprocity in inter-American relations and in the process render future assertions of U.S. hegemony less likely. Thus, the promise of Cartagena conceivably encompassed the evolution of a new inter-American order.

It is too soon to conclude whether the Cartagena Summit initiated a genuine reorientation in inter-American relations and whether its ultimate legacy will be the achievement of a new order in the hemisphere. As of this writing, the results do not appear so momentous. The outlook for cooperation is far less promising than it seemed at the time of the summit; effective collaboration among the three Andean nations and Washington has become chimerical. The prospect of reciprocity in hemispheric relations is scarcely worth discussing as long as the suppression of coca production remains a fixation for U.S. foreign policy.

What went wrong? Why did the spirit of Cartagena not long endure? Superficially, the summit, which produced a kind of détente over the emotionally charged issues of supply and demand, definitely raised expectations that could not be easily met. A brief look at the extent of collaboration or cooperation since the meeting illustrates the point. Between Colombia and the United States there existed what might at best be called asymmetrical cooperation. Arrangements made between the government of César Gaviria Trujillo and major figures in the Medellín cartel allowing the surrender of the cartel members and the disposition of their cases under the Colombian system of justice were greeted as positively as possible by U.S. policymakers. Yet, the likelihood that Fabio Ochoa Vasquez, his brother Jorge Luis, and others would not face extradition—the key to the drug war, according to officials in Washington—had to dismay the Bush administration and Congress.[2]

An equally serious blow to collaboration came in Peru where the DEA announced the suspension of its joint raids with Peruvian police in the coca-rich Upper Huallaga Valley after military officials were discovered selling information about raids to drug traffickers. This development jeopardized a number of U.S. and international aid programs essential to economic planning by the government of President Alberto Fujimori. Also disconcerting was an upswing in political violence directed at U.S. personnel in Bolivia. The violence made it clear that cocaine traffickers—probably associated with Colombia's Cali cartel, which authorities in Bogotá have pursued far less avidly than its counterpart in Medellín—were gaining a foothold in Bolivia. The problem was not so much that the fight against cocaine in that country would be a long one but that it would take place in an atmosphere in which the issue as well as cooperation with the United States in the fight against cocaine could not be divorced from a growing institutional crisis that threatened the survival of Jaime Paz Zamora's regime. Doubts in Washington about the good faith of Bolivia's antidrug commitment, which resurfaced in February and March 1991, were symptomatic of that nation's deeper problems.[3]

The central problem confronting drug control officials and other policymakers at the outset of the 1990s was not just one of unrealistic expectations; something far more basic was involved. The entire history of international drug control, when viewed dispassionately, raises questions about the structure of antidrug efforts and in turn calls for a thorough reconsideration of the conceptual underpinnings of antidrug policies. In other words, any drug control strategy that fails to address the history of antinarcotics activity cannot enjoy more than limited success. This conclusion is no less relevant for a strategy that relies on close collaboration among nations. Before suggesting which strategies might have a role to play in furthering the cause of inter-American drug control, it is worth considering how various strategies have fared in the past.[4]

Unilateral Approaches

Unilateral attempts to control or rationalize the use of illicit drugs permeate the history of antinarcotics activity. In the Philippines at the turn of the twentieth century, the United States managed partially to reduce the incidence of opium smoking among native Filipinos. Smoking had increased after a regulatory scheme established by Spain in 1843 had been abandoned. Chances for complete control were never good, however, because of the presence of around twenty thousand Chinese smokers; yet by 1911 significant progress in reducing the habit throughout the islands had nevertheless been made. The nature, or basic structure, of the antiopium system in the Philippines—prohibition—was unique among Western powers in Asia. Elsewhere—in British and French possessions, for example—it was assumed that opium consumption did not harm even frequent users. Even though the system imposed by the United States soon drove the opium business underground, clandestine enjoyment of opium did not grow appreciably until the eve of World War II, at which time—ironically—efforts to provide better security for U.S. interests across the Pacific undermined the existing system of opium control.

Relative success in the Philippines resulted, it appears, from drug usage being treated as a public health matter and from the operation of an antidrug educational campaign. To be sure, punitive sanctions in the form of law enforcement accompanied the prohibition regime but did not dominate it. What was also special about the situation in the Philippines was that prohibition came about in a colonial situation in which the colonial power—the United States—possessed the will and the ability to enforce its policy and had the support of the indigenous population. All the parties involved believed prohibition was the moral course to follow.[5]

In Formosa as well, where the majority of the population was Chinese, Japan as the colonial power imposed a prohibition regime. (In Japan itself, where relatively few Chinese lived, a system of strict prohibition proved to be extremely effective.) Indeed, it was the Formosan example that induced the United States not to resume a monopoly system in the Philippines based on the earlier Spanish model, which would have adopted a double standard: Adult ethnic Chinese would have been permitted to smoke opium, whereas Filipinos would not have possessed the same right. Instead, U.S. authorities adopted a system of progressive prohibition in which consumption of opium for medical purposes would be illegal after an interim three-year period. The lessons future generations of U.S. policymakers drew from the experience in the Philippines were that narcotics control should be seen as a moral rather than an economic issue and that the objective of prohibition was not negotiable.[6]

A conceptually different model of unilateral drug control found favor in much of Asia from the nineteenth century through World War II and after. This monopoly system operated either under the direct supervision of civil servants or on a contractual basis in which private parties ran the system. The rationale supporting a monopoly was derived from several ostensibly contradictory hypotheses: Complete prohibition of opium consumption was a worthy long-term goal; opium smoking and eating did not necessarily harm those who indulged in such practices; and until conditions were right for prohibition, revenue should be obtained from the monopoly. With revenue as the controlling factor, questions about the morality of opium consumption became largely the province of ethical and religious-affiliated interest groups. Making a strict practical determination that U.S. officials found morally and politically indefensible, European colonial officials evinced no desire to save addicts from themselves. Put differently, these officials did not regard their duties as including the promotion of cultural change.[7]

Opium monopolies were the rule rather than the exception in colonial Asia. In British colonies, for example, the prevailing attitude that the consumption of opium was not harmful followed the report of the Royal Opium Commission in 1895. The opportunity for profit by those who sold smokable opium in Burma made the imposition of any system of drug control highly problematic. In Singapore, by contrast, the traditional institution of opium "farming" gave way in 1910 to the creation of a government monopoly—the result, historian Carl A. Trocki argues, of a trend toward bureaucratic rationalization that allowed greater control than before over opium revenues. Having to contend with a smaller and ultimately less powerful Chinese labor force and commercial elite, the French in Indochina and the Dutch in the East Indies had phased out their respective opium farming systems years earlier and had established government-controlled monopolies in their place.[8]

Another form of drug control combines absolute prohibition with severe penalties exacted for failure to meet government regulations. In both the People's Republic of China in the 1950s and in Iran under Ayatollah Ruhollah Khomeini in the late 1970s and the 1980s, systems mandating total abstinence from drug consumption appear to have been relatively successful. It is not possible to know whether these signal accomplishments resulted more from the revolutionary fervor of the times or from the literal threats to life and limb. Also, extensive illicit opium cultivation was controlled in Turkey in the early 1970s, but this achievement may have had more to do with Turkey's close strategic relationship with the United States than with any firm conviction that opium production is inherently evil.[9]

At least three other unilateral approaches to drug control are readily identifiable. The first might fairly be termed the "great man" or "great woman" theory of drug control. Operationally, this approach entails the incarceration of leading figures in the drug trade, a worthy objective in itself. The removal of the heads of trafficking syndicates or those responsible for related activities such as money laundering can cause a temporary disruption of illicit narcotics operations.

The longtime chief of the Federal Bureau of Narcotics (FBN) Harry J. Anslinger, who was as single-minded in his pursuit of effective drug control as recent Commissioner of Customs William von Raab, compiled what he designated the "Bureau's Mafia files" containing the names of the most notorious international drug traffickers.[10] Yet, neither Anslinger nor von Raab could ignore the possibility of political considerations interfering once a major figure was apprehended. Such seizures have sometimes led to the disclosure of disturbing facts about the relationship between drug traffickers and government policy. Thus, Chiang Kai-shek's Kuomintang in China, fearing revelations about its involvement in the domestic opium traffic, allowed the infamous Yeh Ching-ho to escape into exile in the late 1930s after first congratulating itself on his arrest.[11]

More recently, Colombia and the United States have engaged in what might be interpreted as preventive and perhaps redemptive detention of drug law offenders, incarcerating prominent members of the Medellín cartel or others of the stature of General Manuel Antonio Noriega and Juan Ramón Matta Ballesteros in an effort to curb large-scale operations and at the same time to persuade doubters at home and abroad of a seriousness of purpose. How the individuals were seized has provoked great public controversy, but that tends to miss the point. The more fundamental question relates to the premise that certain key individuals make a significant difference and that their removal from the drug business will have a salutary effect.

Another unilateral approach has centered on interdiction as a means of combatting drugs. Not until the mid-1930s did interdiction become an active part of U.S. antidrug strategy; previously, efforts to halt the flow of illicit drugs depended on the ability of local authorities—sometimes with the assistance of federal drug and customs agents—to keep port cities as free of illegal substances as possible. The earliest efforts at interdiction remained limited in scope, amounting to little more than a few patrols by the coast guard in the waters of the Caribbean and the Gulf of Mexico. Incipient efforts to employ aerial surveillance near the border with Mexico were largely unsuccessful.[12] Only in the wake of Operation Intercept in 1969 did the United States make interdiction in transit as central to its antidrug strategy as control at the source. By the 1980s members of Congress began calling for military participation in the war on drugs, as Bruce M. Bagley has shown in Chapter 9, prompting philosophical and doctrinal questions about the legal and practical extent of the military's mission so far as drug control was concerned.

Finally, experiments with drug maintenance have constituted an effort to control drugs unilaterally. They are discussed here because opposition to maintenance schemes has long colored Washington's narcotic foreign policy. The story of the first drug clinics in the United States is fairly well known. After the passage of the Harrison Narcotics Law in 1914, a number of cities endeavored to handle their addict populations by adopting a maintenance program. Therapeutic or ameliorative in intent, yet established in a social and political environment overwhelmingly receptive to a proscriptive interpretation of the etiology of drug use and addiction, maintenance clinics were quickly condemned as agents of public immorality. To be sure, some clinics were inadequately staffed and poorly run, but they were often misrepresented as fatally flawed and therefore beyond administrative correction only because the guiding spirit favoring drug control at the time was predominantly legalistic and moralistic.[13]

As the clinics in the United States met their demise in the early 1920s, the proponents of drug control in Great Britain were making the opposite and crucial determination that addiction was more a disease than a crime. The famous Rolleston Report (named for the panel chair, Sir Humphrey Rolleston) formally established nothing; nonetheless, it provided a guide for what became known as the "British system" of narcotics control. Lasting well into the 1960s, the basis of treatment for addiction in Great Britain was care rather than punishment or even cure; the judgment of physicians determined the appropriate course of medical action. As Arnold S. Trebach—among others—has shown, this informal system worked, but to this day it is not clear why. A powerful critic of U.S. policy, Trebach forthrightly admits that he wants to believe a humane system for dealing with addiction will ultimately reduce dependence on drugs; yet he also indicates that the homogeneity of British society, which lasted beyond midcentury, may have been a crucial determining factor. This hypothesis acquires greater explanatory power when judged in the context of the rise of a large heterogeneous addict population in Great Britain in the 1960s. The British then turned to a clinic-style program in order to cope with this dramatic change.[14]

In addition to Great Britain and the United States, in the late 1930s the Mexican government briefly attempted to establish a monopoly-cum-clinic scheme for dealing with drug abuse. Domestic opposition and pressure from Anslinger's FBN cut short this effort by Leopoldo Salazar Viniegra, head of Mexico's Federal Narcotics Service. The United States helped to force Salazar, a strident critic of U.S. drug control policy, out of office and made it clear to his successor by embargoing the export of medicinal drugs to Mexico that a monopoly had no place in the hemisphere—at least not in the proximity of the United States. Officials in Washington had reacted to the operation of a monopoly in Uruguay at that same time by doing nothing.[15]

Critics of physician-maintenance or clinic-maintenance drug treatment programs contend that such programs are susceptible to abuse. That assertion is true, but it obfuscates the historical fact that systems relying on either coercion or prohibition to control use have never been more than partially successful. This conclusion does not inexorably lead to support for legalization; that course of action would present new and daunting challenges to any society choosing to experiment with it. Rather, sound public policy seems to dictate consideration of a variation on the clinic system.

A historically informed perspective on unilateral antidrug efforts offers an additional conclusion: Coercive unilateral efforts in themselves cannot seriously affect drug production, trafficking, and consumption. In some instances, unilateralism has led to a worsening of conditions. It is difficult to argue, for example, that the creation of a criminal class in the United States after passage of the Harrison Act served the national interest. At best, unilateral initiatives work in an atmosphere in which human rights abuses matter little. Even then, as Iran's troubles with opium following the death of Ayatollah Khomeini exemplify, absolute prohibition cannot entirely deter drug production and trafficking.[16]

Bilateral Efforts

Given the structural and conceptual limitations of most forms of unilateral drug control, it is fair to ask whether bilateral controls historically have achieved better results. Understanding the strengths and weaknesses of bilateral controls will enable policymakers to assess their utility for the future. In brief, it is possible to identify three principal types of bilateral drug control: mutual, coercive, and what can be termed *derivative*—that is, control that is linked to other foreign policy issues not necessarily related to drugs. Also important for a thorough analysis of bilateral drug control is the issue of motivation on the part of policymakers, both in countries—such as the United States—that advocate strict controls and in those nations that are the object of U.S. antinarcotics initiatives. Another factor to be considered in assessing bilateral antidrug diplomacy concerns the priorities or motivations of those who grow, refine, and distribute illegal drugs. As I have argued elsewhere, lack of attention to this cultural dimension in the pursuit of drug control has usually proven to be problematic and counterproductive.[17]

The United States and China undertook the longest sustained mutual effort to promote comprehensive drug control. From around 1900 through 1949, U.S. authorities worked closely with Chinese officials to curb the domestic and international opiate business in China. The turn of the century was an especially propitious time for the United States and China to join forces against the scourge of opium smoking and the consumption of morphine and heroin, whether imported or domestically manufactured. The Open Door notes of 1899 and 1900 prefigured an increasingly visible U.S. presence in East Asia. And among other things, the Boxer Uprising of 1900 gave additional impetus to the vital spirit that was demanding reforms from the crumbling Ch'ing dynasty. In both prerevolutionary and republican China, leaders as well as common people expressed strong sentiments condemning the impact of opium on their society. A number of antiopium associations kept the fight against opium in the public eye well into the 1930s. With drug control as their objective, authorities in the United States and China consciously sought to perpetuate the myth of a special relationship between the two countries.[18]

The assumption of this common agenda in the struggle against opiates was important on its own terms and because it presumably strengthened, however indirectly, the Sino-U.S. relationship in other, unrelated areas. This is not to argue that mutual control proved to be an effective means of limiting opium production and use: On the contrary, Nationalist China never solved its opium or opiate problems. And on numerous occasions between 1927 and 1949, the United States had reason to doubt whether Chiang's government advocated the control of opium for more than opportunistic political objectives. Nevertheless, Commissioner Anslinger and his counterparts at the Department of State concluded that the Kuomintang was doing what it could to make the best of a bad situation.[19]

The attribution of benign motives to a Chinese leadership that held power as much by dint of force as by popular mandate may appear disingenuous more than fifty years after the fact. Yet, it must be recalled that Nationalist China was the most important Asian supporter of Washington's antinarcotics philosophy. Accordingly, because U.S. officials needed China's backing at international drug control meetings, it was best not to question the good faith of the Kuomintang. Unfortunately, turning a blind eye to the irregularities in China's antiopium record while at the same time blaming the Japanese or Mao Tse-tung's Communist forces for China's opium troubles essentially gave carte blanche to such individuals as Tu Yueh-sheng, among others, who dominated Shanghai's narcotics scene in the 1930s with the blessing of the Kuomintang. As a result, the bilateral drug control relationship fell victim to domestic political priorities in China and was much less effective than both sides publicly claimed.[20]

From this and other experiences, we can see that it is hard to find a historical example of mutual agreement about the desirability of narcotics control that can stand alone without reference to other issues—especially those arising out of domestic politics. One conceivable exception may be the inclusion of drug control on the agenda of the annual U.S.-Mexico interparliamentary conference; without adequate documentation for scholarly inquiry, however, it is not possible to make an informed assessment of the policy relevance of these discussions. Even the relatively amicable U.S.-Mexican relationship that existed by the mid-1970s—dubbed Operation Cooperation in order to repair strained relations after Operation Intercept—grew out of the highly coercive atmosphere surrounding Operation Intercept and evolved into *La Campaña Permanente* in Mexico. Also, it would be seriously misleading to claim that the selective adoption of coca controls in Bolivia and Peru in the mid-1980s came about more because of decades of patient or perhaps coercive diplomatic persuasion by Washington than as a result of an understanding by Bolivian and Peruvian authorities of the ultimately deleterious impact of the coca economy on their political and social institutions. As a result, U.S. officials welcomed the turn toward coca control in the Andes without fully comprehending why it happened.

Because drug control has rarely been treated reciprocally as a self-contained issue in bilateral relations between the United States and other nations, it must therefore be seen as a subject of coercive diplomacy or as a matter relegated to a secondary or derivative status. The history of inter-American drug control is replete with instances of coercion on the part of the United States, as I have shown elsewhere. The same conclusion applies to the history of opium control from about 1900 to midcentury in Asia, where U.S. authorities endeavored to bring about the closure of opium monopolies despite their traditional importance as a source of revenue.

It is tautological to assert that diplomacy is, at least in part, a coercive craft. Accordingly, it is the extent and nature of coercion that become the major issues in drug diplomacy. The United States has employed a remarkable variety of means to impose or promote restrictive forms of drug control in the international arena. In the Western Hemisphere, for example, the more serious U.S. policymakers have judged a situation to be, the more likely they have been to engage in activities that can be interpreted as a challenge or a threat to the sovereignty of Latin American nations. In view of the historical predisposition of the United States to act as hegemon in the Americas, it is easy to understand why efforts to persuade—let alone force—Latin American nations to behave in certain ways have been seen as attempts to undermine their sovereignty. For present analytical purposes, we should imagine a spectrum of challenges to sovereignty that ranges from simple persuasion to outright meddling in domestic politics.

More than any other nation, Mexico has been the object of coercive diplomacy by the United States. In the mid-1930s, for example, in order to gather information about drug trafficking, agents of the Treasury Department were operating in several Mexican states without the approval of the government in Mexico City. Several years later, as discussed previously, the United States helped to force from power the top Mexican drug control official. And in the late 1940s at the Commission on Narcotic Drugs of the United Nations, Anslinger chastised Mexico for what he saw as its inexcusably lax antinarcotic record. At no time did U.S. officials indicate that more than one acceptable road to drug control might exist. On one occasion in 1940, when Mexico capitulated to U.S. pressure and fundamentally altered its drug control policy, a leading Mexican drug official noted that his government would have to hide the fact that Washington was "dictating again."[21]

No matter how far U.S. officials were prepared to intrude into Mexican politics in the 1930s and 1940s, they consistently operated on the assumption that Mexican authorities wanted to adopt an antidrug program much like their own. However fanciful this position, the attribution of what political psychologists call "situational constraints" to the presumed shortcomings of Mexican drug policy prevented Washington from perpetrating a crisis between the two nations. Likewise, Mexican officials had their own reasons for not rupturing ties with their neighbor. Indeed, the frequent exchange of information between the two nations about drug trafficking may have convinced the Mexicans that Anslinger and his State Department colleagues were not ill intentioned despite their highly objectionable tactics. In other words, Mexico chose largely to ignore what could have been construed as serious challenges to its sovereignty.[22]

It is difficult to place as favorable a construction on the coercive aspects of U.S. narcotics diplomacy toward Mexico since 1969. In general, U.S. officials have assumed that drug control has not been a policy priority for Mexico. *La Campaña Permanente* in the mid-1970s was merely the exception that proved the rule. And although the improvement in relations over drugs since President Carlos Salinas de Gortari assumed power has been warmly applauded in Washington, skeptics argue that it has as much to do with Mexico's difficult economic situation as with any desire to control drugs. The reluctance to believe that Mexico's antidrug commitment is genuine underscores the negative impact of the murder of DEA agent Enrique Camarena Salazar on relations between the two countries.

Distrust of Mexico since the days of Operation Intercept reflects in part the need of U.S. authorities and politicians to explain the incidence of domestic drug use and abuse. It is also a manifestation of a struggle between the executive branch and Congress for control of drug policy. Since its creation in 1976, the House Select Committee on Narcotics Abuse and Control has consistently sought to influence the course of drug foreign policy; more recently, this can be said for a number of other committees and subcommittees. Finally, the tension between the two countries over drugs shows how similar to a Gordian knot is the hold of a proscriptive and punitive approach to drug control on U.S. policy.[23]

The attribution of negative dispositional reasons for difficulties with Mexico over drugs has led the United States increasingly to adopt a coercive diplomatic style. The decision of the U.S. government during the presidency of Ronald Reagan to issue annual "certifications" as to whether other nations were making progress against drugs was viewed in Mexico as a direct challenge to its sovereignty, as Attorney General Sergio García Ramírez pointedly observed. Similarly, officials there found objectionable some of the ways in which the United States tried to curb the extensive flow of drugs across the border, including the use of satellite technology. Moreover, the anti-Mexican fervor of Customs Commissioner William von Raab won the United States few friends south of the Rio Grande. Also, anger about the Camarena case has prevented the DEA from speaking with one voice about policy toward Mexico.[24]

Coercive bilateral diplomacy in the pursuit of narcotics control has sometimes differed in form from that practiced toward Mexico in the 1980s. Two variations stand out—one historical, the other contemporary. In two instances the United States sought to compel other nations to change their drug control policies and to rethink their antinarcotics philosophies. And on both of these occasions, U.S. officials attributed the lack of progress in controlling drugs more to dispositional reasons than to adverse situational constraints.

The first case concerns the frequently repeated allegation that Japan deliberately used opiates as a weapon of war against China in the 1930s. Yet, the situation was far more complex than that assertion by U.S. and Kuomintang officials and others would lead us to believe. For the present it is sufficient to note that in strongly condemning the apparent lack of will by authorities in Tokyo to curtail drug-related activities by the Japanese army in occupied China, the United States was not challenging the sovereign prerogatives of Japan—a course of action that would doubtless have been counterproductive. Although hoping that their protests might have an effect, U.S. officials instead were using the drug issue to express their extreme displeasure with Japan's foreign policy throughout East Asia. Thus, coercive narcotics diplomacy as practiced at the Opium Advisory Committee (OAC) of the League of Nations served as a means to a larger end. Japan, refusing to accept the hegemonic pretensions of the United States (and Great Britain) in East Asia, walked out of the OAC in November 1938—never to return. In the sense that it forced Tokyo's hand and thus strengthened anti-Japanese sentiment in U.S. policymaking circles, coercive diplomacy had done its job.[25]

In the contemporary example—which concerns the evolution of coca controls in Bolivia, Colombia, and Peru in the 1980s—the threat to sovereignty as a result of

U.S. pressure was both more subtle and more serious than in the case of Mexico. Since 1961, when the Single Convention on Narcotic Drugs was first opened for ratification, the United States had tried to obtain Bolivian and Peruvian compliance—which by the mid-1980s seemed little more than perfunctory. At the same time, Colombia was home to the world's largest cocaine-processing industry and did not, in the estimation of Congress and the White House, exhibit sufficient interest in the elimination of that industry. Accordingly, in early April 1986 President Reagan determined that drug production and trafficking constituted a security threat in the hemisphere. The rationale behind his action showed the inextricable connection between domestic and foreign policy. Reagan's war on drugs had been far more rhetorical than real as drug abuse, especially in the form of cocaine and crack, mounted in the United States. By 1986 he could no longer ignore congressional and popular demands for action. Yet, in the predictable tradition of U.S. antinarcotic foreign policy, the president looked abroad for a solution to the nation's ills. Strict control at the source along with renewed attention to interdiction would be the bases of U.S. strategy.[26]

The consequences for the three Andean nations were nothing short of momentous. In short order, the political and social institutions of Colombia and Peru became more susceptible to attack by internal revolutionary groups, which had previously been linked only loosely to cocaine merchants. Although arguably the institutional threats would have come about sooner or later, U.S. pressure on the two countries to define the cocaine business as a threat to national security exacerbated existing conditions and thereby hastened that unhappy development. In declaring that drugs were a dire threat, the leaders of Colombia and Peru in effect guaranteed an increased U.S. presence in their countries in the form of DEA agents and operations and through greatly expanded antinarcotics assistance. The threat to Bolivian institutions seemed less immediate during the 1980s; even so, traditional coca growers maintained their way of life, and new areas for cultivation were opened—which, after consultation with emissaries from the Reagan administration, brought the government in La Paz a dramatic increase in anticoca assistance.[27]

Only as this aid was accepted did the United States begin to believe lack of will was not the primary explanation for the explosion in coca production and the cocaine trade in the 1980s. In other words, blaming the U.S. drug problem on external sources has historically been the politically popular thing to do. Yet, the foreign policies derived from that dubious position suggest that on occasion the United States has put the sovereignty of other nations at risk in order to avoid dealing with the vexing issue of domestic demand for drugs. By the beginning of the 1990s, officials of the three Andean countries were trying to work out the limits of a direct U.S. military role in stopping the cocaine trade. Others besides committed revolutionaries were questioning the wisdom of allowing the United States virtually to dictate how the governments of Bolivia, Colombia, and Peru should respond to the increasingly intractable national problems associated with coca growing and cocaine production and trafficking. It would be wrong to discount the prominent role considerations such as these played in the politics of Cartagena and its aftermath.

Aside from such instances of mutual and coercive diplomacy, there is at least one example of drug control occurring as a result of the importance of other foreign policy matters. In 1907 Great Britain and China signed an agreement to reduce the shipment of opium from India by 10 percent per year. To be sure, this accord reflected the growing antiopium sentiment in Great Britain and the strength of the reform movement in China, yet it is unlikely that the British would have bowed to these pressures without additional, larger reasons. First, revenues derived from the sale of Indian opium were declining yearly. Second, in 1902 Great Britain had concluded a treaty of alliance with Japan in order to secure its strategic interests in Asia, especially against Russian adventurism, and to gain a freer hand to attend to interests in Europe. Finally, the development of cordial relations with China, even if that meant abandoning the opium trade, would probably enhance British prospects for greater economic penetration in China proper. Thus, the promotion of opium control in late Ch'ing China resulted partly from considerations essentially separate from the issue of control itself.[28]

This example of derivative opium control may be unique, but that does not necessarily mean it should be consigned to the dustbin of history. In fact, the linkage of opium control and other prominent foreign policy matters could recur under certain circumstances. For example, in Laos—the third-largest producer of opium in the world—the Communist government has recently begun antiopium activities in exchange for economic assistance from the United Nations and the United States in the form of a crop substitution program. The rationale behind Vientiane's decision seems clear: Laos is willing to give up its isolation from the West because of grave economic difficulties. At the same time, the United States has shown an interest in pursuing a better relationship because of the lingering prisoner of war–missing in action issue from the Vietnam War and because of its larger strategic involvement in the region.[29]

Multilateral Prospects

How long the Laotian opening to Washington will persist is uncertain, but U.S. officials took advantage of it to put in place a basic drug control advisory program—complete with equipment and personnel from a number of federal agencies. The Laotian example seems to make the use of linkage all the more appealing in the Americas. If mutual self-interest over a variety of issues, including drug control, exists between the United States and Laos, then the same is a fortiori true between the United States and Latin America—whether on a bilateral or a multilateral basis. The following issues appear to be especially conducive to a strategy of linkage: debt settlement in Peru, widespread crop substitution in Bolivia, commodity price stability in Colombia, and free trade with Mexico, among others. Indeed, linkage permeated the thinking of the Latin American delegations at Cartagena, but George Bush and

James Baker remained largely noncommittal on the issue. For the United States, the fundamental dilemma *may* be one of strong political intent and limited financial capability. Nevertheless, the checkered history of inter-American drug control raises the unsettling question of how important a foreign policy priority comprehensive controls actually are—to both the United States and Latin America. Can drug control ever become a domestic and foreign policy goal of the first order?

In an indirect way, the structure of international drug control as it has evolved since the first antiopium meeting at Shanghai in 1909 provides a partial guide for understanding how linkage might bolster the cause of control. To argue that the international movement has greatly affected illicit drug-related activities would be disingenuous. The conventions and treaties agreed on since the early twentieth century remain only as effective as the willingness of signatory powers to enforce them. The treaty structure itself contains no enforcement mechanisms; these remain the function of individual states pursuant to their own laws.

U.S. policymakers began cooperating with the world antidrug movement in 1931, only after they felt it had accepted as long-term objectives both control at the source and limiting the production and manufacture of narcotics to legitimate scientific and medical purposes. For cultural and economic reasons along with political considerations, producer nations in Latin America historically have not been prone to sign, ratify, and implement international accords. In Bolivia and Peru, for example, pro forma adherence to the various agreements—which were combined in 1961 into the Single Convention on Narcotic Drugs—has been the rule rather than the exception. Mexico's position has consistently been one of selective or intermittent enforcement.

In this light, the work of the Opium Advisory Committee of the League of Nations and the Commission on Narcotic Drugs of the United Nations, the leading agencies of the world movement, might be dismissed as being ultimately futile. To do so would be a mistake. True, neither the manufacturing limitation convention of 1931, nor the 1936 convention to suppress the illicit traffic, nor the international protocol of 1953 restricting legitimate opium production and export to seven countries, let alone the Single Convention have achieved marked success. Yet, these basic agreements affecting raw materials provide a legal and administrative framework for future international activity. And, as historian Arnold H. Taylor suggests, they constitute one possible way of limiting national sovereignty in a noncoercive fashion.[30] In that sense, the infrastructure of a new global drug control regime already exists. Should the signatory powers to the original accords ever agree that limiting sovereignty is in their common interest, then the conceptual basis behind the agreements will have been transformed. No longer would the proscriptive philosophy of the United States dominate attempts to control drugs; in its place, a genuine spirit of reciprocity that recognizes the symbiotic nature of supply and demand might guide the international movement.

Getting to this point anytime soon will not be an easy task. The obstacles to reconceptualizing drug control are many, at both the national and international levels. Are the United States and other manufacturing nations prepared to share power with producer states? Will larger foreign and security policy goals continue to supersede the objective of drug control—especially for the United States, whose leadership in a new drug control regime will be essential? Will the uncertainty of demand reduction prevent an accommodation between producer and consuming nations? Can the political economy of producer nations become less dependent on the lucrative drug business? And finally, concerning the traditional cultural role of coca in Bolivia and Peru, can its recent cultivation in unprecedented amounts be reversed without a destructive assault on indigenous cultures? The historical record of international narcotics control generally and inter-American control specifically does not inspire confidence that these many and diverse obstacles to effective drug control will soon be overcome.

Against this backdrop, it is a wonder that the Cartagena Summit generated as much hope as it did. But if the short-term aftermath of Cartagena suggests a legacy of frustration and the conclusion that it was merely a relic of an old order, it is still possible to find some promise—even opportunities—in the event itself. With boldness and with history as their guide, policymakers in Washington and the Andes, indeed throughout the Americas, might make of Cartagena what the Camp David accords of 1978 offered to Egypt and Israel—a new beginning that over time could put to rest past recriminations. Prolonged disputes over supply, demand, and responsibility for the drug problems in the hemisphere would have no place in the new order.

How might the promise of Cartagena be redeemed? First, it seems clear that unilateral antidrug measures, when employed in the international setting, are rarely effective and create more problems than they solve. In other words, unilateral forms of drug control ought to address domestic problems of use and abuse in a humane, creative fashion. Law enforcement will remain an essential tool for coping with drug traffickers. With some hyperbole, President Bush declared in his 1991 State of the Union message, "We will not rest until the day of the dealer is over, forever."[31] Sentiments such as this should comprise *one* focus of a serious drug control policy.

On a bilateral or multilateral level, the history of drug control dictates the need for a new order as well. Antinarcotic foreign policy, particularly on the part of the United States, must become a diplomacy between and among equals. On this issue the day of the hegemon has passed if drug control is to become a reality in the Americas. If it is too much at once to expect close collaboration over drugs, then all interested parties must accept a period of sporadic ad hoc cooperation—as appeared to exist in early 1991 between the United States and Colombia. And it seems to be productive to link drug control with other outstanding foreign policy issues, when appropriate. Linkage will give all parties a reason for improving the hemisphere's antinarcotics record.

Putting these recommendations into effect will require an appreciation of the history of drug control, both in the Americas and elsewhere, and will demand that policymakers operate from a completely different set of basic assumptions than they have in the past. The punitive ethos and outright suspicions that have traditionally defined the contours of U.S. domestic and foreign drug control policies since their inception are outmoded and must be discarded. Only after this is done will producer states in Latin America not feel compelled to take refuge in a defense of their sovereignty when U.S. authorities propose a drug control program whose specifics require intensive negotiations. Unless some form of the dramatic changes outlined here becomes a reality, drug control in the Americas will never be addressed in other than an ad hoc fashion. And the promise that was Cartagena will recede into oblivion.

Notes

1. *El Tiempo* (Bogotá), February 16, 1990; *New York Times*, February 16, 1990; Washington Post, February 16, 1990.

2. *Washington Post*, December 17, 1990, December 19, 1990, and January 22, 1991.

3. For Peru, see *New York Times*, November 18, 1990, and January 14, 1991; *Washington Post*, November 25, 1990, and December 19, 1990. Concerning Bolivia, see *Washington Post*, November 21, 1990, November 30, 1990, March 4, 1991, and March 14, 1991; *Christian Science Monitor*, November 29, 1990.

4. The following discussion is based on William O. Walker III, *Drug Control in the Americas*, rev. ed. (Albuquerque: University of New Mexico Press, 1989); William O. Walker III, *Opium and Foreign Policy: The Anglo-American Search for Order in Asia, 1912–1954* (Chapel Hill: University of North Carolina Press, 1991); and the work of other historians, including Arnold H. Taylor, *American Diplomacy and the Narcotics Traffic, 1900–1939: A Study in International Humanitarian Reform* (Durham: Duke University Press, 1969); David F. Musto, *The American Disease: Origins of Narcotic Control*, expanded and rev. ed. (New York: Oxford University Press, 1988); and David T. Courtwright, *Dark Paradise: Opiate Addiction in America Before 1940* (Cambridge: Harvard University Press, 1982).

5. Taylor, *American Diplomacy and the Narcotics Traffic*, 31–46.

6. Taylor, *American Diplomacy and the Narcotics Traffic*, 40–44.

7. Generally, see U.S. Congress, Senate, Message from the President of the United States Transmitting the Report of the Committee Appointed by the Philippine Commission to Investigate the Use of Opium and the Traffic Therein, and the Rules, Ordinances, and Laws Regulating Such Use and Traffic in Japan, Formosa, Shanghai, Hong Kong, Saigon, Singapore, Burma, Java, and the Philippine Islands, and Inclosing a Letter from the Secretary of War Submitting the Report for Transmission, *Use of Opium and Traffic Therein*, March 12, 1906, 59th Cong., 1st sess. (Washington, D.C.: U.S. Government Printing Office, 1906).

8. Terry M. Parssinen, *Secret Passions, Secret Remedies: Narcotic Drugs in British Society, 1820–1930* (Philadelphia: Institute for the Study of Human Issues, 1983), 91–92; Senate, *Use of Opium and Traffic Therein*, 36–44, 113–123; Carl A. Trocki, *Opium and Empire: Chinese Society in Colonial Singapore, 1800–1910* (Ithaca, N.Y.: Cornell University Press, 1990); James R. Rush, *Opium to Java: Revenue Farming and Chinese Enterprise in Colonial Indonesia, 1860–1910* (Ithaca, N.Y.: Cornell University Press, 1990).

9. Walker, *Opium and Foreign Policy*, chap. 9. There are indications that by the end of the 1980s, drug consumption was becoming a domestic problem in Iran. Some opium was being grown there, but much was smuggled in from Pakistan and Afghanistan. See U.S. Department of State, Bureau of International Narcotics Matters, *International Narcotics Control Strategy Report* (Washington, D.C.: U.S. Government Printing Office, March 1990), 251–253. For Turkey, see Edward J. Epstein, *Agency of Fear: Opiates and Political Power in America* (New York: G. P. Putnam's Sons, 1977).

10. Harry J. Anslinger and Will Oursler, *The Murderers: The Shocking Story of the Narcotics Gangs* (New York: Farrar, Straus, and Cudahy, 1961), 80.

11. Walker, *Opium and Foreign Policy*, chap. 5.

12. Walker, *Drug Control in the Americas*, 140–141, 151.

13. Courtwright, *Dark Paradise*, 11–15; Musto, *American Disease*, chaps. 6 and 7; Arnold S. Trebach, *The Heroin Solution* (New Haven: Yale University Press, 1982), 145–157.

14. Trebach, *Heroin Solution*, chaps. 5 and 7.

15. Walker, *Drug Control in the Americas*, 122–127, 139–140.

16. Musto, *American Disease*, 121–139; Trebach, *Heroin Solution*, 118–139; Department of State, *International Narcotics Control Strategy Report*, 251–253.

17. William O. Walker III, "Drug Control and the Issue of Culture in American Foreign Relations," *Diplomatic History* 12, no. 4 (Fall 1988): 365–382.

18. Walker, *Opium and Foreign Policy*; Michael H. Hunt, *The Making of a Special Relationship: The United States and China to 1914* (New York: Columbia University Press, 1983).

19. Walker, *Opium and Foreign Policy*; Jonathan Marshall, "Opium and the Politics of Gangsterism in Nationalist China, 1927–1945," *Bulletin of Concerned Asian Scholars* 8, no. 3 (July-September 1976): 19–48.

20. Walker, *Opium and Foreign Policy*; and William O. Walker III, "Decision-Making Theory and Narcotic Foreign Policy: Implications for Historical Analysis," *Diplomatic History* 15, no. 1 (Winter 1991): 31–45.

21. Walker, *Drug Control in the Americas*, 119–133, 177–178, with quote on 131.

22. Walker, "Decision-Making Theory and Narcotic Foreign Policy."

23. William O. Walker III, "After Camarena: U.S. Drug Control Policy and Mexico," paper delivered at the Latin American Studies Association, Fifteenth International Congress, Miami, Florida, December 1989.

24. *Excélsior* (Mexico City), April 15, 1988; *New York Times*, March 17, 1990; Walker, "After Camarena." On the DEA and Mexico, see also Elaine Shannon, *Desperados: Latin Drug Lords, U.S. Lawmen, and the War America Can't Win* (New York: Viking, 1988).

25. Walker, *Opium and Foreign Policy*, chaps. 4–6.

26. Walker, *Drug Control in the Americas*, 197–223.

27. The literature on this issue is extensive. See, for example, Rensselaer W. Lee III, *The White Labyrinth: Cocaine and Political Power* (New Brunswick: Transaction Publishers, 1989); Bruce Michael Bagley, "Dateline Drug Wars: Colombia: The Wrong Strategy," *Foreign Policy* 77 (Winter 1989–1990): 154–171; and a special issue of the *Journal of Interamerican Studies and World Affairs* 30, nos. 2–3 (Summer-Fall 1988).

28. Walker, *Opium and Foreign Policy*, chap. 1; Ian Nish, *The Anglo-Japanese Alliance: The Diplomacy of Two Island Empires, 1894–1907* (London: Athlone Press, University of London, 1966).

29. U.S. Department of State, *International Narcotics Control Strategy Report*, 299–307; U.S. Department of State, *International Narcotics Control Strategy Report, Mid-Year Update* (Washington, D.C.: U.S. Government Printing Office, September 1990), 61–62.

30. Taylor, *American Diplomacy and the Narcotics Traffic*, 326–338.

31. *Washington Post*, January 30, 1991.

19

The United Nations and
the Global Drug Control Regime

Jack Donnelly

National and regional efforts to deal with the drug crisis in the Americas take place within a broader context of multilateral international action that began as far back as the 1909 Shanghai opium conference. Under the League of Nations in the 1920s and early 1930s, a relatively effective international system was established to control the production, trade, and use of dangerous drugs for medical and scientific purposes. Since 1945 the United Nations (UN) has extended and strengthened this system. And over the past decade, in response to growing international concern, the United Nations has substantially increased its attention to drug abuse and drug trafficking—most dramatically in the 1990 Special Session of the General Assembly.

This chapter presents an analytic overview of the norms and procedures of the UN-based global drug control regime. I argue that the United Nations has been remarkably successful in certain areas, most notably in developing international norms and supervising the licit trade in narcotic drugs and psychotropic substances. It also has considerable potential in aspects of the drug war connected with knowledge and information. The UN role in the international war against drugs, however, will remain a supporting one; and the United Nations is likely to play a particularly peripheral role in the Americas.

International Regimes

International regimes can be defined as "principles, norms, rules, and decision-making procedures around which actor expectations converge in a given issue area."[1] An international regime exists when states and other relevant international actors, in order to avoid the costs of uncoordinated national action, agree (more or less explicitly) on normative or procedural constraints on their sovereign freedom of action in an issue-area—and (at least in part) conform their behavior to these norms or procedures.

Regime norms may range from binding international standards that are generally accepted by states as authoritative to international guidelines that are commended in word but rarely heeded in deed. Regime procedures likewise may range from full international decision making, including generally effective enforcement powers, to procedures that amount to little more than international verbal encouragement of sovereign national action. International regimes thus come in an immense variety of forms.

The key to a regime's strength usually lies in the extent of its decision-making powers—that is, the range of activities available to relevant international institutions. Very roughly, there are four principal types of action undertaken by international institutions and thus four general types of international regimes, as follows:[2]

- *Promotion*: encouraging national implementation of international norms by such mechanisms as public information activities and the adoption of hortatory resolutions
- *Assistance*: providing support for national implementation of international norms, typically through financial or technical assistance
- *Implementation*: playing a direct international role in putting regime norms into practice—for example, through systems of international information exchange, policy consultation or coordination, or (unenforceable) international monitoring of national compliance with regime norms or recommended policies
- *Enforcement*: binding and enforceable international implementation of regime norms in which the principal role of states is to give national force to supranational decisions

For completeness I should add a fifth type, declaratory regimes, which involve international norms but have no international decision-making powers.

Most international regimes, regardless of issue-area, have relatively weak decision-making procedures. This is also the case for the global drug control regime. The norms of the global drug control regime are coherent, well-developed, and widely commended by states and nonstate actors alike. Nonetheless, in most cases implementation of these norms remains almost entirely in the hands of national, not international, actors. The result is a largely promotional regime except in the area of licit manufacture and trade, where there is a strong international implementation subregime.

The global drug control regime is neither unimportant nor uninteresting. The work of norm creation has been important. Furthermore, the 1988 United Nations Convention Against Illicit Traffic in Narcotic Drugs and Psychotropic Substances and the February 1990 Special Session of the General Assembly as well as the organizational changes approved by the UN General Assembly in December 1990 indicate serious efforts by the UN system to respond to changes in the nature of the drug problem. The United Nations and its specialized agencies have also been important and are likely to play a growing role in fostering both improvements in national practice and greater levels of bilateral, regional, and international cooperation in the fight against drugs. Nonetheless, I argue that the UN system lacks the resources or the powers necessary for it to play anything more than a subsidiary, supporting role.

Although regional regimes and even certain bilateral agreements are "international regimes" as that term is conventionally defined, this chapter is restricted to what I call the global drug control regime—the most general multilateral norms and procedures, which are universal in the dual sense that they are open to and meant to cover all states. Insofar as it deals with issues of multilateral cooperation, this book is principally concerned with what we might call the inter-American drug control regime. My task in this chapter is to attempt to situate this inter-American regime as well as bilateral cooperation in the Americas within the broader international organizational context, giving particular attention to the role of the United Nations.

The League of Nations
and International Drug Control

There may be an element of truth to the claim that "the history of the human race has also been the history of drug abuse."[3] Prior to the twentieth century, however, drug abuse was not considered an international problem. In fact, not only did Great Britain and Asian colonial powers derive a considerable portion of their imperial revenues from the drug trade, they were even willing to fight to force the Chinese to accept the import of prepared opium. "Free trade" rather than drug control was the prevailing norm throughout the nineteenth century.

China's 1906 antiopium campaign, however, was followed in 1908 by a U.S. proposal for an international conference, which met in Shanghai in February 1909. The Shanghai conference in turn led to a Hague conference that drafted the 1912 International Opium Convention, the first international agreement that sought to regulate trade in and abuse of dangerous drugs.

The early articles of the 1912 convention sought to eliminate gradually the Far Eastern opium trade. For our purposes, however, the more interesting features of the treaty are the initial steps to establish effective domestic control of the manufacture, sale, and use of manufactured opium (especially morphine) and cocaine. The provisions of the convention were often vague and were not strictly binding. The refusals of Germany (a significant manufacturer) and Turkey (a major opium producer) to accept the treaty further limited its practical impact. Nonetheless, it was an important breakthrough that formulated "general principles [that] remain the guide for international drug control to the present day."[4]

After World War I, Article 23(c) of the Covenant of the League of Nations gave the organization "general supervision over the execution of agreements with regard to . . . the traffic in opium and other dangerous drugs." The league assembly, at its first session in 1920, created an Advisory Committee on Traffic in Opium and Other Dangerous Drugs to carry out these responsibilities. Of even greater importance was the development of stronger international rules in two treaties negotiated in Geneva in 1925 and 1931.

The 1925 International Opium Convention extended the range of drugs and raw materials covered and established a relatively aggressive system of import certifications and export authorizations. It also created a Permanent Central Board to supervise and restrict the international narcotics trade. Particularly noteworthy was the power of the board to bring unsatisfactory practices to the attention of the league council and even to recommend suspending exports to a country it felt was not exercising adequate controls. Very few international bodies in the interwar period had such strong monitoring powers.

The 1931 Convention for Limiting the Manufacture and Regulating the Distribution of Narcotic Drugs went even further. In addition to strengthening the trade controls of the 1925 convention and augmenting the powers of the Permanent Central Board, the 1931 convention sought to limit world manufacture to the level required to satisfy medical and scientific needs only. It created a Supervisory Body to enforce production limits through a system of binding estimates of national and international needs. The Supervisory Body was even authorized to provide estimates for both nonparties and contracting parties that failed to submit estimates.

These two conventions were relatively conscientiously implemented. Together with coordinated and increasingly uniform national monitoring programs spurred by the Advisory Committee's 1927 Model Administrative Code, they produced a remarkably effective system of control. For example, world trade in morphine declined from 6,972 kilograms in 1928 to 1,911 kilograms in 1938, and the cocaine trade dropped from 3,230 kilos to 843 in the same period.[5]

The limitations of the interwar regime, however, were also noteworthy. The regime was a system of national controls under international supervision. To be effective, it required essentially universal participation or at least the participation of all countries with a production capacity greater than national consumption. (In the 1920s there were only seven or eight such countries, but by 1945 there were about two dozen.) The only coercive powers available were adverse international publicity and the threat to stop legal supplies from those participating in the regime. In effect, it was an implementation rather than an enforcement regime. Even today, strong international implementation regimes are relatively rare. They were extremely unusual in the interwar period. The problem, in other words, is a generic one in international relations and in fact was less serious in drug control than in most other issue-areas.

The second and much more serious limitation of the interwar regime was conceptual: It dealt solely with the "supply" side. Consumer demand—let alone the problems of preventing addiction and treating addicts—was entirely ignored. As S. D. Stein notes, "Paradoxical though it may seem, much of the history of national and international narcotics control can be written without reference to addicts or addiction."[6]

To a certain extent, supply may create its own demand—the "pusher" model of addiction—but it is at least as true that demand creates its own supply. For example, the decline in the morphine and cocaine trade in the 1930s noted above helped to spur an increase in the production and use of heroin. Only relatively recently has the international drug control regime begun to give serious attention to the demand side of the equation, as we see in greater detail below.

The United Nations:
Extending the Convention Approach

The United Nations initially adopted the general approach of the League of Nations, concentrating on diversions from licit production and trade. The Commission on Narcotic Drugs was established as one of six permanent functional commissions of the Economic and Social Council (ECOSOC), replacing the league's Advisory Committee. The league Secretariat's Drug Control Service was replaced by a similar Division of Narcotic Drugs. The Permanent Board and the Supervisory Body were retained. The United Nations continued to pursue an essentially treaty-based, supply-side approach.

By 1960 six different drug control treaties plus two amending protocols were in force. The 1961 Single Convention on Narcotic Drugs was drafted to simplify and further strengthen the regime, which had evolved in a somewhat haphazard, incremental fashion. The 1961 Single Convention codified, harmonized, and in certain ways extended and strengthened the earlier treaties that it superseded. Even today, as amended by the 1972 protocol, it remains one of the most important documents of the international drug control regime. By October 1989 there were 126 parties to the 1961 convention and 94 parties to the 1972 protocol.

The central principle of the Single Convention is the obligation "to limit exclusively to medical and scientific purposes the production, manufacture, export, import, distribution of, trade in, use, and possession of drugs (Article 4)." The main mechanism to achieve this is an extended version of the estimates system established by the 1931 convention, supervised by the International Narcotics Control Board (created as the successor to the Permanent Board and the Supervisory Body). Each party is required to submit estimates of legitimate (medical and scientific) needs for narcotics in a standardized form. In addition, parties must provide standardized statistical returns on actual annual production or manufacture, consumption, imports, exports, seizures, and stocks. Each party is then limited to the estimated amount in its manufacture and net import of drugs.

The International Narcotics Control Board (INCB) is given extensive supervisory powers over this system of binding estimates and statistical returns. The board may make estimates for parties or nonparties that fail to report. It may even challenge estimates provided by governments. If the INCB is not satisfied with the performance of any government—whether or not it is a party to the convention—it may initiate consultations, call upon that government to adopt remedial measures, bring the problem to the attention of the international community, or even recommend that parties stop trading in drugs with the country in question. Furthermore, if statistical returns reveal that estimated needs have been exceeded, the board may require parties to the convention to halt further exports to that country.

Particularly stringent regulations apply to international trade in scheduled drugs. Exports are permitted only on the basis of a previously obtained import certificate from designated authorities in the receiving country. All such authorities are listed in the annually updated INCB document *National Authorities Empowered to Issue Certificates and Authorizations for the Import and Export of Narcotic Drugs and Psychotropic Substances.* To reduce fraud, a copy of the export authorization must be sent to the government of the importer. After the delivery is made or the authorization expires, the importing government must inform the exporting government of the actual amount delivered. In addition, stringent national controls are required for handling internationally traded drugs.

One of the crucial gaps in the 1961 convention, however, was the limited list of controlled substances. Furthermore, not all actual or potential dangerous drugs were appropriately included in the estimates system that was at the heart of the production limits established through the Single Convention. A parallel system of control for many drugs thus seemed appropriate, and the Single Convention remained single for barely a decade.

The 1971 Convention on Psychotropic Substances—which is explicitly intended to be implemented in conjunction with the 1961 convention—establishes a sliding system of reporting, licensing, and controls for a wide range of drugs. These drugs are listed in four schedules, arranged on the basis of their inherent danger and actual patterns of abuse. To keep up with changes in the nature of the drug problem, the Commission on Narcotic Drugs may add, move, or delete drugs on the schedules. For substances in Schedules I and II, the import and export controls and the required annual statistical reports are essentially the same as those established in the 1961 convention. Slightly less stringent restrictions apply to substances on Schedules III and IV. None of the scheduled drugs, however, is covered by an estimate system of production controls.

By the early 1970s, then, the work begun with the Shanghai conference and the 1912 convention was largely brought to its culmination. The resulting system of estimates, statistics, authorizations, and controls has made diversion from licit international shipments extremely difficult. Legitimate trade has been rather effectively safeguarded, and trafficking for the purposes of drug abuse has been forced into patently illicit channels.

The drug problem has nonetheless continued to intensify. An international drug control regime based primarily on controlling the production of and regulating legal trade in dangerous drugs has proved valuable in safeguarding medical and scientific uses. It has increased the costs and difficulties of illegal trafficking. It also provides a firm basis for further forms of international cooperation. Alone, however, it is completely inadequate to the problem—in large part because of its conceptual narrowness.

From the Vienna Conference
to the Seventeenth Special Session

As I have already noted, the United Nations initially continued the league's treaty-based, supply-side approach to international drug control. In 1970, however, it established the United Nations Fund for Drug Abuse Control (UNFDAC) to provide international technical and financial assistance in the war on drugs. This was the first significant step beyond a treaty-based approach. In the last few years, UNFDAC programs have expanded significantly, giving the United Nations a much greater operational presence in national efforts at drug control (as we will see, however, funding remains very modest).

Even more important has been the expansion of the UN's conceptualization of the nature of the problem over the past decade. Article 38 of the 1961 Single Convention does require that parties "give special attention to and take all practicable measures for the prevention of abuse of drugs and for the early identification, treatment, education, after-care, rehabilitation, and social reintegration of the persons involved and shall co-ordinate their efforts to these ends." This represented a passing nod to the demand side of the drug problem. Today, however, supply and demand are—in theory at least—coequal parts of an integrated plan.[7] Three major events in the past half decade have crystallized the new UN approach: the 1987 International Conference on Drug Abuse and Illicit Traffic, the 1988 United Nations Convention Against Illicit Traffic in Narcotic Drugs and Psychotropic Substances, and the 1990 Seventeenth Special Session of the General Assembly, devoted to drug abuse control.

1987 International Conference

The principal product of the 1987 International Conference on Drug Abuse and Illicit Traffic was the Comprehensive Multidisciplinary Outline of Future Activities in Drug Abuse Control (CMO).[8] The very title of this document suggests a major expansion in focus, as does the first paragraph, which notes that it "is not and was not designed to be a formal legal instrument." Rather, it seeks to provide "a handbook . . . a source of ideas . . . a repertory of recommendations . . . setting forth practical measures which can contribute to the fight against drug abuse and to the suppression of illicit trafficking."

The CMO contains four chapters, dealing with preventing and reducing illicit demand, controlling supply, illicit trafficking, and treatment and rehabilitation. The emphases on demand and treatment in particular go well beyond the earlier treaty-based approach. Each chapter specifies a series of targets, with suggestions for national, regional, and international action. The "multidisciplinary" character of the targets and recommendations is clearest in the emphasis in paragraph 14 on "the participation of many branches of the national governmental machinery . . . and also institutions of higher learning, research, and other academic bodies and private sector organizations." There is also a very strong awareness of the importance of coordinating the activities of a diverse array of actors at both the national and international levels. The thirty-five targets of the CMO are listed below.

Prevention and Reduction of Illicit Demand

1. Assessment of the extent of drug misuse and abuse
2. Organization of comprehensive systems for the collection and evaluation of data
3. Prevention through education
4. Prevention of drug abuse in the workplace
5. Prevention programs by civic, community, and special interest groups and law enforcement officials
6. Leisure-time activities in the service of the continuing campaign against drug abuse
7. Role of the media

Control of Supply

8. Strengthening of the international system of control of narcotic drugs and psychotropic substances
9. Rational use of pharmaceuticals containing narcotic drugs and psychotropic substances
10. Strengthening the control of international movements of psychotropic substances
11. Action related to the increase in the number of controlled psychotropic substances
12. Control of the commercial movement of precursors, specific chemicals, and equipment
13. Control of analogues of substances under international control
14. Identification of illicit narcotic plant cultivation
15. Elimination of illicit plantings
16. Redevelopment of areas formerly under illicit drug crop cultivation

Suppression of Illicit Trafficking

17. Disruption of major trafficking networks
18. Promoting controlled delivery
19. Facilitation of extradition
20. Mutual judicial and legal assistance
21. Admissibility in evidence of samples of bulk seizures of drugs
22. Improved efficacy of penal provisions
23. Forfeiture of the instruments and proceeds of illicit drug trafficking
24. Tightening of controls of movement through official points of entry

25. Strengthening of external border controls and of mutual assistance machinery within economic unions of sovereign states
26. Surveillance of land, water, and air approaches to the frontier
27. Controls over the use of the international mails for drug trafficking
28. Controls over ships on the high seas and aircraft in international airspace

Treatment and Rehabilitation

29. Toward a policy of treatment
30. Inventory of available modalities and techniques of treatment and rehabilitation
31. Selection of appropriate treatment programs
32. Training for personnel working with drug addicts
33. Reduction of the incidence of diseases and the number of infections transmitted through drug-using habits
34. Care for drug-addicted offenders within the criminal justice and prison systems
35. Social reintegration of persons who have undergone programs for treatment and rehabilitation

Many of these targets are very general and rather commonsensical, especially the demand-reduction and treatment targets. Nonetheless, the package as a whole represents a serious effort to see drug abuse as a complex and multifaceted problem that requires national and international attention focused not merely on production and trafficking but also on consumption and rehabilitation. Furthermore, the exemplary effect of this comprehensive approach is important, especially in the many Third World countries in which drug abuse is a relatively new problem. It may even have an impact on public debate in countries such as the United States. At the very least, producer states can use this new international consensus in their negotiations with consumer states to try to increase the amount of assistance they receive.

Even in the more traditional areas of supply and trafficking, the CMO reveals significant innovations. Especially important is Target 16, redevelopment of areas formerly under illicit drug crop cultivation. Many previous supply-side efforts focused on forced eradication with little attention to the large financial incentives for relatively poor, small growers of opium or coca. The idea that supply reduction should be treated in the context of integrated rural development programs was not a major innovation in 1987, having been tried with varying degrees of commitment and success over the preceding decade. It is nonetheless perhaps the most important example of the penetration of a richer understanding of the roots of the problem into the global drug control regime.

The scope and complexity of the Comprehensive Multidisciplinary Outline, however, are also its greatest weaknesses. There is also a danger that the CMO will be treated less as a comprehensive program than as a laundry list, thus undermining the conceptual advance that is perhaps its greatest value. In addition, the CMO entails no binding legal commitments of states.

1988 International Convention

The second major recent advance was, somewhat paradoxically, yet another treaty—the 1988 United Nations Convention Against Illicit Traffic in Narcotic Drugs and Psychotropic Substances. As the title makes clear, its focus is on drug traffic. This treaty represents a significant international effort to deal with a problem that has changed substantially since the early 1970s.

The 1988 convention attempts to give force to the illicit trafficking recommendations of the CMO (which were formulated with the working draft of the convention in mind). Of special importance are provisions relating to the use of controlled delivery,[9] improvements in extradition procedures, attempts to strengthen penal provisions, and provisions for the discovery and seizure of drug-related assets. Parties to the 1988 convention also undertake relatively extensive obligations to provide mutual legal assistance.

Those familiar with recent North American and West European efforts may find little that is truly innovative in these provisions. In fact, they rest on recent experience with programs such as the U.S. seizure of drug-related assets. Law-making treaties, however, can never be far in advance of the most developed practice of their time; if they were, not enough states would ratify them to give them much practical significance. This is a fact of international political life in a world organized around sovereign states. The real impact of any such treaty, if it is successful, will be to raise the average level and intensity of activity among states to something much closer to the highest level prevailing at the time.

The 1988 convention almost certainly requires at least some strengthening of law and practice in any state that takes seriously the obligations imposed by ratification. And it seems likely that the vast majority of states will become parties relatively rapidly. By August 1990, eighty-nine countries had signed the treaty. It entered into force in November 1990.

1990 Special Session

Any changes in state behavior, of course, will rest on the will of governments to discharge their obligations—something that is notoriously difficult to predict in the case of commitments with respect to an unquestionable "good thing" such as drug abuse control. Some indication of that will, however, may be assessed from the results of the February 1990 Special Session of the General Assembly, the principal product of which was the Political Declaration and Global Programme of Action.[10]

The political declaration is a fairly typical solemn declaration from the United Nations. For our purposes, some of the most important elements involve provisions that reaffirm the need for "strategies that are comprehensive and multidisciplinary" (paragraph 6), including the general insistence on the linkages among demand, production, supply, trafficking, and distribution. The representative from Colombia put it well: "We are witnessing an evolution towards a comprehensive, concerted, and joint confrontation of the problem, with recognition of the effects of demand and consumer abuse as the determining factors in this complex area."[11]

The last clause in this quote—although certainly understandable from the Colombian perspective—is overly optimistic, especially when we look at the practice of the major consuming nation, the United States. Nonetheless, the special session does provide substantial evidence of the institutionalization of an expanded conceptualization of the problem. For example, the declaration stresses international support for "viable alternative income schemes" in developing producer countries (paragraph 13) and for the control efforts of developing transit countries. It would be easy for a cynic to dismiss this as mere words, a typical UN confusion of its own resolutions with reality. Certainly, the political declaration alone cannot alleviate the drug problem in any of its dimensions; nonetheless, even mere words can be of value.

As a practical matter, a limited number of issues can be treated as true priority items in the United Nations and by the international community more broadly. The special session and its political declaration can be seen as an important "consciousness-raising" exercise, a major effort to move drugs to a higher place on international agendas.[12] Just getting near the top of the agenda is not enough, as the failure of very high priority efforts to achieve a new international economic order vividly illustrates. But unless drug control rises to the top of international agendas, it is almost certain that we will not achieve the necessary political and especially financial commitments necessary for real progress in international drug control.

In his opening statement to the special session, the secretary-general claimed that "drug abuse is now right at the top of the list of priorities requiring urgent attention from the international community." The real test, however, will come when states must pay for the activities needed to give real meaning to this newly proclaimed priority. As the secretary-general emphasized, "Very considerable additional funding will be required," both in the regular budget and in extra-budgetary contributions to the United Nations Fund for Drug Abuse Control.[13] But U.S. Secretary of State James A. Baker III clearly indicated that the largest UN contributor was not in favor of increased funding unless it came out of existing programs: "We must order our priorities in such a way as to achieve our aims within the framework of a unitary approach to the entire United Nations system and through zero real program growth in budgets."[14]

The issue of funding is critical. In 1988–1989 the regular UN budget was $1.76 billion. Of that, only about $37 million was devoted to drug control. This was only 0.0074 percent of the estimated 1989 drug trade of $500 billion—that is, less than an hour's turnover in the world drug trade.[15] We can contrast this with the budgets of the Universal Postal Union ($32.1 million), the International Maritime Organization ($38.8 million), the World Meteorological Organization ($49.1 million), and the World Intellectual Property Organization ($68.8 million). Such figures make it difficult to take seriously the claims of paramount importance for the war on drugs.

We already have a solid international normative framework for a comprehensive, multidisciplinary international assault on the drug problem (although it will continue to evolve and will be refined incrementally). The report of the Commission on Narcotic Drugs to the special session nicely summarizes the current consensus on general principles.

1. Existing treaties provide a firm basis for current action.
2. The Comprehensive Multidisciplinary Outline provides a generally adequate basis for developing new national policies.
3. States have "primary responsibility" for drug control, but "international co-operation is an indispensable supporting instrument."
4. Success ultimately depends on reducing demand.
5. A comprehensive, multisectoral approach is necessary.
6. The UN role needs to be expanded.
7. Additional financial resources are required.[16]

The central issue now is whether the machinery available throughout the UN system and in related multilateral organizations and forums is sufficient to give force to the often-expressed intention to end drug abuse and the national and international evils with which it is associated. If the special session is to have a lasting positive impact, it must go beyond words to action. As the Administrative Committee on Coordination recently put it, "The major task before the international community now is to translate this unanimous political commitment of Governments into effective action."[17]

The United Nations and Drug Control in the 1990s

As we have seen, the Commission on Narcotic Drugs—a functional commission of the Economic and Social Council—is the principal drug policy body within the United Nations. The General Assembly, as the supreme political organ on drug issues, also plays an important policy role. The principal products of these two groups have been treaties, declarations, resolutions, and plans of action. My concern in this section is with the considerable variety of bodies that are charged with an operational role in the international drug control regime, with special attention to current activities and some of the priority items singled out in the secretary-general's 1990 report on the United Nations System-Wide Plan of Action.[18]

International Narcotics Control Board

The International Narcotics Control Board (INCB), as we saw above, has primary responsibility for supervising the licit supply of drugs under the 1961 and 1971 conventions. Although it has been generally successful in assuring a safe supply for legitimate medical and scientific uses and in preventing regular or systematic diversions into illicit channels, it has only a limited mandate in the international war against drug abuse.

The general level of satisfaction with the efforts of the INCB is perhaps clearest when we turn to the System-Wide Plan of Action. The secretary-general lists no new activities for the INCB, merely incremental improvements in current activities and some improvements in its ability to provide technical assistance. Furthermore, the estimated additional financial needs for 1992–1993 exceed those for 1990–1991 by less than 15 percent.

The system works extremely well for substances controlled under the 1961 convention. It is also largely effective for drugs listed in Schedules I and II of the 1971 convention. And in order to preserve this record, the board pays careful attention to new trends in trafficking. For example, it launched a special program for West Africa in 1989–1990 to deal with the growing use of this area as an intermediate transit site in the drug trade to Europe.

Nonetheless, diversions often do occur from substances listed on Schedules III and IV. Even more troubling is the clear pattern of traffic in new drugs when diversions of previously preferred drugs of abuse are stopped. For example, as controls over amphetamines were tightened in the 1980s, there was a substitution of fenetylline; and as controls on fenetylline are tightened, there is now an apparent move to anorectics and pemoline. In a similar fashion, the move of methaqualone from Schedule IV to Schedule II in 1980 triggered a switch to barbiturates and benzodiazepines.[19]

This problem of control leading more to substitution than to a reduction in demand is an old one, going back at least to the 1930s when reduced opium supplies helped to trigger a switch to heroin. This simply underscores the essential point that in the case of addictive drugs of abuse, demand rather than supply drives the problem (even if a large supply can help to create additional demand). Nonetheless, it remains essential to stop what can be stopped. The INCB has made and will continue to make significant contributions to the war against drugs both by safeguarding licit production, distribution, and use and by reducing the supply of a steadily growing number of drugs.

Division of Narcotic Drugs

The Division of Narcotic Drugs (DND) is the principal unit of the Secretariat dealing with drug issues. Its primary contribution is to gather and make available information and advice. Its informational activities include publications such as the *Bulletin of Narcotic Drugs*, the division's Information Letter, and its *Resource Book on Measures to Reduce Illicit Demand for Drugs*. The division's film and video library is increasingly in demand. In addition, the DND sponsors workshops and expert-group meetings on such technical topics as the use of drug-scenting dogs, pretrial destruction of seized drugs, detecting illicit cultivation through satellite remote sensing and aerial photography, and environmentally sound methods to eradicate drug crops.

As the only body within the United Nations system equipped with a well-outfitted and professionally staffed drug lab, the DND provides a variety of technical services. Its *Manual of Staff Skill Requirements and Basic Equipment for Narcotics Laboratories* is a fundamental standard-setting document for drug labs throughout the world. DND has also developed a series of manuals to assist national laboratories in analyzing and identifying more than a dozen particular narcotic drugs and psychotropic substances subject to extensive abuse.

The Division of Narcotic Drugs has attempted to transfer its knowledge and skills to interested states. It helps to plan, organize, and improve national and regional testing laboratories and provides technical training of various sorts. For example, from July 1989 through June 1990, twenty-one fellows (from Ghana, Iraq, Kenya, Lebanon, Lesotho, Pakistan, Sri Lanka, Tanzania, Yemen, Yugoslavia, and Zambia) received three-month training courses, and another dozen fellows (from Argentina, China, India, Thailand, and Uruguay) received advanced training. The DND has also developed a network of collaborating national training institutions in forensic toxicology. In addition, in 1988–1989 the division distributed over 1,200 samples of controlled drugs, metabolites, and analogues to laboratories in 32 countries and provided 261 field test kits to 25 different countries. The general goal of all of these activities is to foster higher standards and greater uniformity in national testing programs. The DND is also important for facilitating regional and international cooperation among national drug enforcement agencies.

In the area of supply control, DND has studied the effectiveness and environmental consequences of available eradication techniques. It is engaged in a joint program with the Food and Agriculture Organization on detecting illicit opium, coca, and cannabis production. DND has also developed a manual on clandestine manufacture of major drugs of abuse.

The division provides an extensive range of services to national policymakers and drug law enforcement agencies. DND maintains a comprehensive set of national laws on drug abuse and control and provides consulting services to governments on new laws and policies. It publishes quarterly summaries of major seizures in an effort to help chart trends in the traffic. The division has also developed training strategies and materials and regularly provides advisory services to drug law enforcement agencies and projects at both the national and regional levels. Much of the laboratory work described above is also relevant to efforts to interdict the international traffic in drugs.

As the secretary-general's Report on the System-Wide Plan indicates, "The Division will henceforth give higher priority to prevention and reduction of drug abuse with a view to elimination of the illicit demand for narcotic drugs and psychotropic substances."[20] This includes the creation of a new Demand Reduction Section. Current activities include work on using existing community resources in the war on drugs. For example, regional seminars were held in 1989 in Bolivia, Kenya, and Spain.

A particularly important new initiative is the development of the International Drug Abuse Assessment System, a standardized system of information collection and reporting designed to allow national authorities to map the nature of their country's drug problem. In most developed countries, such information is fairly readily available. In many Third World countries, however, even the size and shape of the local drug problem often are largely matters of conjecture. The new assessment system will help to provide national authorities and international agencies with a clearer picture of the nature of the problem they face.

In the area of treatment and rehabilitation as well, the principal functions of the DND are to gather and disseminate information and to stimulate and nurture national efforts through workshops, conferences, and other forms of technical assistance.

Funding is crucial to the effectiveness of all of these activities. The secretary-general's Report on the System-Wide Plan often returns to the need for additional resources in order to meet existing mandates, let alone to move into new activities. In fact, it notes that the division's efforts with respect to illicit traffic have "suffered severely from resource shortages in recent years."[21] The U.S.-triggered financial crisis of the late 1980s forced a reduction in the budget and staff of the Division of Narcotic Drugs and the Secretariat of the International Narcotics Control Board. In 1989 some agencies did not even have the resources to attend interagency meetings. In early 1990 the secretary-general reported that the 1990–1991 budget for the Division of Narcotic Drugs was still about $3 million short of what was needed simply to perform its basic and already well-established tasks.[22] In the area of demand reduction it is estimated that the 1990–1991 regular budget will need to be nearly doubled for 1992–1993, with similar increases in extrabudgetary funding, simply to meet existing mandates.[23] And as more Third World states undertake additional efforts, the need for international assistance will grow rather than remain constant.

Some portion of such funding complaints can be attributed to the voracious and seemingly insatiable appetite of UN bureaucracies. But information—especially the right information delivered in the right place, at the right time, in the right way—is not cheap. Information and expertise alone are hardly solutions to the drug problem. Without the necessary information, however, most other efforts are doomed to inefficiency at best and most often to failure. Especially in the Third World, where the problems of drug abuse and the drug traffic are spreading into areas that traditionally have been relatively untouched, a lack of basic information and expertise remains a serious problem.

The United Nations Fund for Drug Abuse Control

The United Nations Fund for Drug Abuse Control (UNFDAC), which began operations in 1971 and is funded entirely by voluntary contributions, is the principal operational arm of the UN system in the war against drugs. UNFDAC provides much of the funding for the technical assistance activities of the DND mentioned above. Its mandate is to assist developing countries in the general areas of preventive education, integrated rural development and income substitution, drug trafficking, and health and rehabilitation. As the secretary-general's report puts it, UNFDAC's policy "is essentially aimed at creating an anti-drug momentum in countries and strengthening governments' abilities and commitment to tackle the problem of drug abuse and associated trafficking."[24] About a third of UNFDAC expenditures go to reducing supply, another third to reducing demand (primarily through education and public information), and a quarter to strengthening national systems of control.

In Colombia, the country in which it is most involved, UNFDAC had more than twenty programs in operation in 1990. These included prevention programs in six cities plus a program on drug prevention through the mass media, four rural development programs featuring crop replacement, two training programs for educators, and special programs on AIDS and for street children in Bogotá. This pattern is fairly typical for Latin America, although no other countries have more than a few UNFDAC programs in operation.

In Africa, however, there is much greater emphasis on law enforcement. Twelve African countries have UNFDAC current law enforcement programs; there are none in Latin America. In addition, UNFDAC has seven regional programs in operation in Africa (again compared with none in Latin America). This reflects a clear and admirable awareness of differing needs and of the importance of differentiated international responses.

The problem, however, is lack of funds. In 1989 UNFDAC had a budget of $62.5 million supporting 152 projects in 49 countries. Such a sum is ludicrously small given the severity of the problem. This is particularly true in the important and innovative area of integrated rural development and income substitution programs.

In the short run, it is cheaper to spray herbicides on crops or burn fields. But unless peasant producers are offered an attractive alternative, they will simply replant. Providing such alternatives is relatively expensive. It is, however, the only real solution short of eliminating the demand for the crop—something producer countries have little or no control over and that consumer countries, especially the United States, seem entirely unwilling to do. It also has the great attraction of offering positive improvements in the lives of the peasant producers.

The real issue is how deep the normative commitment to an intensified war on drugs really extends—that is, how much states are willing to pay to back their fine-sounding words. Unless the developed countries are willing to increase their contributions to UNFDAC programs dramatically and maintain them for several years, little can be achieved to reduce supply through international action.

One might imagine that some portion of the shortfall in spending on integrated rural development and income substitution would be made up by the United Nations Development Programme (UNDP). Since 1987 UNDP and UNFDAC have operated under a cooperative agreement in which UNDP provides administrative and liaison services and field support and monitoring of UNFDAC projects. UNDP,

however, spends only minuscule amounts of its own resources on drug programs—
less than a quarter of a million dollars in 1988–1989. The International Fund for
Agricultural Development has a somewhat better record, having spent about $92
million in 1990 on rural development programs in or adjacent to areas in which
drug crops are currently cultivated. But even this is at least an order of magnitude
below what would be needed to have a discernible impact on supply.

UN-Sponsored Regional Cooperation

Regional programs are particularly important in the war on drugs. Regional
programs can be much more finely tuned than global programs. And in the areas
of supply and trafficking, a regional approach can help to guard against national
successes leading to little more than a diversion of activity to neighboring countries.
For this reason the United Nations has sponsored a number of regional efforts.

The Commission on Narcotic Drugs has a Sub-Commission on Illicit Drug
Traffic and Related Matters in the Near and Middle East. The most important
institutionalized activities of the United Nations in the field of regional drug control,
however, take place through the regional economic commissions. For example, the
Economic and Social Commission for Asia and the Pacific promotes the development
of national data systems and the sharing of information among countries in the
region. More important than activities in these established forums, however, have
been new regional initiatives. These include the 1988 Tashkent meeting of East
European states, a Balkan states experts meeting in Belgrade in 1989, and the
United Nations Latin American Institute for the Prevention of Crime and the
Treatment of Offenders. One of the oldest and most important activities is the
regional meetings of Heads of Drug Law Enforcement Agencies (HONLEA).

The Asian and Pacific HONLEA dates back to the 1970s. The first HONLEA
meetings for Latin America and the Caribbean and for Africa, by contrast, were
held in 1987; and a European HONLEA was not created until 1990. In addition,
there have been two interregional HONLEA meetings—in 1986 and 1989. The
goal of these meetings is to bring together national authorities to exchange ideas
and experiences and, through the development of personal linkages, to foster
additional cooperative efforts on a regional basis. They also provide a forum for
national drug law enforcement officials to address the international community
collectively.

A number of technical training and advisory service programs have been carried
out on a regional basis. For example, UNFDAC recently developed special (sub-)
regional programs for Southeast Asia, Southwest Asia, the Andean region, and the
so-called "Balkan Route" from Turkey to West Europe. The African region, where
the problem is relatively new and resources are extraordinarily scarce, has recently
received special attention. In 1988–1989 alone, the Division of Narcotic Drugs
helped to establish testing labs in Benin, Côte d'Ivoire, Ghana, Guinea, Kenya,
Mauritania, Senegal, Sierra Leone, and Tanzania. In a five-month period in late
1988 and early 1989, the INCB sent missions to fourteen African countries.

Such regional programs represent an area in which the United Nations can make a notable contribution at relatively low cost. Particularly in Africa—where both funds and experience are unusually scarce—international assistance may greatly accelerate learning by national drug enforcement authorities, and regional cooperation may significantly increase the impact of funds spent. In Latin America, however, greater national experience, the existence of better-established regional and subregional programs, and the availability of U.S. assistance all suggest that the UN role is likely to be especially minor.

Specialized Agencies and Other
International Organizations

In addition to the units discussed above, international organizations exist that are formally independent of but affiliated with the United Nations. Despite their institutional and financial independence, these specialized agencies—which deal with various social, economic, and technical issues—are part of the broader UN system. Many have significant drug control programs.

The World Health Organization (WHO) is active in a variety of areas dealing with the health effects of drug abuse. For example, it has a major project under way on AIDS transmission among drug users and a training program for primary health care workers on identifying and dealing with drug abuse. The International Institute for Health Studies and Information, a WHO research center, is cooperating with the United Nations Interregional Crime and Justice Research Institute on a major multinational information campaign, STOP DROGA, for schools, the workplace, and the media. In 1990 WHO reorganized its various programs of technical assistance. It is also beginning to give greater attention to demand reduction in its work. WHO also provides technical assistance to the INCB and DND concerning scheduling of substances under the 1971 convention and reporting systems.

The United Nations Educational, Scientific, and Cultural Organization (UNESCO) has recently expanded its work in the field of drug information and education. In 1989–1990, for example, it provided technical support for UNFDAC drug education programs in Ghana, Senegal, and Myanmar (Burma) and launched new education programs in Ghana and Senegal based on the findings of epidemiological surveys of emerging patterns of drug abuse in these countries. In summer of 1990, it began work on a regional education center in Quito, Ecuador. UNESCO has also become increasingly active in programs of professional training. For example, it recently obtained a contract to train drug abuse education workers at the University of La Plata in Argentina.

The International Labor Organization has long been concerned with the problem of drugs in the workplace. It has also recently begun to expand its focus to include drug rehabilitation programs. This involves not only the issue of drugs in the workplace but also recognition of the important role employment programs often play in rehabilitation.

Specialized agencies in the transport sector have also become increasingly active in drug control work. The International Civil Aviation Organization is involved in programs to reduce drug use by airline crews and to curb the use of air transport by drug traffickers. The International Maritime Organization has similar programs for water-based transit. In addition, the Universal Postal Union (UPU) has been giving increased attention to the problem of the use of the mails in drug trafficking. In the past three years, the UPU has sponsored regional seminars for postal officials in Asia and the Pacific, Latin America, and Africa.

In addition to the specialized agencies formally affiliated with the United Nations, several other international organizations are active in the field of drug control. Perhaps most prominent is the International Criminal Police Organization (Interpol), which has played a major role in providing information and coordinating national efforts to deal with the international drug trade. The Customs Cooperation Council has played a similar role in sharing information among and coordinating the activities of national customs officials.

A New Structure for UN
Drug Abuse Control Activities

Even this brief review indicates that the range of drug control activities undertaken within the UN system is extensive. Furthermore, international action is increasing in response to growing national and international concern. This is likely to continue for at least the next few years. In light of both the scope and growth of its activities, in 1990 the United Nations decided to centralize and integrate some of its principal drug control activities in order to increase their efficiency.

A group of fifteen international experts met in Vienna in mid-1990 to develop a plan to integrate and upgrade the drug control activities of the Vienna branch of the UN Secretariat, which has responsibility for drugs and other social and humanitarian issues. In December 1990 the General Assembly approved the creation of a United Nations International Drug Control Programme, similar in concept to the United Nations Development Programme and the United Nations Environment Programme. The resulting reorganization began in early 1991.[25]

The work of the Division of Narcotic Drugs, the Secretariat and the International Narcotics Control Board, and the United Nations Fund for Drug Abuse Control has been united under a single head. Activities will now be divided more explicitly on a functional basis in the areas of treaty implementation, policy implementation and research (including both repository services, such as reports and statistics, and substantive services, such as training and laboratory services), and operational activities.

These changes do not directly affect the other parts of the UN system that deal with drug control issues. The hope, however, is that centralizing and upgrading the Vienna Secretariat will facilitate liaison and increase the level of coordination. In addition, the increase in internal administrative efficiency should help to make the resources of the United Nations more readily available to states.

Administrative reform should help the United Nations do more with existing resources. It cannot, however, address vital areas of new work that require additional resources. The 1990–1991 reforms do not increase resources devoted to drug control. In fact, the resolution establishing the programme explicitly reaffirms the practice of funding operational activities (especially UNFDAC) from extrabudgetary resources.[26] The only hope offered is the likelihood that the administrative upgrading will better position the United Nations International Drug Control Programme to make future demands for more funds.

Assessing the Global Drug Control Regime

What has the United Nations accomplished in the field of drug control? What can be done to strengthen the global drug control regime? What is likely to be done? The Comprehensive Multidisciplinary Outline; the Declaration and Plan of Action of the 1990 special session; and the 1961, 1971, and 1988 conventions provide a sound normative framework for international action. The United Nations has also been relatively effective in the related areas of publicity and promotion. Although cynics might dismiss this as mere rhetoric, a substantively sound and widely shared consensus on basic goals and approaches is essential to effective action.

The UN system has also been relatively effective in providing information, advice, and technical support. This has been especially important in Third World countries, most often in Africa, that have only recently faced problems of drug abuse and trafficking. These countries have typically started with little or no drug law enforcement infrastructure. At the same time, their resources are generally scant, and their sensitivity to intrusive bilateral assistance is usually high. The UN system—especially UNFDAC, DND, and INCB—has been able to provide needed assistance with no political strings.

The United Nations has also begun to take significant steps to coordinate its activities in the field of drug control. This is important not only for the fiscal efficiencies it is hoped will result but even more because it is now generally recognized that success is possible only through a coordinated multisectoral effort. It is still much too early to tell whether the Vienna Secretariat, the Administrative Committee on Coordination, and other coordinating bodies will be able to tame the strong centrifugal forces that exist within UN bureaucracies. The effort seems serious, however, and the outcome is crucial.

In the areas of norm creation and coordination, there is no real alternative to the United Nations. Bilateral and regional assistance may supplement UN aid. In some cases, such as the Americas, bilateral aid exceeds multilateral aid. Nonetheless, there is always the need for a neutral source of assistance available to all states more or less equally, largely without political conditions. The real problem faced by proponents of stronger procedures in the global drug control regime is that they lack sufficient political support from states. The simple fact is that most states do not attach sufficient priority to international action against drugs to relinquish much freedom of action or political authority.

Consider the one area of unquestionable UN success—the control of licit manufacture and trade. The authority states transfer to the INCB is in very narrow areas that are of little or no political sensitivity: A few pharmaceutical firms must be regulated according to international norms, a few products must be traded according to specified rules, and certain information must be exchanged. So long as this is done, states do not even have to deal directly with the international supervisory machinery except to file their estimates and statistical reports. In return for these rather modest restrictions, states receive the significant benefit of effective control over and free access to potentially dangerous drugs for medical and scientific purposes.

By contrast, eliminating illicit production is likely to threaten very powerful political and economic interests as well as impose an economic burden on a large number of small producers. And effective international action against drug trafficking would require relinquishing control over parts of the national law enforcement machinery. Virtually no state is likely to find this acceptable, given the centrality of the police power to the very idea of sovereignty. The most that can be hoped for is that a combination of promotion, technical assistance, and coordinating activities can foster more effective cooperation among national authorities—or at best regional agreements (which may appear less threatening, given that one's authority is transferred along with that of one's neighbors to an authority that is not so distant from the state).

We thus should expect the global drug control regime to remain restricted principally to promotion and assistance activities. Assistance in the areas of forensic science and law enforcement can have a significant impact in specific countries. Information and resources in the area of prevention and treatment may help some countries to lessen the damage of drug abuse. If greater regional cooperation can indeed be generated, some progress might even be achieved in reducing rather than simply relocating the drug traffic. A large increase in resources devoted to income-substituting rural development programs might even make a dent in production.

Promotion regimes such as the global drug control regime can help states to discover and define areas of common interest, as has been done in the case of drugs. They also provide a context for negotiating the terms of cooperative action, a process that is ongoing in the global drug control regime. Promotion regimes, however, cannot assure that action will be taken. That still rests on the willingness of states to bear the financial and political costs—a willingness that is not apparent.

In sum, we can look forward to significant international contributions to the war on drugs in those areas that involve ideas, information, and knowledge. There is also some reason to hope for successes that rest on coordinating national action, particularly at the regional level. But the problem of drugs cannot be solved by international organizations alone. The United Nations and related agencies are likely to continue to do their part. That part, however, can only be a supporting one.

Notes

1. Stephen D. Krasner, "Structural Causes and Regime Consequences: Regimes as Intervening Variables," *International Organization* 36, no. 2 (Spring 1982): 185.

2. Within each general type, as defined in the first instance by decision-making procedures, regimes can be further differentiated by the strength and coherence of their norms.

3. Stephen D. Walsh, "Some Aspects of International Drug Control and Illicit Drug Trafficking," in Dennis Rowe, ed., *International Drug Trafficking* (Chicago: Office of International Criminal Justice, 1988), 101.

4. Bertil A. Renborg, *International Drug Control: A Study of International Administration By and Through the League of Nations* (Washington, D.C.: Carnegie Endowment for International Peace, 1947), 16.

5. Renborg, *International Drug Control*, 97.

6. S. D. Stein, *International Diplomacy, State Administrators, and Narcotics Control: The Origins of a Social Problem* (Aldershot, England, and Brookfield, Vt.: Gower, 1985), 5.

7. The growing concern over drugs and the gradual expansion of the focus of the UN response can be traced in a series of resolutions going back at least to General Assembly resolution 35/195 (1980), running through the call for a coordinated system-wide plan of action in resolution 44/141 (1989) and the February 1990 special session, to the administrative reforms approved at the end of 1990 (A/RES/45/179).

8. The CMO is included as Part A of the report of the conference, available as UN Document A/CONF.133/12 (Sales No. E.87.I.18).

9. This is defined in Article 1(g) as "the technique of allowing illicit or suspect consignment . . . or substances substituted for them, to pass out of, through, or into the territory of one or more countries, with the knowledge and under the supervision of their competent authorities, with a view to identifying persons involved in the commission of offenses."

10. A/RES/S-17/2.

11. A/S-17/PV.1, 27.

12. The designation of the decade 1991–2000 as the United Nations Decade Against Drug Abuse represents a major symbolic commitment to continued aggressive activity to assure maximum awareness of the problem. This goes well beyond the 1987 decision designating June 26 as the International Day Against Drug Abuse and Illicit Trafficking.

13. A/S-17/PV.1, 9, 13.

14. A/S-17/PV.2, 34.

15. Total UN spending for drugs, including by specialized agencies such as WHO and units such as UNFDAC that are funded through extrabudgetary (voluntary) contributions, was just over $100 million. Even this figure is scarcely less inadequate.

16. A/S-17/3.

17. E/1990/18, para. 5.

18. E/1990/39 and Add. 1.

19. E/INCB/1989/1, paras. 31–35.

20. E/1990/39, para. 85.

21. E/1990/39, para. 164.

22. E/CN.7/1990/7.

23. E/1990/39, paras. 83, 97, and Annex I.

24. E/1990/39, para. 28.

25. The recommendation of the expert group that the Commission on Narcotic Drugs be given a greater policy role, however, was not approved by the General Assembly.

26. A/RES/45/179, para. 13.

20

The Organization of American States
and Control of Dangerous Drugs

Abraham F. Lowenthal

Today's Western Hemisphere urgently requires effective multilateral cooperation to reduce the high costs and corrosive consequences caused by the illegal production, trafficking, and consumption of dangerous drugs. The Organization of American States is a venerable but somewhat atrophied institution that has outlived its original rationale and badly needs a rejuvenating mission. The potential match is evident, although consummating and then sustaining it may be difficult. That is my main argument.

Facing the Narcotics Challenge:
The Need for International Cooperation

As this book shows clearly, the drug enterprise is transnational in character and scope. Only a small share of illegal narcotics is produced, traded, and consumed entirely within the borders of single nations. In the main, narcotics traffic involves a long international chain—including those who grow, process, transport, smuggle, distribute, and retail the drugs as well as those who handle the financial flows, relations with law enforcement agencies, and the paramilitary aspects of the trade. Indeed, the drug enterprise has become increasingly global as efforts to counter it in one nation lead to new production, processing, or distribution facilities in others and as the financial transactions needed to "launder" illicit proceeds have become more complex and far-flung.

To date, most international efforts against dangerous drugs, especially in the Western Hemisphere, have proceeded on the basis of bilateral agreements between the United States and nations in which drug production or trafficking is important. Through a mixture of incentives and sanctions—conditioning other aspects of bilateral relations on periodic certification by U.S. authorities that Latin American nations are complying sincerely and effectively with antinarcotics programs—the United States has sought to secure concrete actions by individual countries against specific aspects of the drug trade.

Notwithstanding some limited progress, bilateral programs to combat dangerous drugs have proved to be fraught with difficulty. Issues of sovereignty, autonomy, and national identity are inevitably posed when one nation (particularly a large and powerful one) tries—without intermediaries, ambiguity, or even the pretense of collective action—to achieve specific compliance of another on internal matters.

A few examples illustrate the complexities posed by bilateral antidrug programs: conflicts between the United States and Colombia regarding extradition of accused drug traffickers and between the United States and Peru regarding counterinsurgency strategy in narcotics-growing regions; tensions with Mexico over alleged complicity by Mexican officials in the drug trade and even in the murder of a U.S. drug enforcement official as well as frictions concerning the extraterritorial reach of U.S. law enforcement authorities against Mexican citizens; and the intensive clash between the United States and Panama that culminated with the December 1989 U.S. invasion and capture of strongman Manuel Noriega. In each of these cases, antinarcotics considerations and other bilateral issues came into conflict, complicating overall relationships.

In Chapter 19, Jack Donnelly discusses the efforts of the United Nations to develop universal international norms and to supervise the licit trade in narcotic drugs and psychotropic substances; he argues persuasively that the UN role in combatting the illegal drug trade is significant at the level of norms and broad procedures. The UN conception of the international narcotics problem and of its own potential role has slowly expanded over the past decade, culminating with the 1988 UN Convention Against Illicit Traffic in Narcotic Drugs and Psychotropic Substances. As Donnelly points out, however, although the convention and related UN agreements are important exercises in consciousness-raising, all indications so far are that the member states will not provide the United Nations with either the funds or the authority required to play a major direct role in reducing the production, trade, or consumption of illicit drugs. Universal programs, worked out in the UN context, are bound to be longer on norms and rhetoric than on concrete measures and sustained implementation. And the UN role, as Donnelly suggests, is likely to be "particularly peripheral" in the Americas because of a general UN tendency in most circumstances to defer to regional and subregional international organizations.

If effective international efforts to reduce the drug menace are to be forged in the Americas, therefore, they probably must be conducted on a regional and multilateral basis through programs involving both the United States and key Latin American nations directly involved in some aspect of the narcotics enterprise. Multilateral programs on a regional basis must be close enough to the problems to allow for specific and detailed projects but should also avoid the dangers of unilateral imposition.

Fortunately, prospects for inter-American cooperation against dangerous drugs have improved in recent years, for four main reasons. First, the schism between drug-producing nations and the United States, which widened in the early and mid-1980s because of the heavy-handed U.S. certification approach, began to be reduced during the late 1980s as it became clear that Latin American nations themselves would be hurt increasingly by the drug trade and as parallel recognition grew in the

United States that supply-side solutions alone would never work. A regional consensus has been emerging in support of coordinated and simultaneous efforts to reduce both supply and demand. The tendency toward mutual recrimination has consequently been reduced.[1]

Second, significant decreases since the mid-1980s in the number of people consuming drugs in the United States have provided a basis for some hope. It now seems more likely than appeared to be the case ten years ago that demand-reduction efforts can ultimately work and that supply-reduction programs can also begin to become more effective; they will not simply be undermined by the "balloon effect" by which reducing production in one place inevitably means an increase somewhere else.

Third, the United States and several countries in Latin America have begun to show that they are ready to devote substantial priority, including expanded financial and political resources, to drug control efforts. Public opinion in both the United States and Latin America has defined the drug menace as a major concern in the minds of voters and the media. Budgets for the antinarcotics campaign have increased, even in a period of general stringency and reductions.

Fourth, the region can count on some functioning institutional frameworks to structure and reinforce the incipient impulse toward multilateral cooperation. It is for this reason that the possibility that the Organization of American States may revive in the 1990s is so relevant.

The Inter-American System in a World of Change

More than forty years after it was established in the early years of the cold war, the Organization of American States (OAS) shows some indications that it may be reborn under a new sign. Virtually moribund during the 1980s, in the early 1990s the OAS is emitting limited but encouraging signs of life and could come to play an expanding role in a changing world.

The organization's first birth was based on a strategic bargain between the United States and the countries of Latin America. Forged after World War II, it reflected the experience of the several previous decades as well as the cold war preoccupations of that historic moment. The United States in effect undertook to refrain from further unilateral interventions in Latin America and instead to subject itself to multilateral procedures for dealing with regional security concerns. In exchange, Latin America promised support to prevent rival powers—in particular, the international Communist movement led by the Soviet Union—from obtaining a strategic foothold in the Americas. This fundamental deal was embodied in the Rio treaty of 1947 called the Inter-American Treaty of Reciprocal Assistance, which committed all nations of the hemisphere to cooperate in response to an extracontinental military threat. The primary aims of the United States and the American nations were certainly different, but they seemed complementary and compatible. The United

States sought mostly to mobilize Latin Americans for cold war purposes, whereas Latin Americans sought primarily to constrain the United States.

However logical this arrangement seemed in diplomatic theory, it soon began to disintegrate in practice. Except during the Cuban Missile Crisis of 1962, the United States and the Latin American countries rarely agreed on what constituted serious threats to hemispheric security and on what was required to combat them. Divergent views emerged, particularly regarding the nature and extent of the threat posed by the leftist movements that challenged the retrograde social, economic, and political order in many countries.[2] Washington frequently responded to these movements with a hostility most Latin Americans could not fathom, let alone support. The result was a new series of unilateral U.S. interventions, covert and overt: against the Jacobo Arbenz government in Guatemala in 1954, against Fidel Castro's Cuban government in the early 1960s, in the Dominican Republic in 1965, against Salvador Allende in Chile in the 1970s, and against left-nationalist movements in Grenada and Nicaragua during the 1980s. And in the one case in which an extrahemispheric power actually fought against a Latin American nation—when Great Britain sent its forces to the South Atlantic to beat back Argentina's invasion of the disputed Malvinas–Falkland Islands in 1982—the United States bypassed the Rio treaty procedures and sided with Great Britain.

Not surprisingly, the OAS languished and began to atrophy. At least following the Dominican intervention and at an accelerated pace after the Malvinas fiasco, the organization lost stature and significance. It played no important role in coping with the hemisphere's two main problems of the 1980s—the region-wide debt crisis and Central America's civil wars. Once a posting that attracted top-notch diplomats and ambassadors with political clout, the OAS instead became a parking lot for mediocre representatives. Member states—the United States prominent among them—reduced their financial contribution to the organization's budget, thus further crippling its capacity.

A vicious cycle developed because many of the organization's most talented personnel and its various programs were too skimpily funded to be effective. The central administrative structure became increasingly top-heavy in relation to an ever-diminishing set of programs. To an increasing extent, the OAS was reduced to a beautiful old building and a disgruntled staff, both in desperate need of a mission to fulfill. With the decline in the late 1980s of the cold war struggle that had originally provoked its creation, the organization might have been expected to expire.

Instead, the Organization of American States may be gaining a new lease on life.[3] It is too early to be certain because decaying institutions revive only unevenly and uncertainly, if at all; but there are some signs that the United States and several other member governments are trying to reverse the organization's decline. First-class professionals—people such as Heraldo Muñoz of Chile, Luigi Einaudi of the United States, and Samuel Oñate of Mexico—have been working closely to fashion effective consultative procedures and to design action programs. The U.S. government, reversing the aggressive unilateralism of the Reagan years, has begun to pay outstanding contributions to the OAS budget that had been in arrears, has strengthened the U.S. mission to the organization, and has indicated its disposition to rely on the OAS—both by sending Secretary of State James Baker to participate in key OAS debates and by periodic verbal pronouncements. The significant role assigned to the organization in preparing and monitoring the 1990 election in Nicaragua and in several subsequent elections (particularly in Haiti) has further enhanced its standing.

By all accounts, the OAS General Assembly held in June 1991 in Santiago, Chile, was the most productive and significant in many years. A conceptual and political breakthrough occurred in Santiago when the members approved an automatic procedure to convene hemispheric foreign ministers to respond within ten days to a military coup or other interruption of a legitimate elected government. Member governments were unwilling to commit themselves or the organization in advance to any specific course of action in response to unconstitutional changes of government, but for the first time they did enshrine the principle that it is the organization's expected business to *act* to protect democratic consolidation. Beyond this welcome accord, the assembly was noteworthy for its constructive focus on examining a number of other shared Western Hemisphere concerns: how to curb drug traffic, protect the environment, curtail the trade of deadly weapons, and promote expanded regional trade and investment.

Three converging trends help account in broad terms for the incipient revival of the OAS. First, there is more underlying community in the Americas today than has existed in many years. Throughout the hemisphere, as indeed in much of the rest of the world, broad consensus has been emerging on the desirability and appeal of constitutional democratic politics and market-oriented economic reforms. Just a few years ago, self-proclaimed "vanguards" on the Left and "guardians" on the Right openly questioned and criticized the democratic idea, but it is now widely embraced in almost every country and sector. Statist economic approaches have also been discredited, and debates on economic policy now take place within much narrower parameters than used to be the case. There is also widespread and easy accord in Latin America that subregional cooperation is desirable and that feasible partnerships with the United States should be pursued.

Second, in both Latin America and the United States there is a more specific disposition to cooperate multilaterally. During the 1980s many Latin American nations began turning toward what they call *concertación*—that is, improved consultation and cooperative actions on issues such as debt strategy and containing the Central American wars—most often in effect opposing U.S. policy. The Contadora process, the Cartagena initiative on debt negotiations, and especially the formation of the Rio group of eight (later seven) Latin American democracies were all important steps toward regional multilateral undertakings. With the cold war's end, Washington is becoming increasingly receptive to Latin American perspectives and concerns and is far more open to multilateral approaches than was the case during the Reagan years. In an era when burden-sharing is increasingly the name of the broad international game, multilateralism within the Western Hemisphere has a new appeal for both South and North.

Third, changing substantive agendas throughout the Americas have made multilateral cooperation much more important. The key issues on the minds of government leaders and regular citizens in every country today are primarily transnational: trade and investment, migration, drugs, the environment, and public health. It is increasingly clear that no one nation, no matter how powerful, can solve these problems alone; collective action across national boundaries is required. The question is not whether Western Hemisphere nations should cooperate but how best to do so, taking different national interests and prevalent asymmetries into account.

The OAS and the Control of Dangerous Drugs

The control of dangerous drugs is a quintessential example of the new regional agenda and is thus one of the key challenges testing whether the Organization of American States can be made more effective. This is a serious problem of deep concern throughout the hemisphere, is international in scope and character, and requires a sustained multilateral response; yet, no international body is currently meeting the need.

Since the mid-1980s, the OAS has been slowly gearing itself up to play a growing role in combatting the narcotics trade. In 1986 the organization adopted the Program of Action of Rio de Janeiro, actually more an agreement on goals and principles than an active plan for cooperative activities. The Rio program registered regional agreement that the narcotics trade threatened the hemisphere's socioeconomic development as well as its democratic institutions and called for steps to reduce the demand for drugs, prevent drug abuse, and combat unlawful production of and trafficking in drugs.

The Rio program was important in two respects: It was the first international recognition by all the member countries that they share responsibility to control each link in the drug-trafficking chain, and it was the first acknowledgment by the U.S. government—contradicting previous assertions—that equal attention must be given to reducing demand and supply. But all the specific actions recommended were to be taken by individual nations; no effective process for multilateral cooperation was actually proposed. The only practical recommendation for regional cooperation was the suggestion, duly adopted at the next OAS General Assembly (in Guatemala later that year), that an Inter-American Drug Abuse Control Commission (CICAD) be established to monitor the drug problem and the performance of OAS member states in confronting it.

CICAD's formation was accompanied by grandiloquent rhetoric—"The Declaration of Guatemala: The American Alliance Against Drug Trafficking"—but the commission was given little to work with in terms of budget and staff. CICAD's initial capacity was modest—a staff of thirteen and an overall annual budget of about $1 million—and its accomplishments were correspondingly limited. During its first four years, CICAD mainly developed normative goals, collected various forms of relevant data, designed some educational guidelines, organized a few training seminars and workshops, and contributed a small amount to improved consciousness in Latin America of the dimensions of the drug plague.

By 1990, however, CICAD was showing increasing potential to move beyond data-gathering and consciousness-raising. One major CICAD report proposed model legislation and regulations for the control of precursor chemicals essential for narcotics production. Other projects, at varying stages of implementation, emphasize education for drug prevention and the exchange of information about law enforcement agencies. Although CICAD still operates within strict policy and budgetary constraints, it is beginning to acquire a reputation for professional competence and commitment in confronting the drug trade, and it has raised several million dollars—mainly from other international organizations and European governments—to undertake action programs in five priority areas: legal development, education for prevention, community mobilization, data-gathering, and public information.

Enhancing the OAS Role

A question facing the OAS and its member states today is whether the organization can build on CICAD's experience, competence, and growing reputation and play a more central part in the antinarcotics campaign. At least nine areas have been discussed—in the report of the Inter-American Commission on Drug Policy, in CICAD documents, and elsewhere—as possible ways for the OAS to enhance its role in the effort to control dangerous drugs.

1. With cooperation from the United Nations, Interpol, and the Drug Enforcement Administration (DEA), the organization has been devising and encouraging member nations to adopt and apply uniform regulations and export licensing requirements for precursor chemicals. Mechanisms have been developed for consultation and cooperation among CICAD and the Commission of European Communities as well as the DEA.

2. On the instructions of the OAS General Assembly, CICAD has been compiling data on the traffic in small arms and that trade's relationship with illegal drug trafficking. Although no further OAS mandate exists on this issue, the OAS could push for uniform export licensing requirements for firearms and other weapons throughout the Americas.

3. CICAD has already made a good deal of progress in developing model regulations, in line with Article V of the 1988 UN convention, for regional cooperation to prevent money laundering. Concepts developed in the U.S. legal system—for example, the forfeiture of "substitute assets" if illicit profits have been made inaccessible—have been accepted by experts from other OAS member nations as the basis for proposed regulations being readied for formal recommendation to CICAD and then to member states.[4]

4. The OAS could contribute to strengthening the hemisphere's judicial systems by creating regional and subregional commissions to deal with such questions as the status and security of judges, protecting courts against corruption, and extradition issues. Some progress has been registered in establishing programs in this realm, particularly in Central America.

5. The organization could do much more to help structure and facilitate international technical assistance in order to integrate projects for drug education, prevention, and treatment with broad social service programs and to stimulate effective cooperative research programs analyzing the impact of such projects.

6. The organization could work to foster a hemisphere-wide law enforcement training strategy to improve coordination, the exchange of information, and the general professionalism of law enforcement efforts.

7. Building on prior proposals by Brazil and more recently by Brazil and Mexico together, the OAS could promote adoption of one of the key recommendations of the Inter-American Commission on Drug Policy: that the countries of the hemisphere agree to confiscate and monetize the assets seized from drug trafficking and to devote the proceeds to antidrug programs—including a common regional fund for education, prevention, and treatment.

8. The OAS should commission careful studies to determine whether a hemispheric or perhaps subregional tribunal for drug crimes might be warranted as a means of countering particularly heinous activities national legal systems have had great difficulty in handling.

9. Careful study could also be conducted under the auspices of the OAS as to whether a multinational antinarcotic military force—presumably less likely than national forces to be infiltrated, corrupted, or intimidated by drug lords—could be made feasible, at least in the Caribbean region.

It is by no means clear whether the Organization of American States has the political clout and institutional strength to make important contributions in all these areas. Years of inattention—or worse—from the United States and several other member governments have unquestionably weakened the OAS, in fact and in reputation. But the evident need for regional cooperation on issues such as controlling dangerous drugs reminds us that if the Organization of American States did not already exist, it would likely now be invented.

Freed of the cold war visions and concerns that gave it birth but flawed it from the start, the Organization of American States may have a constructive and important role to play in the years to come. To succeed, the organization will need to count on political support from the United States and other member governments, budget resources, talented and committed personnel, and sustained efforts over several years. None of these necessary conditions can yet be assumed, but the cost of failure by the countries of the hemisphere to confront the drug trade together would be very high. With a clear common concern, some past habits of cooperation, and a framework for enhancing them, improved inter-American efforts to control dangerous drugs should be both feasible and efficacious.

Notes

1. See Report of the Inter-American Dialogue, *The Americas in 1989: Consensus for Action* (Lanham, Md.: University Press of America, 1989); and Michael Dziedzic, "Emerging Drug Control Regime in the Americas: Prospects and Limitations," in Scott B. MacDonald and Bruce Zagaris, eds., *International Drug Control Handbook* (Westport, Conn.: Greenwood Publishing Group, Inc., 1992).

2. See Richard J. Bloomfield and Gregory F. Treverton, eds., *Alternatives to Intervention: A New U.S.–Latin American Security Relationship* (Boulder, Colo.: Lynne Rienner, 1990).

3. For a fuller discussion, see Richard J. Bloomfield and Abraham F. Lowenthal, "Inter-American Institutions in a Time of Change," *International Journal* 45, no. 4 (Autumn 1990): 867–888.

4. See Charles A. Intriago, "Money Laundering Forfeiture Laws," *North-South* 2 (August-September 1991): 38–39.

21

Unilateralism and Bilateralism

María Celia Toro

This chapter focuses on the possibilities for cooperation between Mexico and the United States in fighting drug production and trafficking in the Western Hemisphere. The U.S.-Mexican relationship merits attention not only because it offers the longest history of bilateral collaboration against this common problem but also—and more important—because Mexico's efforts likely illustrate the maximum possible commitment for any country in Latin America.[1]

Over the past sixty years, Mexico and the United States have signed an extensive array of joint agreements to promote cooperation against cultivation and commerce in narcotic drugs.[2] During the same period, the U.S. government has led most international initiatives aimed at narcotics control. With the largest drug market in the world, the United States most consistently promotes prohibition as a primary policy instrument to curb narcotics consumption. Most countries, Mexico included, support this approach and have followed the U.S. lead in the design and implementation of antidrug policies.

The United States regards Mexico as a key country in the effort to reduce the supply of drugs to market. Over the past two decades, Mexico has received both the largest amount of financial assistance for antidrug efforts from the U.S. State Department and the largest number of out-of-country agents from the Drug Enforcement Administration (DEA) of any country in its territory. It has often been the most important source of marijuana and heroin for U.S. consumers and in the 1980s was the most important transit point for cocaine. It is the Latin American country that has devoted the greatest resources to curb production and trafficking, and according to quantitative indicators, it has achieved the greatest success in these endeavors.

It could be argued that the United States and Mexico have made great progress in controlling this dangerous market and that their collaboration represents both the possibilities and the limitations of bilateral cooperation on this issue. What can be said about the U.S.-Mexican experience? What are the prospects for future collaboration in the realm of narcotics?

Unilateral Policies

Given the multilateral nature of the worldwide drug problem, unilateral policy initiatives—thus far the most common—are condemned to failure. By unilateral policies I mean those that are designed by a single government and launched independently of any agreement with another country. By now, most governments have learned the limits and costs of these programs, but the negative consequences of their ineffectiveness are often overlooked. These negative consequences result because unilateral programs are wrongly evaluated in terms of their impact on the U.S. drug market. In this light, collaboration between governments to stop illicit trade in narcotics has been conflictive in the past and will probably remain that way in the future.

There are at least three types of limitations on international cooperation: Antidrug policies have been designed to reach unattainable goals; law enforcement, the most important policy instrument, is by definition a national prerogative; and national priorities do not necessarily coincide. Let us examine these issues in turn.

Defining the Goals

U.S. antidrug policy is based on the belief that a reduction in the availability of drugs (marijuana, heroin, and cocaine) will lead to an escalation of market prices and that in response, consumers will forego drug use and abuse. Efforts to curb domestic drug consumption in this manner have naturally led to a search for international collaboration. "No matter how hard we fight the problem of drug abuse at home," in the words of one U.S. policy statement, "we cannot make really significant progress unless we succeed in gaining cooperation from foreign governments, because many of the serious drugs of abuse originate in foreign countries. Thus, our capability to deal with supplies of drugs available in the United States depends strongly on the interest and capability of foreign governments in drug control."[3] Conceived in this manner, the task has been to enlist the cooperation of foreign governments in three areas: eradication of crops, interdiction of drugs bound for the U.S. market, and "immobilization" of traffickers.

As for Latin American governments, most were forced by their own political imperatives—rather than by insistent U.S. diplomacy—to take action against production and traffic in drugs. Today, most countries in the Western Hemisphere are devoting precious resources to efforts to suppress the drug market. Despite the magnitude of these commitments, they have resulted in complete failure. The markets for marijuana, heroin, and cocaine are substantially larger and more skillfully organized than they were when these policies were launched.

Nor have U.S. goals been advanced. The street price of these drugs in the U.S. market has not risen uniformly or dramatically: Marijuana prices have gone up, at least in regional markets, but cocaine and heroin prices have tended to stay fairly level. In fact, there is little reason to believe Latin American governments can affect the price of drugs in the U.S. market and thus dissuade U.S. consumers from taking them.

Given the power of demand, legal prohibition makes the drug business unusually lucrative. In view of this permanent incentive for participation in the illegal market, eradication policies—which still constitute a significant part of Latin American antidrug policies—have proven to be far from cost-efficient. Achievements simply do not justify expenditures. One additional unintended result has been to sustain the wholesale prices for illicit drugs. Another has been to encourage the formation of organized drug rings ready to corrupt or kill law enforcement agents in order to keep their business intact.

Recent efforts to immobilize drug traffickers stemmed essentially from the failure throughout Latin America in the late 1970s and early 1980s to eliminate or curtail the market through eradication and interdiction programs. Peter Reuter has argued convincingly that drug control strategies outside the United States will never be able to increase significantly the price of drugs for U.S. consumers because export prices represent less than 5 percent of the final price on U.S. streets.[4] The Mexican case clearly illustrates this general point.

Antidrug resources have grown substantially over the last decade in Mexico. In the mid-1970s only 5,000 soldiers and around 350 members of the Federal Judicial Police were enrolled in the country's Permanent Campaign against drugs.[5] Upon taking office in late 1988, Carlos Salinas de Gortari created a new law enforcement agency with 1,200 officers dedicated exclusively to the arrest of drug traffickers. The campaign against drugs thus came to involve one-third of the nation's defense budget, one-fourth of the Mexican military (approximately 25,000 soldiers), the largest air fleet of its kind in Latin America (mostly helicopters and light aircraft for aerial spraying and transportation[6]), and 60 percent of the attorney general's budget. Compared with only $20 million (U.S.) in 1987, this same office spent more than $60 million on antidrug programs in 1989, and the U.S. government contributed an additional $14 million.[7]

Narcotics eradication and confiscation figures have grown accordingly. Eradication figures have sometimes become the subject of loud and acrimonious controversy between the United States and Mexico over what some U.S. authorities claim are major inconsistencies in the figures. According to responsible estimates, however, an effective eradication campaign in Mexico would be capable of destroying no more than 40 percent of the annual national output; at the same time, it takes only 15 percent of Mexico's total production of marijuana to satisfy 35 percent of U.S. annual consumption of this drug.[8] Eradication of poppy plants in Mexico is even more unlikely to reduce the availability of heroin. Destruction of opium poppy over the last decade has not modified the relatively stable market of 500,000 heroin addicts in the United States. Coca leaves are not grown in Mexico, so there can be no question of eradication within Mexico.

Confiscation figures also tend to demonstrate the impossibility of significantly reducing the drug market through current enforcement policies. In the case of marijuana, where interdiction might have some plausible chance of affecting prices in the United States, the Mexican government confiscated more than one thousand tons in 1990—an impressive improvement if one considers that only four hundred tons were captured in 1988, which had been the peak year for marijuana seizures. Even if marijuana cigarettes were made more expensive through these crashes on the market, demand for this good is highly inelastic, as Mark Kleiman has shown.[9] A 100 percent increase in the retail price for marijuana would have set the price in 1985 at around fifty cents per joint; every U.S. adult or adolescent would still have had the money to buy one.

Let us take the case of cocaine. Again, seizures have grown dramatically in Mexico. Mexican authorities seized only one-third of a ton of cocaine in 1982–1983; this figure jumped to thirteen tons in 1988[10] and to almost ninety tons in 1990. Nevertheless, the retail price of cocaine in the United States dropped systematically throughout the 1980s. By stopping transshipments of cocaine the Mexican government cannot possibly affect retail prices in the United States simply because, as Peter Reuter has demonstrated, "fully 99 percent of the price of the drug when sold on the streets in the United States is accounted for by payments to people who distribute it."[11]

Increasingly impatient for meaningful reductions in the drug supply, the Reagan administration decided to take a more active part in the "war on drugs" by more than doubling the budget for law enforcement between 1981 and 1988 and by concentrating the bulk of these new resources on interdiction programs.[12] This unilateral policy has yielded impressive results in terms of the absolute quantity of drugs seized; on a relative scale, however, this represents less than 5 percent of the total amount imported by the United States every year.

If the ultimate goal in fighting the drug market is to affect the levels of drug consumption in the United States, or in Mexico for that matter, it will never be attained. Supporters of current policy claim that the real purpose is not to suppress the market but rather to make drugs difficult to obtain and thus to prevent the market from growing. In the absence of enforcement, the argument goes, the number of users would be much higher. According to this logic, which rests on a purely hypothetical foundation, temporary drug shortages provide a "window of opportunity" for education and prevention programs to do their job—hence the need to bolster drug-fighting capabilities in drug-producing and drug-transit countries with U.S. support and, if possible, with U.S. participation.

Law Enforcement: A National Prerogative

As part of its renewed campaign against drugs, the Reagan administration began to increase pressure on drug-producing and drug-transit countries and to bolster the U.S. capacity for extraterritorial assertion of its criminal laws. Toward this end the

Reagan administration introduced important changes in U.S. drug laws—most notably through the Anti-Drug Abuse Act of 1986—and gave narcotics issues higher priority on the international agenda. By resorting to the threat of linkage strategies, the U.S. government came up with a "certification" practice to evaluate other countries' performances. Thus, the Anti-Drug Abuse Act conditions U.S. financial assistance, positive votes in multilateral lending institutions, and trade preferences on cooperation against drug trafficking. Based more on political judgments than on technical assessments, the so-called "certification process" has become a source of considerable irritation for Latin American governments and societies that do not understand why supposedly cooperative endeavors should be judged unilaterally by the country that created the entire problem in the first place. Furthermore, the law considers it a crime to manufacture or distribute drugs outside the United States with the intention of exporting them to U.S. territory. This clause provides the basis for federal grand jury indictments of foreign nationals, which has opened the door to many conflicts over national jurisdictions.

Equally significant has been the development of new forms of joint law enforcement, which reveal that drug dealers and smugglers have become a more serious threat to governments than has drug consumption. In 1986 U.S. authorities and public opinion were prepared to send troops to Bolivia (through Operation Blast Furnace)—not so much to curtail cocaine consumption as to destroy the laboratories and resources of traffickers, who had acquired more powerful fighting capabilities than the Bolivian government. Something similar has happened in Colombia. Funds were channeled to protect Colombian authorities from defiant drug traffickers in Medellín—whereas nobody talks of the Cali cartel, which has been taking advantage of the plight of its beleaguered rivals by increasing its market share in the United States. Similarly, if less dramatically, the U.S. worries in 1985 about Mexico becoming a new transit point for cocaine were centered—as the Camarena affair showed—on the apparent impunity of traffickers and alleged collusion of Mexican authorities rather than on the issue of market availability.

For governments of all these countries, the possibility of U.S. law enforcement agents going abroad in pursuit of traffickers or of U.S. courts assuming that criminal justice can be extended beyond borders represents as important a threat as losing the war against the traffickers themselves. It represents the loss of state control.

It should come as no surprise, then, that extradition treaties in Colombia or hot-pursuit proposals in Mexico exacerbate traditional anti-U.S. feelings. No country wants foreign governments involved in the exercise of such exclusive state prerogatives as law enforcement and criminal justice. Relying only on the principle of sovereignty and on their own capacity to fight traffickers, Latin American governments—and Mexico in particular—expect DEA agents to remember that they lack police powers in other countries. Mexican authorities have always had a hard time explaining to the public what U.S. antidrug agents are doing in Mexico.

From a criminal justice perspective, borders pose a magnificent obstacle to the apprehension of transnational organized criminals, as drug traffickers have come to be called. Sending agents to other countries in search of intelligence and cooperative partnerships is one way of circumventing frontiers.[13] I have no way to evaluate the usefulness of DEA information-gathering operations for the apprehension of traffickers in the United States. What is certain, however, is that unilateral actions in this realm can become a major source of conflict between governments.

National Interests

It is widely believed that Latin America's interest in fighting drugs is to please the U.S. government. If the U.S. government would drop the drug issue from its foreign policy agenda, it therefore follows, Latin American governments would get rid of the problem. In the words of a former Mexican ambassador to Washington: "Drug trafficking is not a Mexican problem in its origin. It is an American problem— a problem caused by demand, not by supply."[14] The Mexican Left has put forward similar arguments.

Drug consumption in Latin America, although admittedly on the rise, is far from constituting the most pressing problem for the region. Most urgent is the need to keep both traffickers and foreign enforcers from challenging governmental authority.

Drug control policies are tailored to address these concerns. In other words, unilateral actions to fight drugs are designed to protect national interests, even when the public evaluation of drug control programs is frequently made in terms of the need to collaborate with the U.S. government. Differences in national interests mean that national policies can work at cross purposes, as the history of antidrug law enforcement shows.

In the case of Mexico, for example, the consumption of marijuana, cocaine, and heroin has not yet become a critical public health problem. The only national survey on drug consumption conducted in Mexico shows that 2.99 percent of the population has used marijuana at least once, 0.33 percent has tried cocaine, and 0.11 percent has tried heroin. Regular use of any one of these drugs is considerably less; during the previous thirty days 0.54 percent of the Mexican population smoked marijuana, 0.14 percent used cocaine, and hardly any of those surveyed reported use of heroin.[15] In other words, most marijuana and heroin manufactured on Mexican soil is bound for the U.S. market; cocaine is in transit to the north. With regard to public health, the Mexican government can only wish that drugs go somewhere else and that drug consumption is neither imported into nor extended within Mexico.

But from this same perspective, current policies may prove to be inadequate. Interdiction efforts to reduce drug smuggling into the United States or more intense eradication and confiscation campaigns by the Mexican government could force drug dealers to keep high inventories until the "storm" is over or until they find new and safer ways of manufacturing and transporting their merchandise. In the meantime, selling part of their drugs at a discount in the domestic market would be an entirely reasonable option. Thus, present policy could have a counterproductive effect on public health in Mexico.

So far, under the assumption that cheap drugs would be a powerful incentive for consumption, the purchasing power of U.S. consumers has protected potential Mexican drug users by keeping the prices of heroin and cocaine too high for the average Mexican. There is little information about the price of these drugs on Mexican streets. According to a former Mexican attorney general, however, one could buy a metric ton of corn in Mexico for the price of a kilo of marijuana,[16] the cheapest drug and the only one with mass consumption potential in Mexico.

Although drug-related crimes in Mexico are classified as "crimes against health" (*delitos contra la salud*, meaning punishment is intended to protect the drug user's health), successive presidential administrations have consistently tried to counter the security rather than public health–related threats of drug production and trafficking.[17] A government that has decided to outlaw a particular type of business is bound to enforce that prohibition, or it will lose its capacity to enforce law and order. The Mexican government therefore must face the consequences that follow from the growth of an illegal market. Its options are constrained by the impossibility of changing, within the prohibition framework, the relationship between the price of drugs in the U.S. market and the price of drugs in Mexico; by the need to rely on antidrug law enforcement as the principal policy instrument to regulate the drug market; and by U.S. demands for cooperation.[18]

The corruption of law enforcement and military personnel that has accompanied the implementation of antinarcotics programs in Mexico is unavoidable. The Mexican state has an interest in reducing the magnitude of this effect. Exposing the criminal justice apparatus to the corrupting influence of traffickers is the most effective way of losing the war against drugs.

But Mexican interests are also conditioned by external events. Mexican policies have always been affected by changes in the international drug market and in U.S. policies. The resourcefulness and adaptability of drug producers and smugglers to different types of enforcement strategies as well as Mexico's interest in keeping drug enforcement activities to itself have given basic shape to Mexican policy. The Mexican government has gradually learned lessons about its vulnerability to enforcement programs of other countries—such as Turkey, Colombia, Bolivia, and the United States—which are ultimately much more decisive than the U.S. demand for narcotics. Any other country's success in disrupting established smuggling routes or traffickers' organizations will almost always affect Mexico. It was as a result of increased enforcement in Colombia and Florida that Mexico became an important transit point for northbound cocaine. Consequently, the Mexican government has been forced to react quickly and effectively to counter further growth in the clandestine market and to guarantee that changes in the international drug market (over which it has little control) do not overwhelm Mexico.

Interdiction of drugs in transit and immobilization of major traffickers in Mexico have recently redressed the traditional emphasis on crop eradication. Other countries will be affected by Mexico's success in making its territory a more dangerous and expensive place for drug dealers. The United States has already become a major producer of marijuana; Guatemala is just now witnessing the emergence of traffickers; Canada has become a newly attractive entrepôt for smuggling drugs into the United States. The development of new export sites and import channels may be welcomed by Mexicans (and may even reduce Mexico's participation in the U.S. market), but it will advance U.S. interests. Unilateral policies thus can further one country's interests in the short term but undermine the interests of other countries in the medium or long term.

Finally, protection against U.S. external pressures and interference in domestic politics has always been a central part of Mexico's national security policy. Drug trafficking has been defined by Mexican presidents de la Madrid and Salinas as a national security threat. To the extent that the United States also defines the problem in national security terms—and advocates the use of drug-related police and military activities in the United States and elsewhere in order to fight "hostile or destructive actions from within or without, overt or covert," including "airborne, amphibious, and overland invasion" of the United States by drug smugglers[19]—the two countries will be pursuing a collision course. Any form of "Americanization" of enforcement[20] will not be in Mexico's best interests and perhaps not in those of the United States. Mexican drug control policies have had one consistent foreign policy objective: stopping U.S. law enforcement at its own borders.

Bilateralism

In addition to this complicated web of national interests and frequently overlooked by those who insist that Mexican antidrug policies are merely a response to pressure from the United States, significant drug control programs in Mexico have been tailored in concert with the United States and with U.S. technical and financial support. Political and diplomatic discourse increasingly emphasizes the need for international cooperation (or regrets the lack of it) in order to eliminate the drug problem.

Most of the literature on the drug connection in U.S.-Mexican relations concludes with similar policy prescriptions: a bilateral approach to solve "the most contentious bilateral issue between the United States and Mexico [and] a mutual program of drug control."[21] To a large extent, policy recommendations calling for joint solutions result from a "market interdependence" framework: Supply and demand are "interrelated aspects of a single market. [Therefore,] producer and consumer countries must share responsibility for dealing with the challenge of illicit drugs. As long as efforts to choke off the drug supply are not accompanied by simultaneous efforts to attack the factors contributing to drug demand, there will always be an overriding economic incentive to keep producing drugs."[22] Such policy-oriented studies are critical of the unilateral actions (typically responding to domestic pressure groups or originating from frustrated police officers or bureaucrats) that have been part of the U.S. strategy to try to influence Mexico and other countries. The most famous incidents—Operation Intercept 1969 and Operation Intercept 1985—are remembered in Mexico as unfair and unreasonable, and they proved to be ineffective as well: Pressure is not the most constructive influence on Mexican drug control policies.

The rationale and possibilities for bilateral cooperation rarely receive much attention. What types of mutual programs could be implemented? For what purposes? At what cost?

At present a good deal of diplomacy—bilateral and multilateral—rests on the summation, assessment, and anticipation of eradication and confiscation figures. These data are usually presented as an unequivocal sign of cooperation; they may only show, however, that countries are being inundated by ever-increasing amounts of narcotics. As I have said, this interpretation of cooperation is bound to lead to frustration on both sides. This type of "bilateralism" serves nobody's interests. From a political perspective, however, it might be expedient to massage the numbers in order to show results and thus limit the practical terms of cooperation in this ultimately purposeless game.

Conclusions on past and present antidrug policy failures point to two types of limitations: technical and political. First, as foreign ministries often proclaim, Latin American countries face important financial, material, human, and technical constraints to effectively fight the drug market. U.S. international programs have tried to support antidrug campaigns in Latin America and elsewhere with funds, helicopters, and police training programs. Second, political factors include corruption amid the ranks of politicians and law enforcement agents as well as the structural weakness of criminal justice systems throughout the continent.

Within this framework of half-true perceptions, some forms of bilateral cooperation have fared well and others have faced insurmountable obstacles. In the case of Mexico and the United States, the late 1970s were considered by both governments as an "example" of what bilateral cooperation could accomplish. After successful eradication programs in Turkey at the end of the 1960s and the disruption of the French Connection in the early 1970s, Mexico became the largest supplier of heroin and marijuana for U.S. consumers. Increasing consumption of marijuana was also viewed as a domestic problem in Mexico,[23] and drug-trafficking organizations had developed considerable power in some states such as Durango and Sinaloa.[24]

The Mexican government launched a major campaign to destroy marijuana and poppy plants through aerial herbicide spraying with the assistance of U.S. funds and equipment. The joint U.S.-Mexican crop eradication program was formalized in 1973, but full implementation did not begin until 1976. Success in these bilateral endeavors was measured by the number of fields destroyed, the share of Mexican heroin and marijuana in the U.S. market, and good working relationships between Mexican and U.S. officials. The destruction of poppy plants and heroin was of particular interest to the United States at that time. Mexico's share in the U.S. market for marijuana dropped from more than 80 percent in 1973 to around 20 percent in 1980, whereas Mexico's share of U.S. heroin supplies tumbled from 85 percent to 31 percent in that same period.[25]

Operation Condor was the core of the major year-round chemical defoliant eradication campaign initiated by the Mexican government in 1976. According to Richard Craig, the "coordination and cooperation that typified the eradication program also characterized the interdiction phase."[26] Drug-related information and intelligence were gathered and exchanged between the Mexican police and around thirty DEA agents to build conspiracy cases involving drug traffickers in both countries, especially those in transit from South America to the United States.[27]

The Mexican government was able to destroy most of the clandestine market for marijuana and poppy plants with the use of advanced technology and thus managed to benefit from the abandonment (although it was incomplete) of what had become a politically costly scheme to counter illegal production: manual eradication of crops and governmental harassment of peasants. At the same time, major drug traffickers were forced to leave the business.

Both U.S. and Mexican authorities were pleased with the results. The Mexican government invested an average of $4 for each dollar coming from the United States. The nature of these programs allowed the Mexican government to maintain control over most of the activities in which the U.S. government was involved.

This kind of technical cooperation has been formalized in more than fifty bilateral letters of agreement plus amendments—mostly for the provision of telecommunications and aerial photographic equipment, helicopters and specialized aircraft, spare parts, and training for Mexican pilots.[28] The Mexican attorney general takes responsibility for carrying out eradication campaigns of opium poppy and marijuana fields with Mexican pilots and troops and agrees to ensure that U.S. aircraft and equipment are used for the eradication and confiscation of drugs. U.S. government personnel are allowed to oversee these operations, and they offer assistance in the targeting of fields. The Mexican government has also agreed to participate in mutually developed training programs. Agreements to establish links between customs agencies on both sides of the border as well as between the DEA and Mexican Judicial Police have been signed as well. A Mutual Legal Assistance Treaty is meant to formalize and limit legal cooperation between the two attorney generals on legal matters, some of which relate to drug smugglers.

More troublesome has been cooperation between the Mexican Judicial Police and DEA agents. Sending DEA agents abroad to promote the development of similar agencies in other countries and to gather drug-related intelligence has been at the core of U.S. international strategy. Yet, the DEA presence in Mexican territory has always been ridden with conflict. Antidrug agents have been in Mexico at least since the 1930s, with or without Mexican government permission. From time to time the DEA has crossed over the Mexican border in pursuit of criminals. Whenever Mexican administrations have sought to formalize agreements with the United States regarding the presence of agents on Mexican soil, they have usually been responding to activities already under way.[29]

Past experience coupled with the intrusive nature of intelligence-gathering by foreigners might be part of the reason cooperation with the United States in law enforcement matters is inherently suspect in Mexico. In the minds of Mexican policymakers, bilateral agreements that go beyond technical and financial assistance have always raised the potential for U.S. encroachment on Mexican territorial sovereignty, especially in the borderlands.

Many U.S. policymakers and experts nonetheless believe interdiction at the U.S.-Mexican border is the most promising way to reduce availability of illicit drugs in the U.S. market.[30] It is also assumed that joint law enforcement can substantially improve interdiction efforts. The U.S. President's Commission on Organized Crime offered its advice to improve drug interdiction and the capture of smugglers: "Facilitate Customs pursuit of suspected airborne drug traffickers into Mexican air space" and encourage "joint enforcement and intelligence operations by source and transshipment countries" with the participation of U.S. personnel.[31]

Mexican authorities have consistently rejected such proposals. Military cooperation has also been considered unacceptable by Mexican officials. They fear these schemes may lead not only to the loss of the sovereign power over enforcement but also to subordination of the police force. (This can happen, for example, when Mexican antidrug agents redirect their activities toward the capture of fugitive Mexicans charged with drug violations in the United States. And unless they proffer this type of collaboration, the United States might respond by kidnapping Mexican suspects.)

Subordinate relations can also result from the simple fact that DEA agents have superior intelligence and special training to capture middle- and high-level traffickers. Thus, they are able to identify and locate targets almost anywhere in the world and ask for assistance from national police. Although the pursuit of a foreign criminal who is hiding in Mexican territory would be considered a form of law enforcement cooperation, it also means national police distract time and resources from their own internal duties in order to engage in such pursuit.

Doubts arise about the likelihood of reciprocity.[32] The relative weakness of the Mexican police and military as well as the lack of Mexican interest in running after criminals beyond its territory would make "hot pursuit" a one-way endeavor and "joint task forces" a bilateral enforcement program within only one country. The fundamental problem for Mexico in these requests is one of setting limits because such requests are potentially expandable.

Beyond the exchange of information, cooperation between enforcement agencies can work only if the national interests of the two countries coincide, as they often have in the past. Training of special antinarcotics units in Mexico to perform specific and limited tasks worked well in the late 1970s. Similar programs could be resumed or expanded in pursuit of high-level traffickers, who can make a difference in the availability of drugs (if only temporarily) and who are politically dangerous for Mexico. This type of trafficker will obviously not be apprehended at the border. I doubt the potential for success of an inter-American strike force, however, because it will inevitably become a U.S.-led enforcement unit hunting traffickers in Latin

America. For similar reasons, the creation of some sort of international police is utterly impossible.

Crop substitution programs, in my opinion, will not work in Mexico. They have had very limited success in other Latin American countries. No agricultural product can be made as profitable as any commodity that is to be sold on the black market. The gap between the prices of legal and illegal crops is enormous. Short of decriminalization or legalization, little can be done to eliminate the economic incentives that spur drug production and smuggling.

Conclusion

Under the current regulatory framework and allocation of resources, bilateral or multilateral collaboration to reduce drug consumption in the United States or elsewhere through the repression of supply has scant prospects for success. Pressing collaboration in this direction will only lead to increasing conflict and misunderstanding in which both (or all) sides feel disappointed and deceived. At best, it will end in the new revelation of always "unprecedented" destruction figures, which are taken as evidence of true and honest cooperation in exchange for which governments feel legitimately entitled to international recognition.

Regardless of how much cooperation from other countries is requested and obtained, reducing the use of drugs in the United States will remain an essentially domestic affair simply because no other country can effectively eliminate such a lucrative market. Inasmuch as the drug problem is a public health concern, reducing drug consumption within any country can only be a national issue and responsibility. Governments can share experiences in the areas of prevention, education, and treatment, but they cannot go much farther than that.

In the meantime, Latin American governments and societies continue to face the problem of keeping the illegal drug market under control to the best of their abilities and capacities. Efforts to equip these countries with better means to fight the drug trade should go only as far as the requesting governments stipulate. It is fundamentally incorrect to assume that U.S. drug law enforcement can extend beyond U.S. borders without causing adverse consequences. The most acrimonious fights—at least in the case of Mexico and the United States—have resulted from unauthorized police practices and from U.S. incursions into Mexican airspace and territory.

By definition, governments do not want to share enforcement activities. It is only in desperate situations, such as those of Bolivia and Colombia, that governments ask for help in these matters, and it occurs at very high internal cost. Even assuming that Mexican decision makers and public opinion can interpret hitherto forbidden practices as a form of collaboration rather than a violation of sovereignty, the new mode would only open the door for new sources of conflict with little gain in terms of either country's national interests—unless friendly relations with the neighbor is taken as a desirable objective in and of itself.

If corruption and violence in Latin America are taken as the principal obstacles to more successful antidrug campaigns rather than as pernicious and inevitable consequences of present policies, the "war" against drugs will become a war between governments. Unfortunately, the U.S. government can do little to stop these negative effects of enforcement in other countries. If the goal of reducing drug consumption in the United States by relying on other countries' antidrug campaigns is unattainable, it is an even greater mistake to use drug policy and diplomacy as instruments to eradicate corruption and other maladies in Latin America.

Yet, there are collaborative practices that have proven fruitful in the past and that could continue at the bilateral, and even better, at the multilateral levels. These include intelligence-sharing, police training, and technical assistance—provided they have clearly stated objectives and are tailored to meet specific needs that reflect the genuine interests of the nations involved. There is evidence that the United States and Mexico can work together when the targets and the limits are established beforehand and when selected groups of enforcers are set to perform the task. Open-ended collaboration involving different types of joint law enforcement or any kind of "hot pursuit" will at best push traffickers into finding new routes for reaching U.S. consumers.

Unilateral actions—when they include "bashing" other governments or cajoling weaker countries into enlisting in the war on drugs (or worse, from an international relations perspective, deceiving U.S. public opinion)—are thoroughly regrettable. But when unilateral action means governments take the problem into their own hands and launch renewed programs against traffickers, there can be positive effects. Unilateral action in this sense means addressing urgent problems, identifying national interests, and—in the case of drug smuggling—preventing the undesirable relocation of trafficking routes and trafficking groups. (So far, at least, in this way Mexico has managed to avoid scenarios such as those of Colombia and Bolivia.) Despite their limitations, unilateral policies of this kind have largely proven to be more effective than bilateral or multilateral approaches.

The belief that Latin American countries need to be pressed to fight the drug market in their territories overlooks the fact that no government welcomes the growth of black markets within its territory. Equally wrong are the beliefs, so widespread in Latin America, that the drug problem is only one of U.S. consumption and that Latin American governments are graciously helping their ungrateful northern neighbor at considerable cost.

All countries suffer the consequences of ill-conceived drug enforcement policies and problematic collaboration frameworks. If this is indeed the case, it seems sensible to move away from some types of enforcement and to reduce the level of some operations. Less and more-focused enforcement might prove beneficial to all countries; this option has not yet been seriously explored. Such a step requires collaboration. To assure that individual countries will not suffer adverse consequences from a unilateral reduction of law enforcement campaigns, international cooperation is essential.

Notes

1. This argument is made by Peter Reuter and David Ronfeldt in *Quest for Integrity: The Mexico-U.S. Drug Problem* (Santa Monica, Calif.: RAND Corporation, 1991).

2. A list of these and other agreements can be found in U.S. House of Representatives, Report prepared for the Committee on Foreign Affairs, *Compilation of Narcotics Laws, Treaties, and Executive Documents* (Washington, D.C.: U.S. Government Printing Office, 1990).

3. Report to the president from the Domestic Council Drug Abuse Task Force, *White Paper on Drug Abuse* (Washington, D.C.: U.S. Government Printing Office, 1975), 50.

4. A sound discussion of the effect of source countries' efforts to eradicate drug crops on drug prices in the U.S. market is Peter Reuter, "Eternal Hope: America's Quest for Narcotics Control," *Public Interest* 79 (Spring 1985): 79–95.

5. Richard Craig, "La Campaña Permanente: Mexico's Antidrug Campaign," *Journal of Interamerican Studies and World Affairs* 20, no. 2 (May 1978): 110–111.

6. Sergio García Ramírez, *El narcotráfico: Un punto de vista mexicano* (México: Editorial Porrúa, 1988), 141.

7. Office of the Assistant Attorney General for Investigation and Combat of Drug Trafficking, *Mexico's Efforts in the Fight Against Drug Trafficking* (Mexico City: Office of the Attorney General, 1990).

8. Javier Treviño, "Evaluación de la estrategia internacional de erradicación de cultivos," paper presented at El Colegio de México, Mexico City, April 28–29, 1988.

9. Mark Kleiman has made a convincing argument in favor of reducing federal enforcement efforts against marijuana in the United States in "Allocating Federal Drug Enforcement Resources: The Case of Marijuana," Ph.D. diss., Department of Government, Harvard University, 1985.

10. García Ramírez, *El narcotráfico*, 584.

11. Peter Reuter, "Can the Borders Be Sealed?" *Public Interest* 92 (Summer 1988): 56.

12. For figures about federal government expenditures, see Ethan Nadelmann, "U.S. Drug Policy: A Bad Export," *Foreign Policy* 70 (Spring 1988): 83–108; and Reuter, "Can the Borders Be Sealed?"

13. Ethan A. Nadelmann, "Cops Across Borders: Transnational Crime and International Law Enforcement," unpublished Ph.D. diss., John F. Kennedy School of Government, Harvard University, 1987.

14. José Juan de Olloqui, former Mexican ambassador to the United States, "On the Formulation of U.S. Policy Toward Mexico," in Susan Kaufman Purcell, ed., *Mexico in Transition: Implications for U.S. Policy* (New York: Council on Foreign Relations, 1988), 115.

15. María Elena Medina-Mora and Roberto Tapia et al., "Encuesta nacional de adicciones," *Anales de la Quinta Reunión de Investigación del Instituto Mexicano de Psiquiatría* (México: Instituto Mexicano de Psiquiatría, 1990), 48–55. See also the discussion by Medina-Mora and Mariño in Chapter 3 of the present volume.

16. García Ramírez, *El narcotráfico*, 146–148.

17. María Celia Toro, "The United States and Mexico: Drug Trafficking from a National Security Perspective," paper presented to the Latin American Studies Association, Miami, Florida, December 1989.

18. María Celia Toro, "El control del narcotráfico: ¿podemos cooperar?" in Blanca Torres, ed., *La interdependencia: ¿Un enfoque útil para el análisis de las relaciones México-Estados Unidos?* (México: El Colegio de México, 1990), 231–252.

19. National security was defined in these terms by the U.S. Joint Chiefs of Staff. See President's Commission on Organized Crime, Report to the President and the Attorney General, *America's Habit: Drug Abuse, Drug Trafficking, and Organized Crime* (Washington, D.C.: U.S. Government Printing Office, 1986), 473.

20. Bruce Bagley talks about the "Americanization" of enforcement in Latin America as a possible but unwise U.S. government decision in "Colombia and the War on Drugs," *Foreign Affairs* 67, no. 1 (Fall 1988): 70–92.

21. Riordan Roett, ed., *Mexico and the United States: Managing the Relationship* (Boulder: Westview Press, 1988), 13, 18.

22. Report of the Bilateral Commission on the Future of United States–Mexican Relations, *The Challenge of Interdependence: Mexico and the United States* (Lanham, Md.: University Press of America, 1989), 116.

23. Craig, "La Campaña Permanente"; Ethan A. Nadelmann, "International Drug Trafficking and U.S. Foreign Policy," *Washington Quarterly* 8, no. 4 (Fall 1985): 90.

24. Peter A. Lupsha, "Drug Trafficking: Mexico and Colombia in Comparative Perspective," *Journal of International Affairs* 35, no. 1 (Spring 1981): 99.

25. Bilateral Commission, *Challenge*, 124–126.

26. Richard Craig, "Operation Condor: Mexico's Antidrug Campaign Enters a New Era," *Journal of Interamerican Studies and World Affairs* 22, no. 3 (August 1980): 345–363.

27. Craig, "La Campaña Permanente," 120.

28. Files of the Secretaría de Relaciones Exteriores. For a summary of the most important bilateral agreements, see Connie M. lvarez, "Drugs, Guns, and Money: The Death of Enrique Camarena Salazar and Its Effects on U.S.-Mexican Cooperation in Drug Law Enforcement," unpublished manuscript, June 1988.

29. For the history of these negotiations, see William O. Walker III, *Drug Control in the Americas* (Albuquerque: University of New Mexico Press, 1981).

30. Reuter, "Can the Borders Be Sealed?"

31. President's Commission on Organized Crime, *America's Habit*, 467, 471.

32. For more detail, see García Ramírez, *El narcotráfico*, 146–148.

22

The Logic of Inter-American
Cooperation on Drugs

David R. Mares

Why have governments in the Americas cooperated on international antidrug policy? One might be tempted to answer from a normative perspective: Drugs are evil, and therefore all virtuous people will seek ways to control them. Because a number of ways of collaboration exist, however—each with distinct distributions of costs and benefits—the question of cooperation inevitably becomes a matter of choice. Because choice is possible, noncooperation becomes possible as well. The question of *why* collaboration thus becomes tied into the question of how nations agree on *how* to collaborate.

In this chapter I suggest an analytical framework to understand how domestic and international factors interact to facilitate or obstruct international cooperation on drug policy. The framework is grounded in insights from the theory of games but seeks to go beyond the mathematical logic of strategic choice in order to be of direct relevance to policymakers. The structure of a game and the strategies and preferences of its players may allow us to predict the terms of collaboration or its absence; but policymakers must discover the game they are playing, the strategies available to themselves and their counterparts, and the preferences of all players.

The analytic framework proposed here integrates game theory with theories about domestic and international politics. The result is not a predictive framework; the complexity of policymaking is too great and negotiation outcomes are too contingent, especially on the domestic level, for predictive accuracy. But analysts and especially policymakers need some framework to interpret, evaluate, and plan. I offer this analysis in this spirit.

My approach suggests that inter-American collaboration on illicit drug control has gone through two phases in the past twenty years. The U.S. ability to impose collaboration and the Latin American ability to implement the terms of that collaboration only partially during the first phase can best be understood through the logic of a particular game known as Bully, played out at the international level. By the mid-1980s major changes occurred at the domestic and international levels, resulting in a change in the structure of the international drug policy game. U.S. and Latin-Caribbean negotiators found themselves playing two-level games: Strategies and preferences at home were affected by strategies and preferences internationally.

As a result of these changes, inter-American drug policy is now in a state of flux. In the future a number of new games may characterize the new logic that will come to underpin hemispheric drug interactions. We could find ourselves in a Deadlock game, with all players refusing to concede anything. Or we might discover cooperation itself rather than a continuation of U.S.-enforced collaboration. We might even encounter a new version of Bully, with Latin American producer countries in the role of the dominant player.

At the outset of this chapter I review some elementary concepts in game theory. In particular, I focus on applications of game theory to international policy. The next section presents game-theoretic examples for interpreting inter-American drug policy over the past twenty to thirty years, with practical suggestions for negotiators from both consumer and producer nations. A concluding section advances ideas about how to encourage the conditions that would promote cooperative inter-American drug games.

Games as Models: Contributions
and Limits for Policymakers

Models allow social scientists to illuminate causal relationships. They may be created through an inductive or a deductive process, but in either case they require abstraction from reality. The purpose of the model is to reduce reality to its bare essentials in order to understand the logic of the particular phenomena under study. Although analytically necessary, abstraction creates a tension between the elegance of a model and its application to policymaking.[1]

The basic challenge is to provide a logical structure for evaluating the strategies available to the players and for understanding the impact of players' preferences on the outcome. For this instrumental purpose it is necessary to understand only the basics of game theory and to elaborate a simple model. Five concepts are fundamental: strategy, strategic rationality, payoffs, preferences, and structure.

A *strategy* is "a complete plan for action" that can be usefully understood as "simplified representations of general policy stances."[2] Rationality is a contentious subject in social science, but it is essential if we are to make sense of social phenomena. In game-theoretic terms, rationality simply means making logically correct calculations with the available information in pursuit of specified goals. It implies nothing about the inherent value of those goals. *Strategic rationality* recognizes that one player's pursuit of his or her own interest requires consideration of the other player's choices. The implication of strategic rationality is that actors will choose their strategies "based on preferences and expectations of how others will behave."[3]

Payoff is the outcome of the choice of strategies each player makes. As we can see in Figure 22-1, in a two-by-two game there are four payoffs, with the first letter

FIGURE 22-1
Generalized Bargaining Game

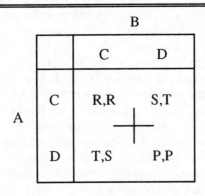

Options
    C=cooperate (make concession)
    D=defect (no concessions)
Payoffs
    P=payoff for deadlock
    R=payoff for compromise concessions
    S=payoff for making unilateral concessions
    T=payoff for getting one's way

in a pair representing A's payoff and the second representing that of B. *Preferences* refer to the values actors assign to the payoffs. *Structure* means the ordinal ranking by the players of their values for each of the possible payoffs.[4]

The basic point of game theory is that *if we know* the strategies available to players and their preference structure, we may be able to discover which game they are playing (out of a mathematically possible array of seventy-eight two-by-two games),[5] and we may be able to predict the outcome of the game. (Not all games have determinate solutions.)

One major limitation is that we must incorporate conclusions about strategies and preferences drawn from other theories about the political economy of the subject in question. In the case of inter-American drug relations, we need to know something about the characteristics of the drug trade. The market determinants of supply and demand—including substitution possibilities—will influence what strategies are available, their potential distribution of costs and benefits, and their potential effectiveness. The relative position of consumer and producer countries in the international political economy will also have an effect on the ability of one actor to sanction or reward another actor's choice of strategy.

A second important limitation lies in the perceptual realm. The analyst may be able to determine after the fact which game was being played, but the actors may each think they are playing a different game. Because negotiators may wish to distort their actual preferences in order to gain more,[6] a misreading of the preference structure and therefore of the game can pose real problems for policymakers.

With these limitations in mind, we can still benefit from thinking in game-theoretic terms. Let me demonstrate the point through two games that illuminate the logic of inter-American drug policy over the last twenty years. Two caveats are in order. First, I focus on two-by-two games because inter-American drug policy has essentially been bilateral rather than multilateral. The United States prefers it this way, and Latin American countries seem to as well—despite the rhetoric of meetings such as that in 1990 in Cartagena.[7] Given the different drugs involved (marijuana, cocaine, and heroin), the varying positions of countries in the drug cycle (producer, processor, transshipper, money launderer), and differences in the domestic socioeconomic-political characteristics of the various actors in the drug business, it should come as no surprise that Latin America finds it difficult to develop a coordinated response to U.S. drug policy preferences.

Second, let me explain my definition of *cooperation*. Given the nature of the drug market, demand and supply both have an impact. The inter-American drug issue, therefore, is captured either in terms of U.S. *demand* and Latin American *supply* or of U.S. *demand and supply* and Latin American *supply*. In either case, inter-American policy has two general outcomes: Both parties accept compromise, or one dictates terms and the other accedes. Only in the former case do I consider mutual cooperation to have occurred; in the latter case, one side cooperates whereas the other retains an essentially unilateral approach. The existence of an inter-American policy, therefore, does not necessarily constitute cooperation.

One final observation on this point: Given that international policy on any issue is virtually never built on trust (essentially because states are sovereign), cooperation requires explicit linkages between policy—that is, if country A does something (for example, attempt to control supply), country B will also do something (for example, attempt to control demand). "Cooperation" in this sense requires explicit linking of policies on supply and demand.

Inter-American Drug Policy Games

As noted earlier, the game structure depends on the available strategies and the distribution of actor preferences across the payoffs produced by those strategies. For our two-by-two games, the strategies can be thought of as various combinations of cooperation and defection. In terms of the international drug policy game, we can define the relevant elements as follows:

Players

A = consuming country
B = producing country

Strategies (combinations of cooperation and defections on controlling drugs)

DD= no control on supply or demand
CD= control on demand, no control on supply
DC= control on supply, no control on demand
CC= control on both supply and demand.

Preferences

To derive preferences, we need to think about what each strategy means to each player in terms of both his or her goal and potential responses by the other actor. Each strategy implies a distinct distribution of costs and benefits. Two examples from inter-American drug policy illustrate the point.

Let us take a traditional U.S. policy approach, one that focuses on crop eradication in the producing country with no link established to demand-control policies in the consuming country (combination DC, as displayed above). In this case the cost to the United States comes from money to help fund eradication. But for a country such as Peru, the cost is found in increased peasant alienation from the government, in loss of life among soldiers and civilians (innocent as well as guilty), in decreased domestic legitimacy for the government vis-à-vis some domestic groups (for example, nationalists, including the military), in possible ecological damage if herbicides are used, in violation of human rights and due process, and in expenditures of money (because U.S. funds do not cover the entire cost). This policy option clearly places the burden of cost on the producing nation.

What about the distribution of benefits: Are they likewise skewed in favor of one party? The benefits to the United States include a possible decrease in supply to the U.S. market and a possible decrease in the number of users of the drug (although they may switch to alternatives, including synthetics such as methamphetamines produced in the United States). For Peru the benefits would include some economic aid (because other aid is usually tied to performance on drug programs), the possibility of a decline in production (although production is likely to shift to new regions, perhaps even within Peru), and an increased domestic legitimacy vis-à-vis some domestic groups (such as those worried about production).

Let us examine an alternative policy—one that targets the street-level trafficker in the United States—this time without drawing specific links to performance on supply control in Peru (combination CD). In this case, the costs to Peru are zero (assuming it does not see a decrease in foreign exchange earnings from the coca trade as negative). The costs to the United States, however, are high: increased tension in ghettos and universities; a strong likelihood of violation of due process legislation; increased deaths and casualties among police, innocent bystanders, and traffickers; an increased number of prison inmates, with overcrowding in both prisons and the court system (fueling tension and forcing increased budgets); and substantially increased costs for preventive and rehabilitation programs. In terms of benefits, Peru would possibly depart from the drug business if Europe and Japan did not significantly increase their demand, whereas the United States would experience a possible decrease in drug use.

We can clearly see that both producer and consumer countries pay costs and receive benefits from each policy. The distributional consequences, however, are heavily skewed in favor of the consuming country in the crop eradication program and are skewed in favor of the producing country in the street-level trafficker program.[8]

Different policies may also have distinct probabilities of significantly influencing drug consumption. As other chapters in this book have shown, a policy focusing strictly on supply controls is unlikely to have a fundamental impact on consumption. In addition, users, producers, traffickers, and money launderers are not homogeneous groups; hence, different policy responses may be necessary to target subgroups. For example, education campaigns may have a dramatic impact on middle-class drug use but will likely have to be supplemented by socioeconomic and community development programs to significantly impact ghetto and barrio youth. As with all public policy issues, efficiency and efficacy gains interact with political costs and benefits to influence which policy is actually adopted.

The Bully Game

Let us begin by assuming that the goal of severely limiting socially disruptive drug use is valued by social groups and policymakers in the consuming countries but that both would prefer that foreigners shoulder the bulk of the burden. The negative externalities of drug use are just beginning to alarm the consuming society. Action is demanded, but the existence of a foreign actor in the drug trade means that hard choices at home can initially be avoided by demanding that the foreigner act first.

Now some assumptions about producing countries. Producing countries recognize that drug consumption is a problem but see this as demand-induced; hence, they believe consuming countries should take the lead. But producing countries are weaker internationally than consuming countries, leading to a situation in which consumer countries can impose significant sanctions on producers. The cost of these sanctions outweighs the costs of initially meeting consumer countries' demands for controls.

These initial assumptions lead us to the following preferences for consuming and producing countries:

A: DC > DD > CC > CD

B: DC > CC > CD > DD

When we examine the normal form of the game that corresponds to these preferences (called Bully, as shown in Figure 22-2), we can clearly see the great advantage of A. (The numbers represent the ordinal ranking of preferences, from least [1] to most [4].) The great bargaining advantage for A is that no matter what

FIGURE 22-2
Bully Game

		B	
		C	D
A	C	2,3	1,4
	D	4,2	3,1

B does, A is assured of at least a 3 (if B chooses C, A gets 3; if B chooses D, A gets 4). A's dominant strategy, therefore, forces B to cooperate even as A defects. B is so weak in this game that B is willing to concede (cooperate while A defects, therefore B gets 2) rather than fight (defect and get a 1). The incentive is for A to defect and coerce, or "bully," B to give A its maximum payoff.[9]

Note that the structure of the game is derived from the payoffs as they are valued by each player. A game-theoretic framework by itself cannot tell us why the players value the payoffs as they do. To discover those payoffs, we must move to the empirical case.

If Bully is indeed the correct structure of the international drug game, we should expect one of the players to be able to exact significant costs relative to benefits from the other for defecting. This has indeed been the case. In the inter-American component of the game, the United States has been able to use a variety of sanctions to keep Latin American and Caribbean countries from refusing to accept some type of control on supply, even as the United States refused to link control on supply to efforts to control demand. This refusal to recognize the fundamental power of demand on supply may seem perplexing for a country imbued with a liberal economic ideology. But because controlling demand implied payment of domestic costs and because it appeared possible to shift the costs to producing countries, this became a rational first move. U.S. preferences would not change until it became clear that controls on foreign supply alone would have little impact on the U.S. drug problem (because demand continued to grow, its socioeconomic locus changed and spilled over to challenge new groups, and the United States itself was becoming an important producer).

Of course, cost imposed by U.S. sanctions is not the only item in the calculation of the supplier countries. Here the distinction between policy formulation and implementation helps us better understand supplier preferences. As long as the

United States did not insist on intimate oversight of antidrug policy in supplier countries, implementation could be sporadic and selective. Hence, the domestic costs of policy cooperation on the bully's terms were not as great as one might expect. The marginalization of domestic factors thus helps explain the persistence of such a skewed inter-American drug policy.

Two-Level Games

When international negotiators must deal not only with their counterparts but also with domestic interests, they find themselves playing two simultaneous and overlapping games. These two-level games are significantly more complex than one-level games. Because the players are involved in two games at the same time, a move that may be rational in one game may not be rational in the other; moves in one game may result in a realignment of positions in the other game, thereby making possible outcomes that were previously unattainable.[10]

The empirical richness of the two-level game framework means it is potentially of great value to policymakers, although academics may find it too inelegant for theoretical purposes. (In fact, it is not even formally a "game.") Its benefit for policy analysis is that it tells us where to look for a more complex derivation of strategies and preferences: the interplay between international and domestic politics.

The two games entail (1) international negotiations to reach an agreement, and (2) domestic negotiations to ratify international agreements. The basic argument is that the domestic game drives the international game, although there may be some international sources for the derivation of domestic preferences.[11] Negotiators have a sense of the domestic "win-set" that constrains their bargaining at the international level. A win-set is all the possible international agreements that would "win"—that is, "gain the necessary majority among constituents, when simply voted up or down."[12]

Examination of the win-sets in the domestic game, therefore, provides an important starting point in the study of international diplomacy. Ceteris paribus, the larger the win-sets at the domestic level, the more likely will be cooperation at the international level. At the same time, larger win-sets have paradoxical results because size affects the distribution of joint gains: "The larger the win-set at home, the more the negotiator can be pushed around; the smaller the win-set at home, the less the negotiator can accept."[13]

What determines the size of the win-set? Here we must turn to theoretical debates about the impact of state and society on the making of foreign policy.[14] Essentially, we need to know the identity of the relevant political groups in society, the institutional structure within which the specific foreign policy issue is negotiated and ratified at home, and the ability of state policymakers to influence societal preferences and create policy coalitions. Although two-level game frameworks do not provide these answers, they demonstrate how they will matter.

The domestic win-set is not the determinant of international policy: Negotiators at the international level must still play their game. All the classic strategies for bargaining become relevant here but with the caveat that any bargains must fall within the domestic win-set.

By now we can see that a two-level game will probably produce a contingent and not a determinate outcome because of its theoretical inelegance. There are too many variables that cannot be clearly specified to begin with (for example, the range of policy coalitions), so it is difficult to investigate preference orderings with a high degree of confidence. But for logically ordering and interconnecting our arguments about the domestic and international determinants of international policymaking, the two-level game framework represents an important advance for both analysts and policymakers.

What are the characteristics of the two-level game of inter-American drug policy? A number of games become possible for understanding drug policy, depending on the preference orderings coming out of the domestic game for both parties. Let us return to the Bully game. There the United States had a dominant strategy, which shifted all the costs of international cooperation to the producing countries. But the characteristics of the market for drugs are impossible to ignore for long. Demand is a fundamental determinant of supply. Without some attack on demand, the drug problem in the consuming country will not go away.

Domestic constituents become involved in policy because they do not believe the current policies are producing the preferred outcome. Because the issue here is consumption of illegal drugs, users will not be a powerful domestic political force. But others who believe they are suffering at the hands of drug users or traffickers may become motivated to participate in the policy process. If so, they will demand effective drug policies.

Two possible impacts on the game structure may result from this domestic preference, and each would probably change the structure of the inter-American drug policy game. If domestic society did not wish to pay the costs of controlling demand, U.S. negotiators could insist on better implementation of supply controls in Latin America and the Caribbean. Alternatively, if domestic society realized that demand was the fundamental determinant of the drug phenomenon, international negotiators would not be able to sell the supply control–only strategy at home even if they could force the producing country to accept it.

When U.S. negotiators respond to domestic demands for a supply-focused policy with significantly better implementation in foreign lands, the game is likely to shift from Bully to Deadlock (see Figure 22-3). Because sporadic and selective implementation by Latin American and Caribbean governments would no longer be acceptable to the United States, the domestic costs of those programs to the Latin and Caribbean governments would increase. As those costs increase, domestic groups would begin to pressure these governments to insist that the United States shoulder more of the cost. Because in this example U.S. domestic politics rejects linking international policy to domestic controls on demand, the United States would not alter its dominant strategy of no cooperation. Because foreign governments now find the domestic costs of capitulating to U.S. demands too high, they will also

FIGURE 22-3
Deadlock Game

		B	
		C	D
A	C	2,2	1,4
	D	4,1	3,3

prefer to defect. The result would be a breakdown in inter-American collaboration on drug policy. The state of U.S.-Peruvian relations throughout early 1991 was aptly characterized by this game.

A surprising possibility arises if U.S. domestic groups searching for effective drug policies insist that their government allocate more of its scarce resources to the fight against demand at home. In this scenario U.S. preferences in the inter-American drug policy game would be for control on both demand and supply; *but* if producer countries reject controls on supply, the United States would still adopt policies to control demand. If Latin American preferences were to free-ride on U.S. demand control and U.S. demand were to fall dramatically, supply would fall as well without significantly increased European and Japanese demand. The result of strategic interaction in accord with these preferences would be to keep us in a Bully game, displayed in Figure 22-4, but with Latin America having the dominant strategy.

A more likely scenario would involve U.S. domestic groups clamoring for controls on both demand and supply as a way to speed up the fight against drug consumption at home. U.S. negotiators thus would seek cooperation with Latin and Caribbean governments. Because the United States still retains significant sanctions and would be willing to cooperate in good faith, other governments would probably be willing to cooperate as well. The solution would then revolve around the mix of policies this cooperation would represent. Here the win-set in each country becomes both more complex and more fundamental.

Rather than hypothesize specific payoffs to the two-level game at this point, it would be more useful to explore how those win-sets might overlap. Figure 22-5 presents some illustrative but not exhaustive examples of which policy strategies could lie outside and within those win-sets. Figure 22–5 suggests that for the United States, legalization and a punitive domestic drug war against users with few constraints of due process are most likely outside of the win-set. For Latin and

FIGURE 22-4
Bully Game #2

		B	
		C	D
A	C	4,2	3,4
	D	2,1	1,3

Caribbean governments and societies these may be attractive policy options, but a U.S. negotiator would be unlikely to get them ratified at home. On the other hand, Latin and Caribbean societies would prefer to leave a punitive drug war against producers with few constraints of due process as well as extradition out of their domestic win-sets. (The Peruvian and Colombian cases, respectively, demonstrate the high political cost of these measures.)

But Figure 22-5 also suggests that there is potential overlap between win-sets. For a consumer country, these would include education and a punitive drug war against demand that operated within the constitutional process. The win-set in producing countries—which would overlap with that in consuming countries— probably includes policies of crop diversion, a punitive drug war against producers within constitutional guidelines, and military aid as long as it is tied to developmental aid.

Conclusion

The logic of inter-American cooperation on drug policy can be more clearly understood if we use an analytic framework incorporating elementary game theory. I have suggested that inter-American drug policy has gone through two phases in the last twenty years. In the first phase, the U.S. ability to impose collaboration and Latin American governments' abilities to respond with selective compliance resulted in a Bully game at the international level. Domestic politics played a minor role within the United States; and although domestic politics were very important to Latin leaders, their inability to move the United States from its dominant strategy resulted in their playing two parallel games—one with the United States and the other at home. Because these games were parallel, Latin leaders' strategies at home were independent of what strategies were available in the international game.

FIGURE 22-5
Win-Sets in a Two-Level Game

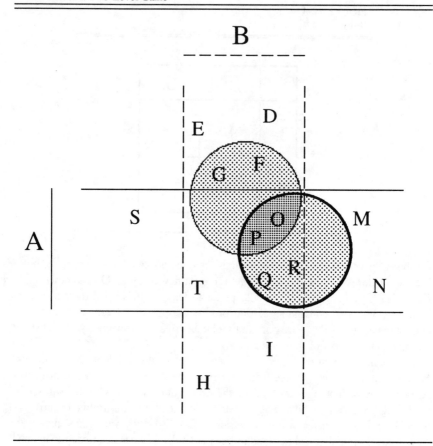

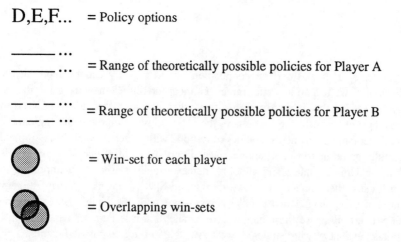

D,E,F... = Policy options

___ ... = Range of theoretically possible policies for Player A

_ _ _ ... = Range of theoretically possible policies for Player B

= Win-set for each player

= Overlapping win-sets

In the second phase, two major changes occurred at the domestic and international levels, resulting in a change in the structure of the inter-American drug policy game. First, drugs became an important issue in domestic policy within the United States. Consequently, policymakers had to address domestic issues while they negotiated with Latin leaders. Second, the United States was no longer able to impose its policy choice on Latin America and the Caribbean at the international level; consequently, policy negotiations suddenly became "real." U.S. and Latin-Caribbean negotiators found themselves playing interconnected games: Strategies and preferences at home were affected by strategies and preferences internationally.

The result is a more complex strategic interaction on international drug policy. But because domestic politics is now an integral part of the negotiation, for the first time there is hope that international cooperation will lead to policies that will have a serious impact on the drug trade. For demand especially and supply to a lesser extent, effective policies must be accepted by domestic constituencies.

How might preferences and the game structure itself be changed to make possible more meaningful inter-American drug policy? There are essentially three ways in which we might alter the inter-American drug game for the better: introduce a new actor(s), have the players operate within a regime, and change U.S. preferences.

Introducing new actors turns our two-by-two games into n-person games. One fundamental difference is that coalition-building takes center stage. If the new actor(s) recognizes that demand is a fundamental aspect of the problem or that punitive action can be only a secondary factor in controlling supply, the new alliance could possibly force the consuming country to play a more responsible role.

A second possibility would be to construct a regime (which might include revamping relevant international institutions to facilitate cooperation on international drug policy).[15] Regimes consist of norms and principles to guide behavior as well as rules and decision-making procedures to diminish cheating.[16] Regime creation is difficult, but a hegemonic power may be able to impose a regime, which could then gain legitimacy by demonstrating to participants that they are better off supporting the regime even when the hegemonic power declines.[17] The United States so far has exercised hegemony over international antidrug policy. Unfortunately, it has not used that power to create a cooperative regime. If U.S. policy preferences change, a cooperative drug trade regime could still be constructed.

Changing U.S. policy preferences could facilitate cooperation either through regime creation or on its own. In the Bully game, the United States has the dominant strategy: It can force producer countries to cooperate whether it does so or not. Consequently, if the United States prefers cooperation, it can achieve it in the Bully game. Even in the Deadlock game, a U.S. decision to link control on supply in Latin America to control on demand within the United States might break the impasse. We must be careful, however, not to believe the United States can produce cooperation merely by recognizing that demand factors are the principal determinants of the problem. If U.S. domestic groups simply focus on U.S. demand and ignore foreign-supply issues, Latin American negotiators may find themselves in an unaccustomed role: that of the Bully.

Notes

1. The principal exponent of this view is Alexander L. George. See, for example, his critique of deterrence theory's impact on U.S. foreign policy in Alexander L. George and Richard Smoke, *Deterrence in American Foreign Policy* (New York: Columbia University Press, 1974).

2. Duncan Snidal, "The Game *Theory* of International Politics," in Kenneth A. Oye, ed., *Cooperation Under Anarchy* (Princeton: Princeton University Press, 1986), 37.

3. Snidal, "The Game *Theory*," 39.

4. Glenn Snyder and Paul Diesing, *Conflict Among Nations: Bargaining, Decision Making, and System Structure in International Crisis* (Princeton: Princeton University Press, 1977), 481–482.

5. Ordinal rather than cardinal preferences are used. For a full discussion, see Anatol Rapoport and Melvin Guyer, "A Taxonomy of 2x2 Games," as cited in Snyder and Diesing, *Conflict Among Nations*, 41–42.

6. The classic analysis is found in Thomas Schelling, *The Strategy of Conflict* (Cambridge: Harvard University Press, 1960), 21–52.

7. Peter H. Smith, "Drug Wars in Latin America," *Iberoamericana* 12, no. 1 (Summer 1990): 13–14.

8. For further discussion, see Smith, "Drug Wars"; Report of the Inter-American Dialogue, *The Americas in 1989: Consensus for Action* (Lanham, Md.: University Press of America, 1989), 31–39.

9. Snyder and Diesing, *Conflict Among Nations*, 46–47.

10. This discussion is taken from Robert D. Putnam, "Diplomacy and Domestic Politics: The Logic of Two-Level Games," *International Organization* 42, no. 3 (Summer 1988): 427–460.

11. Putnam seems to mean links through the transnational alliances discussed in the context of complex interdependence (Joseph S. Nye and Robert O. Keohane, *Power and Interdependence* [Boston: Little, Brown, 1971]) rather than those that derive from the position of a domestic actor in an international market (Peter A. Gourevitch, *Politics in Hard Times* [Ithaca, N.Y.: Cornell University Press, 1987]). For our purposes, both are appropriate.

12. Putnam, "Diplomacy and Domestic Politics," 437.

13. Putnam, "Diplomacy and Domestic Politics," 437–440; Schelling, *Strategy of Conflict*, 21–52.

14. For the current state of the debate, see Gourevitch, *Politics in Hard Times*; Peter Hall, *Governing the Economy* (New York: Oxford University Press, 1987); and a special issue of *International Organization* 42, no. 1 (Winter 1988).

15. See the call for strengthening regional institutions in *The Americas in a New World: The 1990 Report of the Inter-American Dialogue* (Queenstown, Md.: Aspen Institute, 1990), 16.

16. Stephen D. Krasner, "Structural Causes and Regime Consequences: Regimes as Intervening Variables," *International Organization* 36, no. 2 (Spring 1982): 185–205.

17. Robert O. Keohane, *After Hegemony: Cooperation and Discord in the World Political Economy* (Princeton: Princeton University Press, 1984).

About the Book
and Editor

Drug use and drug trafficking pose intractable policy dilemmas for the United States and Latin America. Despite repeated declarations of a "war on drugs" and occasional pronouncements of imminent victory, serious problems persist. Efforts to reduce consumption have not been effective, the costs of curtailing the drug trade have multiplied, and violence has intensified as narco-terrorists have unleashed a deadly challenge to governmental authority. Confusion over drug policy, moreover, leads to mutual recrimination. How have governments responded? What *can* governments do? What *should* governments do?

Presenting the perspectives of specialists from both Latin America and the United States, this book offers a fresh and thorough assessment of national and regional drug policies as well as alternative approaches. Contributors analyze the magnitude and structure of the illicit drug market, the impact of the "war on drugs," the utility of therapy and treatment, and the implications of legalization. The result is an incisive portrait of a drug network that stretches from the Andes through Mexico and the Caribbean to the United States and a dispassionate—often critical—evaluation of official policies. The book places special emphasis on the long-term, frequently unintended consequences of antidrug policies, the feasibility of stressing demand reduction rather than supply control, and realistic possibilities for regional collaboration among nations of the Americas.

Peter H. Smith is professor of political science and director of the Center for Iberian and Latin American Studies at the University of California, San Diego. A specialist on comparative politics, Latin American politics, and U.S.–Latin American relations, he has written numerous books and articles, including *Modern Latin America* (with Thomas E. Skidmore). He is a past president of the Latin American Studies Association and has served as codirector of the Bilateral Commission on the Future of United States–Mexican Relations.

About the Contributors

Elena Alvarez is Research Associate Professor at the University Center for Policy Research at the State University of New York in Albany, where she is directing a multiyear project on the political economy of coca production in the Andes. An economist, she has written extensively on agrarian reform and agricultural development in Peru. Her publications include *Política agraria y estancamiento de la agricultura, 1969–1979* (1983) and *Política económica y agricultura en el Perú, 1969–1979* (1983).

Naya Arbiter is Director of Services at Amity, Inc., an educational and treatment facility for adolescent and adult substance abusers in Tucson, Arizona. She has taken special interest in the development of effective treatment programs for underserved populations, such as women and minorities, and in the design of interventions for people at high risk of HIV infection. In 1987 Arbiter took part in the White House Conference for a Drug-Free America, and in 1990 she was a panelist at the National Conference on State and Local Drug Policy.

Bruce M. Bagley is Associate Dean and Associate Professor at the University of Miami's Graduate School of International Studies. He has specialized in the politics of Colombia, Central America, and inter-American relations. He has published articles in *Foreign Affairs* and other journals, and he is editor of *Contadora and the Diplomacy of Peace in Central America* (1987). His current research interests focus on the effect of the international drug trade on Latin American source countries.

Jack Donnelly is Associate Professor of Political Science at the University of North Carolina. He has written extensively on international organization and human rights; his publications include *Universal Human Rights in Theory and Practice* (1989) and *Human Rights and World Politics* (1991). He has lectured in Asia, Canada, Europe, and South America.

Mathea Falco is Senior Research Associate at Hunter College, a lawyer, and a consultant on public health issues. From 1977 through 1981 she was U.S. Assistant Secretary of State for International Narcotics Matters. She is the author of *Winning the Drug War* (1989) and of many articles on drug-related questions.

Guy Gugliotta is a reporter at the *Washington Post* and served for ten years as Latin American correspondent for the *Miami Herald*. He has been a Nieman Fellow and an Alicia Patterson Fellow. He is coauthor of *Kings of Cocaine: Inside the Medellín Cartel* (1989), a book based on a prize-winning series of articles in the *Miami Herald* in 1987.

Michael C. Hoffmann is founder and Chairman of the Board of the Inter-American Consortium for Human Development in San Antonio, Texas. He has conducted seminars and symposia on community mobilization throughout Europe and Latin America, often with the sponsorship of the U.S. government or the Organization of American States. He has also

344

served as Director of the International Office of Substance Abuse Prevention at the University of Oklahoma.

José Guillermo Justiniano, an agriculturalist and private consultant, is former Minister of Agriculture of Bolivia. A graduate of the Universidad Nacional de La Plata in Argentina, he has published several papers and books on agricultural economics in Bolivia. Justiniano has represented his country at numerous international gatherings, including the 1988 United Nations Anti-Narcotics Convention in Vienna.

Mark A.R. Kleiman is Lecturer in Public Policy and Research Fellow in Criminal Justice at the John F. Kennedy School of Government, Harvard University. His work embraces drug policy, crime control, and policy on AIDS. His publications include *Marijuana: Costs of Abuse, Costs of Control* (1989) and *Choosing a Drug Problem* (forthcoming).

Roberto Lerner is former Deputy Director of the Centro de Información y Educación para la Prevención del Abuso de Drogas and currently Associate Professor of Psychology at the Pontificia Universidad Católica in Lima, Peru. He holds a Ph.D. in psychiatry and is the author of *Drugs in Peru: Reality and Representation* (1991) and editor of the journal *Psychoactiva*.

Abraham F. Lowenthal is Executive Director of the Inter-American Dialogue and Professor of International Relations at the University of Southern California. He has written extensively on Latin American politics, especially in Peru, and on U.S.–Latin American relations. His most recent book is *Partners in Conflict: The United States and Latin America* (1987).

Flavio Machicado serves as Director of Civil Services for the Project on Economic Management of the Public Sector in Bolivia. A specialist in public policy, he served as Minister of Planning in 1970 and as Minister of Finance in 1971 and 1983–1984. He has been a faculty member at the University of Bolivia in La Paz and a visiting lecturer at universities in Chile, Colombia, Guatemala, and the United States. Machicado has also been an adviser to the United Nations and the Food Assistance Organization.

David R. Mares is Associate Professor of Political Science at the University of California, San Diego. A specialist on international political economy, he is the author of *Penetrating the International Market: Theoretical Considerations and a Mexican Case* (1987). He has been a visiting researcher in Mexico and Chile and a consultant to the Mexican government.

María del Carmen Mariño is Associate Researcher at the National Institutes of Health in Mexico and a full-time researcher at the Instituto Mexicano de Psiquiatría. She collaborated on a national household survey on addictions and has published numerous scientific articles on epidemiology.

Lisa L. Martin has been Assistant Professor of Political Science at the University of California, San Diego, with emphasis on international relations. She is the author of *Coercive Cooptation: Explaining Multilateral Economic Sanctions* (1992) and the recipient of an Advanced Foreign Policy Fellowship from the Social Science Research Council. She has recently accepted a faculty position at Harvard University.

María Elena Medina-Mora is a Researcher at the National Institutes of Health in Mexico and Division Chief at the Instituto Mexicano de Psiquiatría. She has served as an adviser to the World Health Organization and the Pan American Health Organization. Author of more than fifty scientific publications, Medina-Mora has received two national awards from the Mexican government for her outstanding contributions to the fields of epidemiology, addictions, and mental health.

Rod Mullen is Executive Director of Amity, Inc., in Tucson, Arizona. Formerly a program director at Synanon, he has been a consultant to local, state, and federal agencies and has contributed frequently to national and international conferences on drug policy. He is a member of the Advisory Committee on Substance Abuse Prevention of the Alcohol, Drug Abuse, and Mental Health Administration.

David F. Musto is Professor of Psychiatry and the History of Medicine at Yale University. Awarded the M.D. in 1963, he conducts research on social history and public health policy. He is the author of *The American Disease: Origins of Narcotic Control* (1973, revised 1987), and he has been a member of the White House Strategy Council on Drug Abuse Policy.

Peter Reuter is Senior Economist at the Washington office of the RAND Corporation and codirector of the RAND Drug Policy Research Center. He has applied tools of economic analysis to such illicit activities as gambling and drug trafficking. Reuter is author of *Disorganized Crime: The Economics of the Visible Hand* (1983), which received the 1984 Leslie Wilkens Award as the outstanding study in criminal justice. He is senior author of *Sealing the Borders: The Effects of Increased Military Participation in Drug Interdiction* (1988), a classic in the field.

Miguel Ruiz-Cabañas I. is a member of the Mexican diplomatic corps and has represented his country at numerous international conferences on drug abuse and illicit drug trafficking. A Ph.D. candidate at Columbia University, he has contributed essays to *The Drug Connection in U.S.-Mexican Relations* (1989) and to numerous prominent journals.

Aaron Saiger is Resident Consultant at the RAND Corporation, where he conducts research on illicit drug use and crime control. He is project manager for RAND's National Assessment of the Bureau of Justice Assistance Formula Grant Program, the federal government's largest grants-in-aid program for state and local drug enforcement, and of a study on drug crime in public housing developments. He has been chief executive officer of BOTEC, a public policy consulting firm.

Francisco E. Thoumi is a Research Economist at the Inter-American Development Bank in Washington, D.C. Born in Colombia, he earned his Ph.D. from the University of Minnesota and has published important studies on regional economic integration, economic development patterns, and industrial policy. In recent years he has worked on underground economies and the economics of drug trafficking.

María Celia Toro is a faculty member in the Centro de Estudios Internacionales at El Colegio de México and a Ph.D. candidate in international relations at Stanford University. She has published articles on U.S.-Mexican relations and is working on a study of the politics of drug trafficking.

William O. Walker III is Professor of History at Ohio Wesleyan University. A specialist in international relations, Walker is the author of *Drug Control in the Americas* (1981, revised 1989) and of *Opium and Foreign Policy: The Anglo-American Search for Order in Asia, 1912–1954* (1991). In 1987 he received a Social Science Research Council–MacArthur Foundation Fellowship in International Peace and Security.

Index